I FIGURED I'D AT LEAST TRY HARD
TO NOT BE SO WORDY HERE.
I'M FINE AND I'M WORKING HARD.
- TSUGUMI OHBA

Tsugumi Ohba
Born in Tokyo.
Hobby: Collecting teacups.
Day and night, develops manga plots
while holding knees on a chair.

Takeshi Obata was born in 1969 in Niigata, Japan, and
is the artist of the wildly popular SHONEN JUMP title
**Hikaru no Go**, which won the 2003 Tezuka Shinsei
"New Hope" award and the Shogakukan Manga award.
Obata is also the artist of **Arabian Majin Bokentan
Lamp Lamp, Ayatsuri Sakon,** and **Cyborg Jichan G.**

**DEATH NOTE VOL 5**
**SHONEN JUMP ADVANCED Manga Edition**

STORY BY TSUGUMI OHBA
ART BY TAKESHI OBATA

Translation & Adaptation/Alexis Kirsch
Touch-up Art & Lettering/Gia Cam Luc
Design/Sean Lee
Editor/Pancha Diaz

DEATH NOTE © 2003 by Tsugumi Ohba, Takeshi Obata
All rights reserved. First published in Japan in 2003 by SHUEISHA Inc.,
Tokyo. English translation rights arranged by SHUEISHA Inc.

Printed in the U.S.A.

Published by VIZ Media, LLC
P.O. Box 77010
San Francisco, CA 94107

17
First printing, May 2006
Seventeenth printing, February 2014

SHONEN JUMP ADVANCED MANGA

# DEATH NOTE

デスノート

白紙
5

## Vol. 5

## Whiteout

Story by Tsugumi Ohba
Art by Takeshi Obata

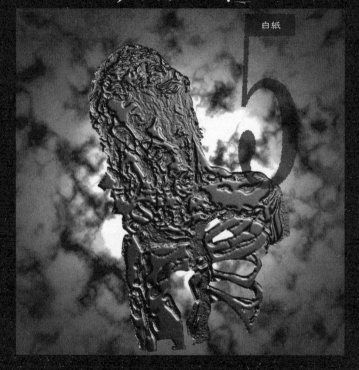

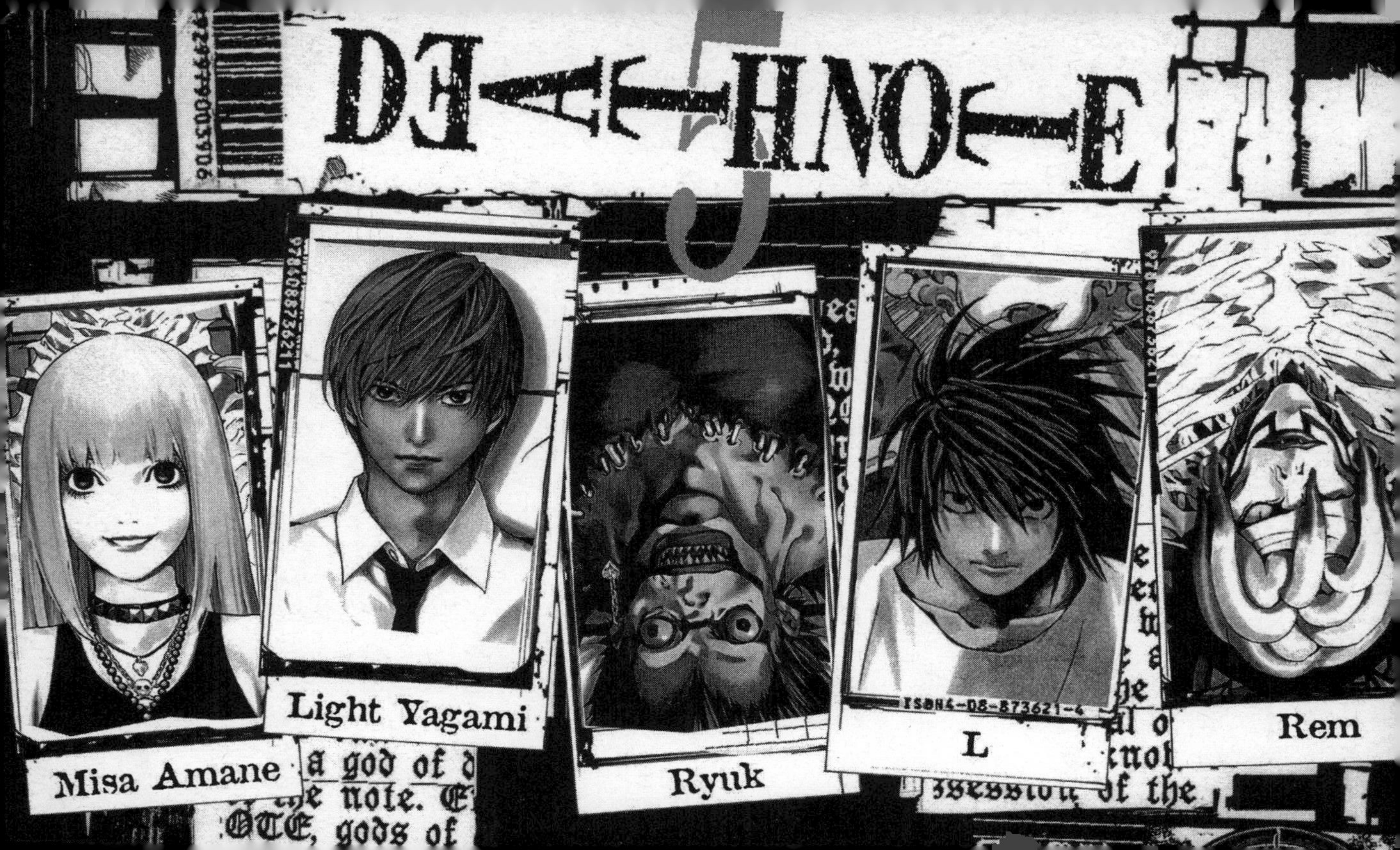
DEATH NOTE
Misa Amane
Light Yagami
Ryuk
L
Rem
ISBN4-08-873621-4

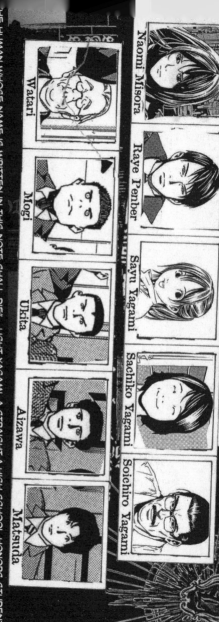

Naomi Misora
Raye Penber
Sayu Yagami
Sachiko Yagami
Soichiro Yagami
Watari
Mogi
Ukita
Aizawa
Matsuda

"THE HUMAN WHOSE NAME IS WRITTEN IN THIS NOTE SHALL DIE"... LIGHT YAGAMI, A STRAIGHT-A HIGH SCHOOL HONORS STUDENT, PICKS UP THE "DEATH NOTE" DROPPED BY THE SHINIGAMI RYUK INTO THE HUMAN WORLD. HALF DISBELIEVING, LIGHT USES THE NOTEBOOK, ONLY TO SEE THE PEOPLE WHOSE NAMES HE HAS WRITTEN DROP DEAD! INITIALLY HORRIFIED BY THE NOTEBOOK'S POWERS, LIGHT EVENTUALLY DECIDES TO USE THE DEATH NOTE TO PURGE THE WORLD OF VIOLENT CRIMINALS AND CREATE AN IDEAL SOCIETY. MEANWHILE, AS CRIMINALS WORLDWIDE START DYING MYSTERIOUSLY, THE ENIGMATIC L, A SECRETIVE GENIUS WHO SPECIALIZES IN SOLVING UNSOLVED CASES, ENTERS THE PICTURE. HE USES A TV BROADCAST TO ANNOUNCE HE WILL CATCH WHOEVER IS RESPONSIBLE, SETTING OFF AN ALMIGHTY BATTLE OF WITS BETWEEN LIGHT AND HIMSELF...

LIGHT BEGINS KILLING ALL THOSE WHO STAND IN HIS WAY. HOWEVER, L'S POWERS OF DEDUCTION SOON PICK OUT LIGHT AS A POSSIBLE SUSPECT. AFTER BATTLING OUT VARIOUS MIND GAMES, THE TWO DECIDE TO JOIN FORCES TO INVESTIGATE THE SECOND KIRA. LIGHT DOES SO IN ORDER TO LOCATE THE SECOND KIRA BEFORE L, AND L DOES SO TO KEEP HIS EYES ON LIGHT...AFTER FIGURING OUT THE HIDDEN MESSAGES SENT BY THE SECOND KIRA, LIGHT HEADS TO AOYAMA, BUT IS UNEXPECTEDLY DISCOVERED BY MISA, THE SECOND HUMAN WHO POSSESSES A DEATH NOTE. AFTER THAT, MISA SHOWS UP AT LIGHT'S HOME AND PLEDGES TO HELP HIM REACH HIS GOALS. LIGHT DECIDES TO USE HER SHINIGAMI, REM, TO KILL OFF L. WHEN MISA, WHO POSSESSES THE SHINIGAMI EYES, UNEXPECTEDLY RUNS INTO L, LIGHT IS CONFIDENT IN HIS VICTORY. BUT BEFORE HE CAN ACT, THE TASK FORCE SUDDENLY APPREHENDS MISA! PUSHED TO THE BRINK, LIGHT ASKS THAT HE BE PUT

# DEATH NOTE
## Vol. 5

## CONTENTS

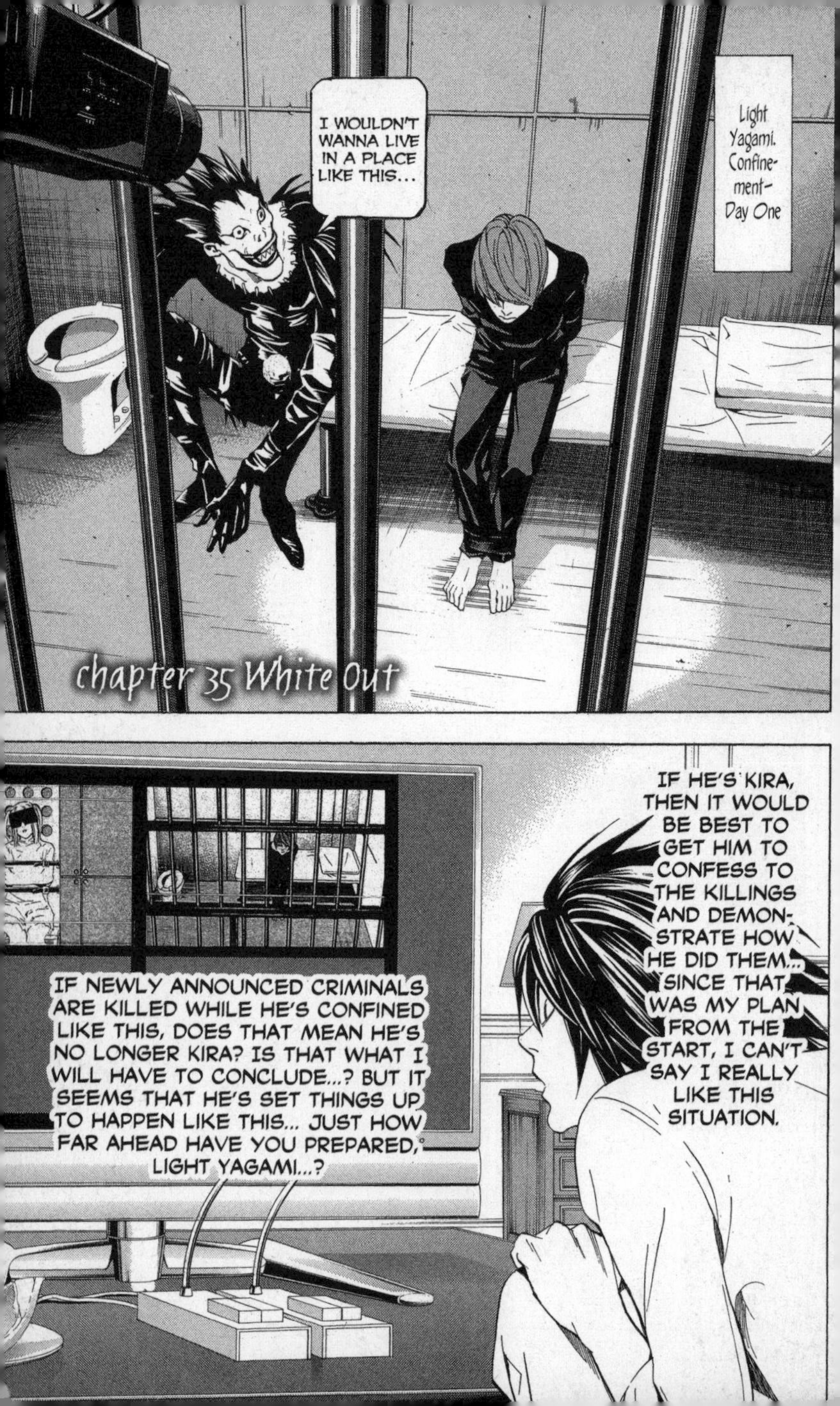
Light Yagami. Confinement-Day One
I WOULDN'T WANNA LIVE IN A PLACE LIKE THIS...
chapter 35 White Out
IF HE'S KIRA, THEN IT WOULD BE BEST TO GET HIM TO CONFESS TO THE KILLINGS AND DEMONSTRATE HOW HE DID THEM... SINCE THAT WAS MY PLAN FROM THE START, I CAN'T SAY I REALLY LIKE THIS SITUATION.
IF NEWLY ANNOUNCED CRIMINALS ARE KILLED WHILE HE'S CONFINED LIKE THIS, DOES THAT MEAN HE'S NO LONGER KIRA? IS THAT WHAT I WILL HAVE TO CONCLUDE...? BUT IT SEEMS THAT HE'S SET THINGS UP TO HAPPEN LIKE THIS... JUST HOW FAR AHEAD HAVE YOU PREPARED, LIGHT YAGAMI...?

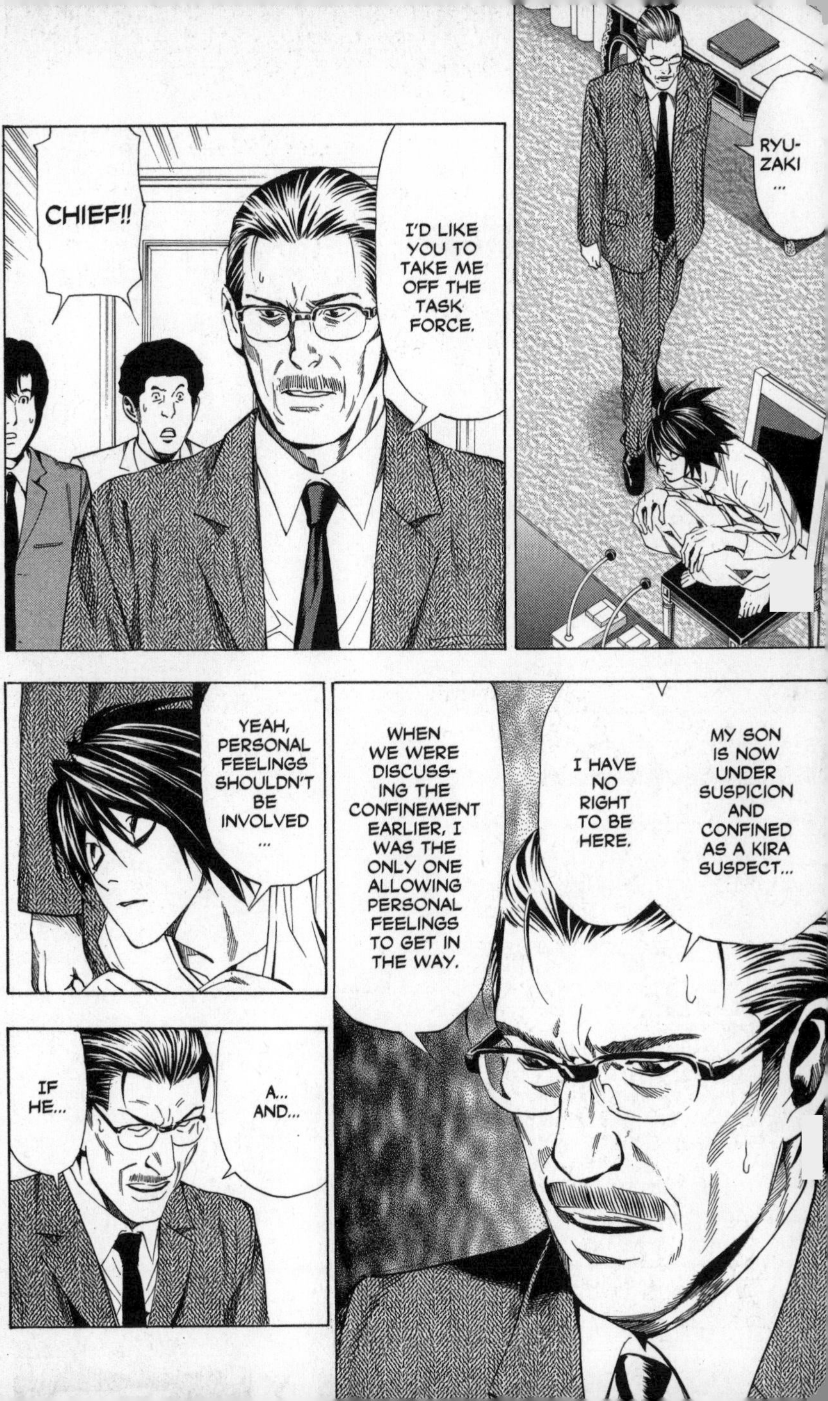
RYU-ZAKI ...
I'D LIKE YOU TO TAKE ME OFF THE TASK FORCE.
CHIEF!!
MY SON IS NOW UNDER SUSPICION AND CONFINED AS A KIRA SUSPECT...
I HAVE NO RIGHT TO BE HERE.
WHEN WE WERE DISCUSS-ING THE CONFINEMENT EARLIER, I WAS THE ONLY ONE ALLOWING PERSONAL FEELINGS TO GET IN THE WAY.
YEAH, PERSONAL FEELINGS SHOULDN'T BE INVOLVED ...
A... AND...
IF HE...

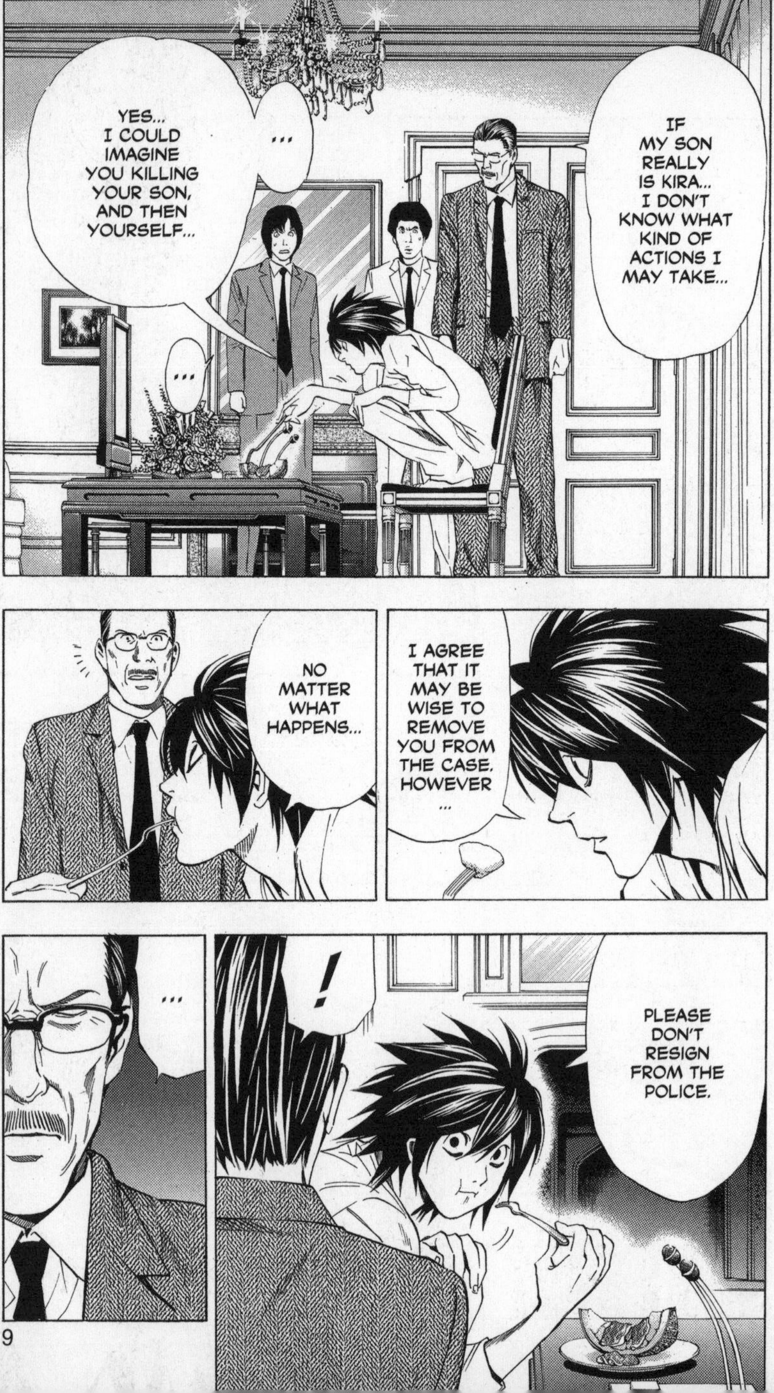
IF MY SON REALLY IS KIRA... I DON'T KNOW WHAT KIND OF ACTIONS I MAY TAKE...
...
YES... I COULD IMAGINE YOU KILLING YOUR SON, AND THEN YOURSELF...
...
I AGREE THAT IT MAY BE WISE TO REMOVE YOU FROM THE CASE. HOWEVER ...
NO MATTER WHAT HAPPENS...
PLEASE DON'T RESIGN FROM THE POLICE.
!
...

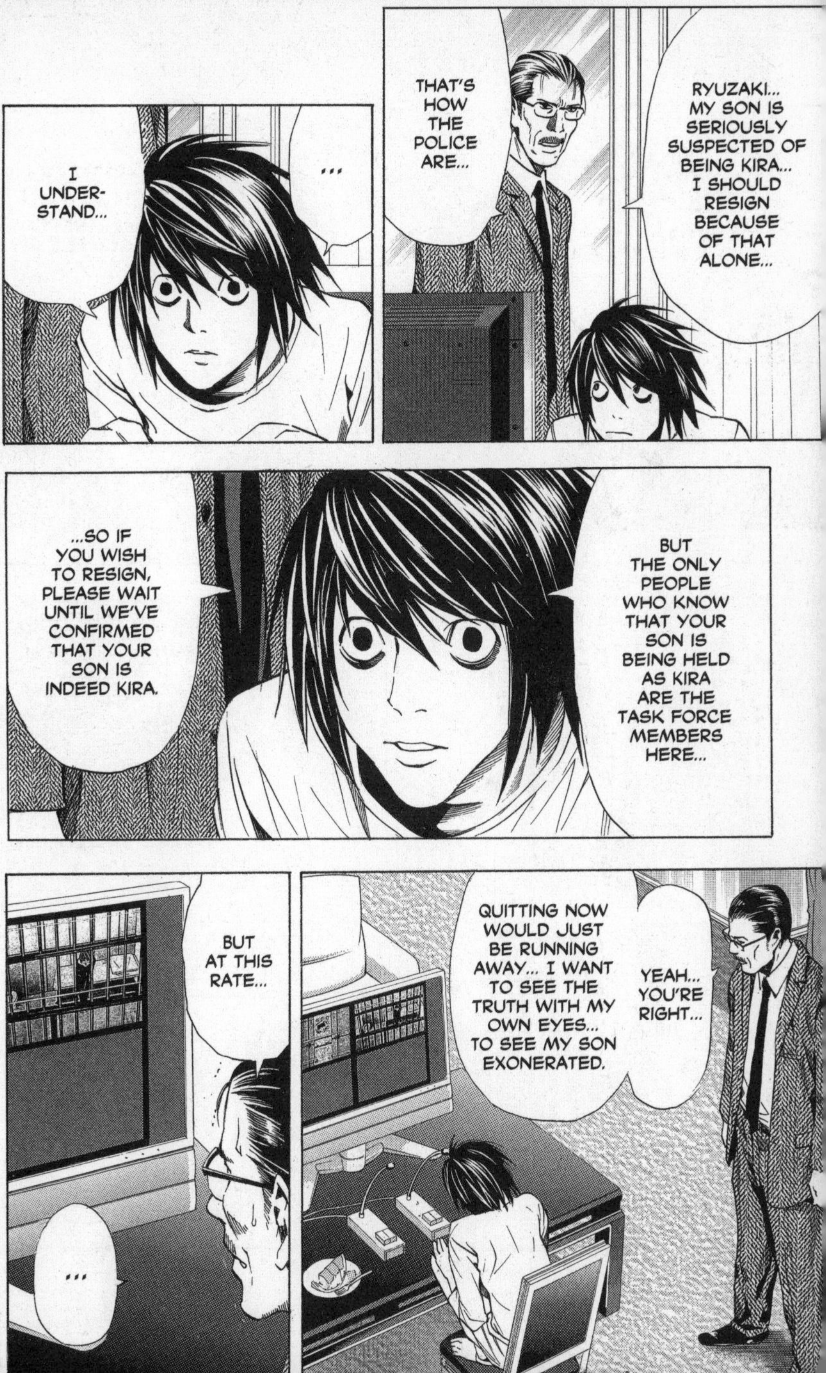
RYUZAKI... MY SON IS SERIOUSLY SUSPECTED OF BEING KIRA... I SHOULD RESIGN BECAUSE OF THAT ALONE...
THAT'S HOW THE POLICE ARE...
...
I UNDER-STAND...
BUT THE ONLY PEOPLE WHO KNOW THAT YOUR SON IS BEING HELD AS KIRA ARE THE TASK FORCE MEMBERS HERE...
...SO IF YOU WISH TO RESIGN, PLEASE WAIT UNTIL WE'VE CONFIRMED THAT YOUR SON IS INDEED KIRA.
YEAH... YOU'RE RIGHT...
QUITTING NOW WOULD JUST BE RUNNING AWAY... I WANT TO SEE THE TRUTH WITH MY OWN EYES... TO SEE MY SON EXONERATED.
BUT AT THIS RATE...
...

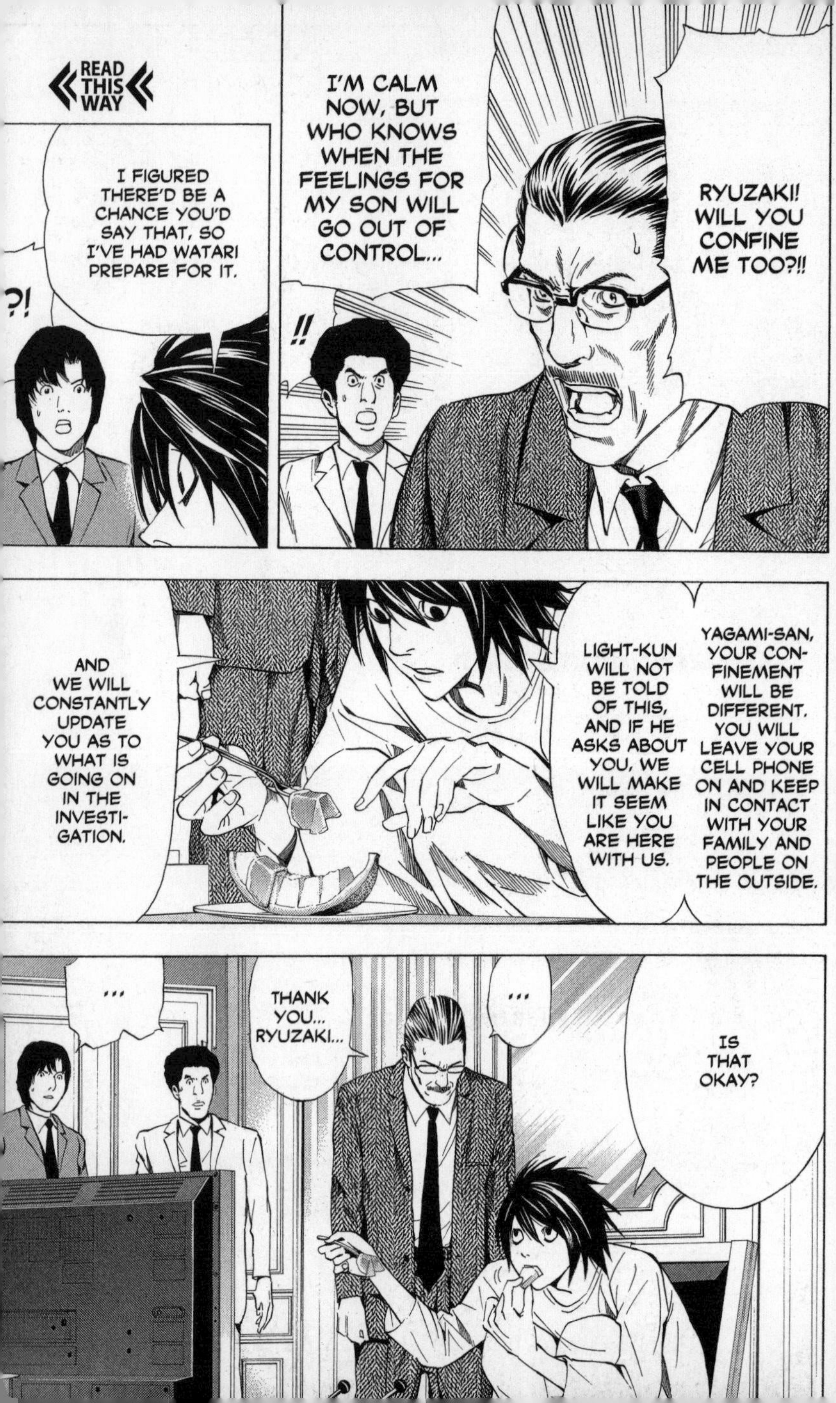
READ THIS WAY
RYUZAKI! WILL YOU CONFINE ME TOO?!!
I'M CALM NOW, BUT WHO KNOWS WHEN THE FEELINGS FOR MY SON WILL GO OUT OF CONTROL...
!!
I FIGURED THERE'D BE A CHANCE YOU'D SAY THAT, SO I'VE HAD WATARI PREPARE FOR IT.
?!
YAGAMI-SAN, YOUR CON-FINEMENT WILL BE DIFFERENT. YOU WILL LEAVE YOUR CELL PHONE ON AND KEEP IN CONTACT WITH YOUR FAMILY AND PEOPLE ON THE OUTSIDE.
LIGHT-KUN WILL NOT BE TOLD OF THIS, AND IF HE ASKS ABOUT YOU, WE WILL MAKE IT SEEM LIKE YOU ARE HERE WITH US.
AND WE WILL CONSTANTLY UPDATE YOU AS TO WHAT IS GOING ON IN THE INVESTI-GATION.
IS THAT OKAY?
...
THANK YOU... RYUZAKI...
...

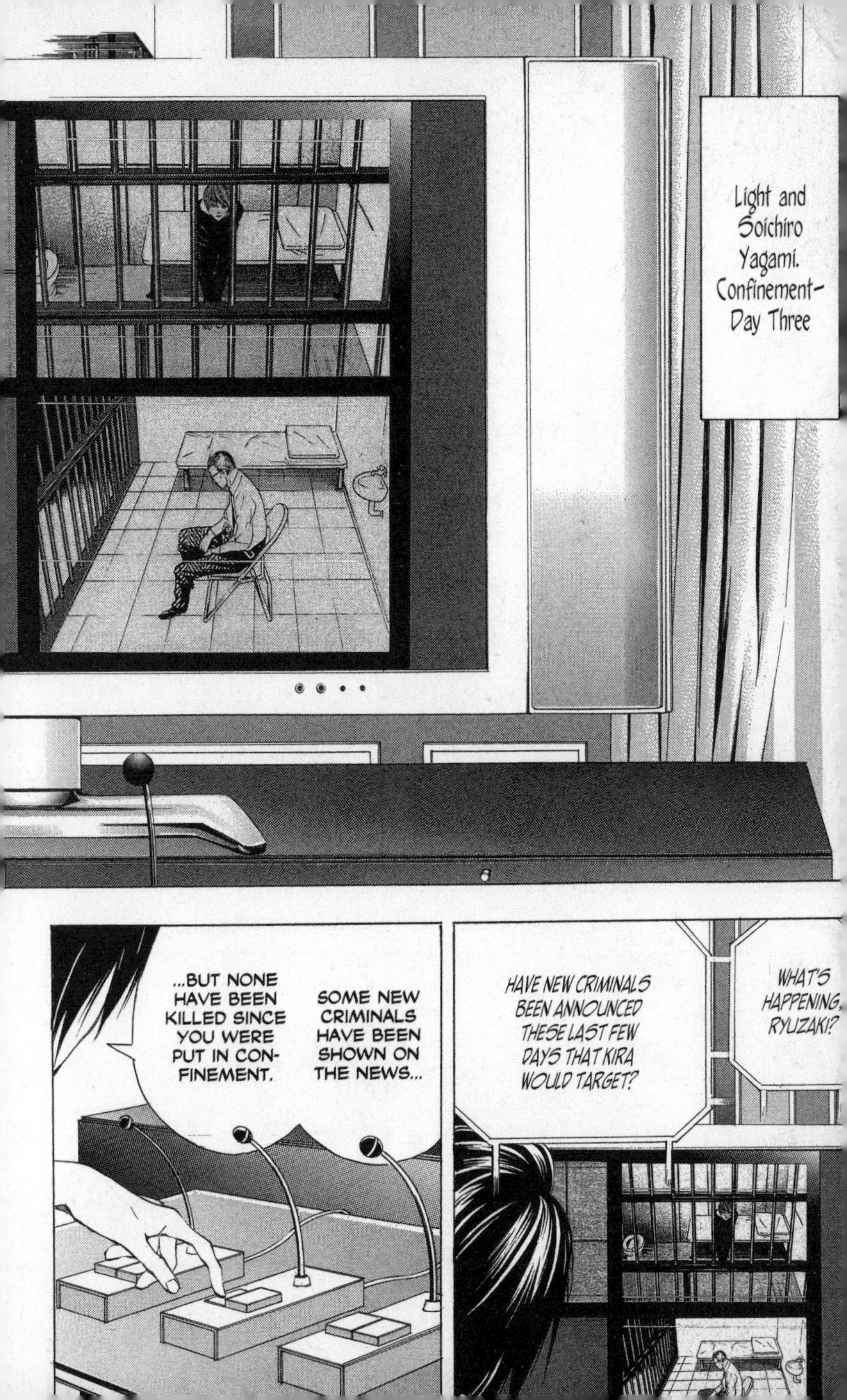
Light and Soichiro Yagami. Confinement–Day Three
WHAT'S HAPPENING, RYUZAKI?
HAVE NEW CRIMINALS BEEN ANNOUNCED THESE LAST FEW DAYS THAT KIRA WOULD TARGET?
SOME NEW CRIMINALS HAVE BEEN SHOWN ON THE NEWS...
...BUT NONE HAVE BEEN KILLED SINCE YOU WERE PUT IN CON-FINEMENT.

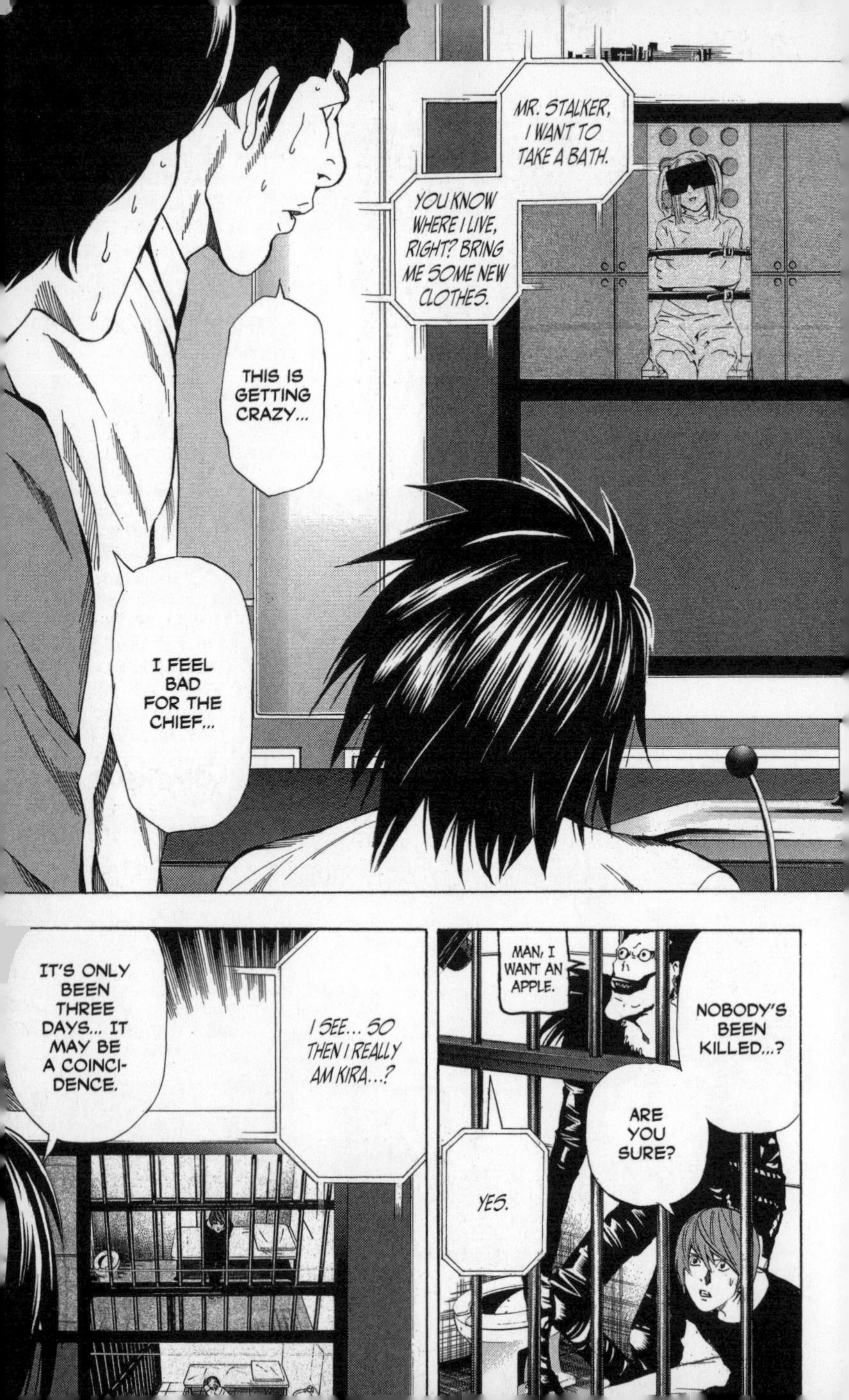
MR. STALKER, I WANT TO TAKE A BATH.
YOU KNOW WHERE I LIVE, RIGHT? BRING ME SOME NEW CLOTHES.
THIS IS GETTING CRAZY...
I FEEL BAD FOR THE CHIEF...
NOBODY'S BEEN KILLED...?
MAN, I WANT AN APPLE.
ARE YOU SURE?
YES.
I SEE... SO THEN I REALLY AM KIRA...?
IT'S ONLY BEEN THREE DAYS... IT MAY BE A COINCI-DENCE.

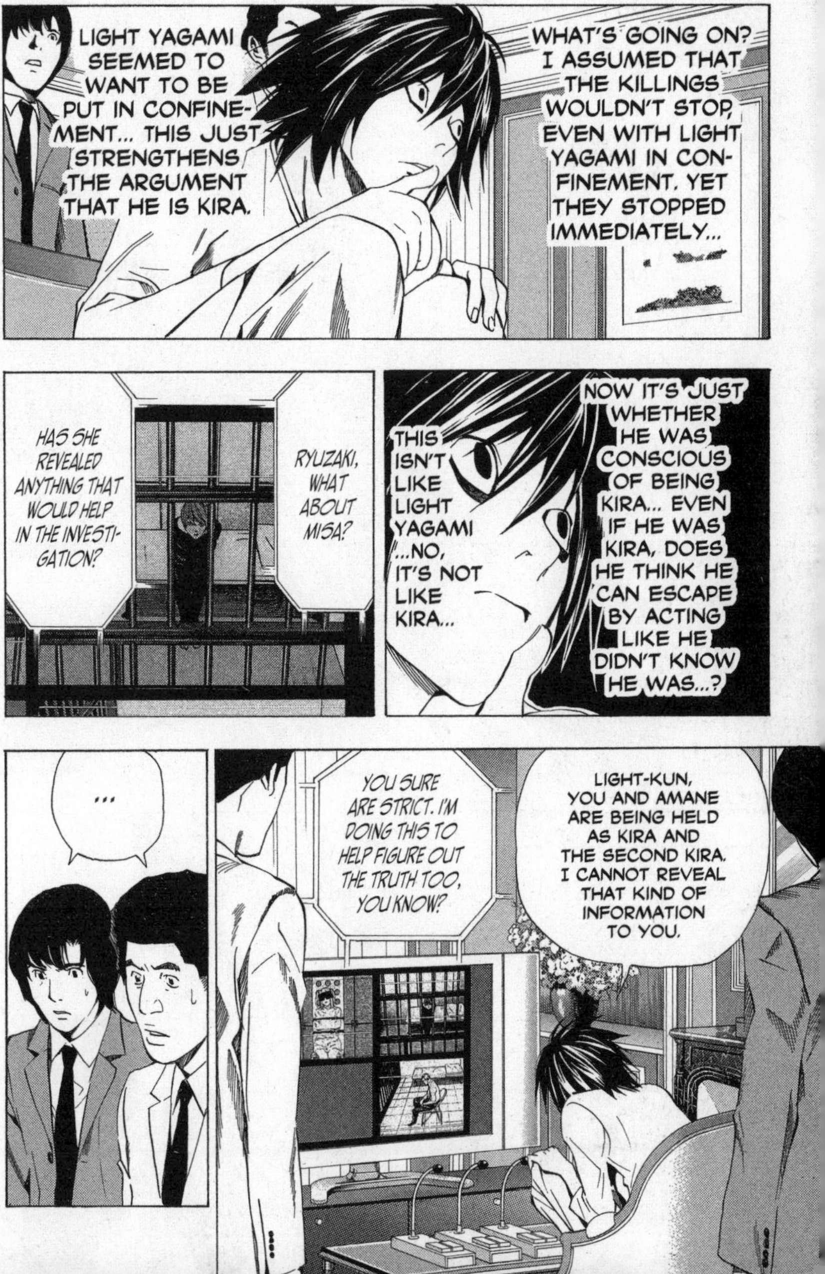
WHAT'S GOING ON? I ASSUMED THAT THE KILLINGS WOULDN'T STOP, EVEN WITH LIGHT YAGAMI IN CONFINEMENT. YET THEY STOPPED IMMEDIATELY...
LIGHT YAGAMI SEEMED TO WANT TO BE PUT IN CONFINEMENT... THIS JUST STRENGTHENS THE ARGUMENT THAT HE IS KIRA.
NOW IT'S JUST WHETHER HE WAS CONSCIOUS OF BEING KIRA... EVEN IF HE WAS KIRA, DOES HE THINK HE CAN ESCAPE BY ACTING LIKE HE DIDN'T KNOW HE WAS...?
THIS ISN'T LIKE LIGHT YAGAMI ...NO, IT'S NOT LIKE KIRA...
RYUZAKI, WHAT ABOUT MISA?
HAS SHE REVEALED ANYTHING THAT WOULD HELP IN THE INVESTIGATION?
LIGHT-KUN, YOU AND AMANE ARE BEING HELD AS KIRA AND THE SECOND KIRA. I CANNOT REVEAL THAT KIND OF INFORMATION TO YOU.
YOU SURE ARE STRICT. I'M DOING THIS TO HELP FIGURE OUT THE TRUTH TOO, YOU KNOW?
...

READ THIS WAY

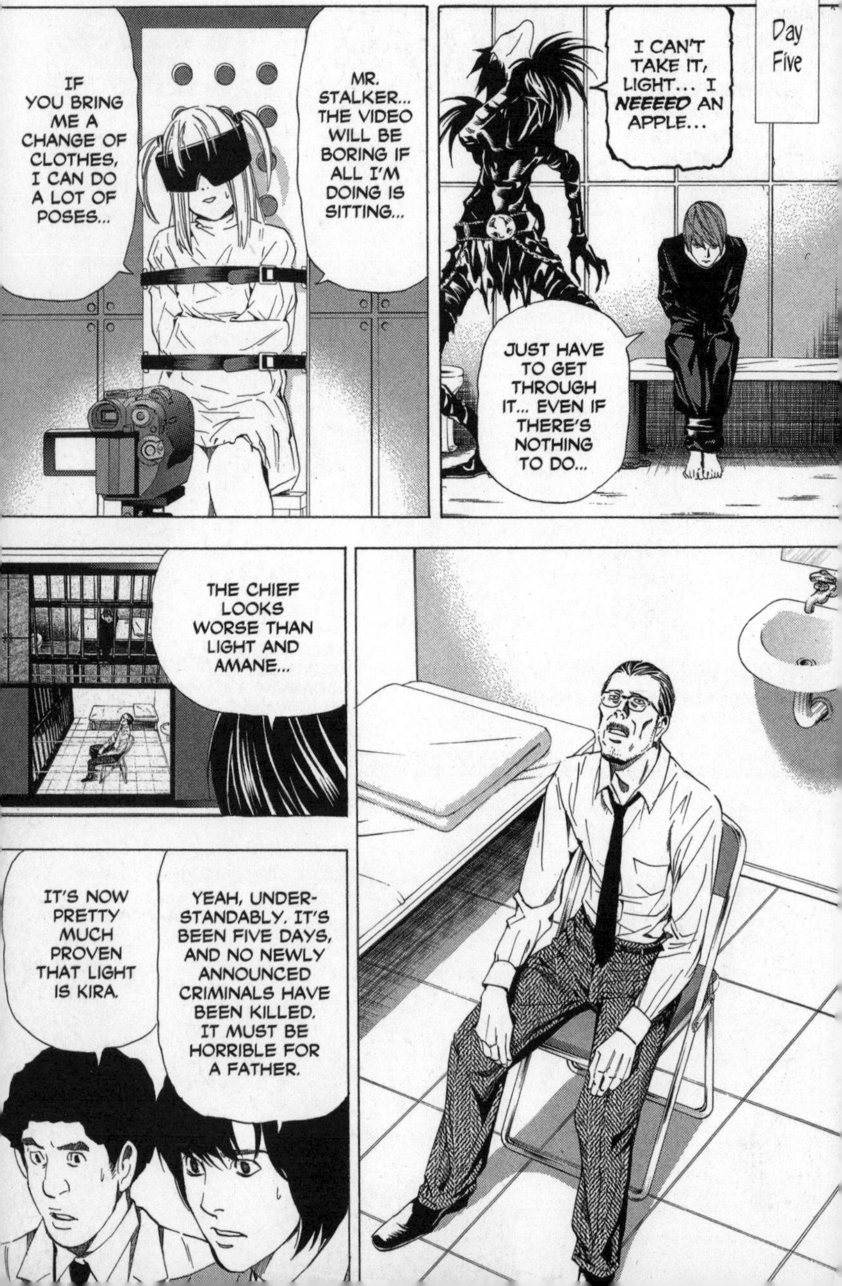
Day Five
I CAN'T TAKE IT, LIGHT... I NEEEED AN APPLE...
JUST HAVE TO GET THROUGH IT... EVEN IF THERE'S NOTHING TO DO...
MR. STALKER... THE VIDEO WILL BE BORING IF ALL I'M DOING IS SITTING...
IF YOU BRING ME A CHANGE OF CLOTHES, I CAN DO A LOT OF POSES...
THE CHIEF LOOKS WORSE THAN LIGHT AND AMANE...
YEAH, UNDER-STANDABLY. IT'S BEEN FIVE DAYS, AND NO NEWLY ANNOUNCED CRIMINALS HAVE BEEN KILLED. IT MUST BE HORRIBLE FOR A FATHER.
IT'S NOW PRETTY MUCH PROVEN THAT LIGHT IS KIRA.

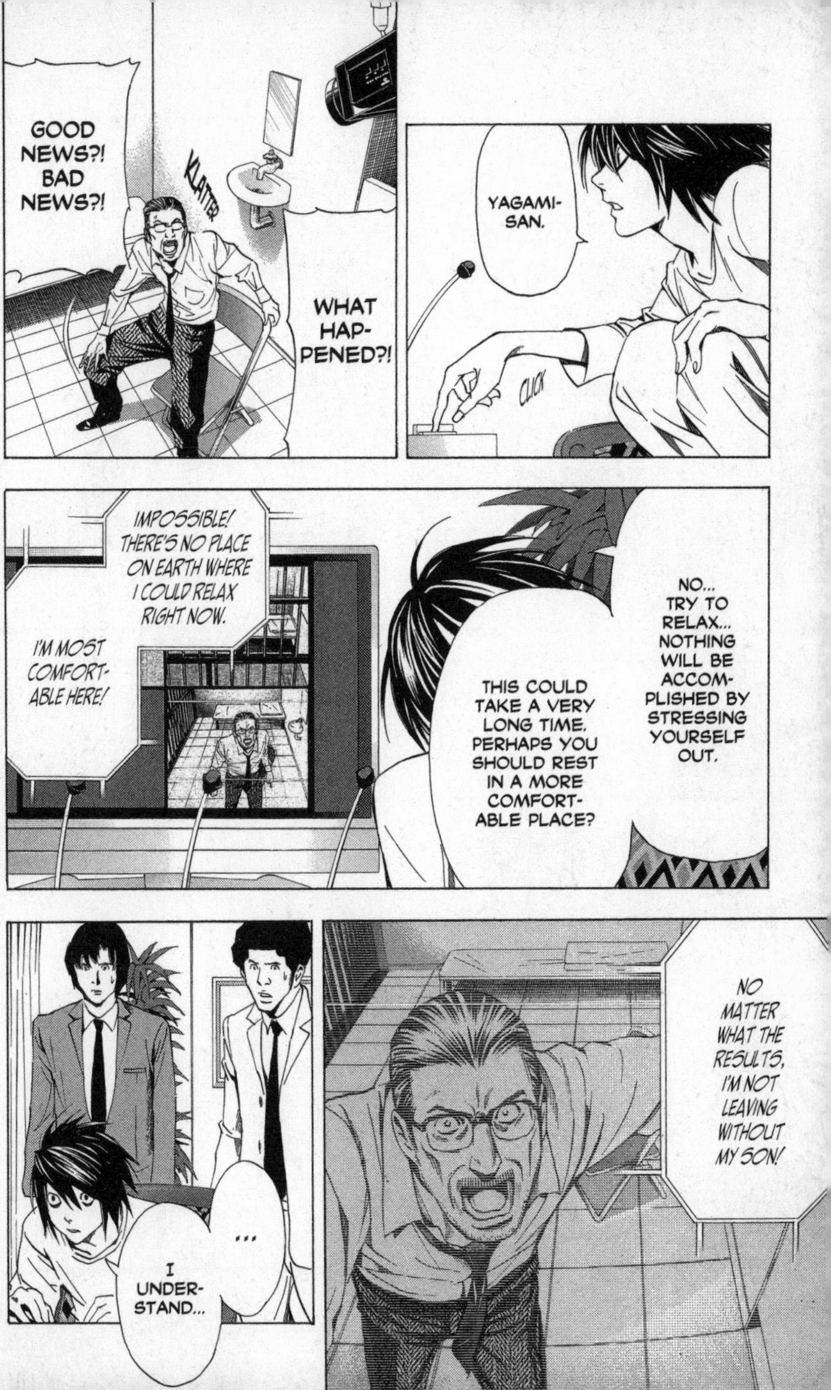
YAGAMI-SAN.
CLICK
KLATTER
WHAT HAPPENED?!
GOOD NEWS?! BAD NEWS?!
NO... TRY TO RELAX... NOTHING WILL BE ACCOMPLISHED BY STRESSING YOURSELF OUT.
THIS COULD TAKE A VERY LONG TIME. PERHAPS YOU SHOULD REST IN A MORE COMFORTABLE PLACE?
IMPOSSIBLE! THERE'S NO PLACE ON EARTH WHERE I COULD RELAX RIGHT NOW.
I'M MOST COMFORTABLE HERE!
NO MATTER WHAT THE RESULTS, I'M NOT LEAVING WITHOUT MY SON!
...
I UNDERSTAND...

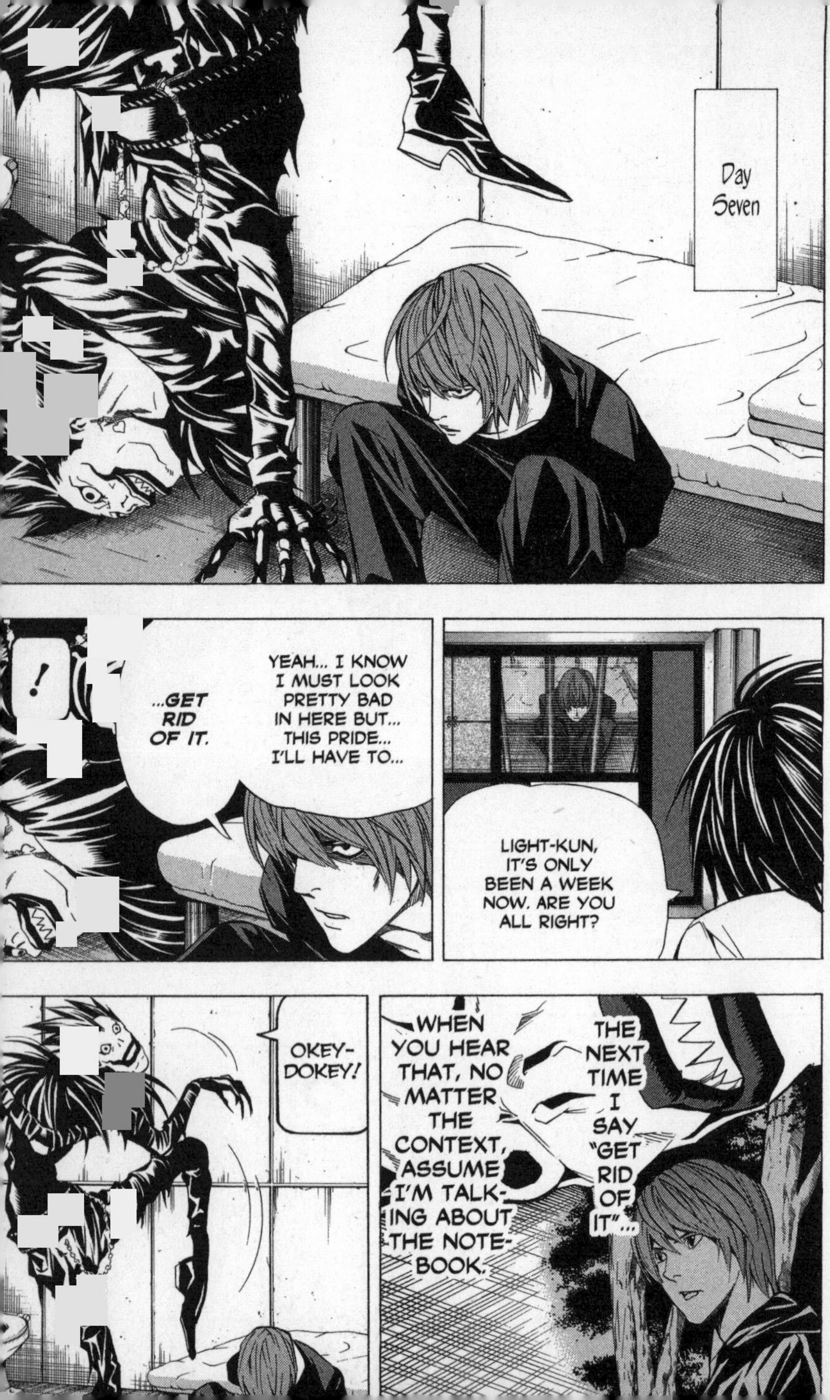
Day Seven
LIGHT-KUN, IT'S ONLY BEEN A WEEK NOW. ARE YOU ALL RIGHT?
YEAH... I KNOW I MUST LOOK PRETTY BAD IN HERE BUT... THIS PRIDE... I'LL HAVE TO...
...GET RID OF IT.
!
THE NEXT TIME I SAY "GET RID OF IT"...
WHEN YOU HEAR THAT, NO MATTER THE CONTEXT, ASSUME I'M TALKING ABOUT THE NOTEBOOK.
OKEY-DOKEY!

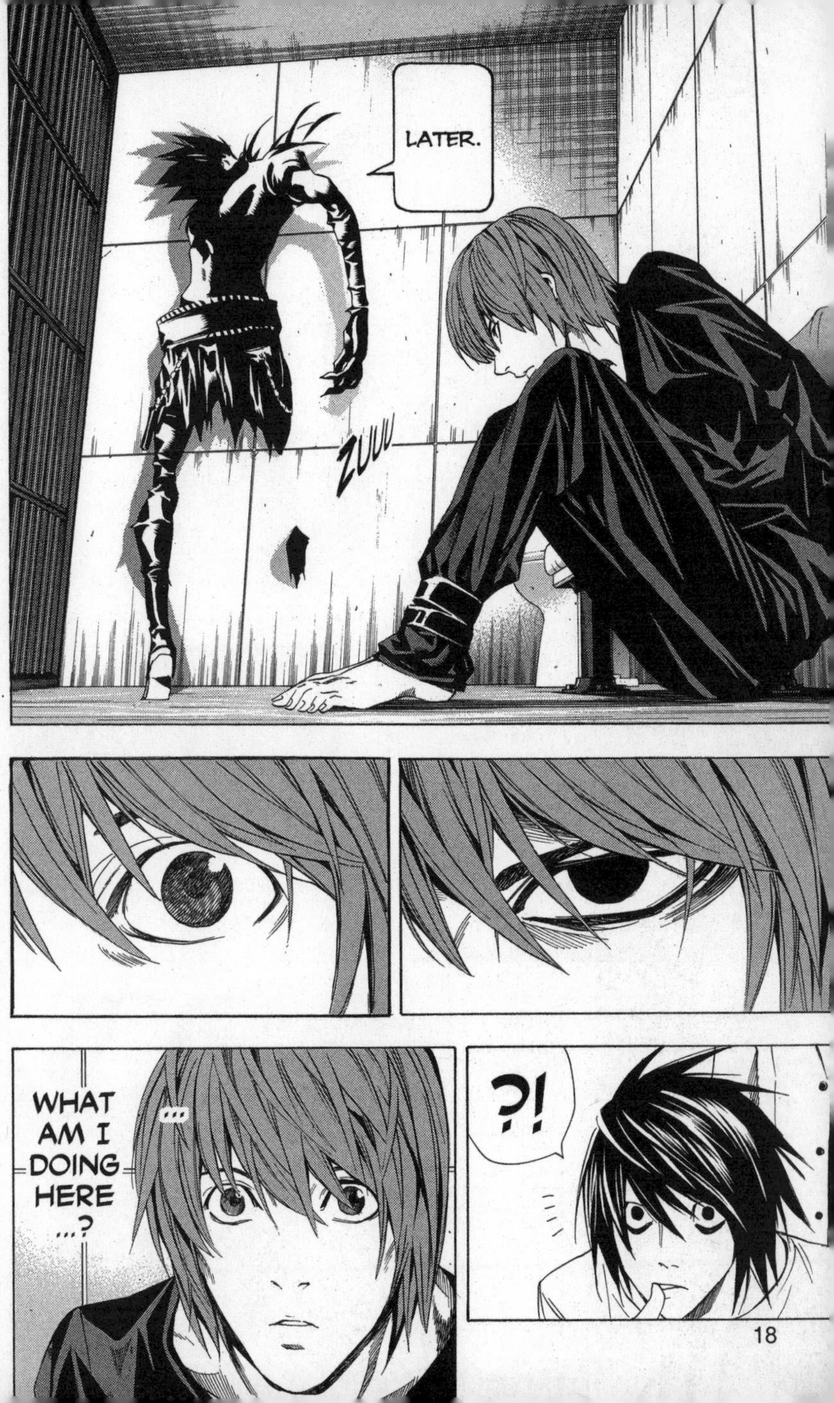
LATER.
ZUUU
?!
...
WHAT AM I DOING HERE ...?

READ THIS WAY

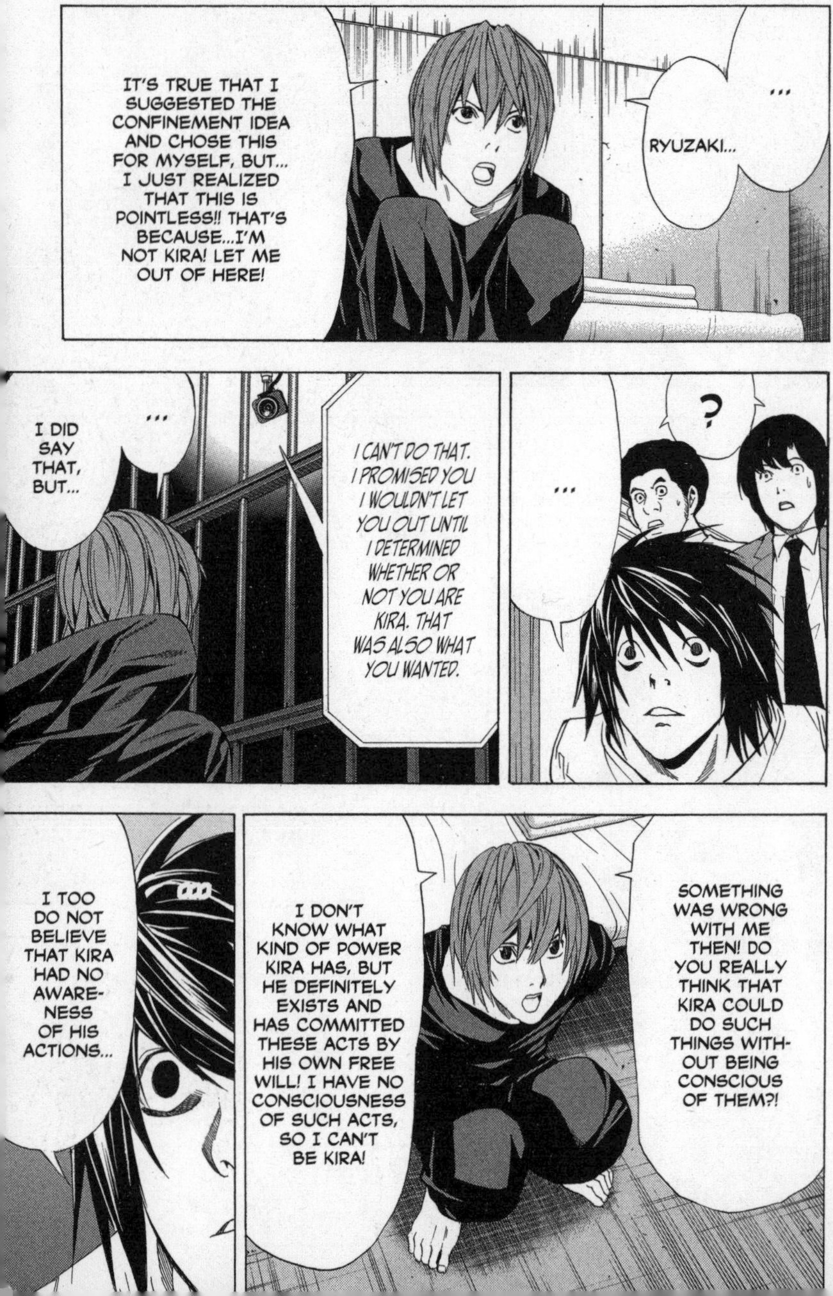
...
RYUZAKI...
IT'S TRUE THAT I SUGGESTED THE CONFINEMENT IDEA AND CHOSE THIS FOR MYSELF, BUT... I JUST REALIZED THAT THIS IS POINTLESS!! THAT'S BECAUSE...I'M NOT KIRA! LET ME OUT OF HERE!
?
...
I CAN'T DO THAT. I PROMISED YOU I WOULDN'T LET YOU OUT UNTIL I DETERMINED WHETHER OR NOT YOU ARE KIRA. THAT WAS ALSO WHAT YOU WANTED.
...
I DID SAY THAT, BUT...
SOMETHING WAS WRONG WITH ME THEN! DO YOU REALLY THINK THAT KIRA COULD DO SUCH THINGS WITH-OUT BEING CONSCIOUS OF THEM?!
I DON'T KNOW WHAT KIND OF POWER KIRA HAS, BUT HE DEFINITELY EXISTS AND HAS COMMITTED THESE ACTS BY HIS OWN FREE WILL! I HAVE NO CONSCIOUSNESS OF SUCH ACTS, SO I CAN'T BE KIRA!
I TOO DO NOT BELIEVE THAT KIRA HAD NO AWARE-NESS OF HIS ACTIONS...

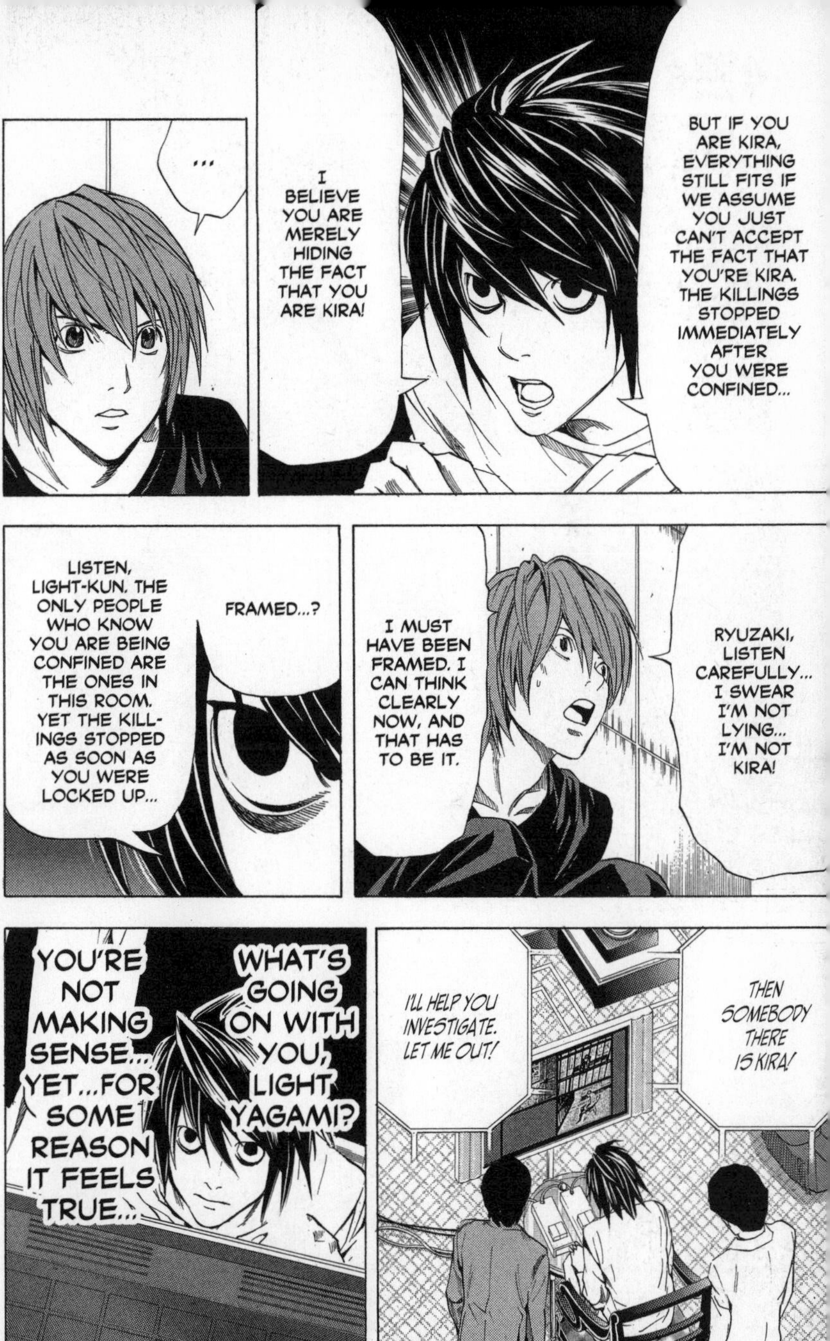
BUT IF YOU ARE KIRA, EVERYTHING STILL FITS IF WE ASSUME YOU JUST CAN'T ACCEPT THE FACT THAT YOU'RE KIRA. THE KILLINGS STOPPED IMMEDIATELY AFTER YOU WERE CONFINED...
I BELIEVE YOU ARE MERELY HIDING THE FACT THAT YOU ARE KIRA!
...
RYUZAKI, LISTEN CAREFULLY... I SWEAR I'M NOT LYING... I'M NOT KIRA!
I MUST HAVE BEEN FRAMED. I CAN THINK CLEARLY NOW, AND THAT HAS TO BE IT.
FRAMED...?
LISTEN, LIGHT-KUN. THE ONLY PEOPLE WHO KNOW YOU ARE BEING CONFINED ARE THE ONES IN THIS ROOM. YET THE KILL-INGS STOPPED AS SOON AS YOU WERE LOCKED UP...
THEN SOMEBODY THERE IS KIRA!
I'LL HELP YOU INVESTIGATE. LET ME OUT!
WHAT'S GOING ON WITH YOU, LIGHT YAGAMI?
YOU'RE NOT MAKING SENSE... YET...FOR SOME REASON IT FEELS TRUE...

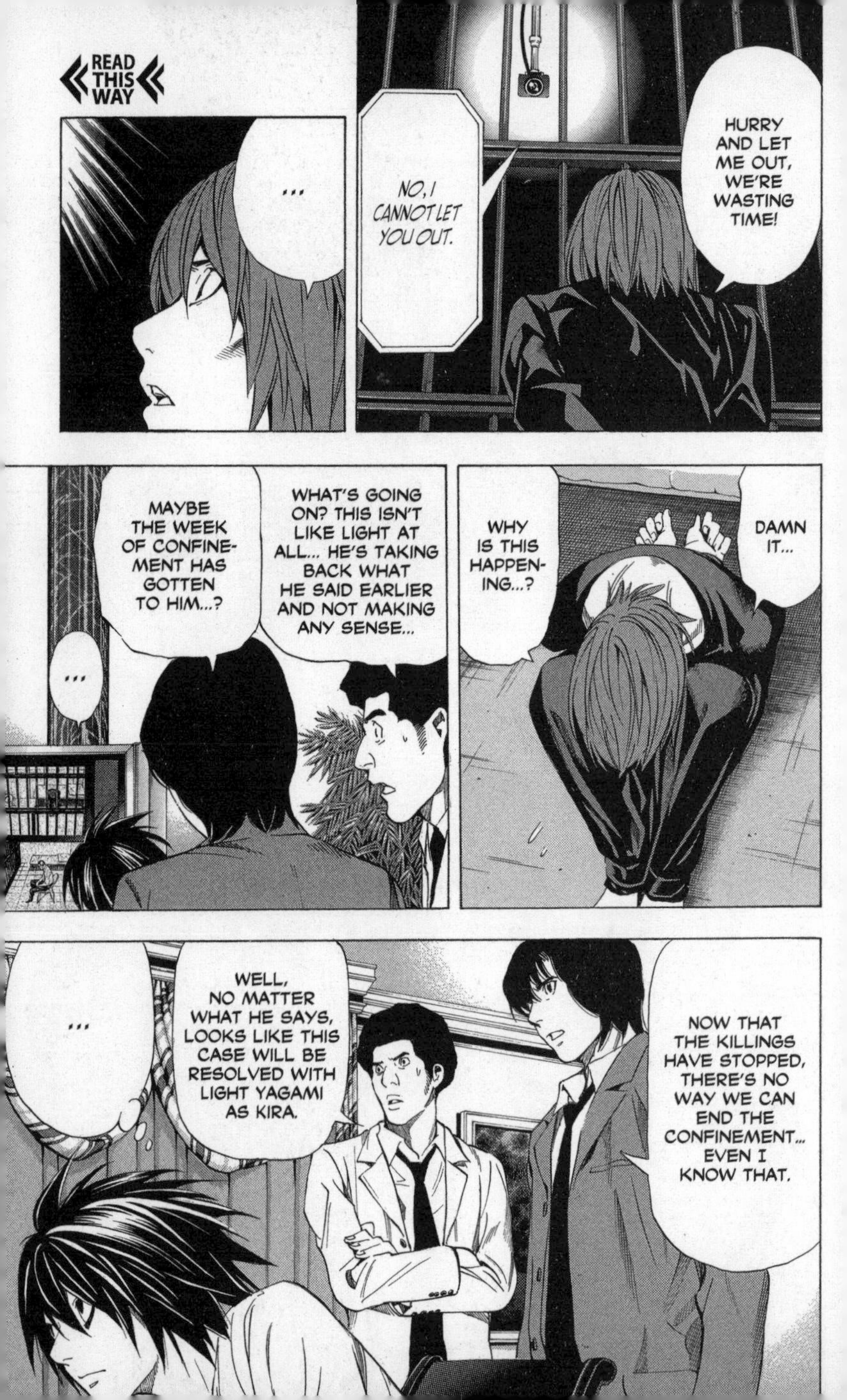
READ THIS WAY
HURRY AND LET ME OUT, WE'RE WASTING TIME!
NO, I CANNOT LET YOU OUT.
...
DAMN IT...
WHY IS THIS HAPPEN-ING...?
WHAT'S GOING ON? THIS ISN'T LIKE LIGHT AT ALL... HE'S TAKING BACK WHAT HE SAID EARLIER AND NOT MAKING ANY SENSE...
MAYBE THE WEEK OF CONFINE-MENT HAS GOTTEN TO HIM...?
...
NOW THAT THE KILLINGS HAVE STOPPED, THERE'S NO WAY WE CAN END THE CONFINEMENT... EVEN I KNOW THAT.
WELL, NO MATTER WHAT HE SAYS, LOOKS LIKE THIS CASE WILL BE RESOLVED WITH LIGHT YAGAMI AS KIRA.
...

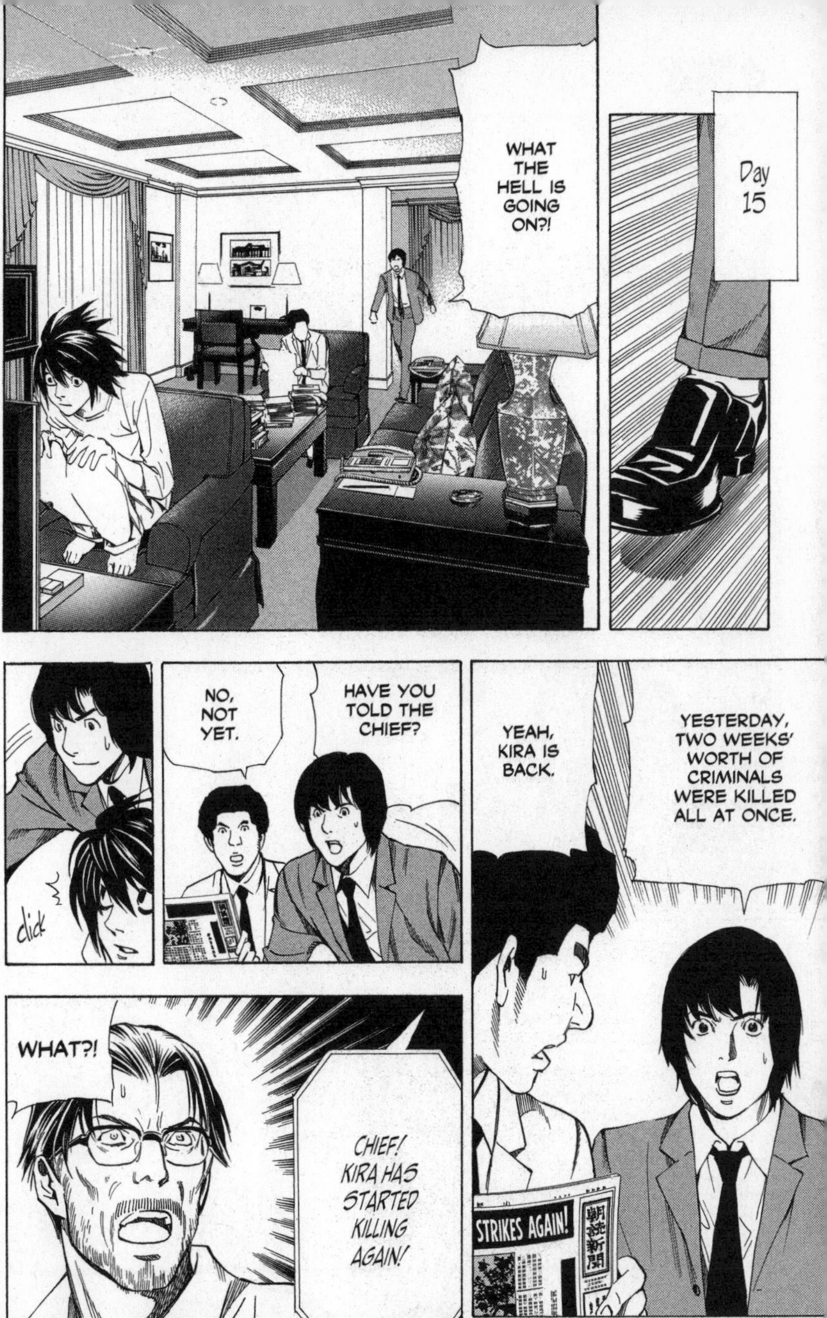
Day 15
WHAT THE HELL IS GOING ON?!
YESTERDAY, TWO WEEKS' WORTH OF CRIMINALS WERE KILLED ALL AT ONCE.
YEAH, KIRA IS BACK.
STRIKES AGAIN!
HAVE YOU TOLD THE CHIEF?
NO, NOT YET.
click
CHIEF! KIRA HAS STARTED KILLING AGAIN!
WHAT?!

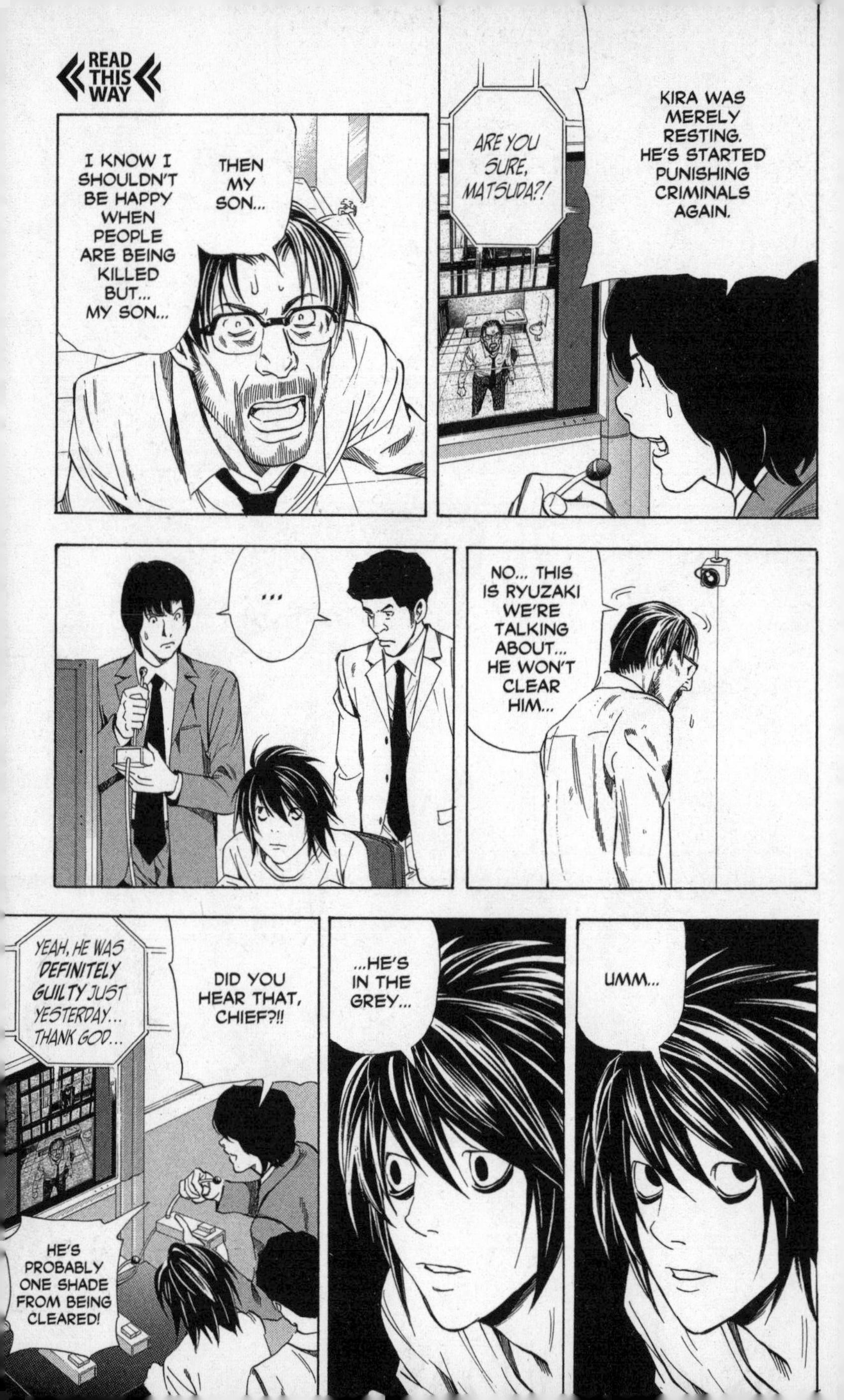
READ THIS WAY
KIRA WAS MERELY RESTING. HE'S STARTED PUNISHING CRIMINALS AGAIN.
ARE YOU SURE, MATSUDA?!
THEN MY SON...
I KNOW I SHOULDN'T BE HAPPY WHEN PEOPLE ARE BEING KILLED BUT... MY SON...
NO... THIS IS RYUZAKI WE'RE TALKING ABOUT... HE WON'T CLEAR HIM...
...
UMM...
...HE'S IN THE GREY...
DID YOU HEAR THAT, CHIEF?!!
YEAH, HE WAS DEFINITELY GUILTY JUST YESTERDAY... THANK GOD...
HE'S PROBABLY ONE SHADE FROM BEING CLEARED!

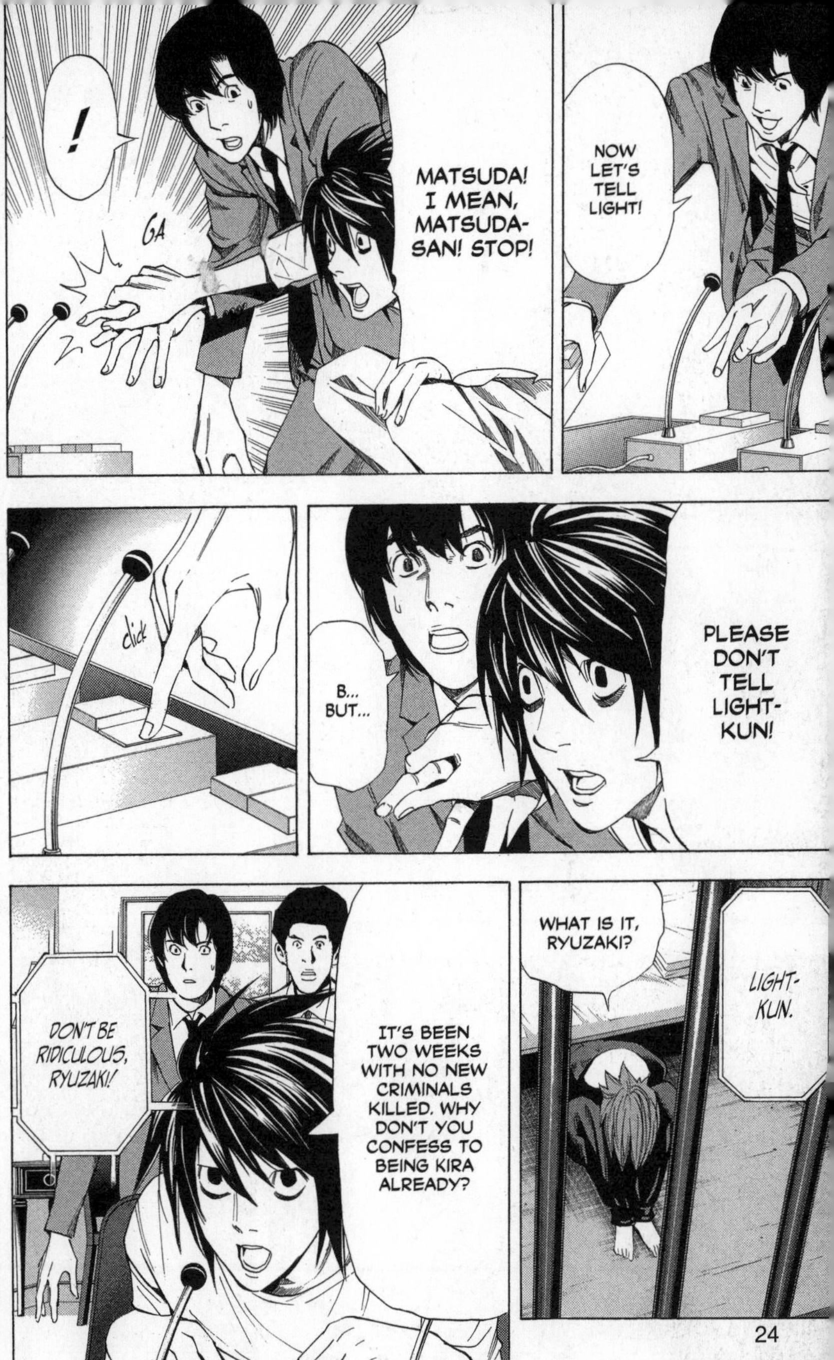
NOW LET'S TELL LIGHT!
MATSUDA! I MEAN, MATSUDA-SAN! STOP!
!
GA
PLEASE DON'T TELL LIGHT-KUN!
B... BUT...
click
LIGHT-KUN.
WHAT IS IT, RYUZAKI?
IT'S BEEN TWO WEEKS WITH NO NEW CRIMINALS KILLED. WHY DON'T YOU CONFESS TO BEING KIRA ALREADY?
DON'T BE RIDICULOUS, RYUZAKI!

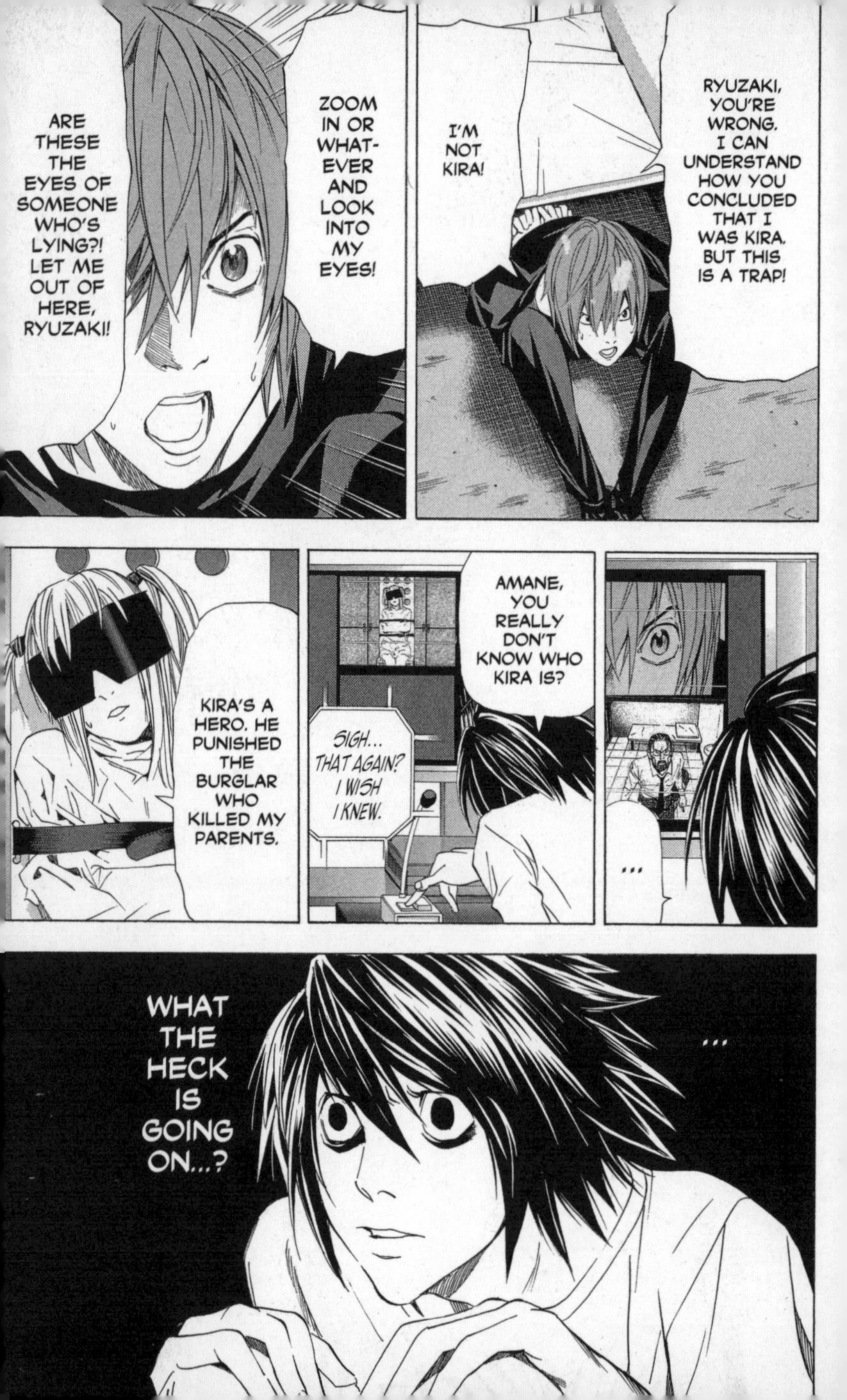
RYUZAKI, YOU'RE WRONG. I CAN UNDERSTAND HOW YOU CONCLUDED THAT I WAS KIRA. BUT THIS IS A TRAP!
I'M NOT KIRA!
ZOOM IN OR WHATEVER AND LOOK INTO MY EYES!
ARE THESE THE EYES OF SOMEONE WHO'S LYING?! LET ME OUT OF HERE, RYUZAKI!
...
AMANE, YOU REALLY DON'T KNOW WHO KIRA IS?
SIGH... THAT AGAIN? I WISH I KNEW.
KIRA'S A HERO. HE PUNISHED THE BURGLAR WHO KILLED MY PARENTS.
...
WHAT THE HECK IS GOING ON...?

# DEATH NOTE
## How to Use It
### XXIV

○ The god of death must not stay in the human world without a particular reason. Conditions to stay in the human world are as follows:

死神は無闇に人間界に居てはならない。
人間界に居てよい条件は、

I.    When the god of death's DEATH NOTE is handed to a human.

Ⅰ. 自分が所持していたノートを人間に持たせている時。

II.    Essentially, finding a human to pass on the DEATH NOTE should be done from the world of the gods of death, but if it is within 82 hours this may also be done in the human world.

Ⅱ. ノートを渡す人間を物色するのは、本来、死神界からするべきではあるが、82時間以内であれば、人間界に居て物色しても構わない。

III.    When a god of death stalks an individual with an intention to kill them, as long as it is within 82 hours of haunting them, the god of death may stay in the human world.

Ⅲ. 人間を殺す目的でより深くその個人を観察する場合も、82時間以内でその人間に憑いていれば人間界に居てもよい。

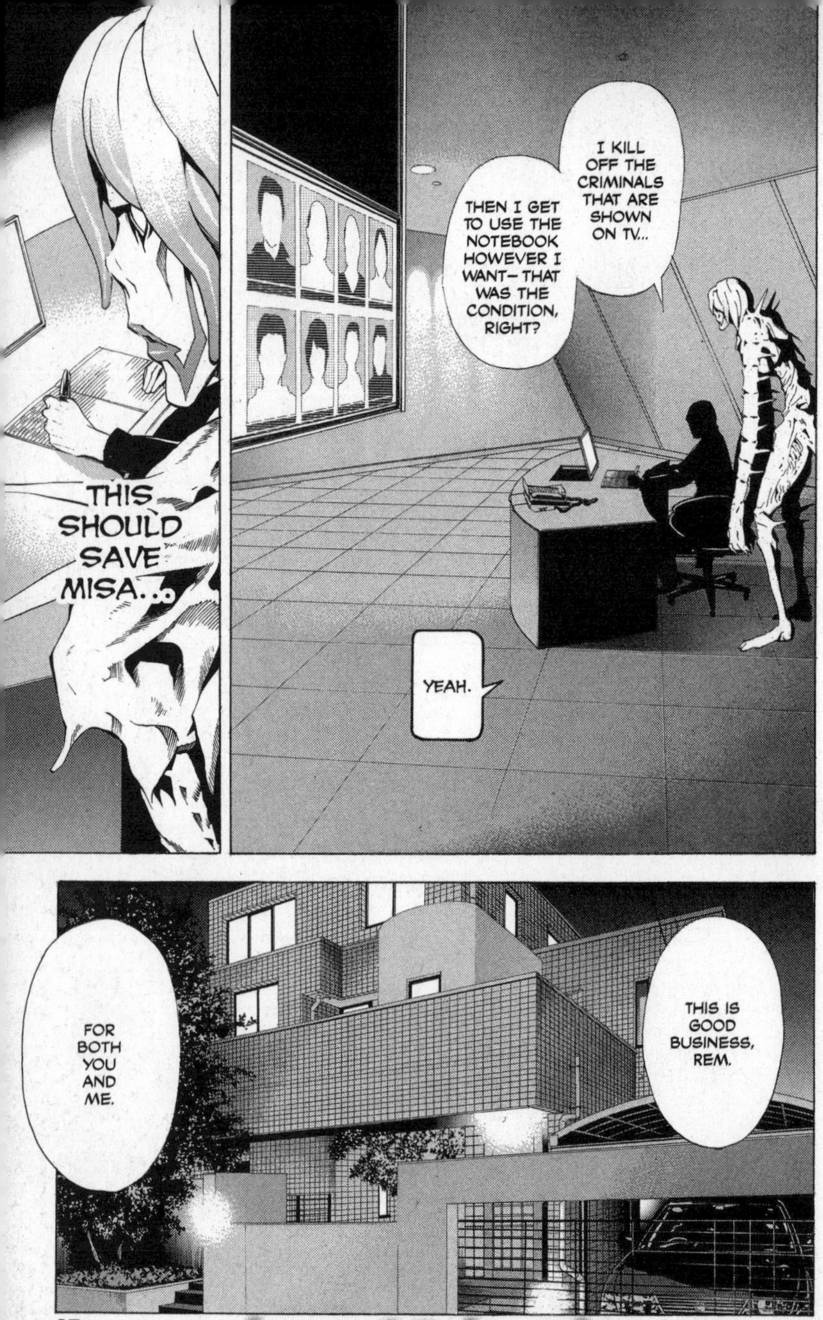
I KILL OFF THE CRIMINALS THAT ARE SHOWN ON TV...
THEN I GET TO USE THE NOTEBOOK HOWEVER I WANT—THAT WAS THE CONDITION, RIGHT?
YEAH.
THIS SHOULD SAVE MISA...
THIS IS GOOD BUSINESS, REM.
FOR BOTH YOU AND ME.



# chapter 36 Father and Son

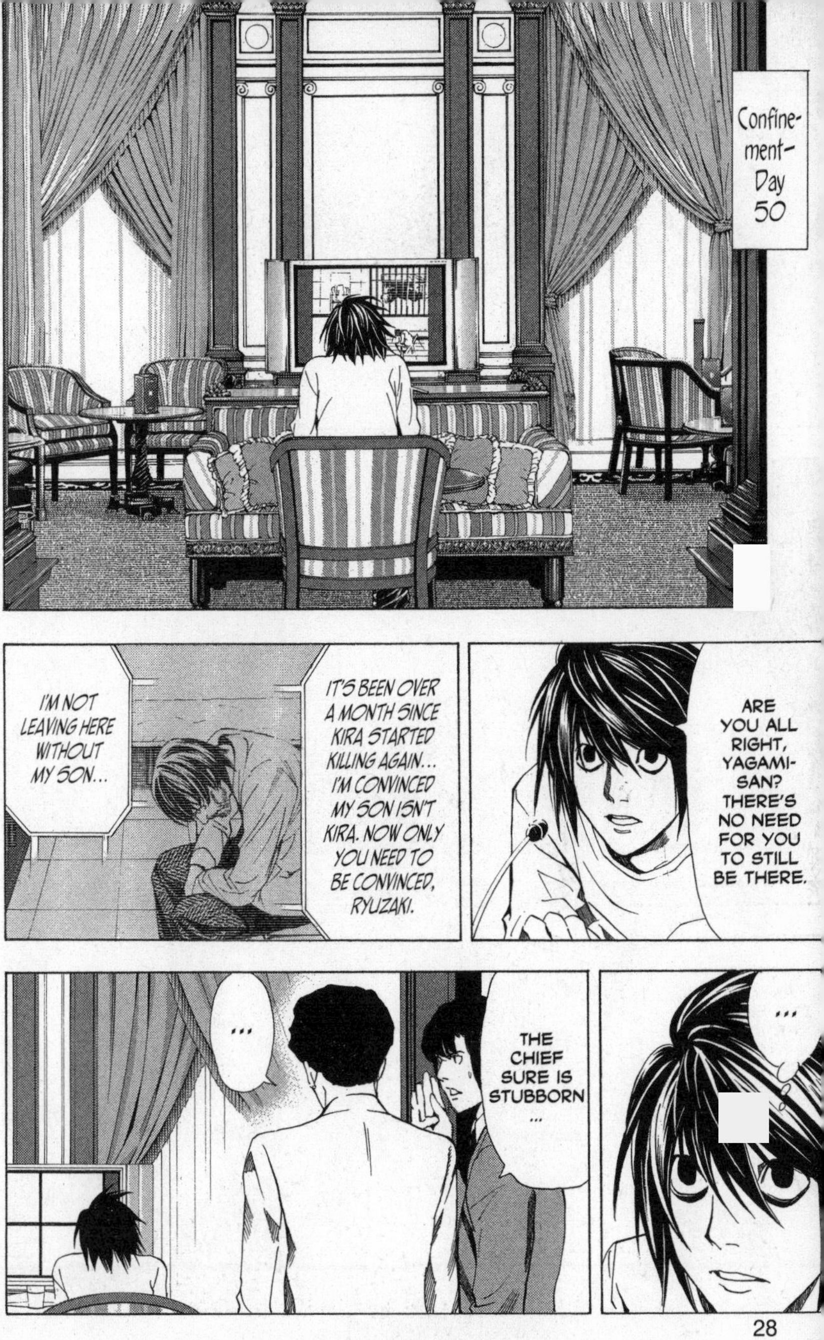
Confinement-Day 50
ARE YOU ALL RIGHT, YAGAMI-SAN? THERE'S NO NEED FOR YOU TO STILL BE THERE.
IT'S BEEN OVER A MONTH SINCE KIRA STARTED KILLING AGAIN... I'M CONVINCED MY SON ISN'T KIRA. NOW ONLY YOU NEED TO BE CONVINCED, RYUZAKI.
I'M NOT LEAVING HERE WITHOUT MY SON...
...
THE CHIEF SURE IS STUBBORN ...
...

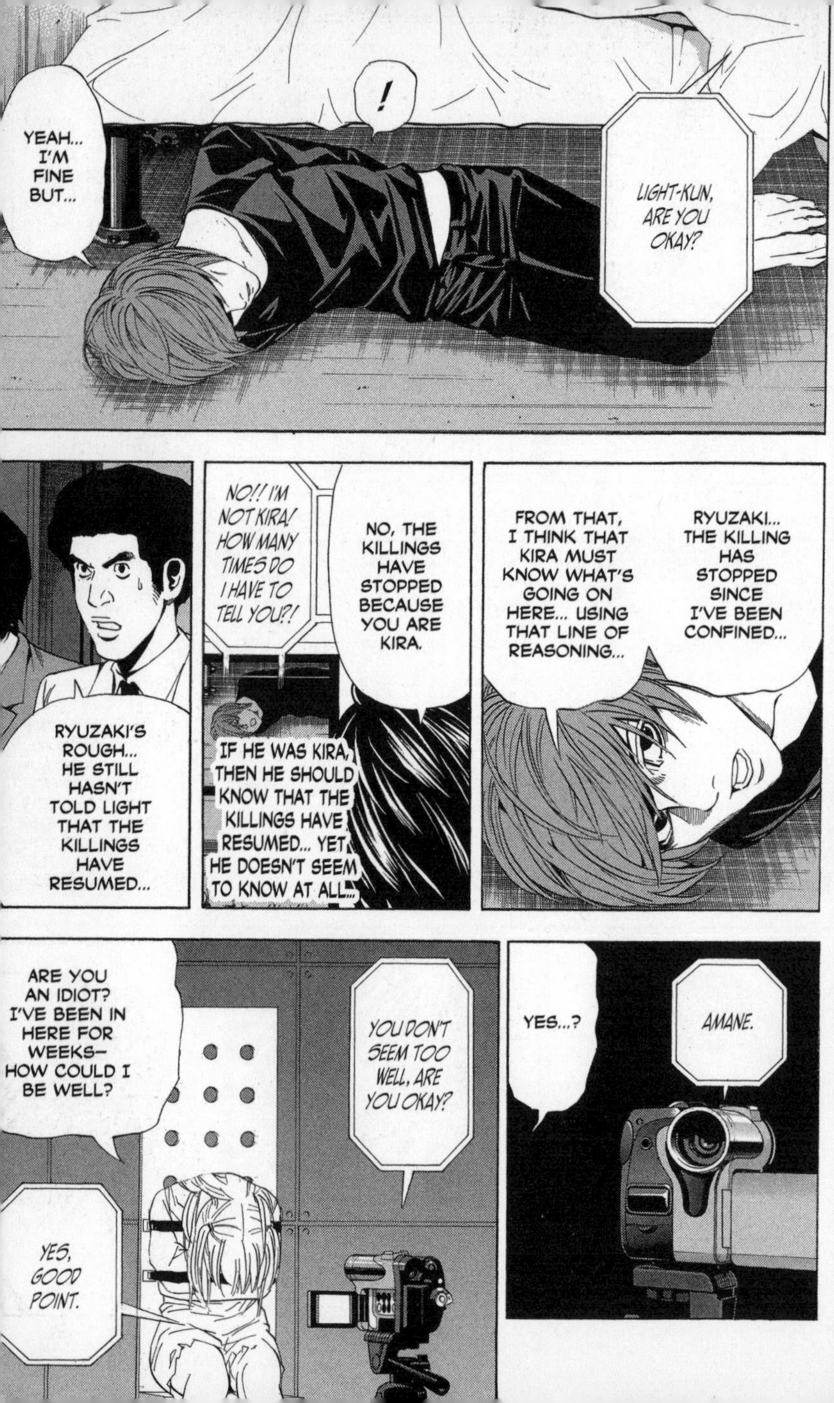
LIGHT-KUN, ARE YOU OKAY?
!
YEAH... I'M FINE BUT...
RYUZAKI... THE KILLING HAS STOPPED SINCE I'VE BEEN CONFINED...
FROM THAT, I THINK THAT KIRA MUST KNOW WHAT'S GOING ON HERE... USING THAT LINE OF REASONING...
NO, THE KILLINGS HAVE STOPPED BECAUSE YOU ARE KIRA.
NO!! I'M NOT KIRA! HOW MANY TIMES DO I HAVE TO TELL YOU?!
IF HE WAS KIRA, THEN HE SHOULD KNOW THAT THE KILLINGS HAVE RESUMED... YET HE DOESN'T SEEM TO KNOW AT ALL...
RYUZAKI'S ROUGH... HE STILL HASN'T TOLD LIGHT THAT THE KILLINGS HAVE RESUMED...
AMANE.
YES...?
YOU DON'T SEEM TOO WELL, ARE YOU OKAY?
ARE YOU AN IDIOT? I'VE BEEN IN HERE FOR WEEKS– HOW COULD I BE WELL?
YES, GOOD POINT.

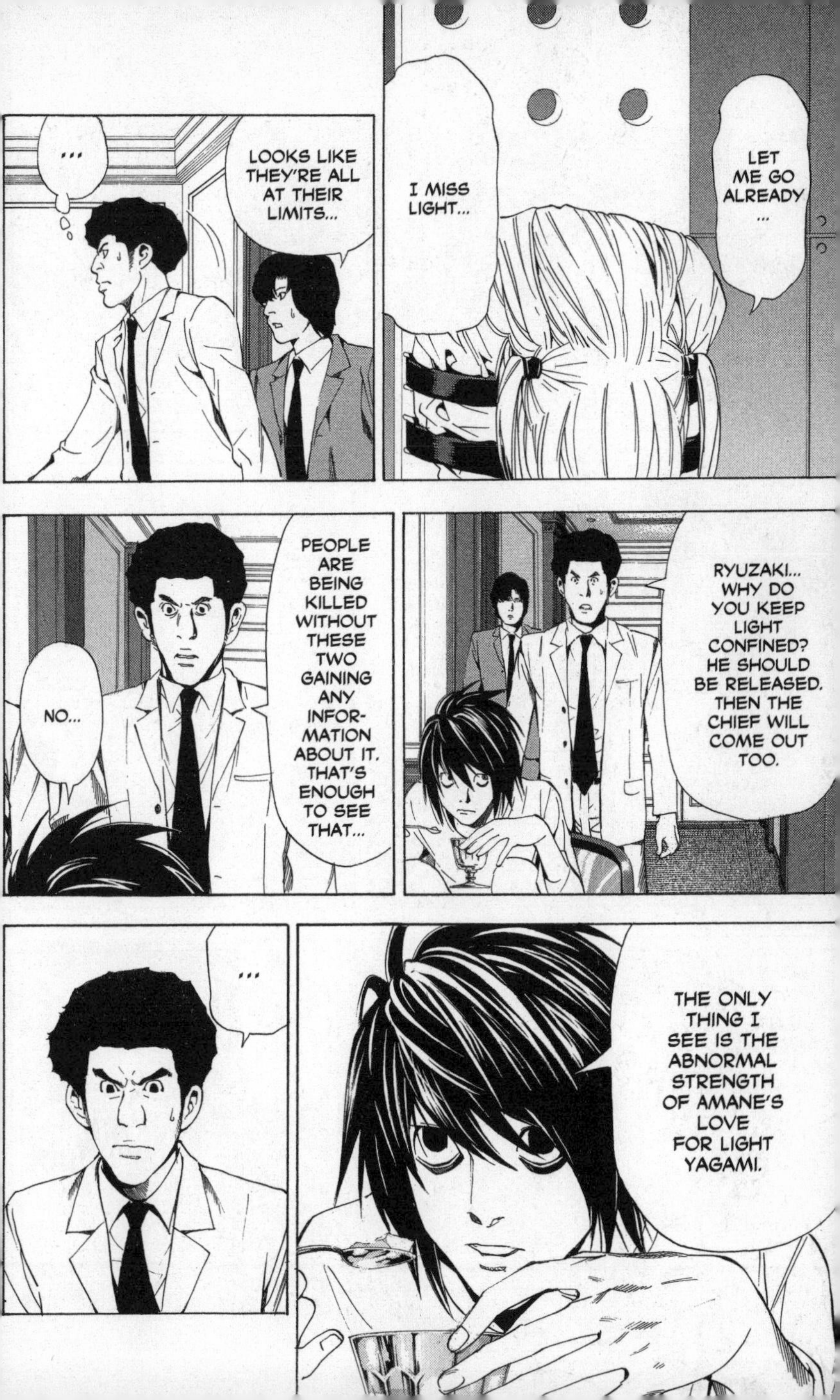
LET ME GO ALREADY ...
I MISS LIGHT...
LOOKS LIKE THEY'RE ALL AT THEIR LIMITS...
...
RYUZAKI... WHY DO YOU KEEP LIGHT CONFINED? HE SHOULD BE RELEASED. THEN THE CHIEF WILL COME OUT TOO.
PEOPLE ARE BEING KILLED WITHOUT THESE TWO GAINING ANY INFORMATION ABOUT IT. THAT'S ENOUGH TO SEE THAT...
NO...
THE ONLY THING I SEE IS THE ABNORMAL STRENGTH OF AMANE'S LOVE FOR LIGHT YAGAMI.
...

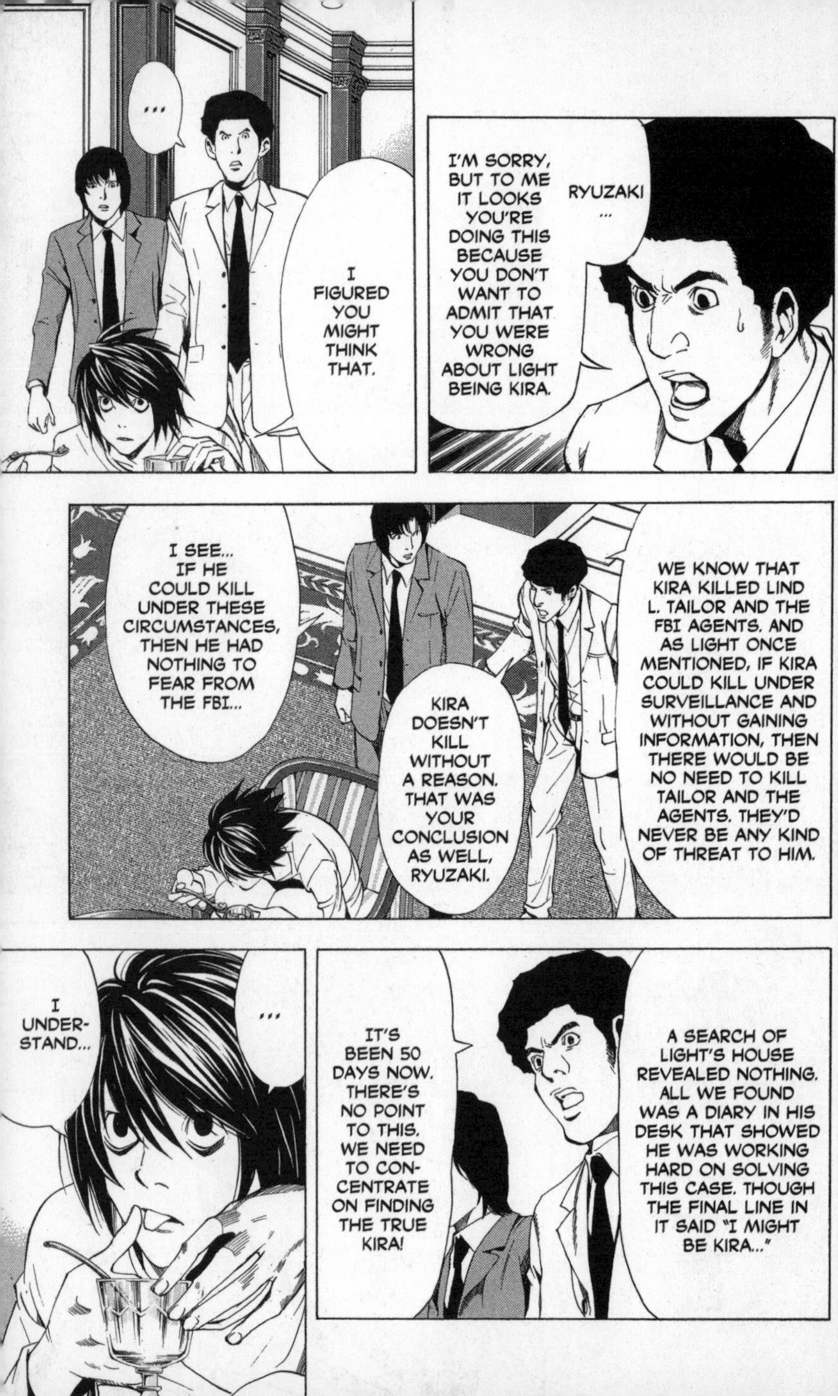
RYUZAKI ...
I'M SORRY, BUT TO ME IT LOOKS YOU'RE DOING THIS BECAUSE YOU DON'T WANT TO ADMIT THAT YOU WERE WRONG ABOUT LIGHT BEING KIRA.
...
I FIGURED YOU MIGHT THINK THAT.
WE KNOW THAT KIRA KILLED LIND L. TAILOR AND THE FBI AGENTS. AND AS LIGHT ONCE MENTIONED, IF KIRA COULD KILL UNDER SURVEILLANCE AND WITHOUT GAINING INFORMATION, THEN THERE WOULD BE NO NEED TO KILL TAILOR AND THE AGENTS. THEY'D NEVER BE ANY KIND OF THREAT TO HIM.
KIRA DOESN'T KILL WITHOUT A REASON. THAT WAS YOUR CONCLUSION AS WELL, RYUZAKI.
I SEE... IF HE COULD KILL UNDER THESE CIRCUMSTANCES, THEN HE HAD NOTHING TO FEAR FROM THE FBI...
A SEARCH OF LIGHT'S HOUSE REVEALED NOTHING. ALL WE FOUND WAS A DIARY IN HIS DESK THAT SHOWED HE WAS WORKING HARD ON SOLVING THIS CASE. THOUGH THE FINAL LINE IN IT SAID "I MIGHT BE KIRA..."
IT'S BEEN 50 DAYS NOW. THERE'S NO POINT TO THIS. WE NEED TO CON-CENTRATE ON FINDING THE TRUE KIRA!
...
I UNDER-STAND...

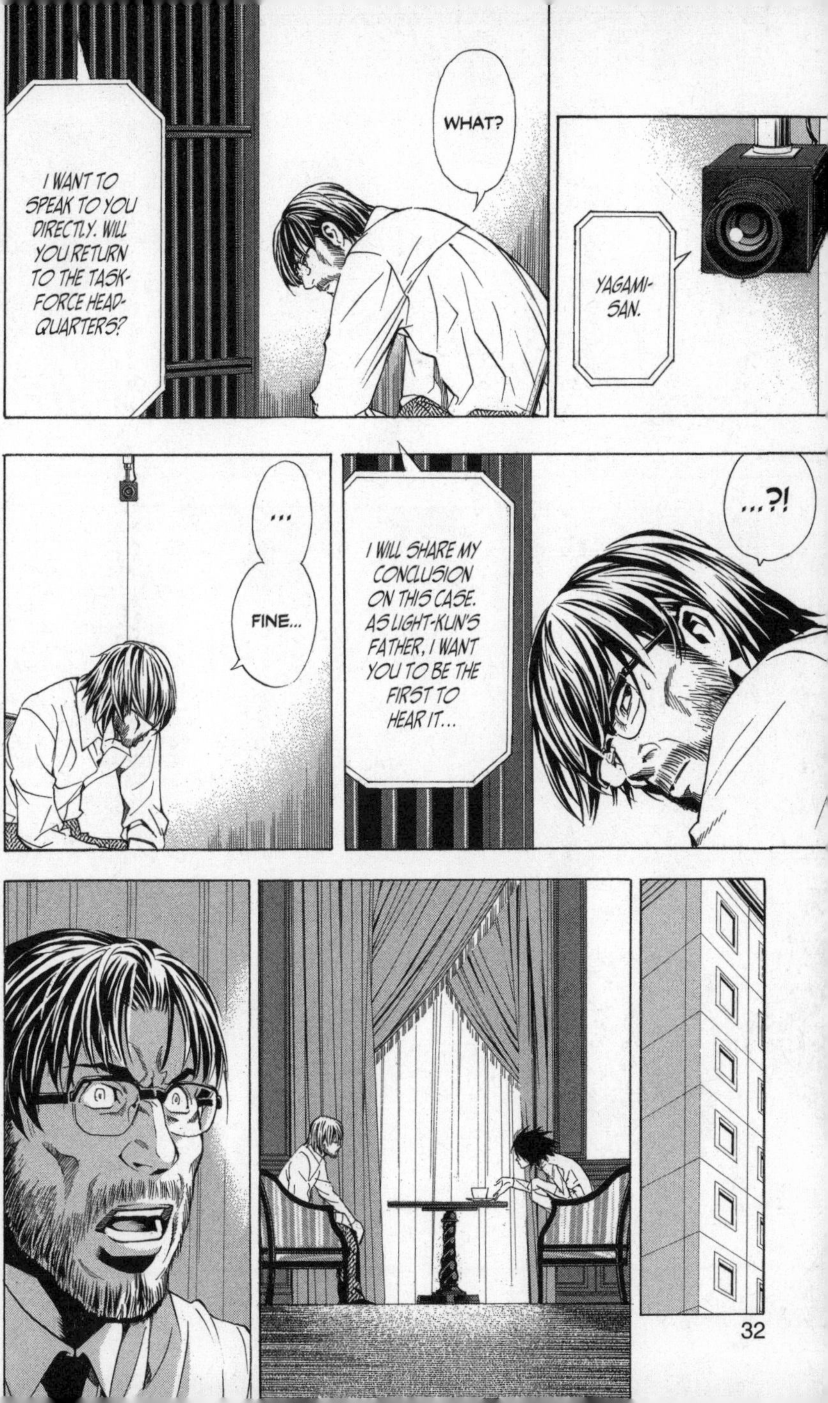
YAGAMI-SAN.
WHAT?
I WANT TO SPEAK TO YOU DIRECTLY. WILL YOU RETURN TO THE TASK-FORCE HEAD-QUARTERS?
...?!
I WILL SHARE MY CONCLUSION ON THIS CASE. AS LIGHT-KUN'S FATHER, I WANT YOU TO BE THE FIRST TO HEAR IT...
...
FINE...

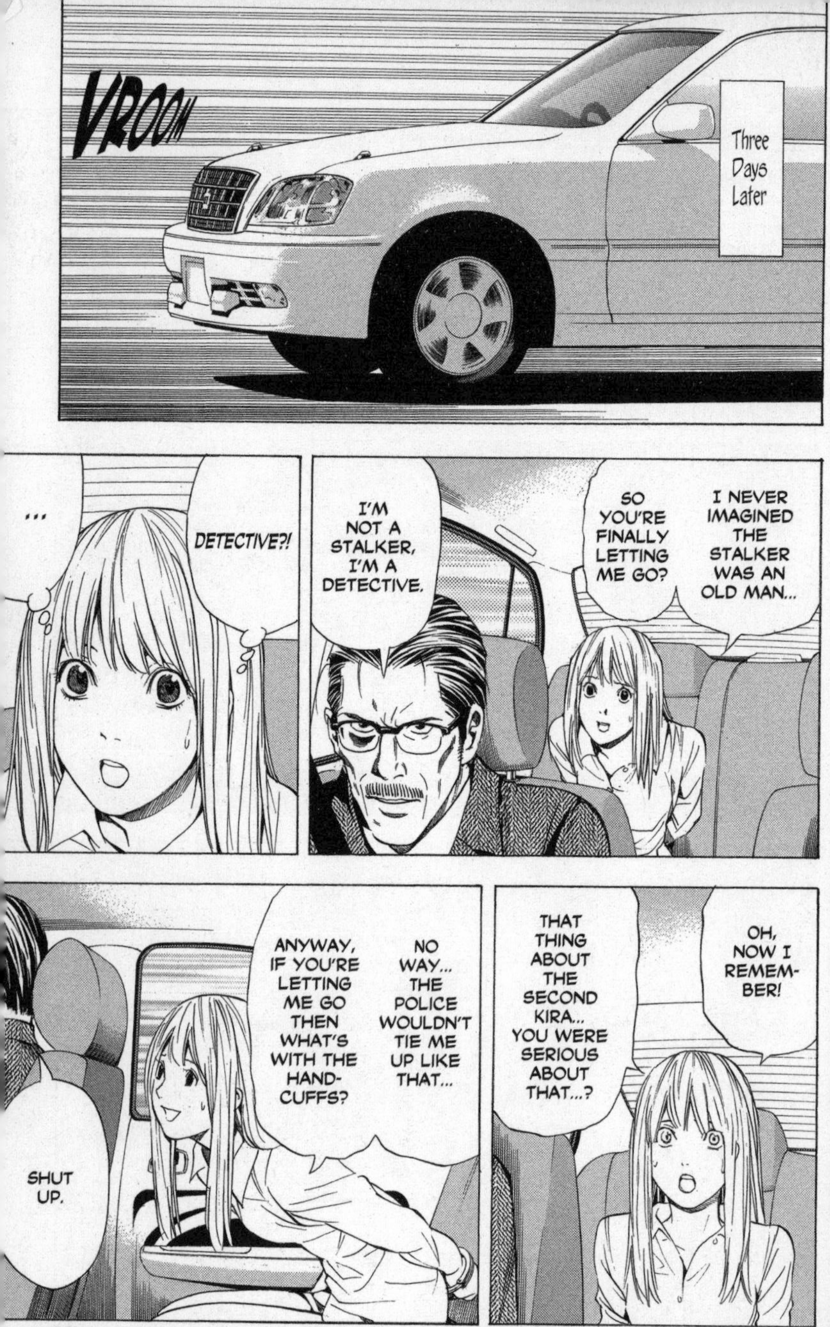

VROOM
Three Days Later
I NEVER IMAGINED THE STALKER WAS AN OLD MAN...
SO YOU'RE FINALLY LETTING ME GO?
I'M NOT A STALKER, I'M A DETECTIVE.
DETECTIVE?!
...
OH, NOW I REMEMBER!
THAT THING ABOUT THE SECOND KIRA... YOU WERE SERIOUS ABOUT THAT...?
NO WAY... THE POLICE WOULDN'T TIE ME UP LIKE THAT...
ANYWAY, IF YOU'RE LETTING ME GO THEN WHAT'S WITH THE HAND-CUFFS?
SHUT UP.

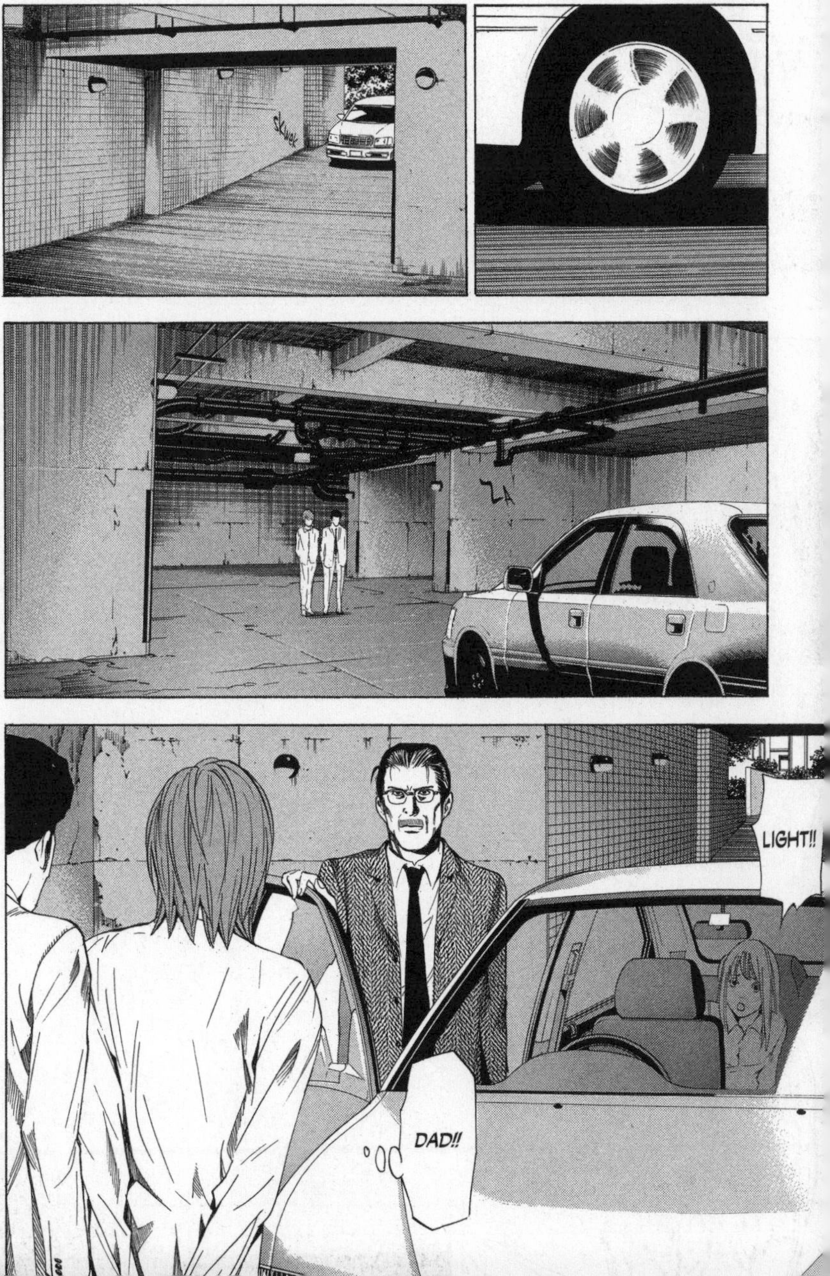
LIGHT!!
DAD!!

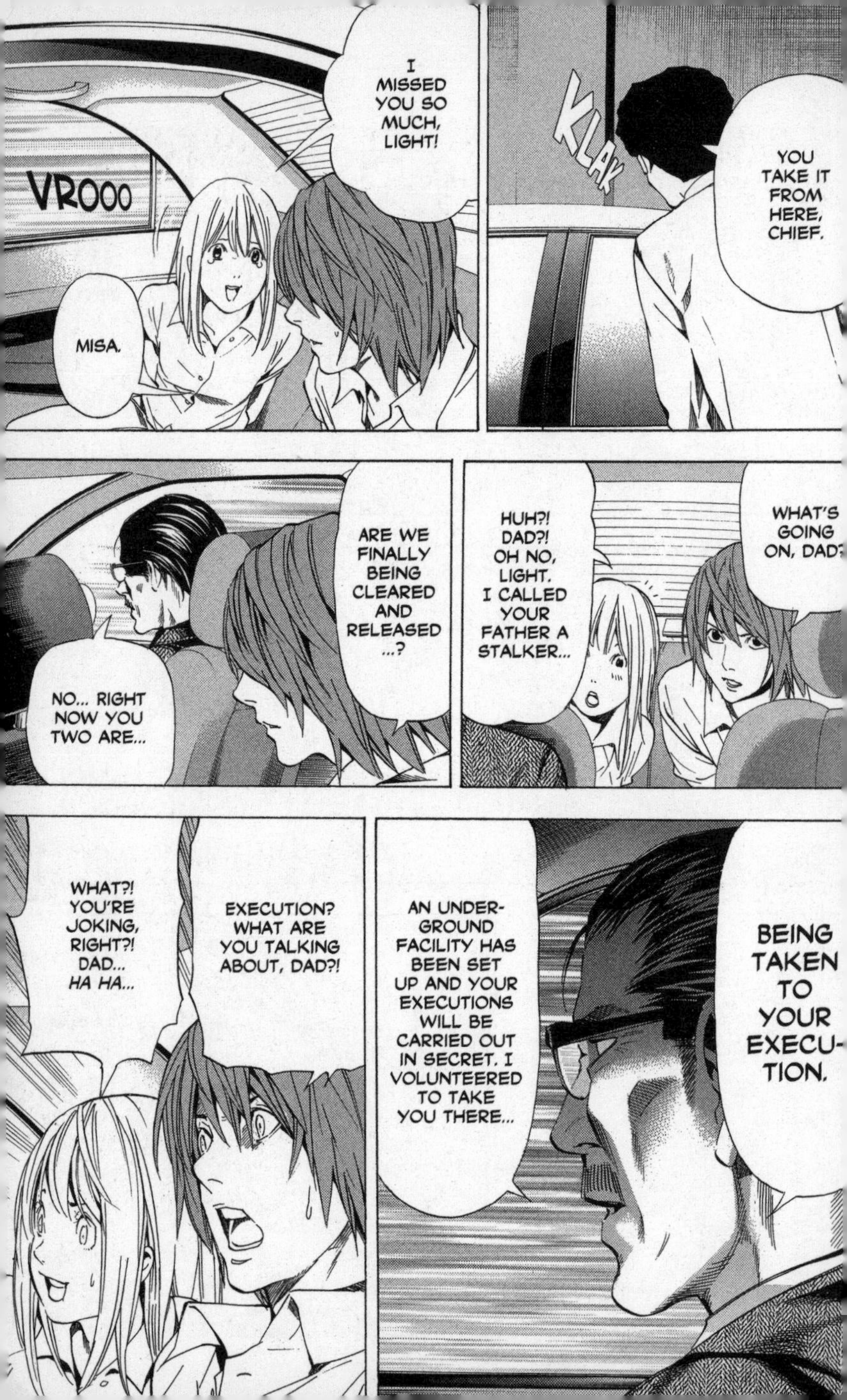
KLAK
YOU TAKE IT FROM HERE, CHIEF.
I MISSED YOU SO MUCH, LIGHT!
VROOO
MISA.
WHAT'S GOING ON, DAD?
HUH?! DAD?! OH NO, LIGHT. I CALLED YOUR FATHER A STALKER...
ARE WE FINALLY BEING CLEARED AND RELEASED ...?
NO... RIGHT NOW YOU TWO ARE...
BEING TAKEN TO YOUR EXECUTION.
AN UNDERGROUND FACILITY HAS BEEN SET UP AND YOUR EXECUTIONS WILL BE CARRIED OUT IN SECRET. I VOLUNTEERED TO TAKE YOU THERE...
EXECUTION? WHAT ARE YOU TALKING ABOUT, DAD?!
WHAT?! YOU'RE JOKING, RIGHT?! DAD... *HA HA...*

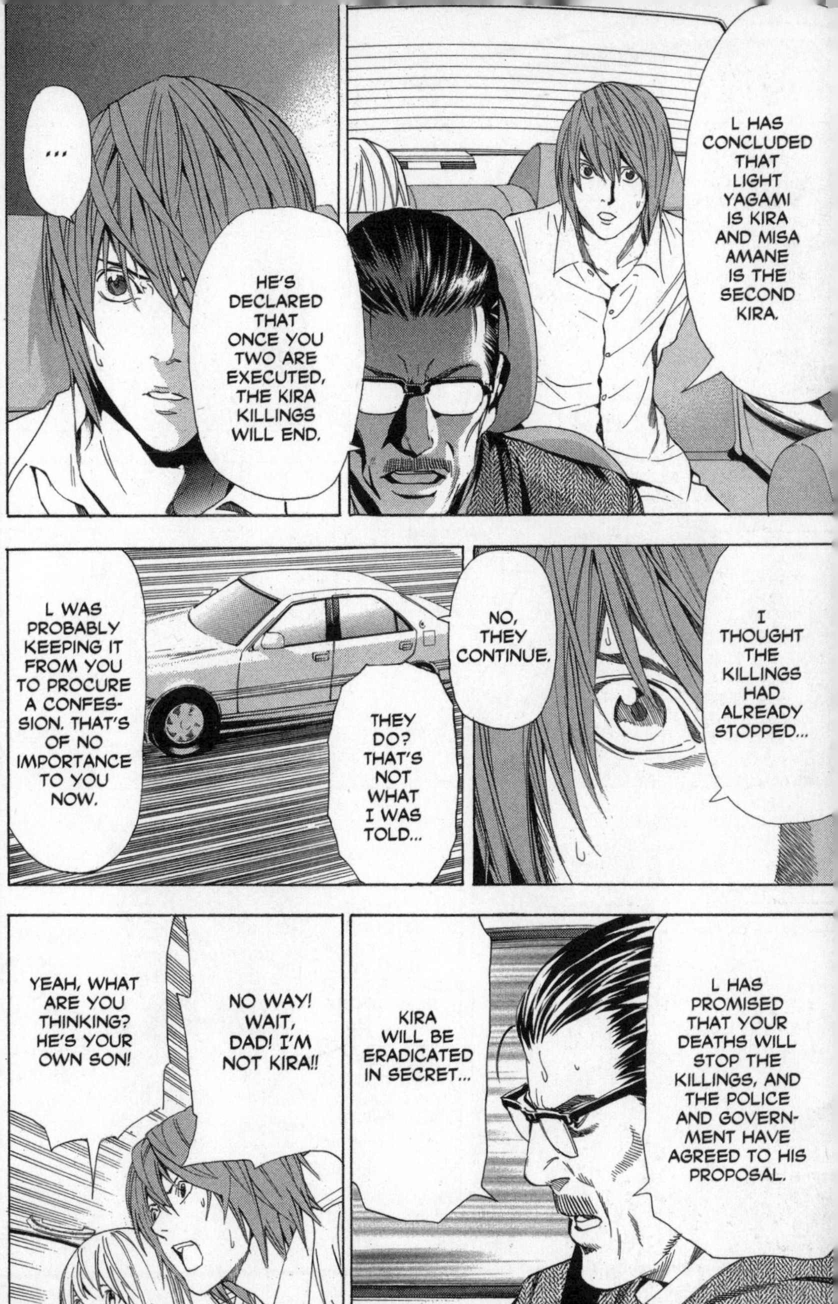
L HAS CONCLUDED THAT LIGHT YAGAMI IS KIRA AND MISA AMANE IS THE SECOND KIRA.
HE'S DECLARED THAT ONCE YOU TWO ARE EXECUTED, THE KIRA KILLINGS WILL END.
...
I THOUGHT THE KILLINGS HAD ALREADY STOPPED...
NO, THEY CONTINUE.
THEY DO? THAT'S NOT WHAT I WAS TOLD...
L WAS PROBABLY KEEPING IT FROM YOU TO PROCURE A CONFES-SION. THAT'S OF NO IMPORTANCE TO YOU NOW.
L HAS PROMISED THAT YOUR DEATHS WILL STOP THE KILLINGS, AND THE POLICE AND GOVERN-MENT HAVE AGREED TO HIS PROPOSAL.
KIRA WILL BE ERADICATED IN SECRET...
NO WAY! WAIT, DAD! I'M NOT KIRA!!
YEAH, WHAT ARE YOU THINKING? HE'S YOUR OWN SON!

READ THIS WAY

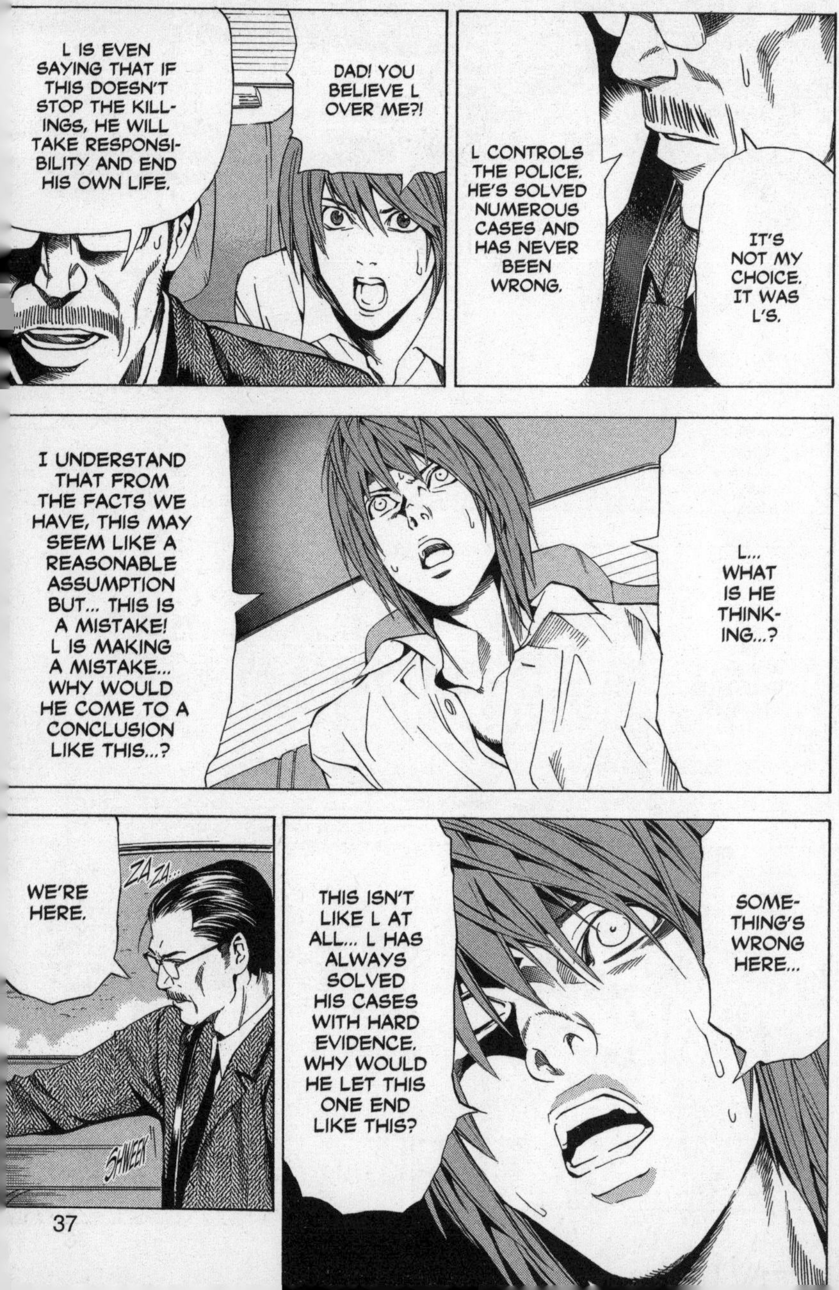
L CONTROLS THE POLICE. HE'S SOLVED NUMEROUS CASES AND HAS NEVER BEEN WRONG.
IT'S NOT MY CHOICE. IT WAS L'S.
DAD! YOU BELIEVE L OVER ME?!
L IS EVEN SAYING THAT IF THIS DOESN'T STOP THE KILLINGS, HE WILL TAKE RESPONSIBILITY AND END HIS OWN LIFE.
L... WHAT IS HE THINKING...?
I UNDERSTAND THAT FROM THE FACTS WE HAVE, THIS MAY SEEM LIKE A REASONABLE ASSUMPTION BUT... THIS IS A MISTAKE! L IS MAKING A MISTAKE... WHY WOULD HE COME TO A CONCLUSION LIKE THIS...?
SOMETHING'S WRONG HERE...
THIS ISN'T LIKE L AT ALL... L HAS ALWAYS SOLVED HIS CASES WITH HARD EVIDENCE. WHY WOULD HE LET THIS ONE END LIKE THIS?
ZA ZA...
WE'RE HERE.
SHWEEK

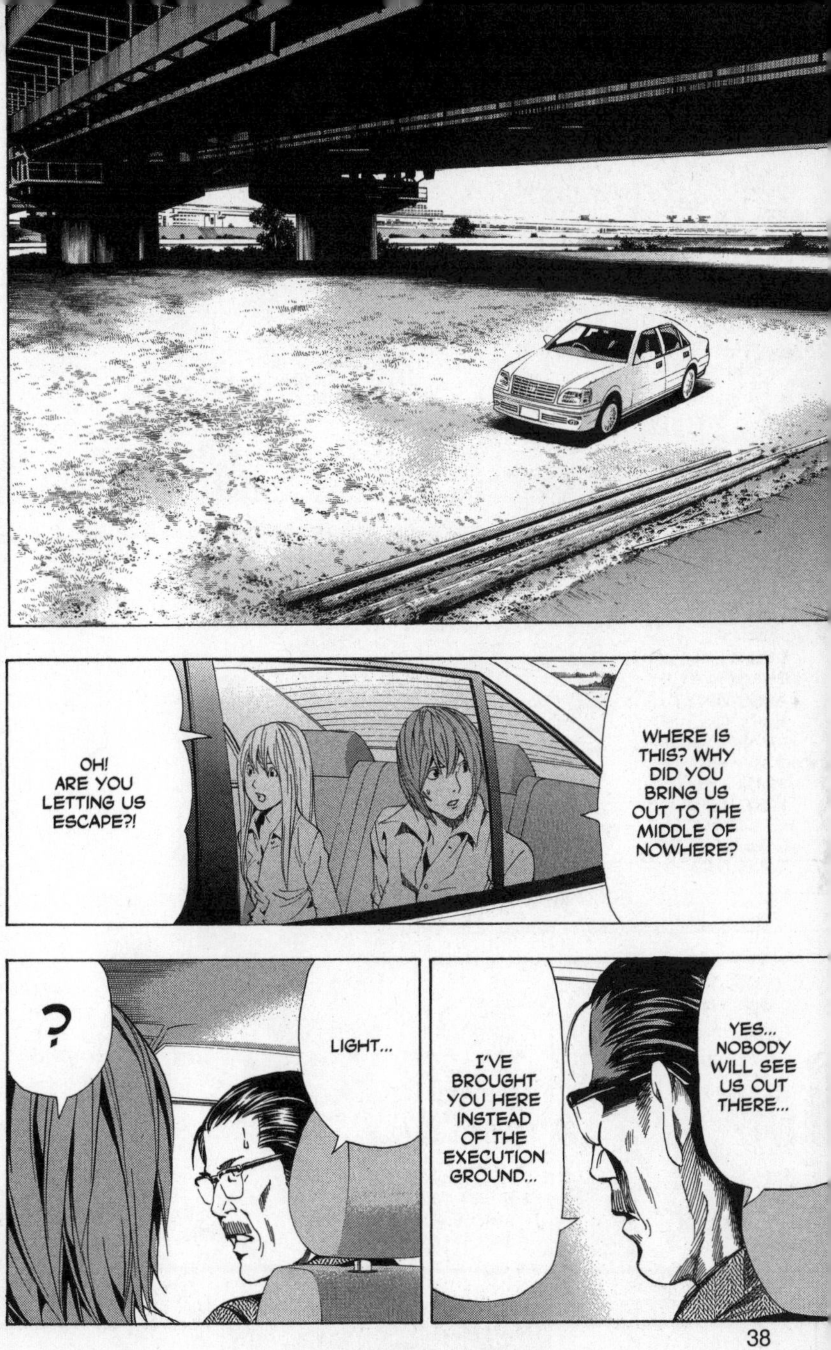
WHERE IS THIS? WHY DID YOU BRING US OUT TO THE MIDDLE OF NOWHERE?
OH! ARE YOU LETTING US ESCAPE?!
YES... NOBODY WILL SEE US OUT THERE...
I'VE BROUGHT YOU HERE INSTEAD OF THE EXECUTION GROUND...
LIGHT...
?

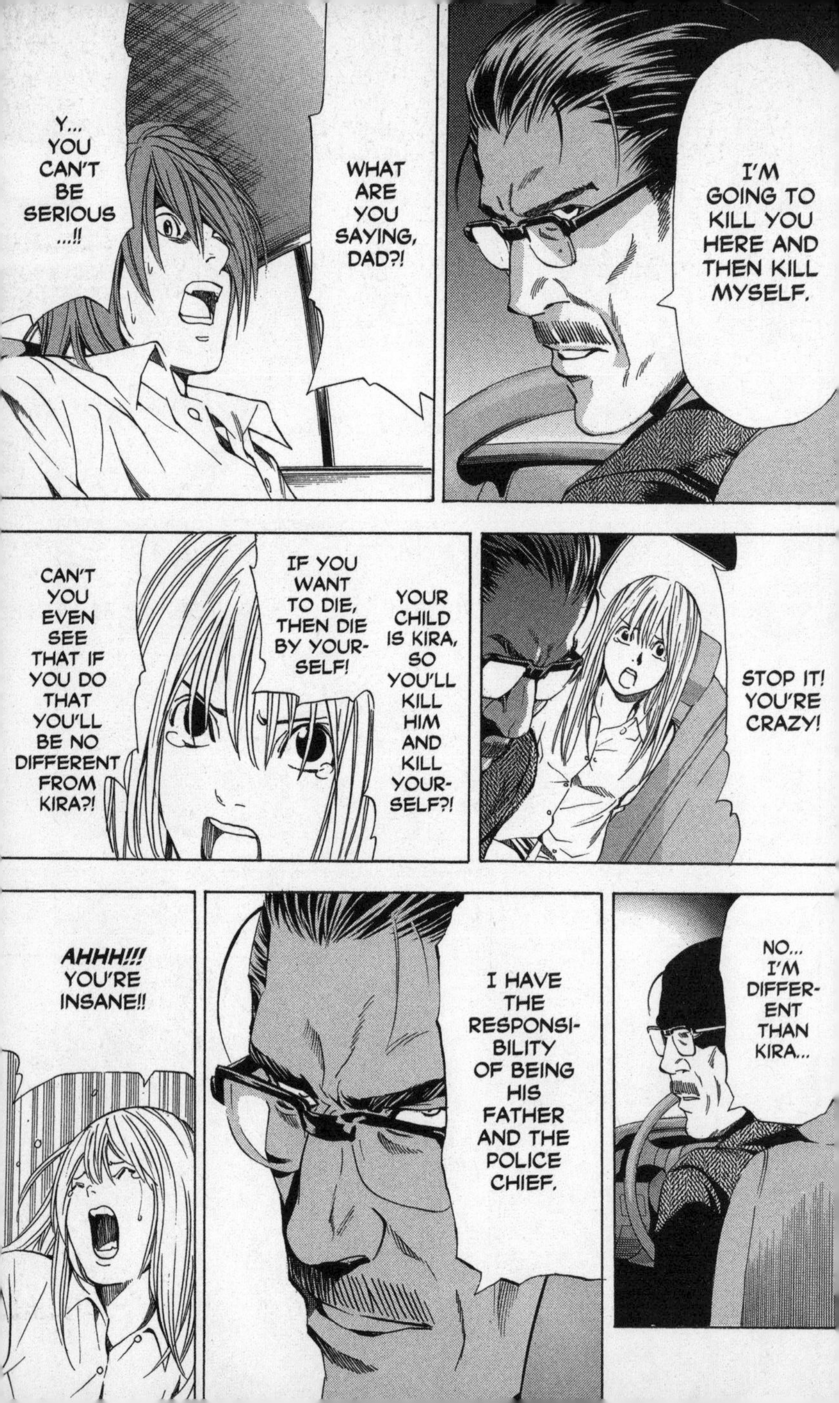

I'M GOING TO KILL YOU HERE AND THEN KILL MYSELF.
WHAT ARE YOU SAYING, DAD?!
Y... YOU CAN'T BE SERIOUS ...!!
STOP IT! YOU'RE CRAZY!
YOUR CHILD IS KIRA, SO YOU'LL KILL HIM AND KILL YOURSELF?!
IF YOU WANT TO DIE, THEN DIE BY YOURSELF!
CAN'T YOU EVEN SEE THAT IF YOU DO THAT YOU'LL BE NO DIFFERENT FROM KIRA?!
NO... I'M DIFFERENT THAN KIRA...
I HAVE THE RESPONSIBILITY OF BEING HIS FATHER AND THE POLICE CHIEF.
AHHH!!! YOU'RE INSANE!!

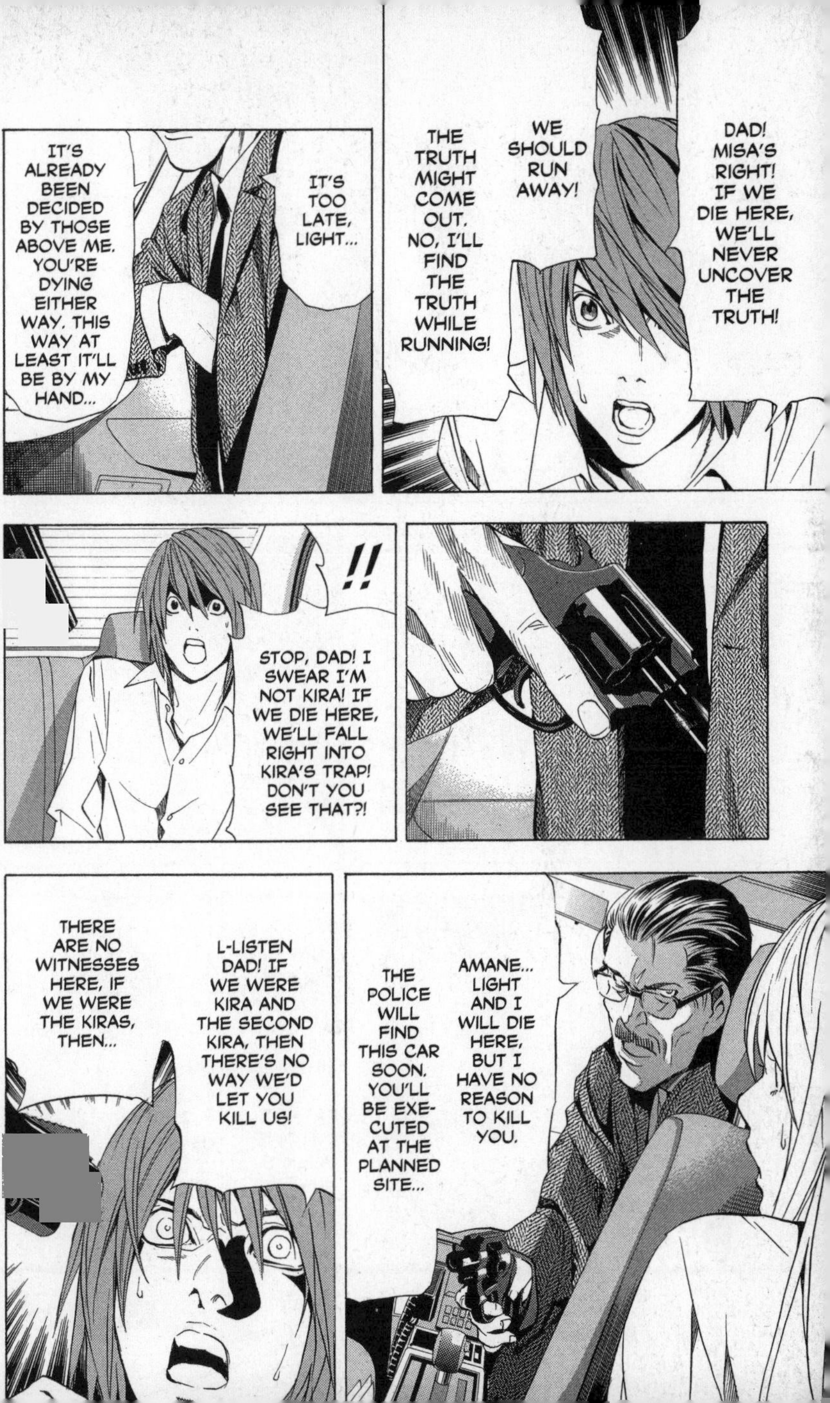
DAD! MISA'S RIGHT! IF WE DIE HERE, WE'LL NEVER UNCOVER THE TRUTH!
WE SHOULD RUN AWAY!
THE TRUTH MIGHT COME OUT. NO, I'LL FIND THE TRUTH WHILE RUNNING!
IT'S TOO LATE, LIGHT...
IT'S ALREADY BEEN DECIDED BY THOSE ABOVE ME. YOU'RE DYING EITHER WAY. THIS WAY AT LEAST IT'LL BE BY MY HAND...
!!
STOP, DAD! I SWEAR I'M NOT KIRA! IF WE DIE HERE, WE'LL FALL RIGHT INTO KIRA'S TRAP! DON'T YOU SEE THAT?!
AMANE... LIGHT AND I WILL DIE HERE, BUT I HAVE NO REASON TO KILL YOU.
THE POLICE WILL FIND THIS CAR SOON. YOU'LL BE EXE-CUTED AT THE PLANNED SITE...
L-LISTEN DAD! IF WE WERE KIRA AND THE SECOND KIRA, THEN THERE'S NO WAY WE'D LET YOU KILL US!
THERE ARE NO WITNESSES HERE, IF WE WERE THE KIRAS, THEN...

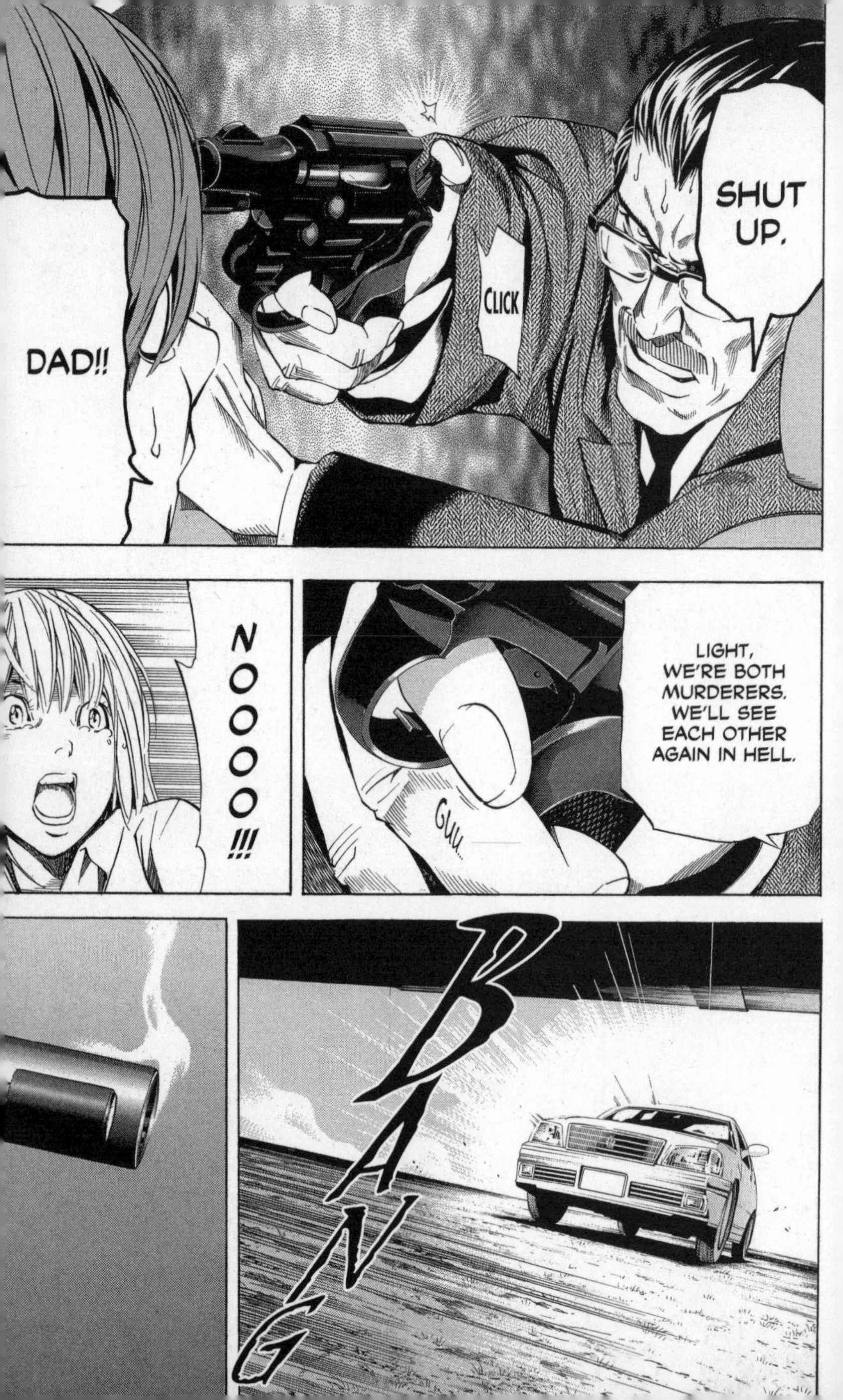
SHUT UP.
CLICK
DAD!!
LIGHT, WE'RE BOTH MURDERERS. WE'LL SEE EACH OTHER AGAIN IN HELL.
Guu...
NOOOOO!!!
BANG

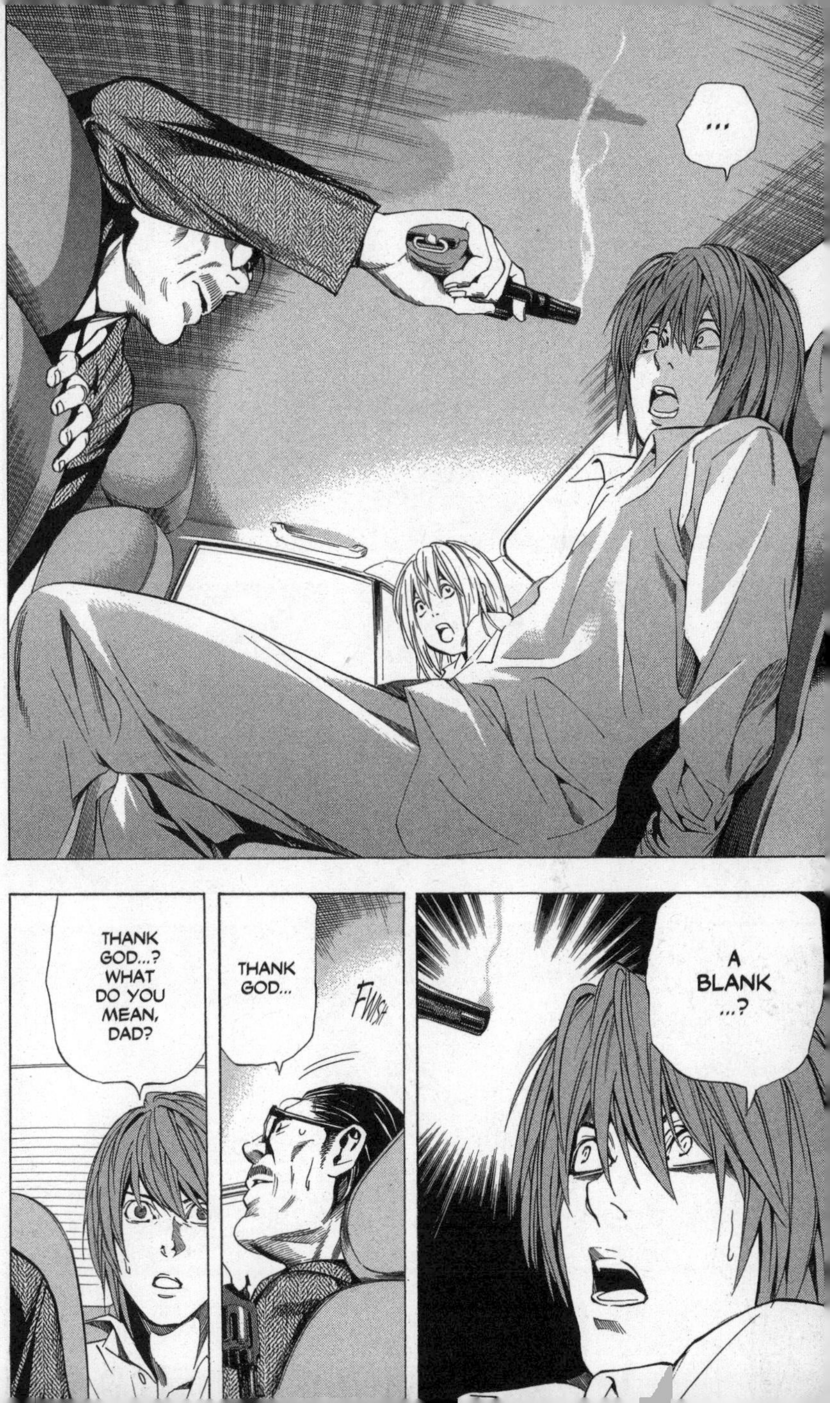
...
A BLANK ...?
THANK GOD...
FWISH
THANK GOD...? WHAT DO YOU MEAN, DAD?

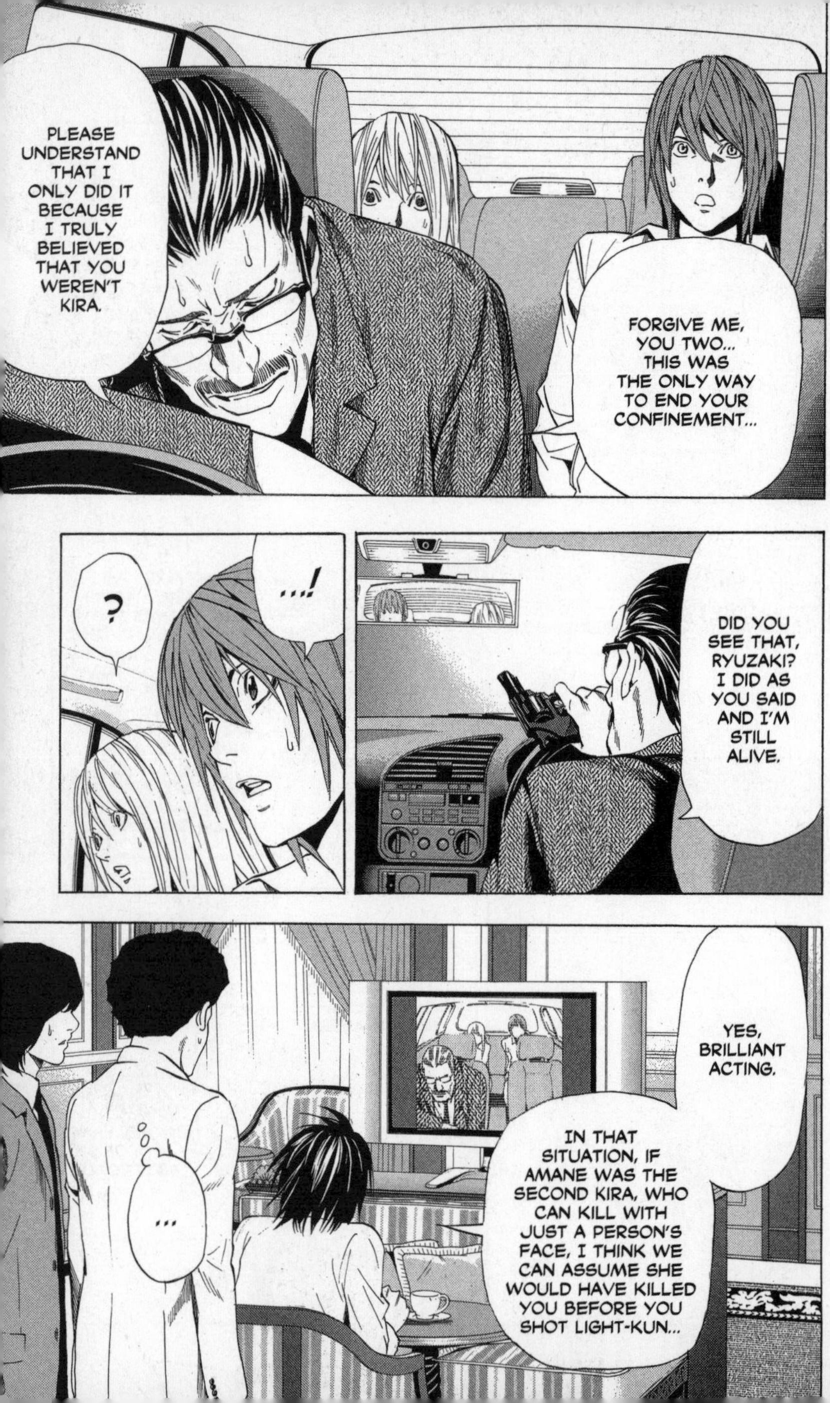
FORGIVE ME, YOU TWO... THIS WAS THE ONLY WAY TO END YOUR CONFINEMENT...
PLEASE UNDERSTAND THAT I ONLY DID IT BECAUSE I TRULY BELIEVED THAT YOU WEREN'T KIRA.
DID YOU SEE THAT, RYUZAKI? I DID AS YOU SAID AND I'M STILL ALIVE.
...!
?
YES, BRILLIANT ACTING.
IN THAT SITUATION, IF AMANE WAS THE SECOND KIRA, WHO CAN KILL WITH JUST A PERSON'S FACE, I THINK WE CAN ASSUME SHE WOULD HAVE KILLED YOU BEFORE YOU SHOT LIGHT-KUN...
...

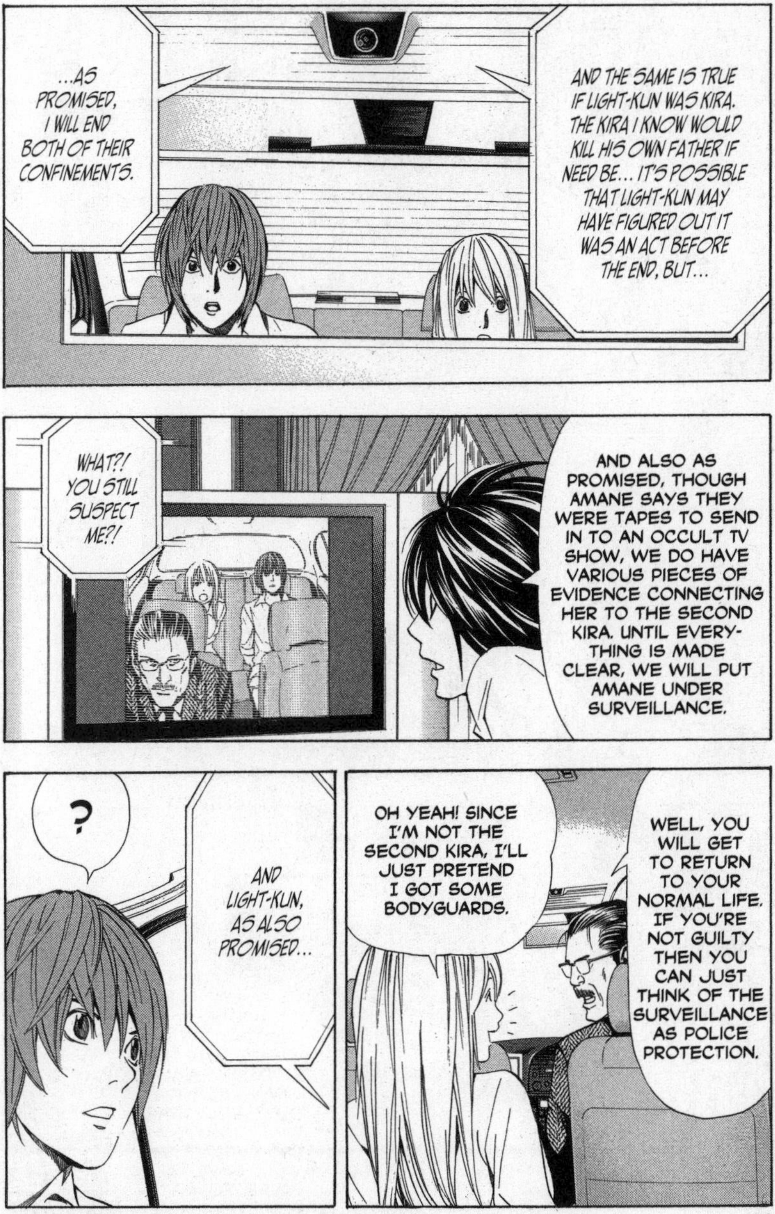
AND THE SAME IS TRUE IF LIGHT-KUN WAS KIRA. THE KIRA I KNOW WOULD KILL HIS OWN FATHER IF NEED BE... IT'S POSSIBLE THAT LIGHT-KUN MAY HAVE FIGURED OUT IT WAS AN ACT BEFORE THE END, BUT...
...AS PROMISED, I WILL END BOTH OF THEIR CONFINEMENTS.
AND ALSO AS PROMISED, THOUGH AMANE SAYS THEY WERE TAPES TO SEND IN TO AN OCCULT TV SHOW, WE DO HAVE VARIOUS PIECES OF EVIDENCE CONNECTING HER TO THE SECOND KIRA. UNTIL EVERY-THING IS MADE CLEAR, WE WILL PUT AMANE UNDER SURVEILLANCE.
WHAT?! YOU STILL SUSPECT ME?!
WELL, YOU WILL GET TO RETURN TO YOUR NORMAL LIFE. IF YOU'RE NOT GUILTY THEN YOU CAN JUST THINK OF THE SURVEILLANCE AS POLICE PROTECTION.
OH YEAH! SINCE I'M NOT THE SECOND KIRA, I'LL JUST PRETEND I GOT SOME BODYGUARDS.
AND LIGHT-KUN, AS ALSO PROMISED...
?

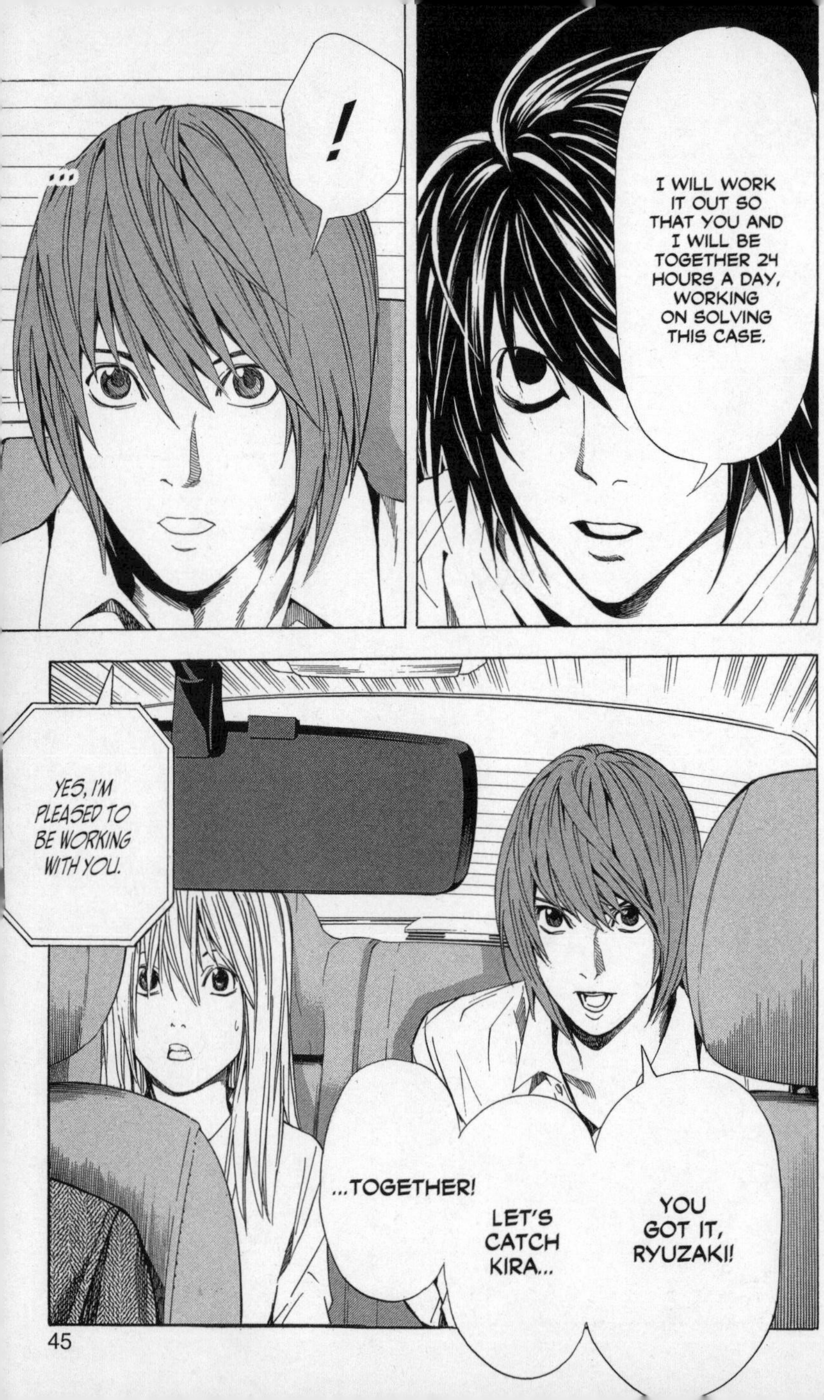
I WILL WORK IT OUT SO THAT YOU AND I WILL BE TOGETHER 24 HOURS A DAY, WORKING ON SOLVING THIS CASE.
!
...
YES, I'M PLEASED TO BE WORKING WITH YOU.
YOU GOT IT, RYUZAKI!
LET'S CATCH KIRA...
...TOGETHER!

# DEATH NOTE
## How to use it
## XXV

○ The god of death must not hand the DEATH NOTE directly to a child under 6 years of age (based on the human calendar).

死神は人間にデスノートを直接渡す場合、
人間界単位で満6歳に満たない人間にノートを渡してはならない。

○ The DEATH NOTE must not be handed to a child under 6 years of age, but DEATH NOTES that have been dropped into the human world, and are part of the human world, can be used upon humans of any age with the same effect.

満6歳未満の人間に渡してはならないが、
人間界に落とし人間界の物になったノートは、
何歳の人間に使われようとその効力は同じである。

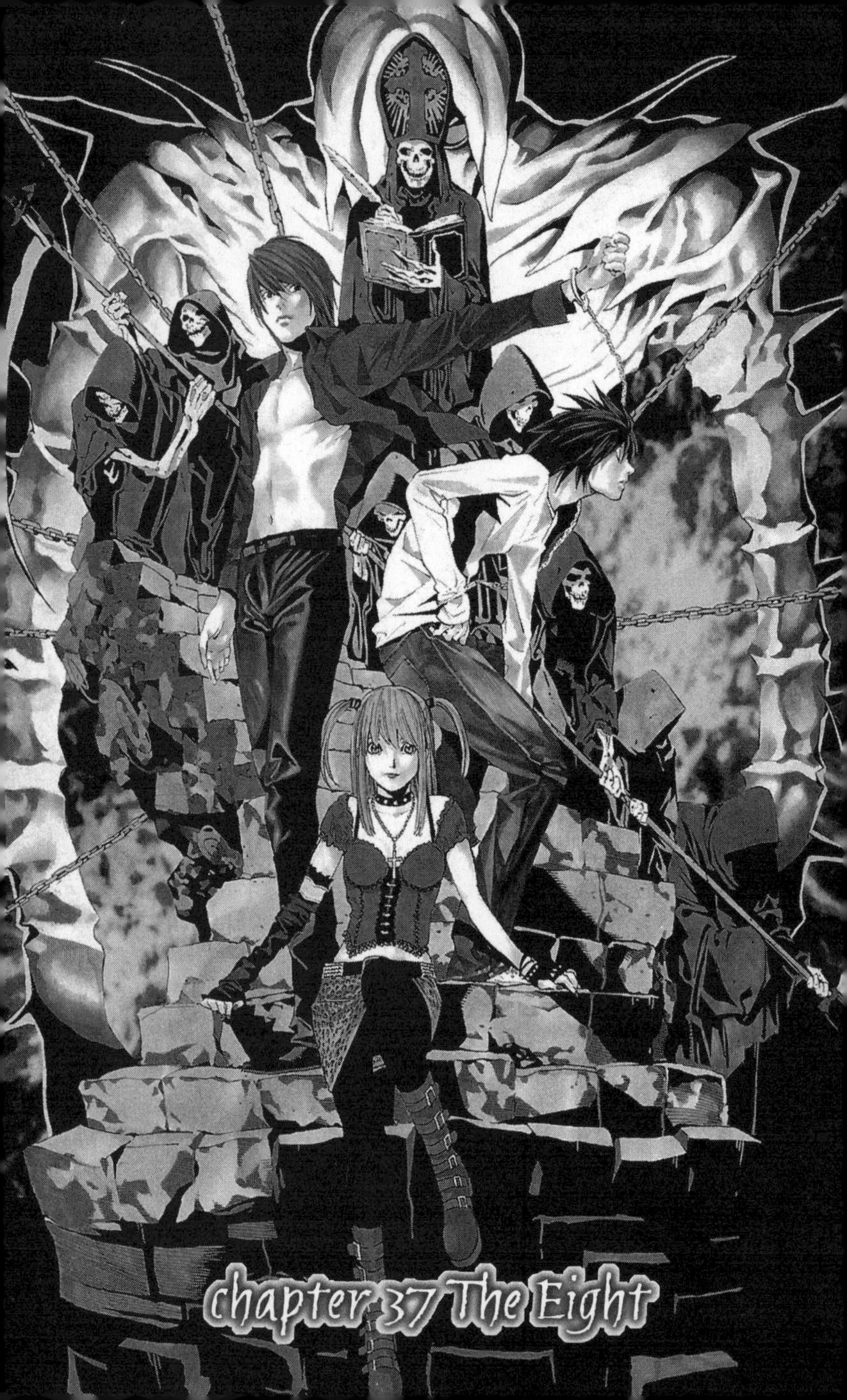
chapter 37 The Eight

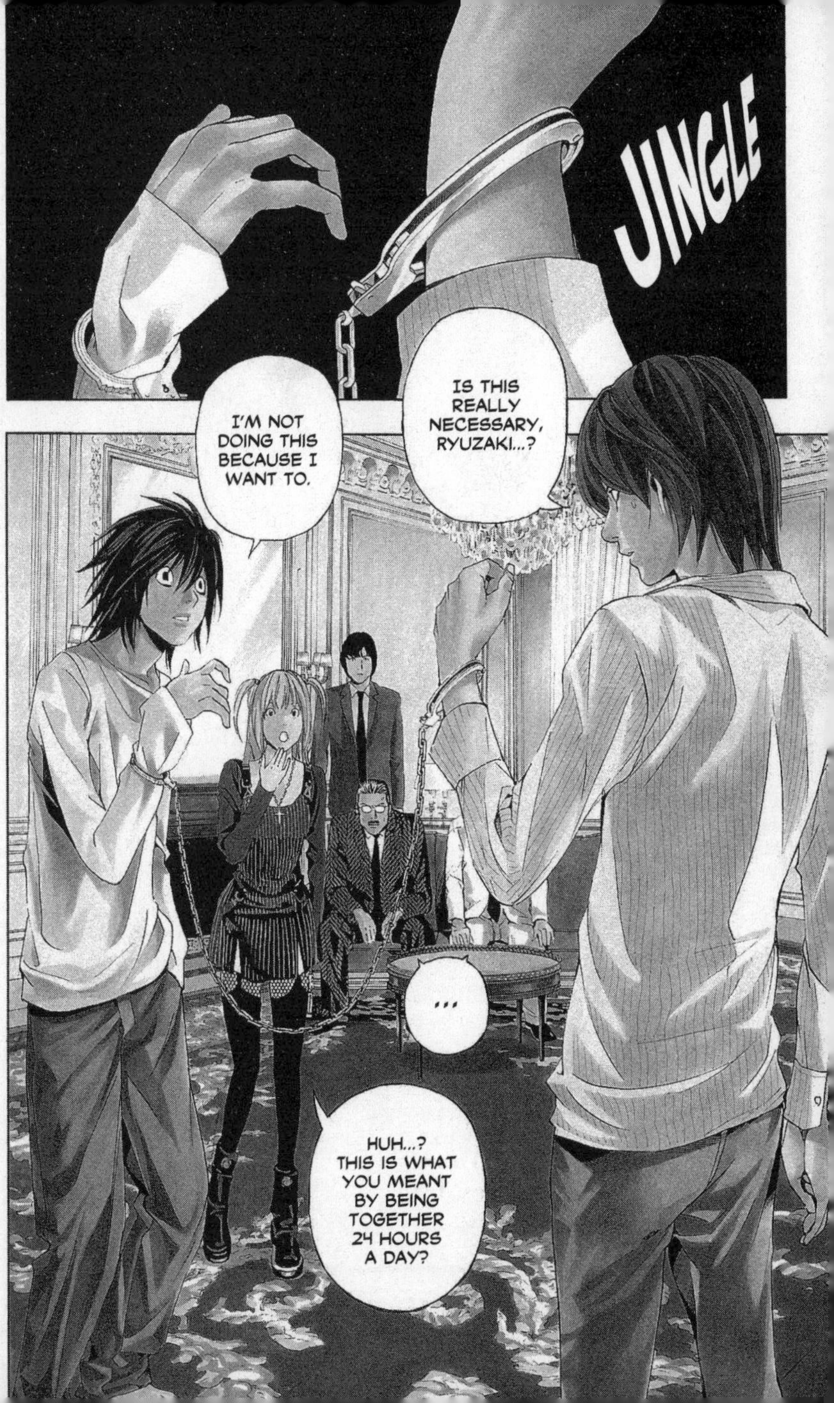

JINGLE
IS THIS REALLY NECESSARY, RYUZAKI...?
I'M NOT DOING THIS BECAUSE I WANT TO.
...
HUH...? THIS IS WHAT YOU MEANT BY BEING TOGETHER 24 HOURS A DAY?

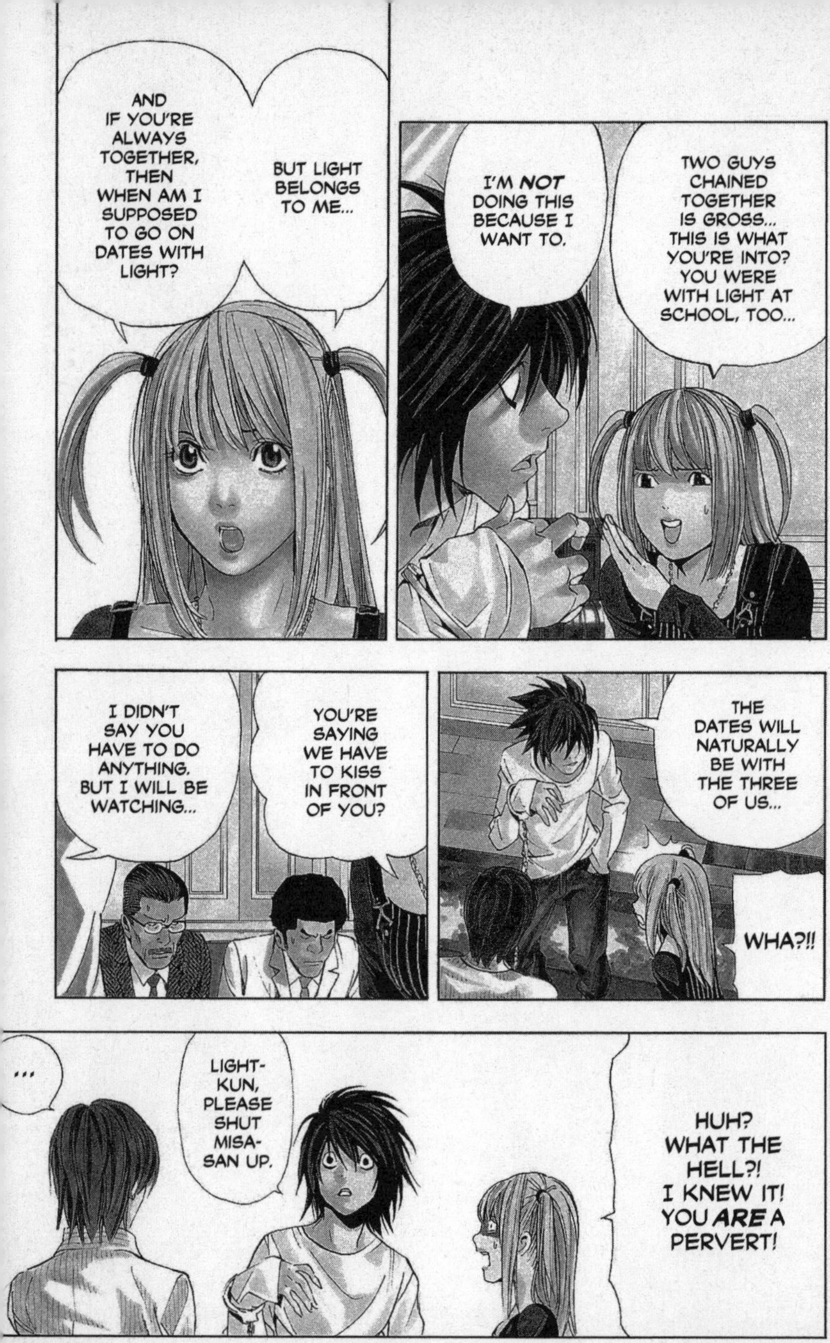
TWO GUYS CHAINED TOGETHER IS GROSS... THIS IS WHAT YOU'RE INTO? YOU WERE WITH LIGHT AT SCHOOL, TOO...
I'M **NOT** DOING THIS BECAUSE I WANT TO.
BUT LIGHT BELONGS TO ME...
AND IF YOU'RE ALWAYS TOGETHER, THEN WHEN AM I SUPPOSED TO GO ON DATES WITH LIGHT?
THE DATES WILL NATURALLY BE WITH THE THREE OF US...
WHA?!!
YOU'RE SAYING WE HAVE TO KISS IN FRONT OF YOU?
I DIDN'T SAY YOU HAVE TO DO ANYTHING. BUT I WILL BE WATCHING...
HUH? WHAT THE HELL?! I KNEW IT! YOU **ARE** A PERVERT!
LIGHT-KUN, PLEASE SHUT MISA-SAN UP.
...

READ THIS WAY

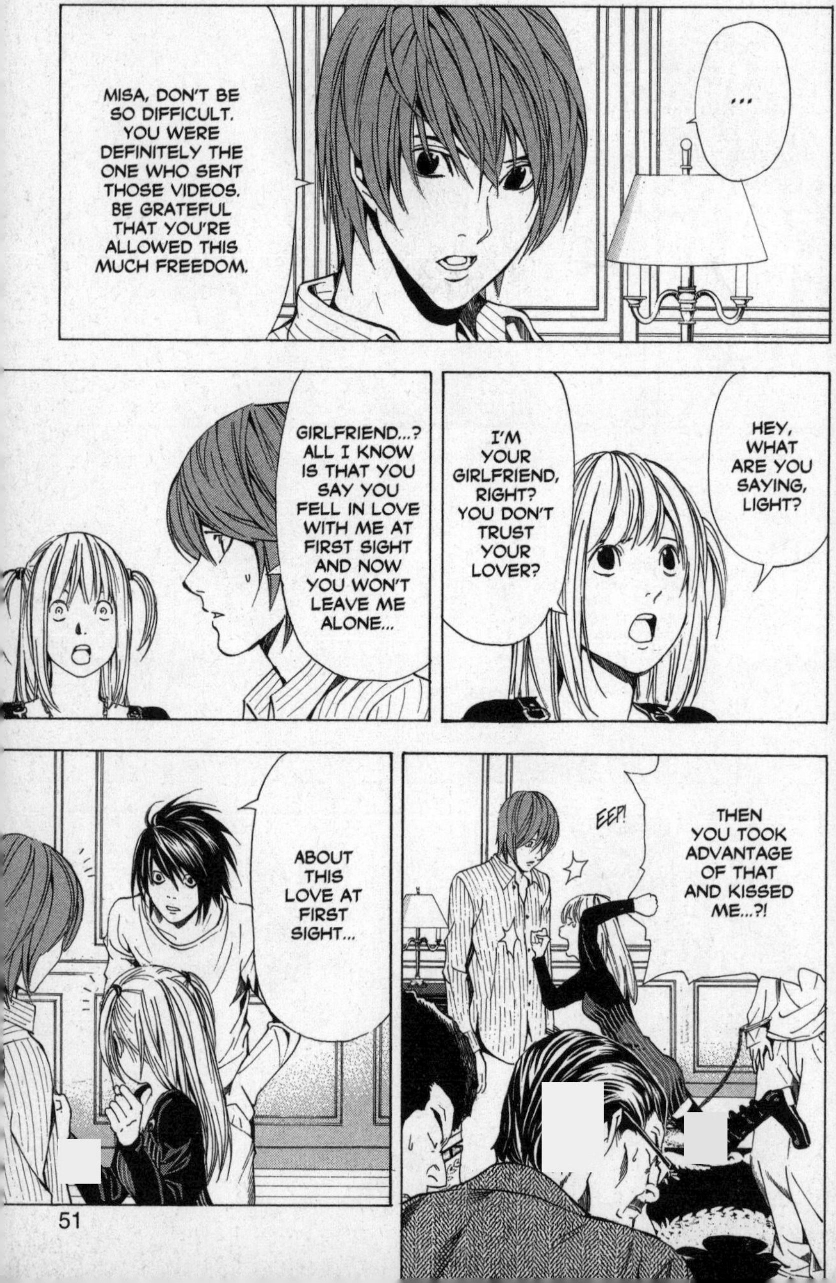
...
MISA, DON'T BE SO DIFFICULT. YOU WERE DEFINITELY THE ONE WHO SENT THOSE VIDEOS. BE GRATEFUL THAT YOU'RE ALLOWED THIS MUCH FREEDOM.
HEY, WHAT ARE YOU SAYING, LIGHT?
I'M YOUR GIRLFRIEND, RIGHT? YOU DON'T TRUST YOUR LOVER?
GIRLFRIEND...? ALL I KNOW IS THAT YOU SAY YOU FELL IN LOVE WITH ME AT FIRST SIGHT AND NOW YOU WON'T LEAVE ME ALONE...
THEN YOU TOOK ADVANTAGE OF THAT AND KISSED ME...?!
EEP!
ABOUT THIS LOVE AT FIRST SIGHT...

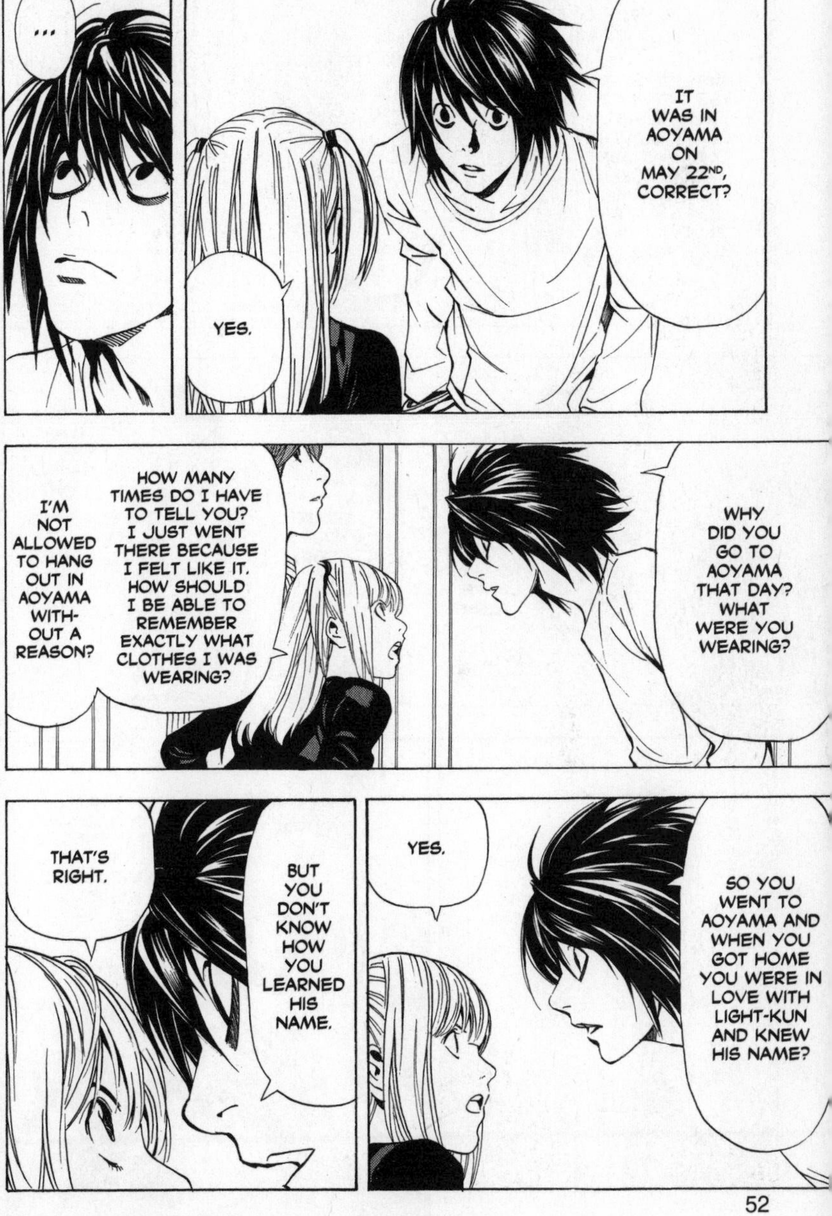
IT WAS IN AOYAMA ON MAY 22ND, CORRECT?
YES.
...
WHY DID YOU GO TO AOYAMA THAT DAY? WHAT WERE YOU WEARING?
HOW MANY TIMES DO I HAVE TO TELL YOU? I JUST WENT THERE BECAUSE I FELT LIKE IT. HOW SHOULD I BE ABLE TO REMEMBER EXACTLY WHAT CLOTHES I WAS WEARING?
I'M NOT ALLOWED TO HANG OUT IN AOYAMA WITH-OUT A REASON?
SO YOU WENT TO AOYAMA AND WHEN YOU GOT HOME YOU WERE IN LOVE WITH LIGHT-KUN AND KNEW HIS NAME?
YES.
BUT YOU DON'T KNOW HOW YOU LEARNED HIS NAME.
THAT'S RIGHT.

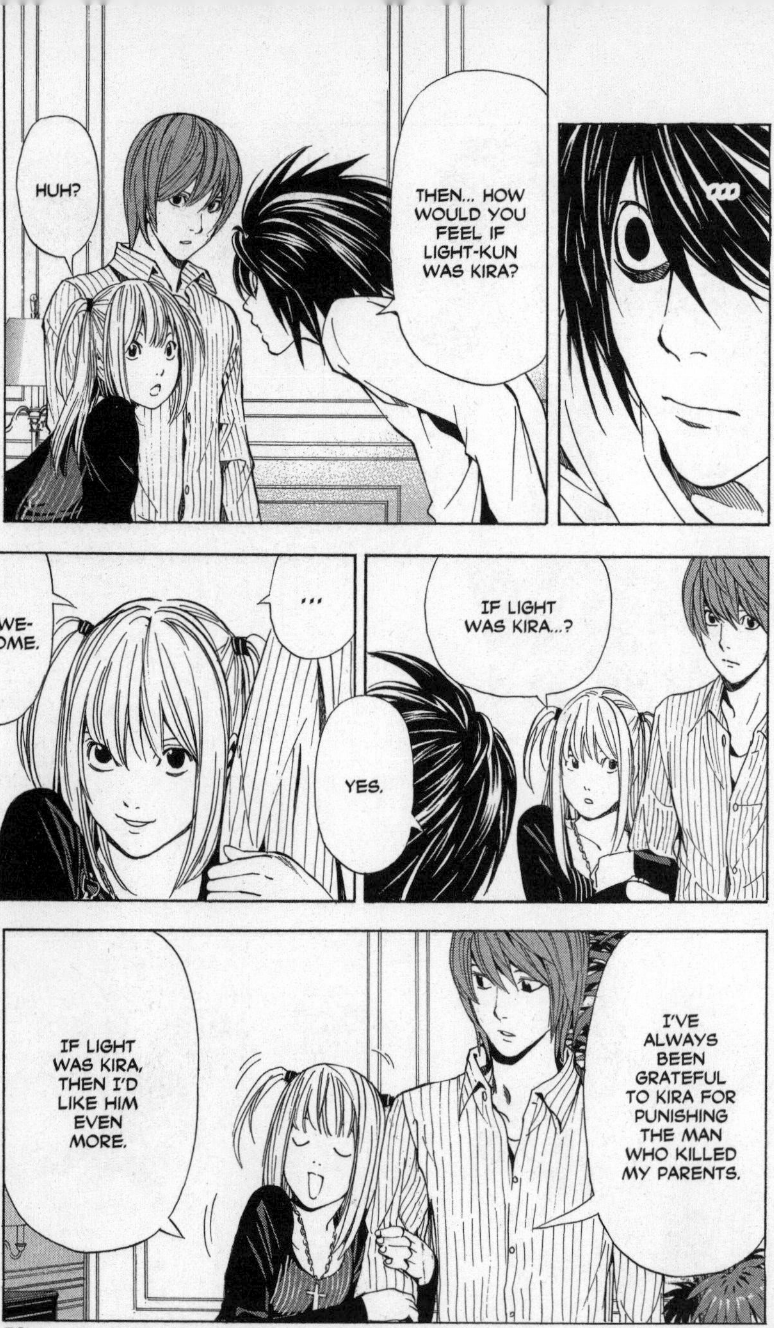
THEN... HOW WOULD YOU FEEL IF LIGHT-KUN WAS KIRA?
HUH?
IF LIGHT WAS KIRA...?
YES.
...
AWE-SOME.
I'VE ALWAYS BEEN GRATEFUL TO KIRA FOR PUNISHING THE MAN WHO KILLED MY PARENTS.
IF LIGHT WAS KIRA, THEN I'D LIKE HIM EVEN MORE.

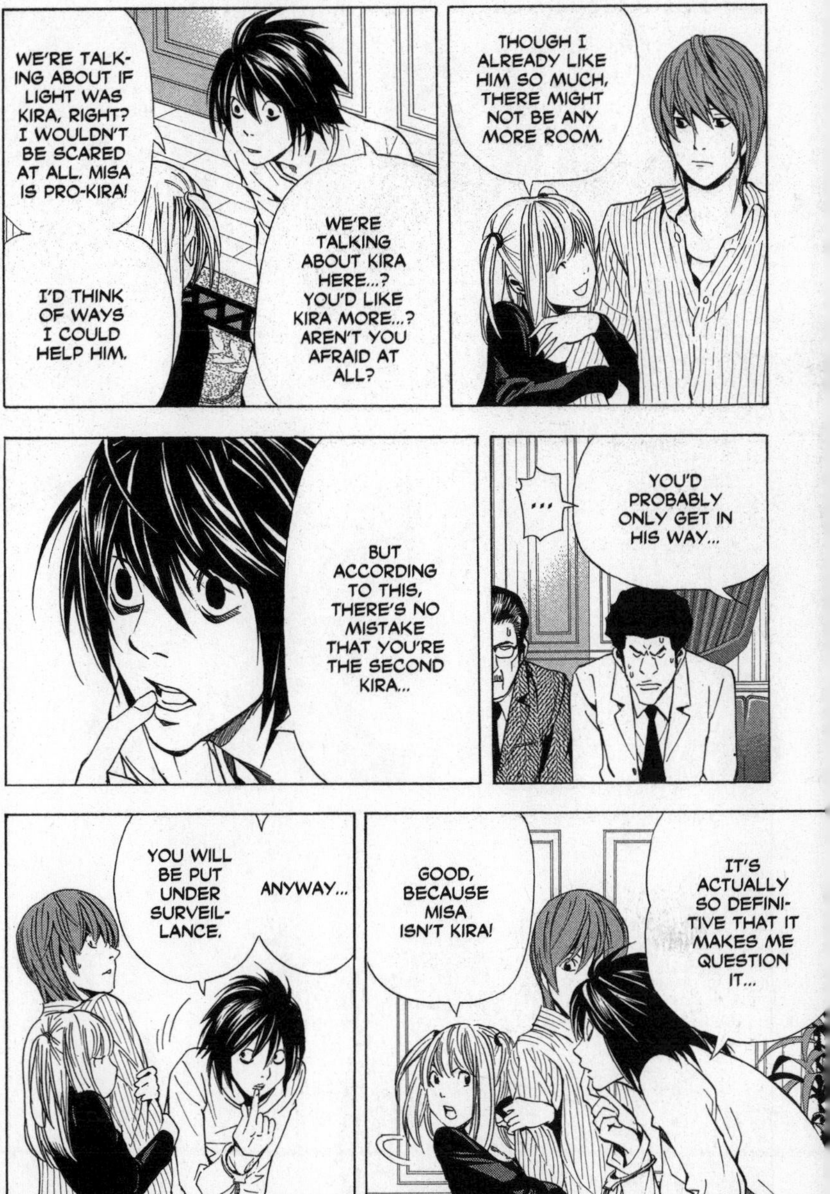
THOUGH I ALREADY LIKE HIM SO MUCH, THERE MIGHT NOT BE ANY MORE ROOM.
WE'RE TALKING ABOUT KIRA HERE...? YOU'D LIKE KIRA MORE...? AREN'T YOU AFRAID AT ALL?
WE'RE TALK-ING ABOUT IF LIGHT WAS KIRA, RIGHT? I WOULDN'T BE SCARED AT ALL. MISA IS PRO-KIRA!
I'D THINK OF WAYS I COULD HELP HIM.
YOU'D PROBABLY ONLY GET IN HIS WAY...
...
BUT ACCORDING TO THIS, THERE'S NO MISTAKE THAT YOU'RE THE SECOND KIRA...
IT'S ACTUALLY SO DEFINI-TIVE THAT IT MAKES ME QUESTION IT...
GOOD, BECAUSE MISA ISN'T KIRA!
ANYWAY...
YOU WILL BE PUT UNDER SURVEIL-LANCE.

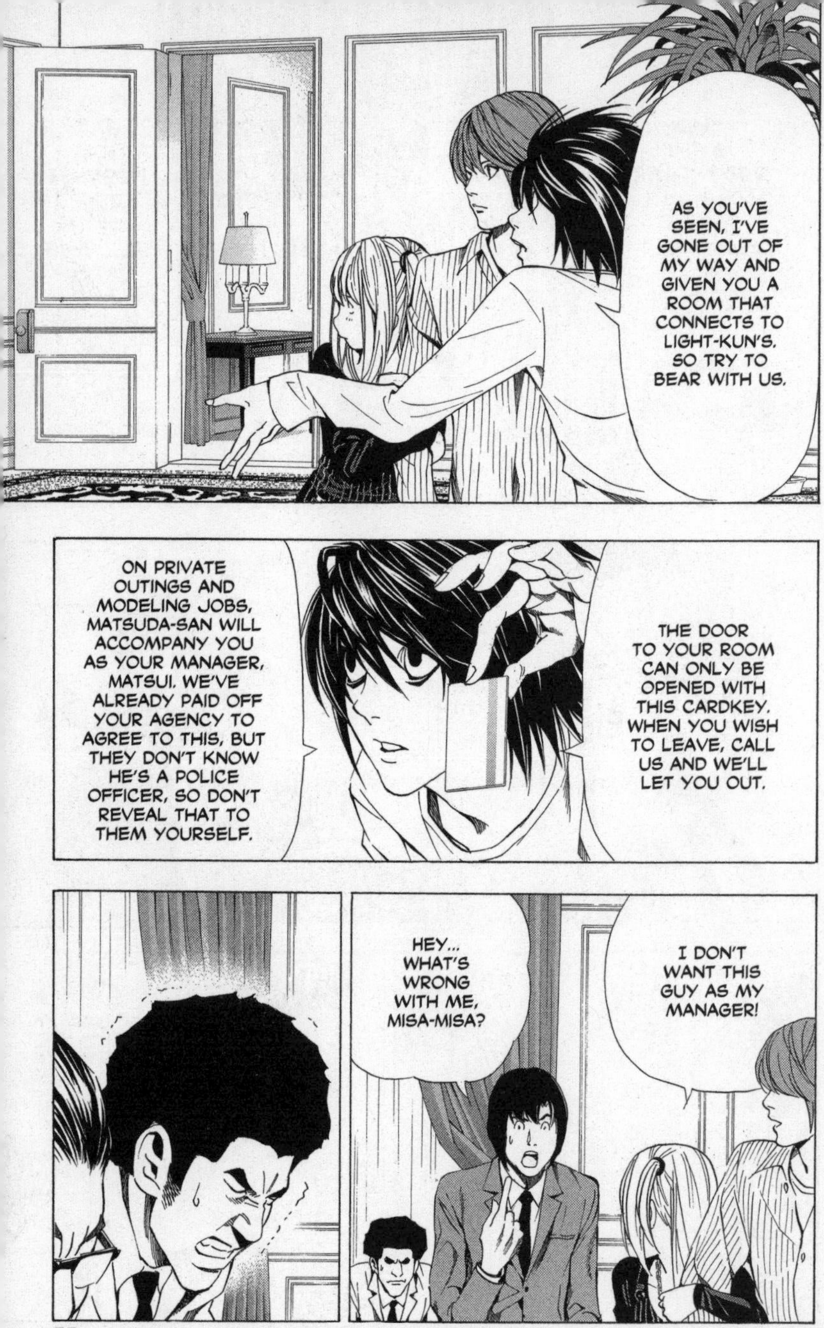
AS YOU'VE SEEN, I'VE GONE OUT OF MY WAY AND GIVEN YOU A ROOM THAT CONNECTS TO LIGHT-KUN'S. SO TRY TO BEAR WITH US.
THE DOOR TO YOUR ROOM CAN ONLY BE OPENED WITH THIS CARDKEY. WHEN YOU WISH TO LEAVE, CALL US AND WE'LL LET YOU OUT.
ON PRIVATE OUTINGS AND MODELING JOBS, MATSUDA-SAN WILL ACCOMPANY YOU AS YOUR MANAGER, MATSUI. WE'VE ALREADY PAID OFF YOUR AGENCY TO AGREE TO THIS, BUT THEY DON'T KNOW HE'S A POLICE OFFICER, SO DON'T REVEAL THAT TO THEM YOURSELF.
I DON'T WANT THIS GUY AS MY MANAGER!
HEY... WHAT'S WRONG WITH ME, MISA-MISA?

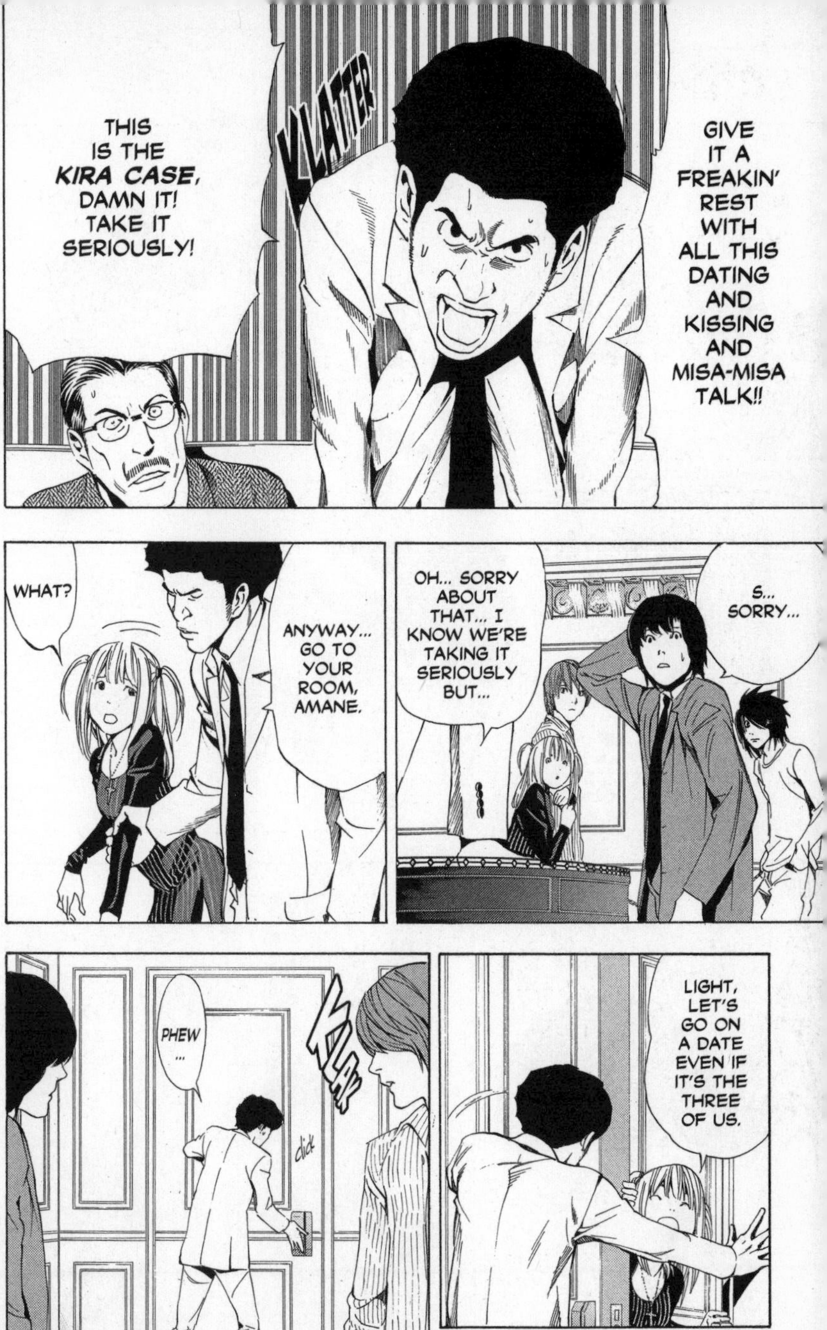
GIVE IT A FREAKIN' REST WITH ALL THIS DATING AND KISSING AND MISA-MISA TALK!!
KLATTER
THIS IS THE *KIRA CASE*, DAMN IT! TAKE IT SERIOUSLY!
S... SORRY...
OH... SORRY ABOUT THAT... I KNOW WE'RE TAKING IT SERIOUSLY BUT...
ANYWAY... GO TO YOUR ROOM, AMANE.
WHAT?
LIGHT, LET'S GO ON A DATE EVEN IF IT'S THE THREE OF US.
KLAK
PHEW ...
click

READ THIS WAY

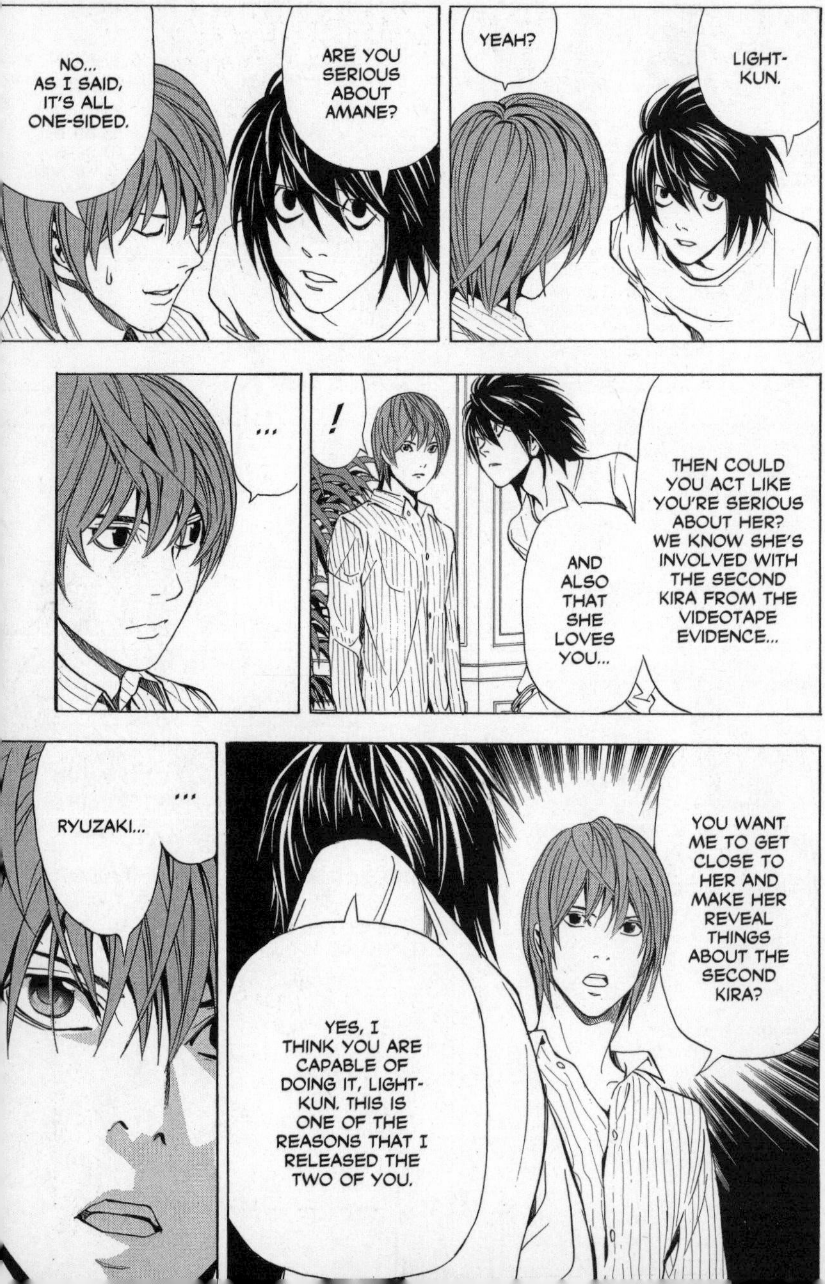
LIGHT-KUN.
YEAH?
ARE YOU SERIOUS ABOUT AMANE?
NO... AS I SAID, IT'S ALL ONE-SIDED.
THEN COULD YOU ACT LIKE YOU'RE SERIOUS ABOUT HER? WE KNOW SHE'S INVOLVED WITH THE SECOND KIRA FROM THE VIDEOTAPE EVIDENCE...
AND ALSO THAT SHE LOVES YOU...
!
...
YOU WANT ME TO GET CLOSE TO HER AND MAKE HER REVEAL THINGS ABOUT THE SECOND KIRA?
YES, I THINK YOU ARE CAPABLE OF DOING IT, LIGHT-KUN. THIS IS ONE OF THE REASONS THAT I RELEASED THE TWO OF YOU.
...
RYUZAKI...

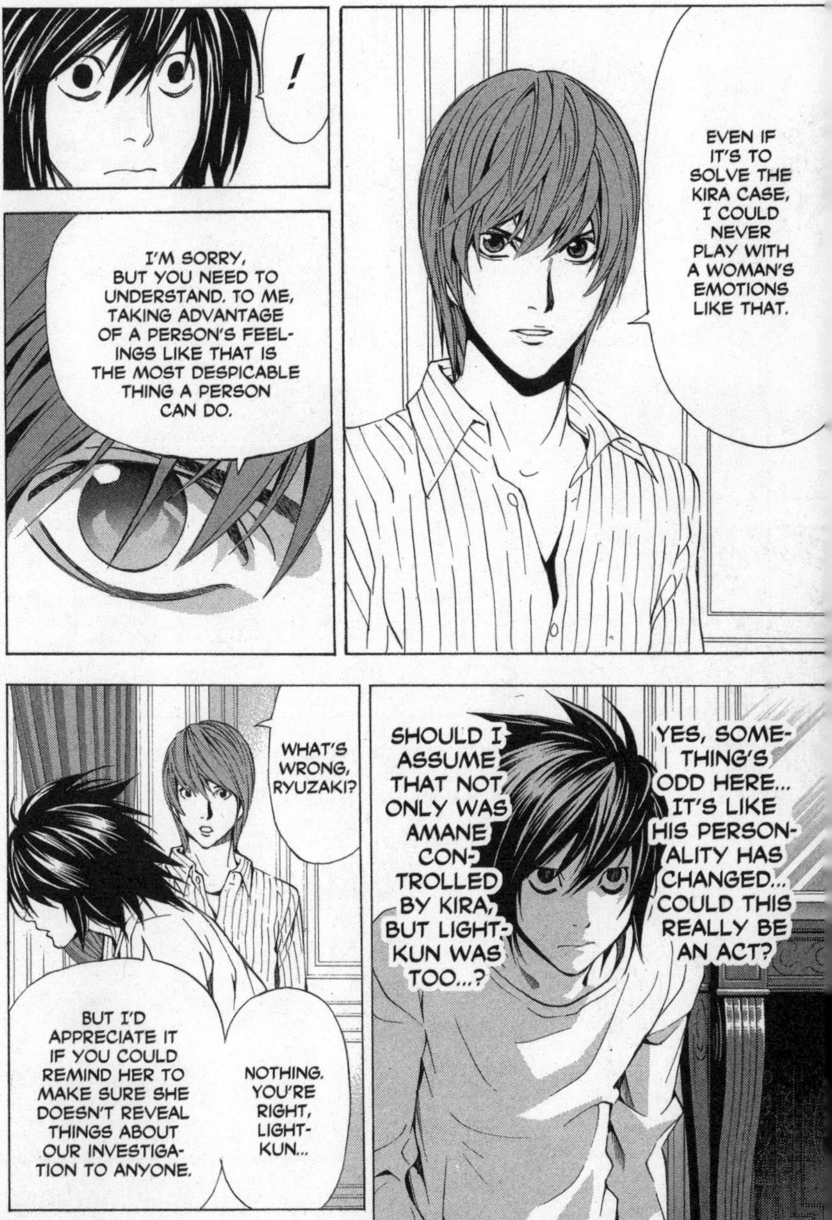
EVEN IF IT'S TO SOLVE THE KIRA CASE, I COULD NEVER PLAY WITH A WOMAN'S EMOTIONS LIKE THAT.
!
I'M SORRY, BUT YOU NEED TO UNDERSTAND. TO ME, TAKING ADVANTAGE OF A PERSON'S FEEL-INGS LIKE THAT IS THE MOST DESPICABLE THING A PERSON CAN DO.
YES, SOME-THING'S ODD HERE... IT'S LIKE HIS PERSON-ALITY HAS CHANGED... COULD THIS REALLY BE AN ACT?
SHOULD I ASSUME THAT NOT ONLY WAS AMANE CON-TROLLED BY KIRA, BUT LIGHT-KUN WAS TOO...?
WHAT'S WRONG, RYUZAKI?
NOTHING. YOU'RE RIGHT, LIGHT-KUN...
BUT I'D APPRECIATE IT IF YOU COULD REMIND HER TO MAKE SURE SHE DOESN'T REVEAL THINGS ABOUT OUR INVESTIGA-TION TO ANYONE.

READ THIS WAY

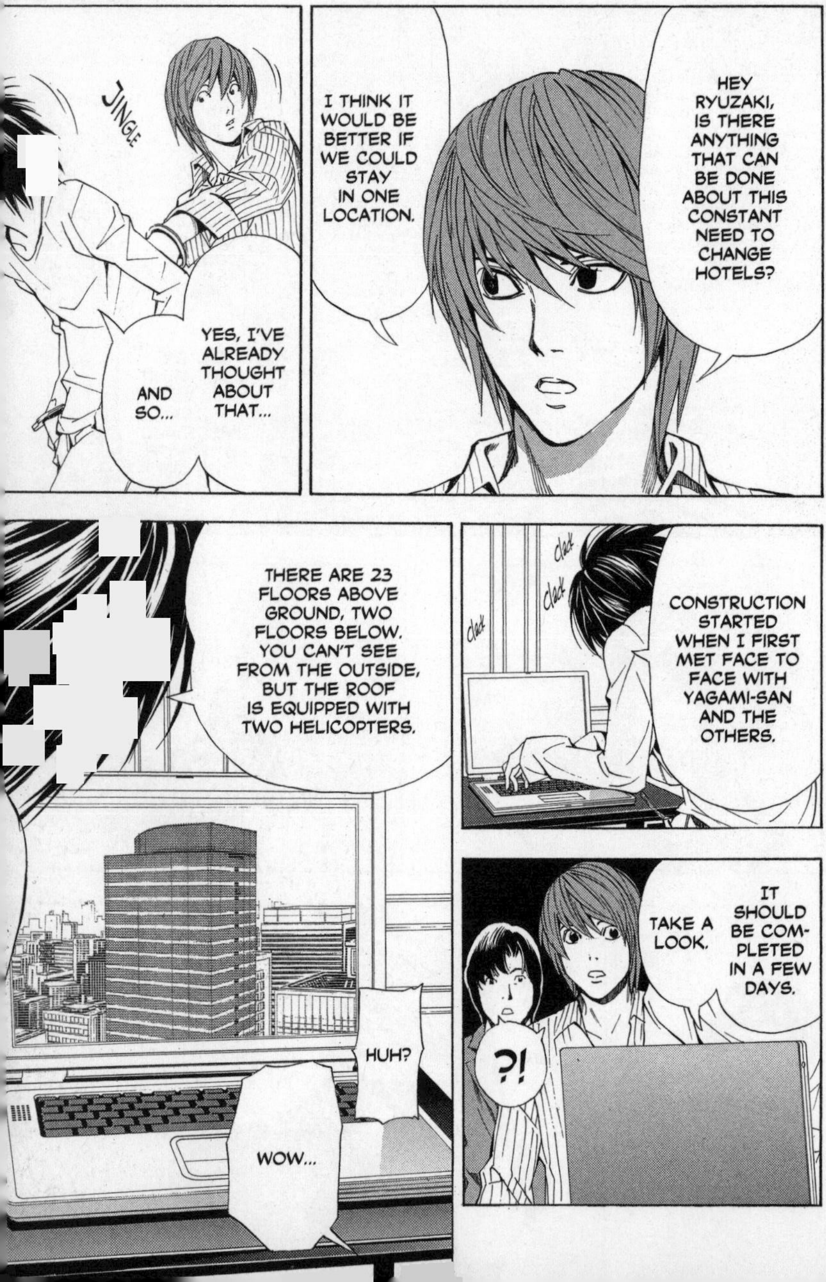
HEY RYUZAKI, IS THERE ANYTHING THAT CAN BE DONE ABOUT THIS CONSTANT NEED TO CHANGE HOTELS?
I THINK IT WOULD BE BETTER IF WE COULD STAY IN ONE LOCATION.
JINGLE
YES, I'VE ALREADY THOUGHT ABOUT THAT...
AND SO...
clack
clack
clack
CONSTRUCTION STARTED WHEN I FIRST MET FACE TO FACE WITH YAGAMI-SAN AND THE OTHERS.
IT SHOULD BE COM-PLETED IN A FEW DAYS.
TAKE A LOOK.
?!
THERE ARE 23 FLOORS ABOVE GROUND, TWO FLOORS BELOW. YOU CAN'T SEE FROM THE OUTSIDE, BUT THE ROOF IS EQUIPPED WITH TWO HELICOPTERS.
HUH?
WOW...

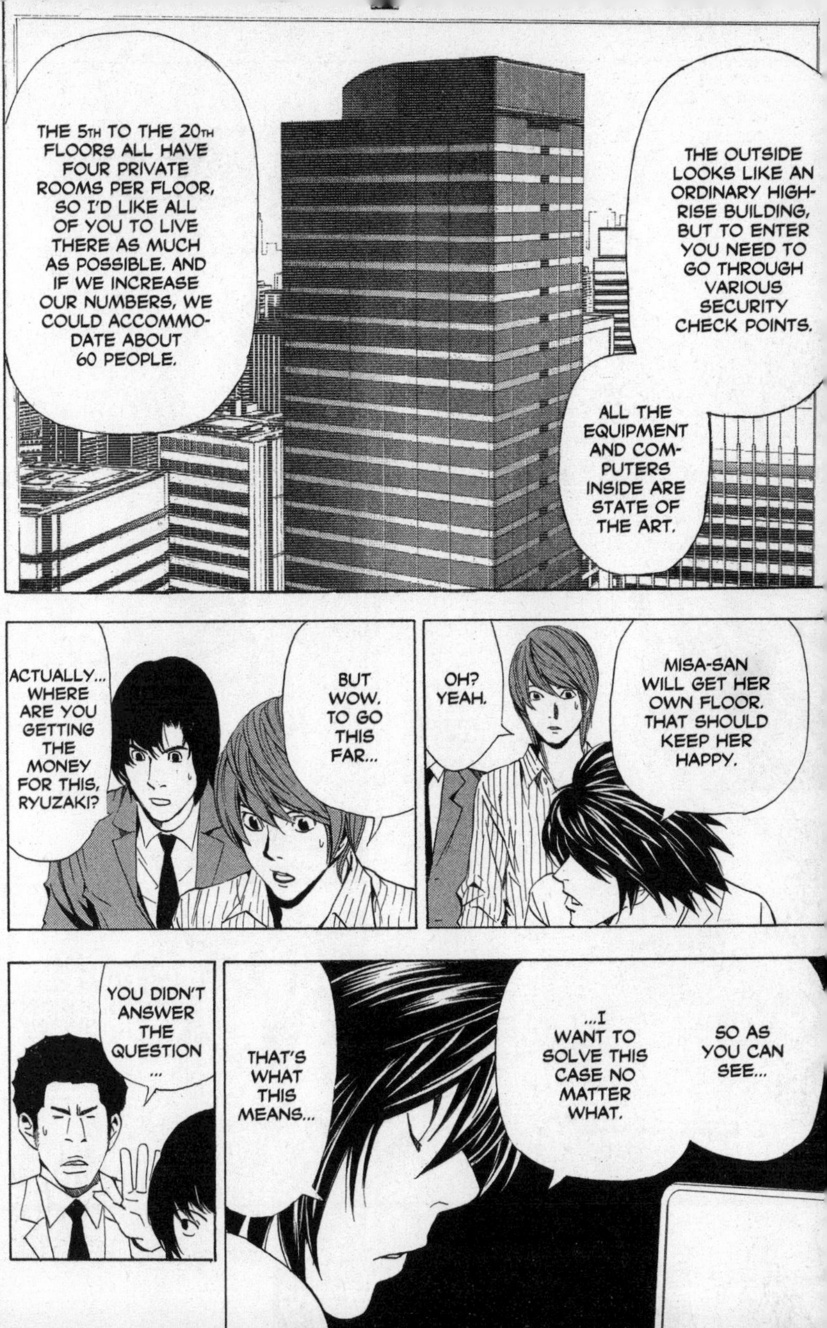
THE OUTSIDE LOOKS LIKE AN ORDINARY HIGH-RISE BUILDING, BUT TO ENTER YOU NEED TO GO THROUGH VARIOUS SECURITY CHECK POINTS.
ALL THE EQUIPMENT AND COMPUTERS INSIDE ARE STATE OF THE ART.
THE 5TH TO THE 20TH FLOORS ALL HAVE FOUR PRIVATE ROOMS PER FLOOR, SO I'D LIKE ALL OF YOU TO LIVE THERE AS MUCH AS POSSIBLE. AND IF WE INCREASE OUR NUMBERS, WE COULD ACCOMMODATE ABOUT 60 PEOPLE.
MISA-SAN WILL GET HER OWN FLOOR. THAT SHOULD KEEP HER HAPPY.
OH? YEAH.
BUT WOW. TO GO THIS FAR...
ACTUALLY... WHERE ARE YOU GETTING THE MONEY FOR THIS, RYUZAKI?
SO AS YOU CAN SEE...
...I WANT TO SOLVE THIS CASE NO MATTER WHAT.
THAT'S WHAT THIS MEANS...
YOU DIDN'T ANSWER THE QUESTION ...

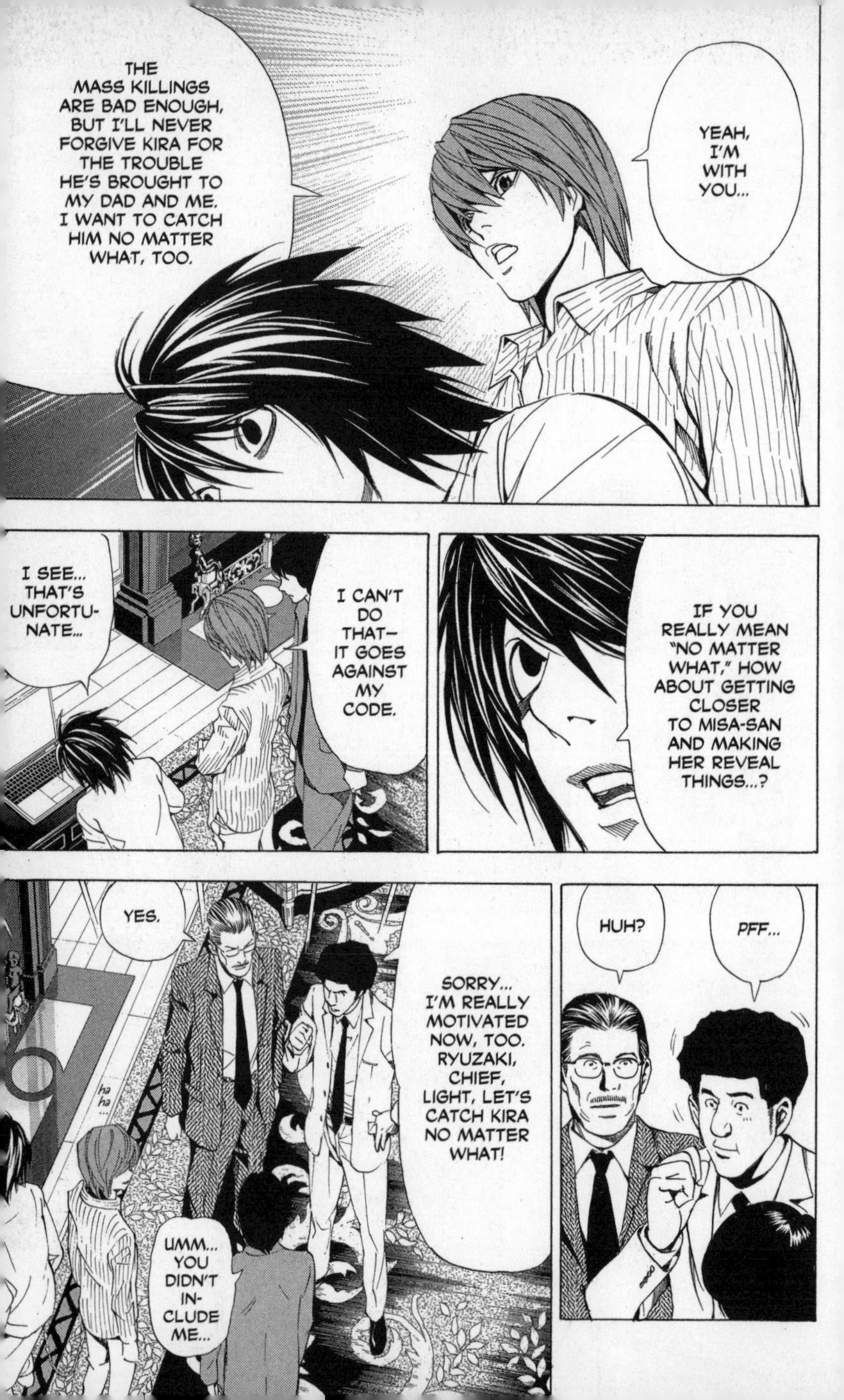
YEAH, I'M WITH YOU...
THE MASS KILLINGS ARE BAD ENOUGH, BUT I'LL NEVER FORGIVE KIRA FOR THE TROUBLE HE'S BROUGHT TO MY DAD AND ME. I WANT TO CATCH HIM NO MATTER WHAT, TOO.
IF YOU REALLY MEAN "NO MATTER WHAT," HOW ABOUT GETTING CLOSER TO MISA-SAN AND MAKING HER REVEAL THINGS...?
I CAN'T DO THAT— IT GOES AGAINST MY CODE.
I SEE... THAT'S UNFORTU-NATE...
PFF...
HUH?
SORRY... I'M REALLY MOTIVATED NOW, TOO. RYUZAKI, CHIEF, LIGHT, LET'S CATCH KIRA NO MATTER WHAT!
YES.
ha ha...
UMM... YOU DIDN'T IN-CLUDE ME...

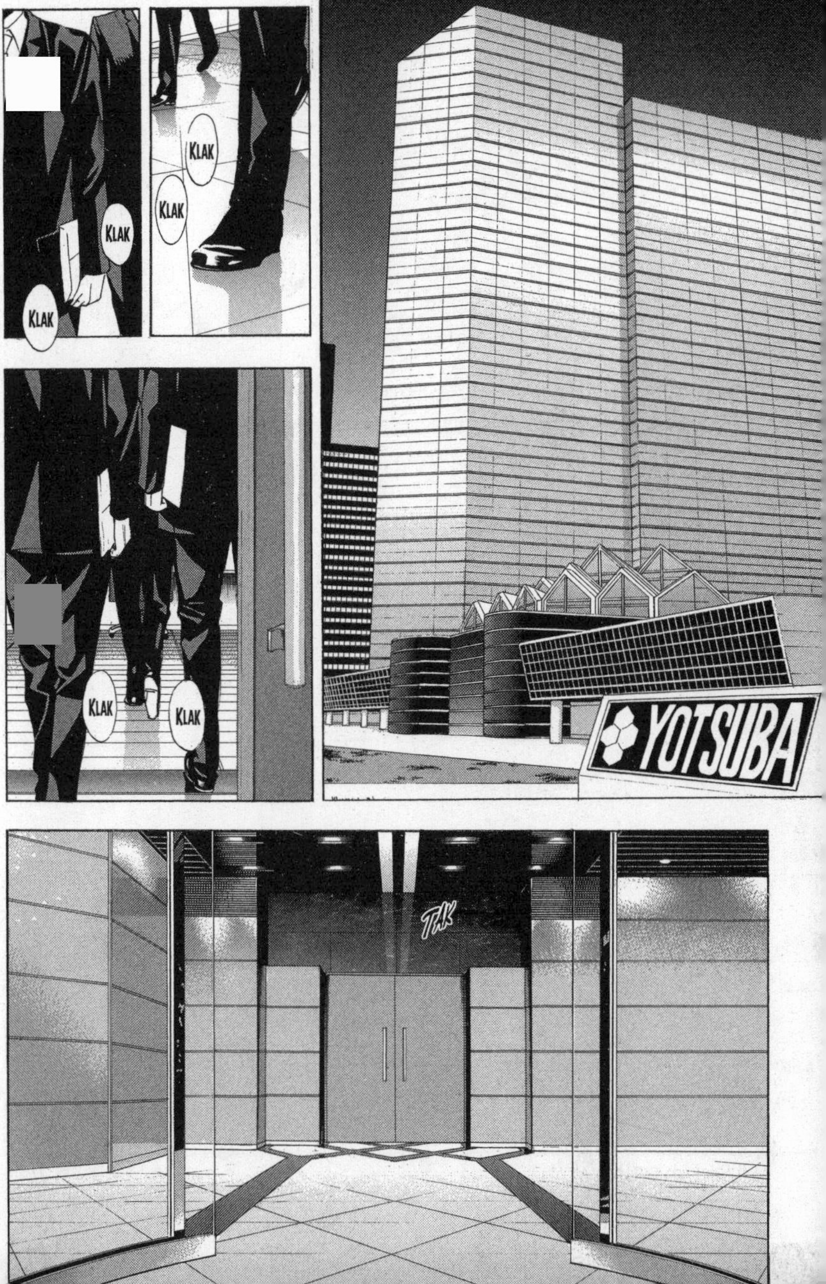
YOTSUBA
KLAK
KLAK
KLAK
KLAK
KLAK
KLAK
TAK

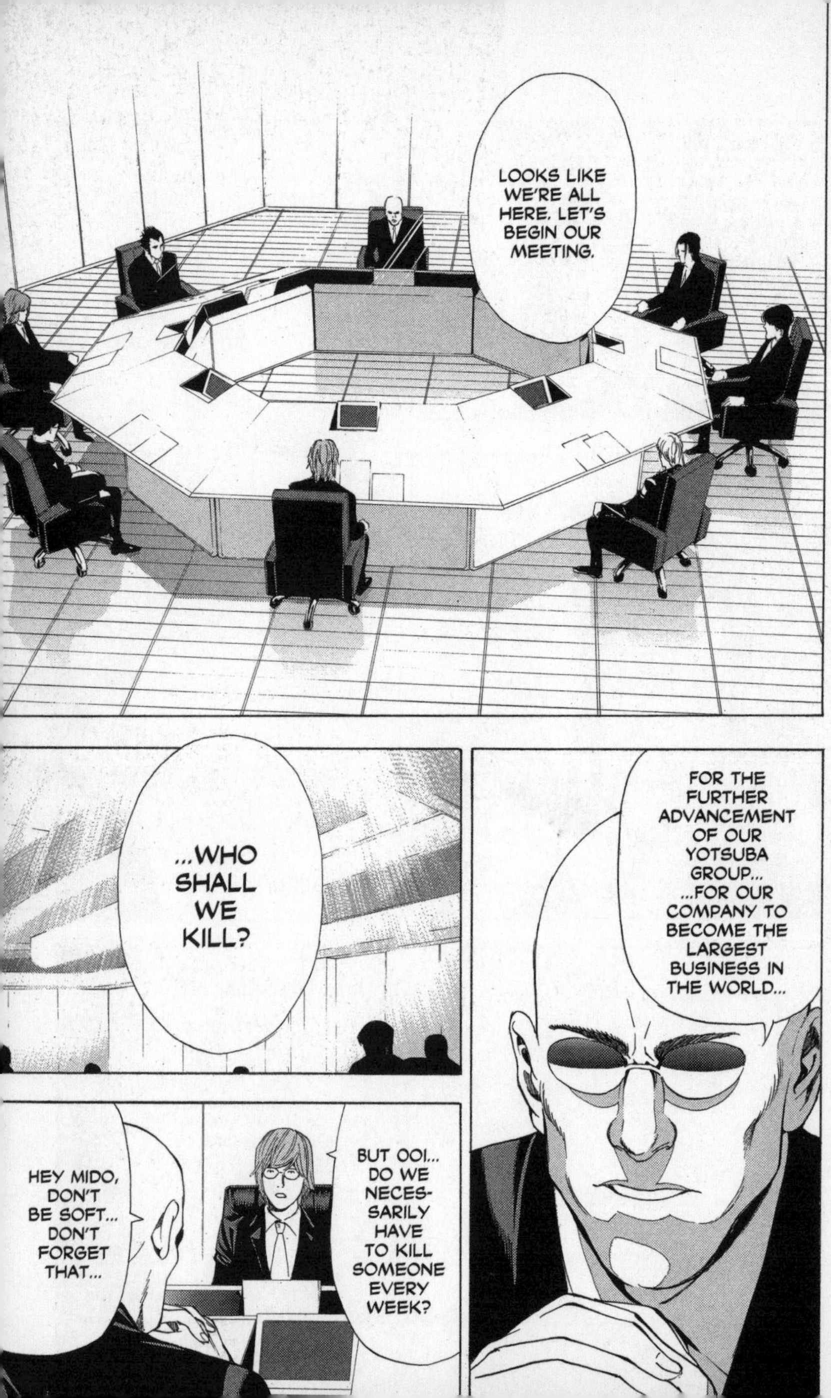
LOOKS LIKE WE'RE ALL HERE. LET'S BEGIN OUR MEETING.
FOR THE FURTHER ADVANCEMENT OF OUR YOTSUBA GROUP... ...FOR OUR COMPANY TO BECOME THE LARGEST BUSINESS IN THE WORLD...
...WHO SHALL WE KILL?
BUT OOI... DO WE NECES-SARILY HAVE TO KILL SOMEONE EVERY WEEK?
HEY MIDO, DON'T BE SOFT... DON'T FORGET THAT...

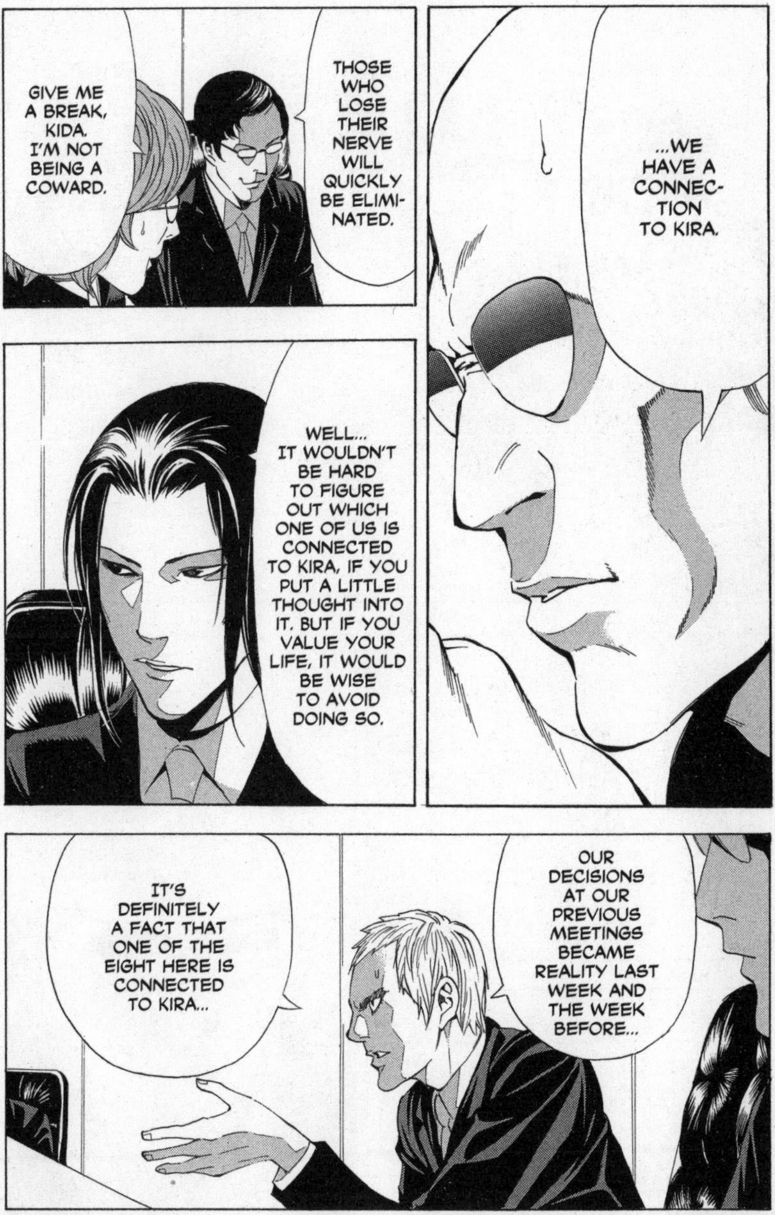
...WE HAVE A CONNECTION TO KIRA.
THOSE WHO LOSE THEIR NERVE WILL QUICKLY BE ELIMINATED.
GIVE ME A BREAK, KIDA. I'M NOT BEING A COWARD.
WELL... IT WOULDN'T BE HARD TO FIGURE OUT WHICH ONE OF US IS CONNECTED TO KIRA, IF YOU PUT A LITTLE THOUGHT INTO IT. BUT IF YOU VALUE YOUR LIFE, IT WOULD BE WISE TO AVOID DOING SO.
OUR DECISIONS AT OUR PREVIOUS MEETINGS BECAME REALITY LAST WEEK AND THE WEEK BEFORE...
IT'S DEFINITELY A FACT THAT ONE OF THE EIGHT HERE IS CONNECTED TO KIRA...

READ THIS WAY

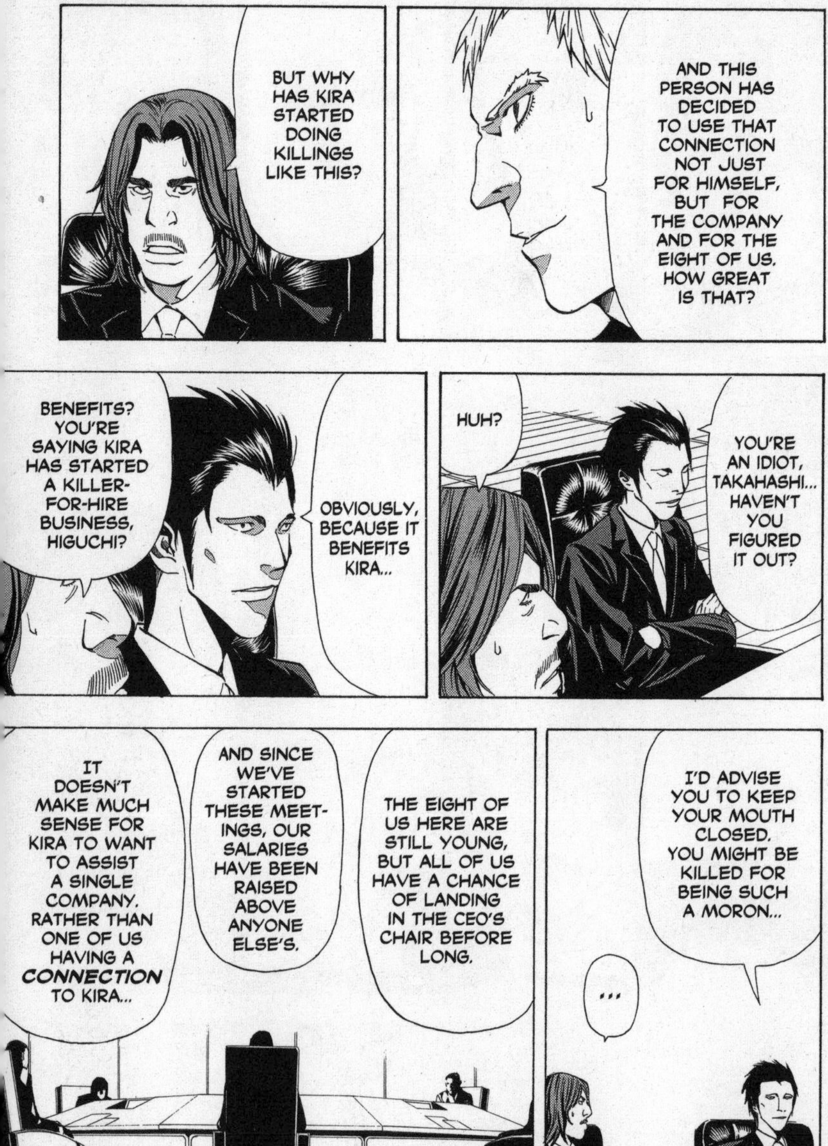
AND THIS PERSON HAS DECIDED TO USE THAT CONNECTION NOT JUST FOR HIMSELF, BUT FOR THE COMPANY AND FOR THE EIGHT OF US. HOW GREAT IS THAT?
BUT WHY HAS KIRA STARTED DOING KILLINGS LIKE THIS?
YOU'RE AN IDIOT, TAKAHASHI... HAVEN'T YOU FIGURED IT OUT?
HUH?
OBVIOUSLY, BECAUSE IT BENEFITS KIRA...
BENEFITS? YOU'RE SAYING KIRA HAS STARTED A KILLER-FOR-HIRE BUSINESS, HIGUCHI?
I'D ADVISE YOU TO KEEP YOUR MOUTH CLOSED. YOU MIGHT BE KILLED FOR BEING SUCH A MORON...
...
THE EIGHT OF US HERE ARE STILL YOUNG, BUT ALL OF US HAVE A CHANCE OF LANDING IN THE CEO'S CHAIR BEFORE LONG.
AND SINCE WE'VE STARTED THESE MEETINGS, OUR SALARIES HAVE BEEN RAISED ABOVE ANYONE ELSE'S.
IT DOESN'T MAKE MUCH SENSE FOR KIRA TO WANT TO ASSIST A SINGLE COMPANY. RATHER THAN ONE OF US HAVING A CONNECTION TO KIRA...

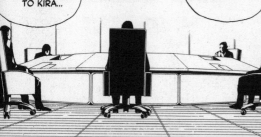

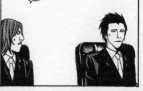

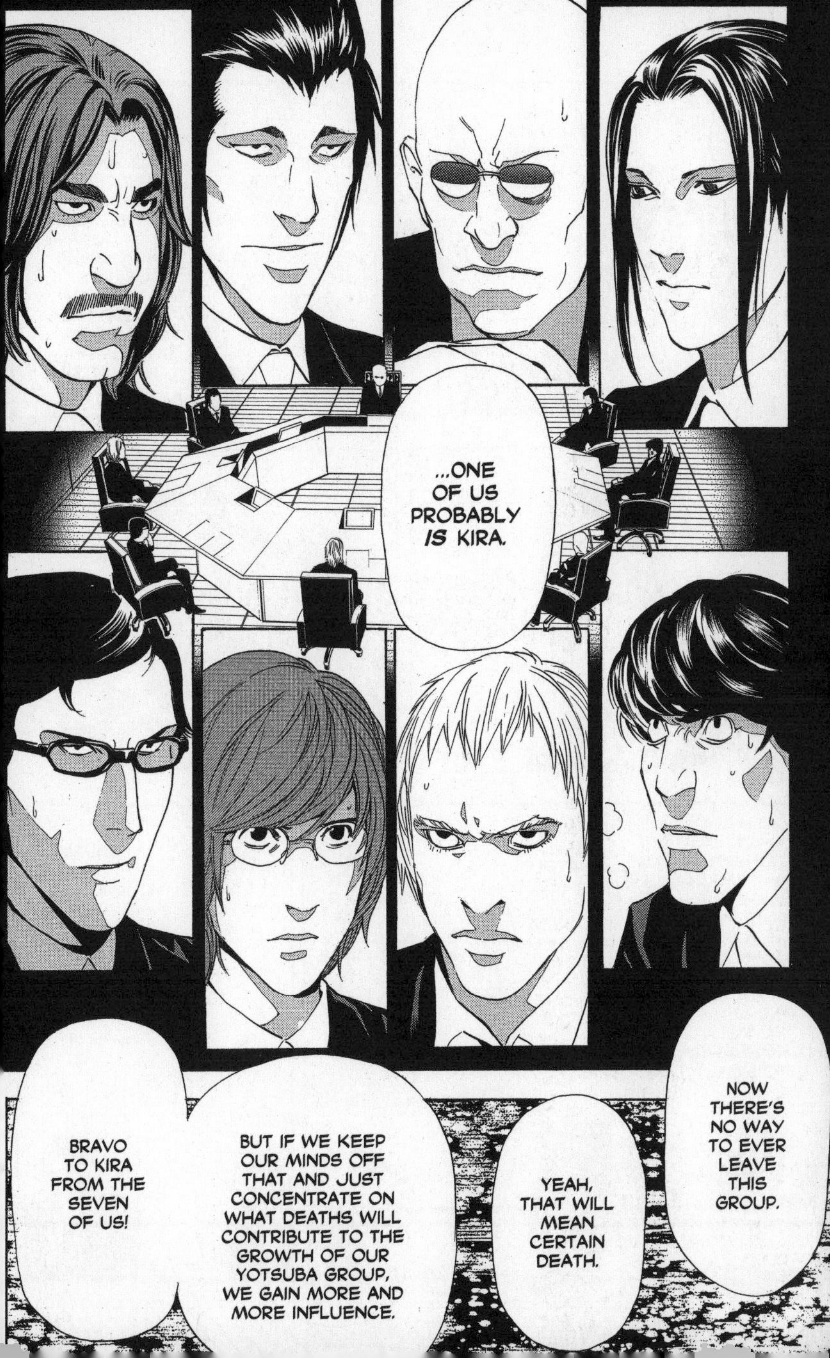
...ONE OF US PROBABLY *IS* KIRA.
NOW THERE'S NO WAY TO EVER LEAVE THIS GROUP.
YEAH, THAT WILL MEAN CERTAIN DEATH.
BUT IF WE KEEP OUR MINDS OFF THAT AND JUST CONCENTRATE ON WHAT DEATHS WILL CONTRIBUTE TO THE GROWTH OF OUR YOTSUBA GROUP, WE GAIN MORE AND MORE INFLUENCE.
BRAVO TO KIRA FROM THE SEVEN OF US!

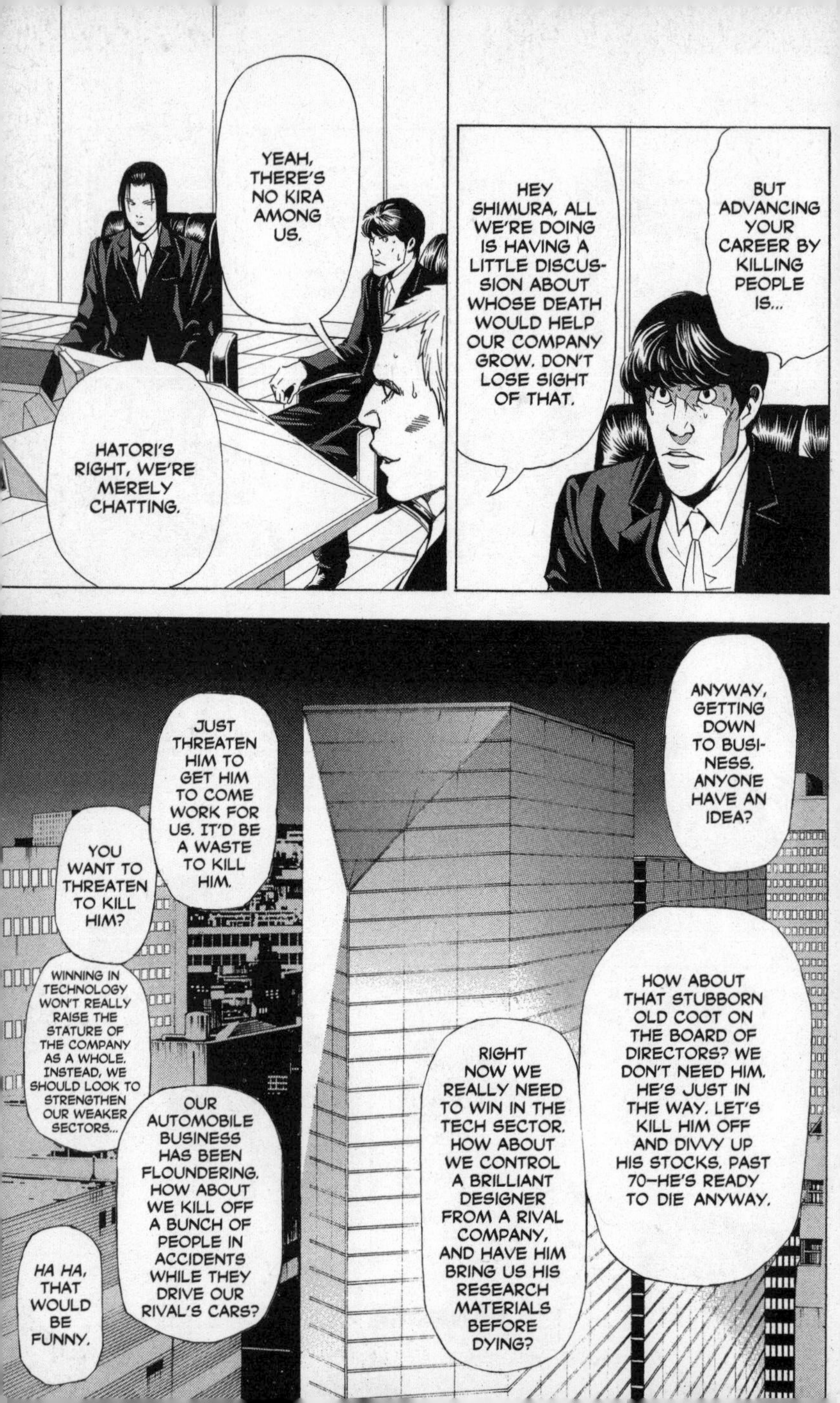
BUT ADVANCING YOUR CAREER BY KILLING PEOPLE IS...
HEY SHIMURA, ALL WE'RE DOING IS HAVING A LITTLE DISCUSSION ABOUT WHOSE DEATH WOULD HELP OUR COMPANY GROW. DON'T LOSE SIGHT OF THAT.
YEAH, THERE'S NO KIRA AMONG US.
HATORI'S RIGHT, WE'RE MERELY CHATTING.
ANYWAY, GETTING DOWN TO BUSINESS. ANYONE HAVE AN IDEA?
HOW ABOUT THAT STUBBORN OLD COOT ON THE BOARD OF DIRECTORS? WE DON'T NEED HIM. HE'S JUST IN THE WAY. LET'S KILL HIM OFF AND DIVVY UP HIS STOCKS. PAST 70—HE'S READY TO DIE ANYWAY.
RIGHT NOW WE REALLY NEED TO WIN IN THE TECH SECTOR. HOW ABOUT WE CONTROL A BRILLIANT DESIGNER FROM A RIVAL COMPANY, AND HAVE HIM BRING US HIS RESEARCH MATERIALS BEFORE DYING?
JUST THREATEN HIM TO GET HIM TO COME WORK FOR US. IT'D BE A WASTE TO KILL HIM.
YOU WANT TO THREATEN TO KILL HIM?
WINNING IN TECHNOLOGY WON'T REALLY RAISE THE STATURE OF THE COMPANY AS A WHOLE. INSTEAD, WE SHOULD LOOK TO STRENGTHEN OUR WEAKER SECTORS...
OUR AUTOMOBILE BUSINESS HAS BEEN FLOUNDERING. HOW ABOUT WE KILL OFF A BUNCH OF PEOPLE IN ACCIDENTS WHILE THEY DRIVE OUR RIVAL'S CARS?
*HA HA, THAT WOULD BE FUNNY.*

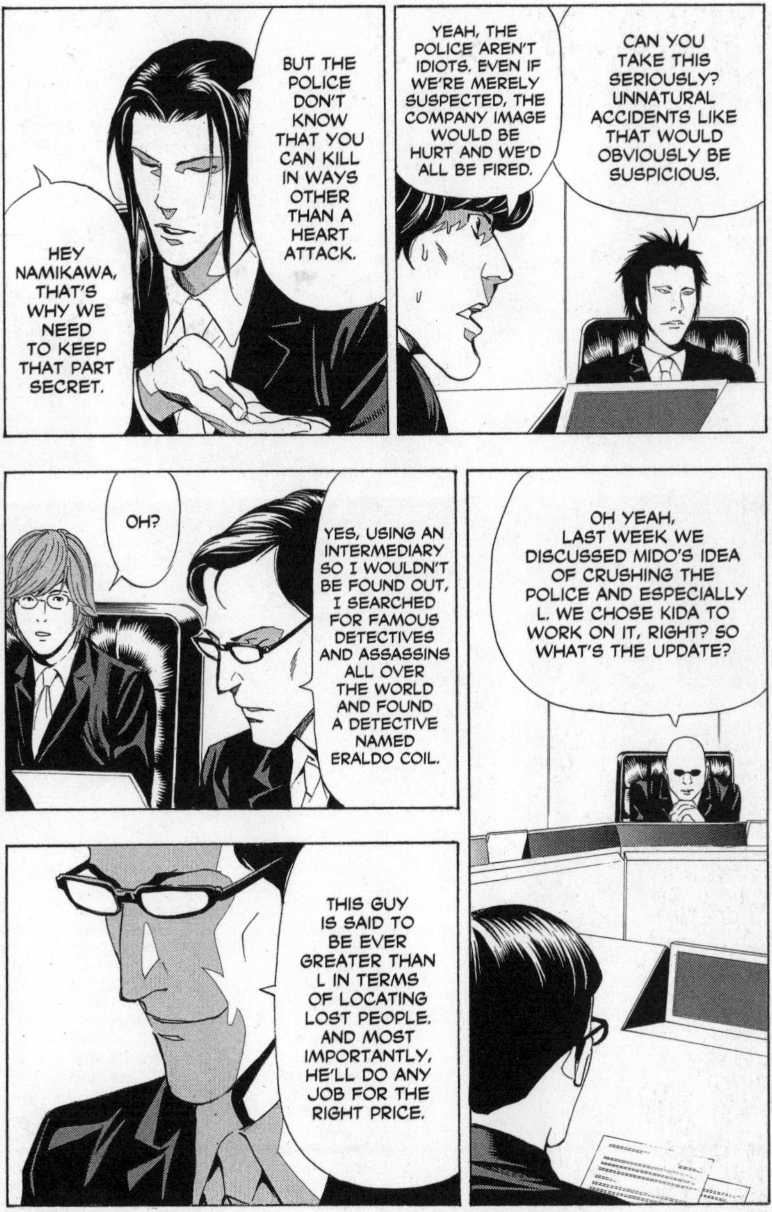
CAN YOU TAKE THIS SERIOUSLY? UNNATURAL ACCIDENTS LIKE THAT WOULD OBVIOUSLY BE SUSPICIOUS.
YEAH, THE POLICE AREN'T IDIOTS. EVEN IF WE'RE MERELY SUSPECTED, THE COMPANY IMAGE WOULD BE HURT AND WE'D ALL BE FIRED.
BUT THE POLICE DON'T KNOW THAT YOU CAN KILL IN WAYS OTHER THAN A HEART ATTACK.
HEY NAMIKAWA, THAT'S WHY WE NEED TO KEEP THAT PART SECRET.
OH YEAH, LAST WEEK WE DISCUSSED MIDO'S IDEA OF CRUSHING THE POLICE AND ESPECIALLY L. WE CHOSE KIDA TO WORK ON IT, RIGHT? SO WHAT'S THE UPDATE?
YES, USING AN INTERMEDIARY SO I WOULDN'T BE FOUND OUT, I SEARCHED FOR FAMOUS DETECTIVES AND ASSASSINS ALL OVER THE WORLD AND FOUND A DETECTIVE NAMED ERALDO COIL.
OH?
THIS GUY IS SAID TO BE EVER GREATER THAN L IN TERMS OF LOCATING LOST PEOPLE. AND MOST IMPORTANTLY, HE'LL DO ANY JOB FOR THE RIGHT PRICE.

READ THIS WAY

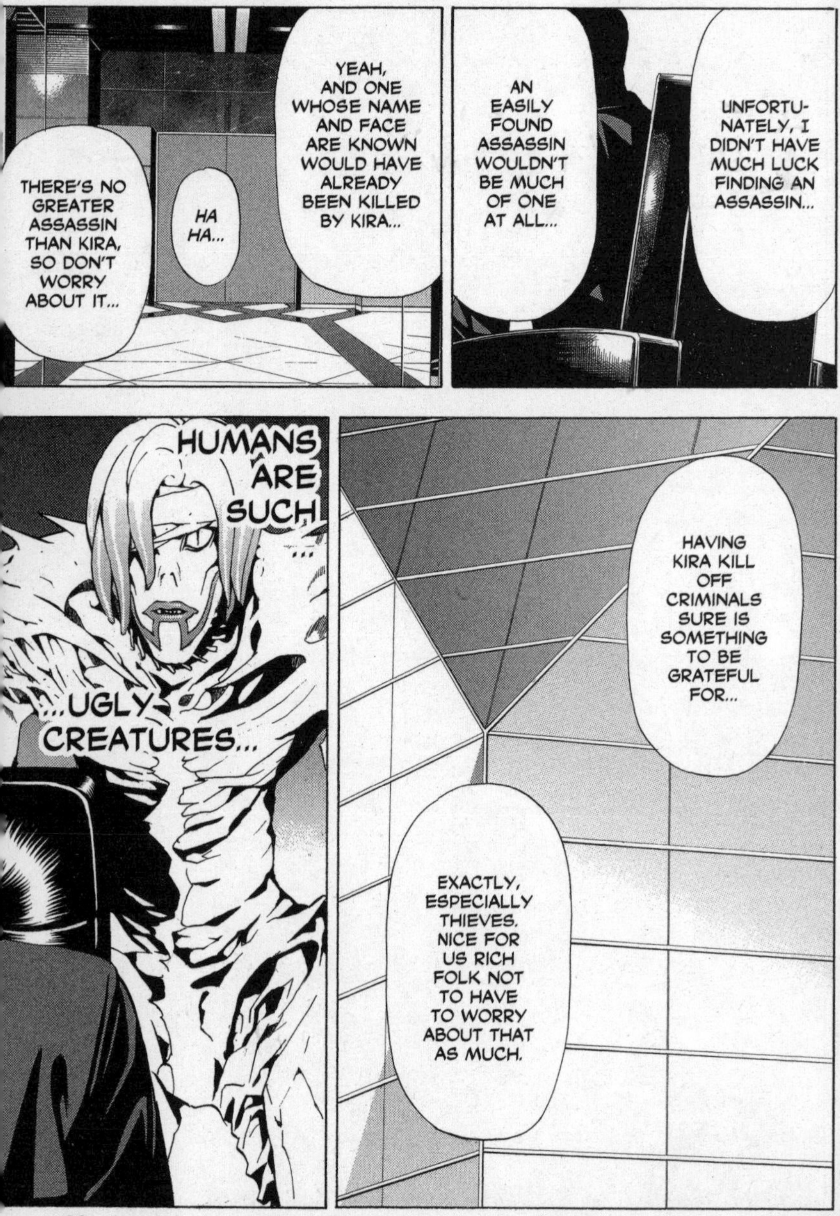

UNFORTUNATELY, I DIDN'T HAVE MUCH LUCK FINDING AN ASSASSIN...
AN EASILY FOUND ASSASSIN WOULDN'T BE MUCH OF ONE AT ALL...
YEAH, AND ONE WHOSE NAME AND FACE ARE KNOWN WOULD HAVE ALREADY BEEN KILLED BY KIRA...
HA HA...
THERE'S NO GREATER ASSASSIN THAN KIRA, SO DON'T WORRY ABOUT IT...
HAVING KIRA KILL OFF CRIMINALS SURE IS SOMETHING TO BE GRATEFUL FOR...
EXACTLY, ESPECIALLY THIEVES. NICE FOR US RICH FOLK NOT TO HAVE TO WORRY ABOUT THAT AS MUCH.
HUMANS ARE SUCH...
...UGLY CREATURES...

# chapter 38 Strike

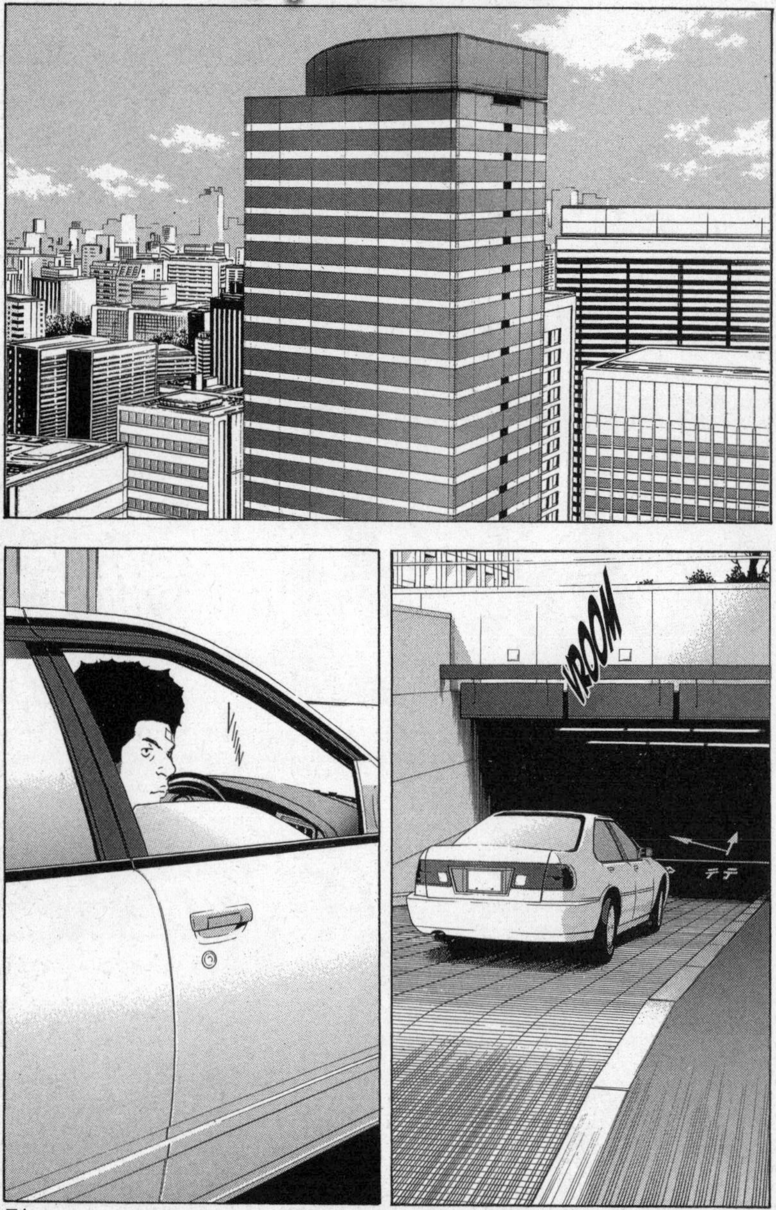
VROOM
VIIN

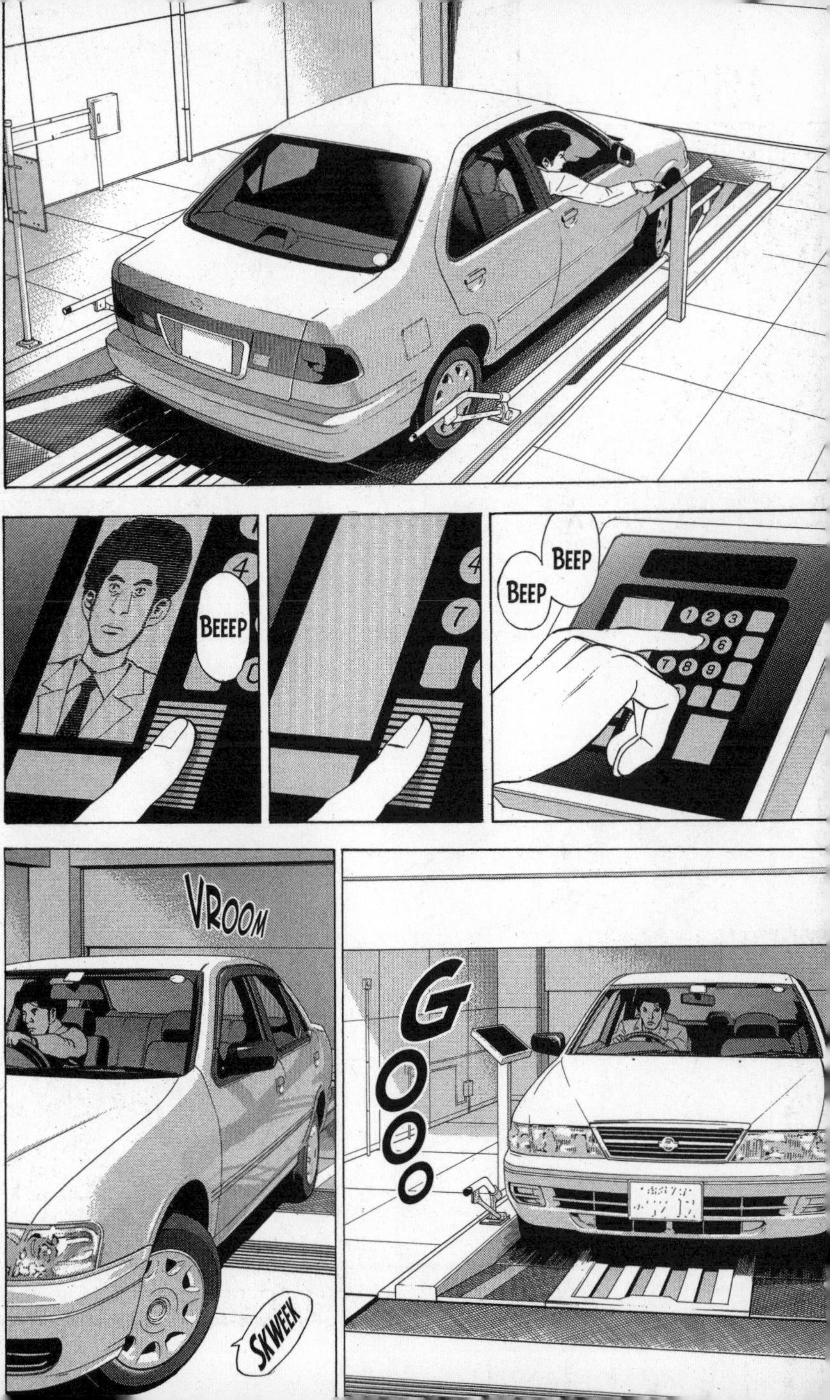
BEEP
BEEP
BEEEP
GOOO
VROOM
SKWEEK

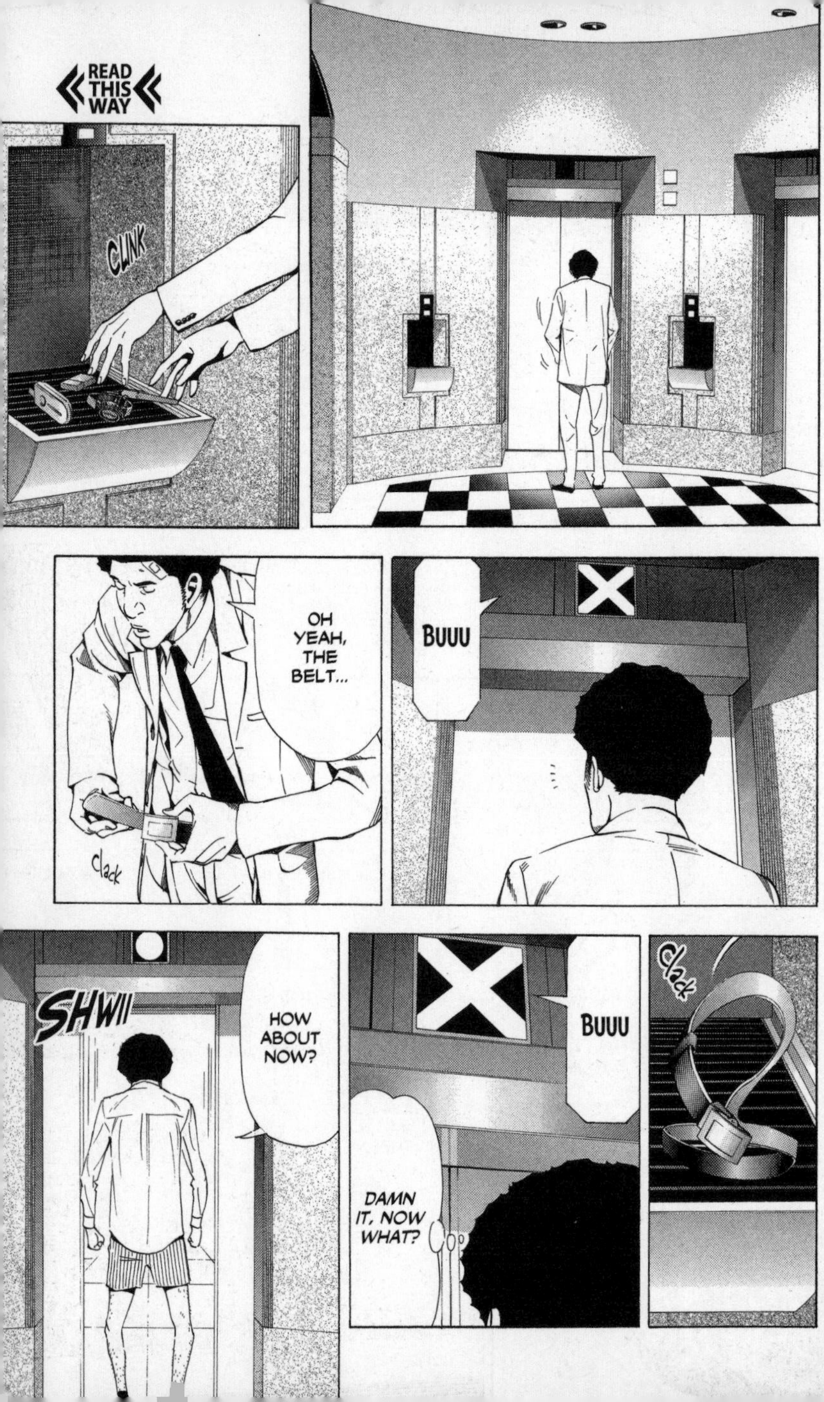
READ THIS WAY
CLINK
BUUU
OH YEAH, THE BELT...
clack
clack
BUUU
DAMN IT, NOW WHAT?
SHWII
HOW ABOUT NOW?

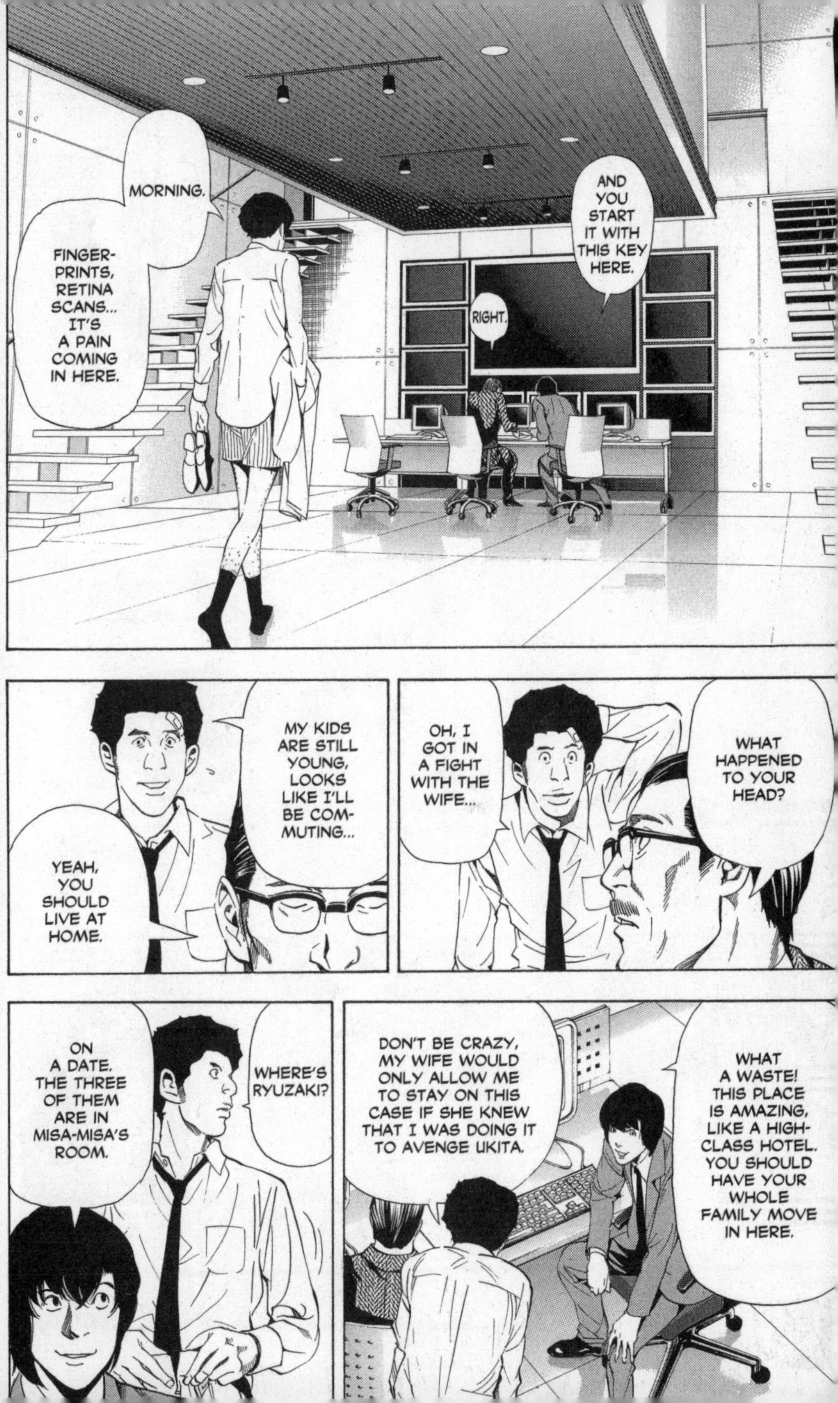
AND YOU START IT WITH THIS KEY HERE.
RIGHT.
MORNING.
FINGER-PRINTS, RETINA SCANS... IT'S A PAIN COMING IN HERE.
WHAT HAPPENED TO YOUR HEAD?
OH, I GOT IN A FIGHT WITH THE WIFE...
MY KIDS ARE STILL YOUNG, LOOKS LIKE I'LL BE COM-MUTING...
YEAH, YOU SHOULD LIVE AT HOME.
WHAT A WASTE! THIS PLACE IS AMAZING, LIKE A HIGH-CLASS HOTEL. YOU SHOULD HAVE YOUR WHOLE FAMILY MOVE IN HERE.
DON'T BE CRAZY, MY WIFE WOULD ONLY ALLOW ME TO STAY ON THIS CASE IF SHE KNEW THAT I WAS DOING IT TO AVENGE UKITA.
WHERE'S RYUZAKI?
ON A DATE. THE THREE OF THEM ARE IN MISA-MISA'S ROOM.

READ THIS WAY

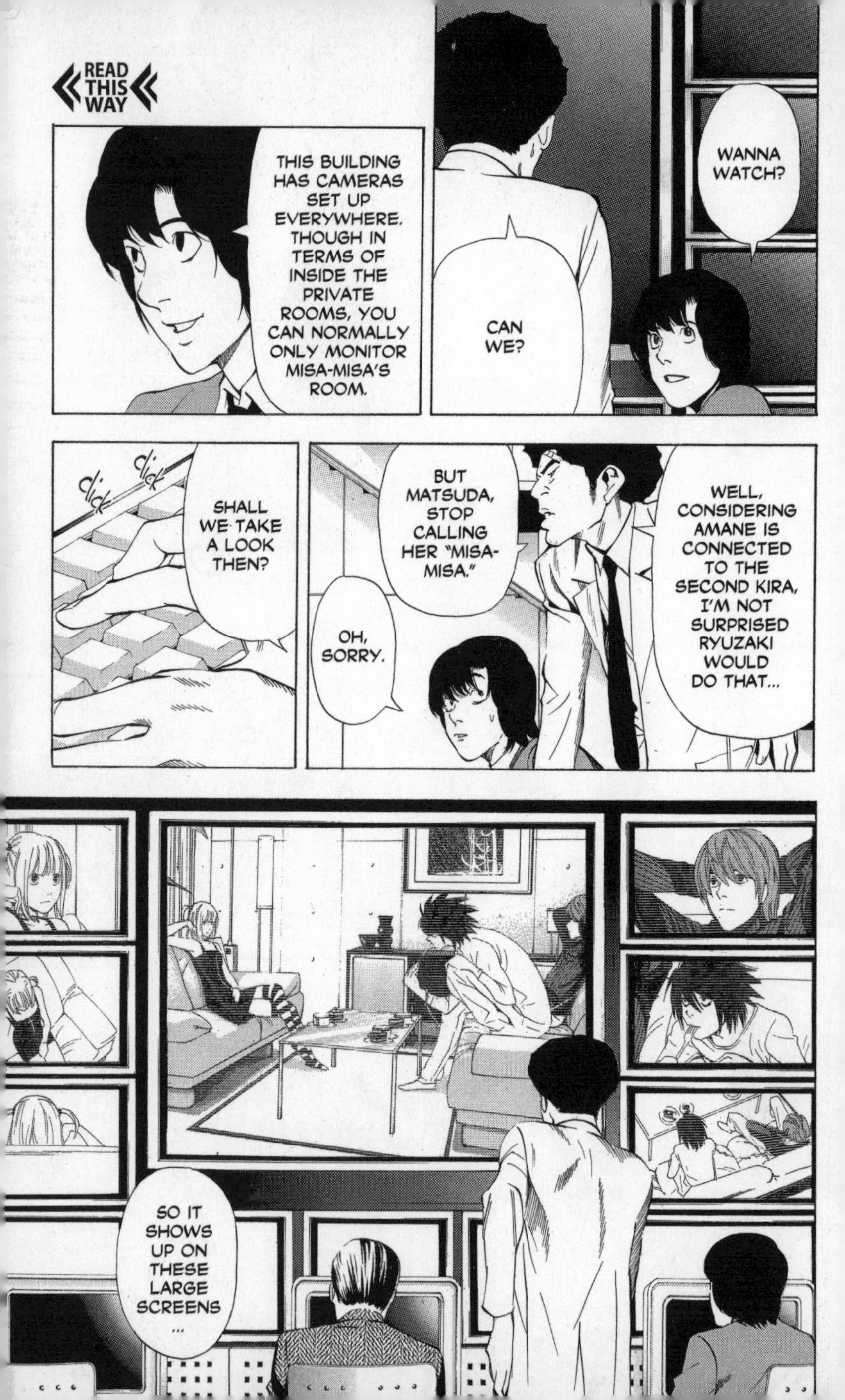
WANNA WATCH?
CAN WE?
THIS BUILDING HAS CAMERAS SET UP EVERYWHERE. THOUGH IN TERMS OF INSIDE THE PRIVATE ROOMS, YOU CAN NORMALLY ONLY MONITOR MISA-MISA'S ROOM.
WELL, CONSIDERING AMANE IS CONNECTED TO THE SECOND KIRA, I'M NOT SURPRISED RYUZAKI WOULD DO THAT...
BUT MATSUDA, STOP CALLING HER "MISA-MISA."
OH, SORRY.
SHALL WE TAKE A LOOK THEN?
click
click
SO IT SHOWS UP ON THESE LARGE SCREENS ...

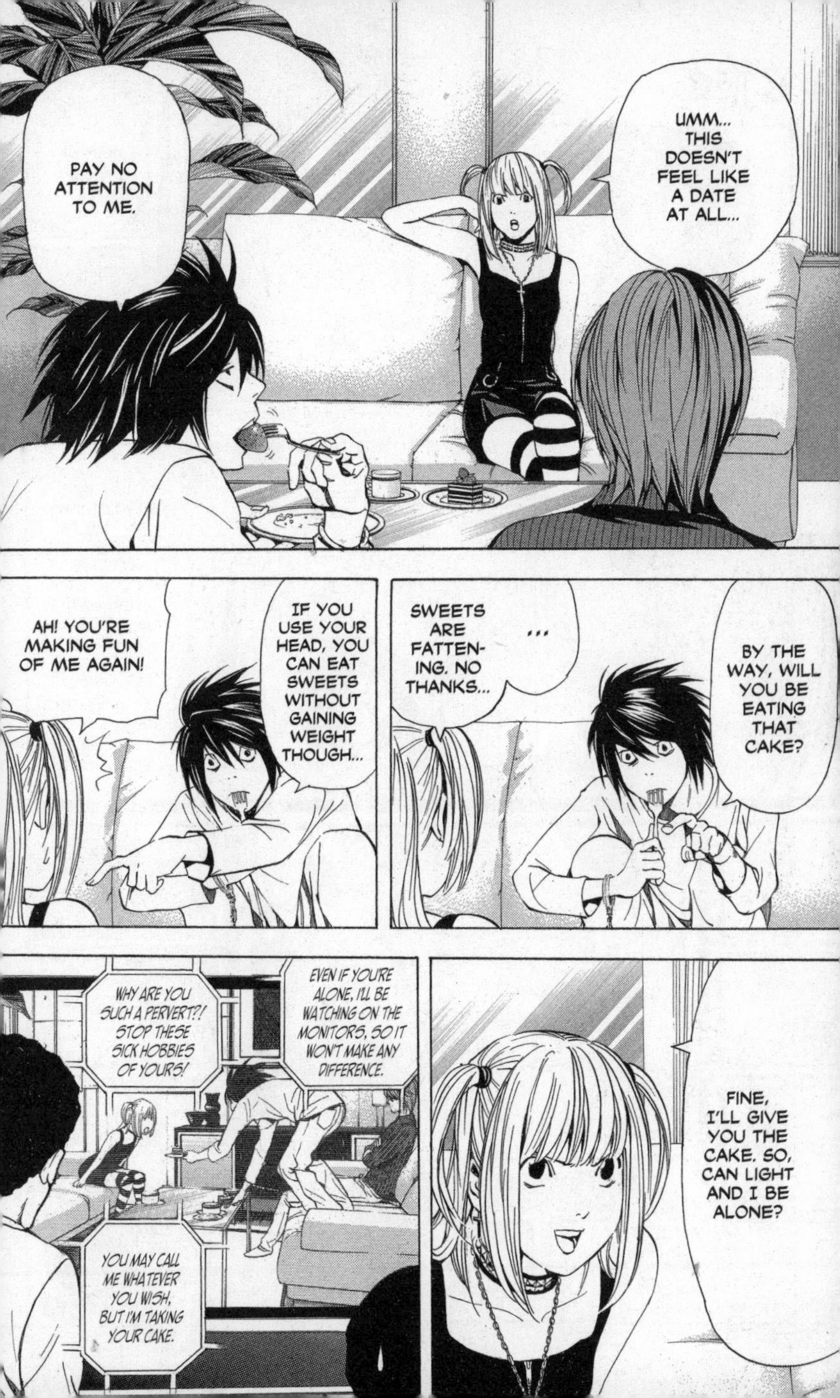
UMM... THIS DOESN'T FEEL LIKE A DATE AT ALL...
PAY NO ATTENTION TO ME.
BY THE WAY, WILL YOU BE EATING THAT CAKE?
...
SWEETS ARE FATTEN-ING. NO THANKS...
IF YOU USE YOUR HEAD, YOU CAN EAT SWEETS WITHOUT GAINING WEIGHT THOUGH...
AH! YOU'RE MAKING FUN OF ME AGAIN!
FINE, I'LL GIVE YOU THE CAKE. SO, CAN LIGHT AND I BE ALONE?
EVEN IF YOU'RE ALONE, I'LL BE WATCHING ON THE MONITORS, SO IT WON'T MAKE ANY DIFFERENCE.
WHY ARE YOU SUCH A PERVERT?! STOP THESE SICK HOBBIES OF YOURS!
YOU MAY CALL ME WHATEVER YOU WISH, BUT I'M TAKING YOUR CAKE.

READ THIS WAY

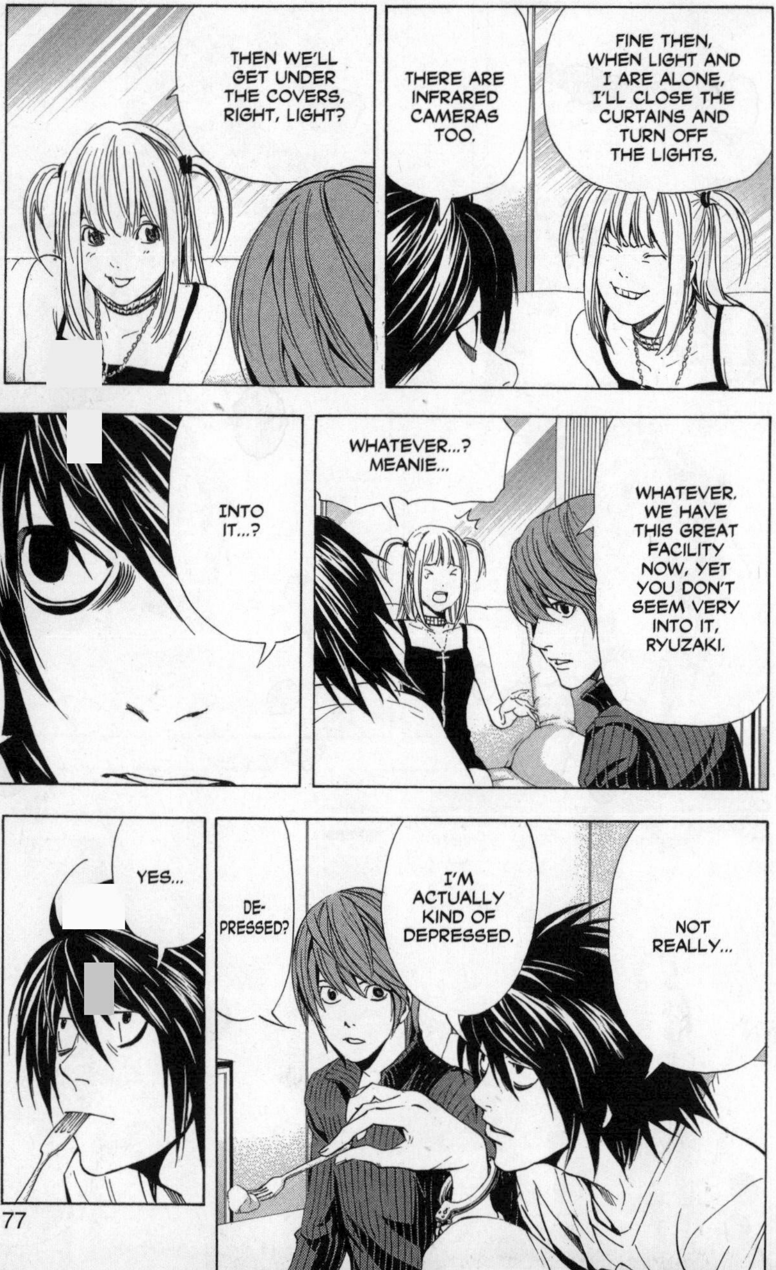
FINE THEN, WHEN LIGHT AND I ARE ALONE, I'LL CLOSE THE CURTAINS AND TURN OFF THE LIGHTS.
THERE ARE INFRARED CAMERAS TOO.
THEN WE'LL GET UNDER THE COVERS, RIGHT, LIGHT?
WHATEVER. WE HAVE THIS GREAT FACILITY NOW, YET YOU DON'T SEEM VERY INTO IT, RYUZAKI.
WHATEVER...? MEANIE...
INTO IT...?
NOT REALLY...
I'M ACTUALLY KIND OF DEPRESSED.
DE-PRESSED?
YES...

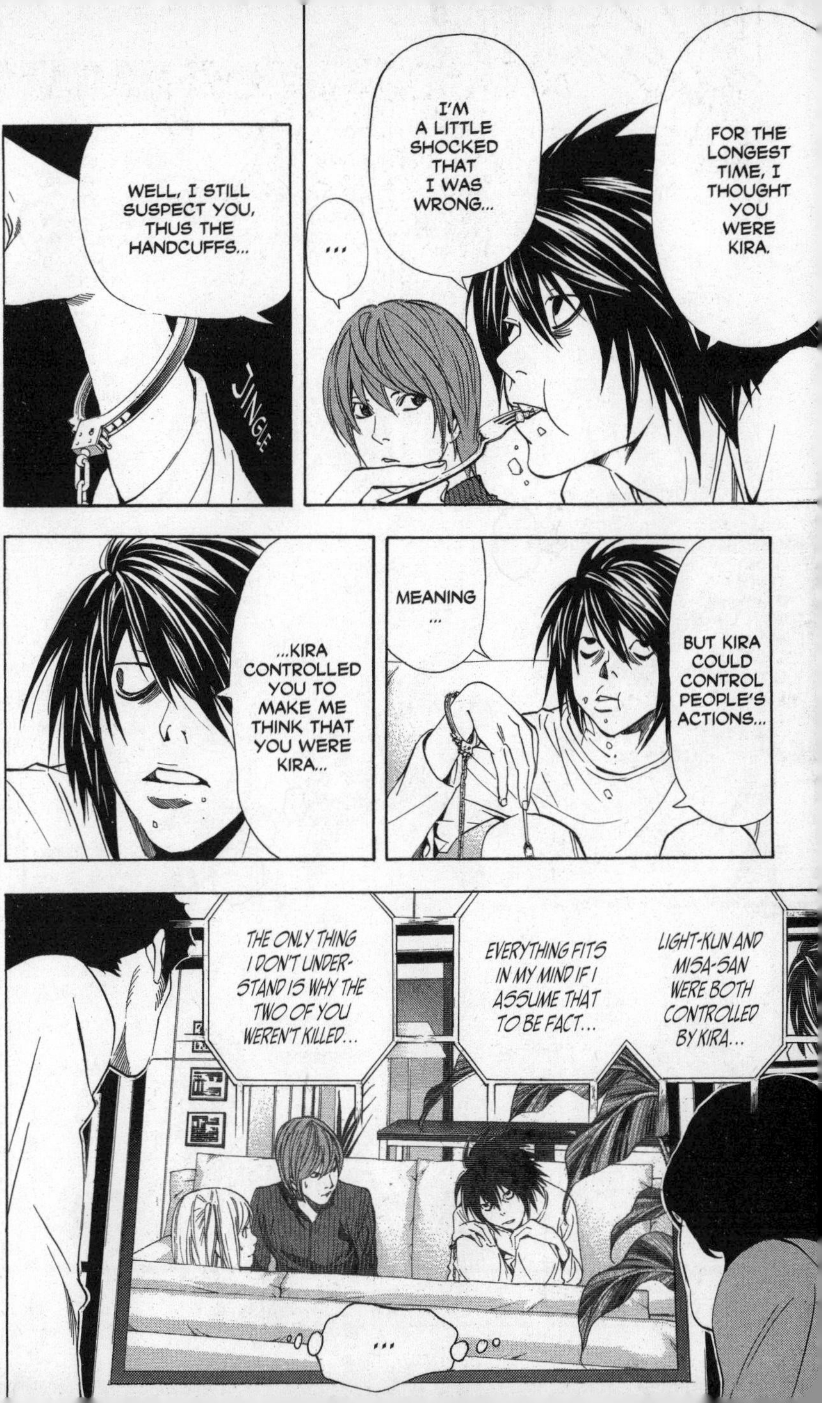
FOR THE LONGEST TIME, I THOUGHT YOU WERE KIRA.
I'M A LITTLE SHOCKED THAT I WAS WRONG...
...
WELL, I STILL SUSPECT YOU, THUS THE HANDCUFFS...
JINGLE
BUT KIRA COULD CONTROL PEOPLE'S ACTIONS...
MEANING ...
...KIRA CONTROLLED YOU TO MAKE ME THINK THAT YOU WERE KIRA...
LIGHT-KUN AND MISA-SAN WERE BOTH CONTROLLED BY KIRA...
EVERYTHING FITS IN MY MIND IF I ASSUME THAT TO BE FACT...
THE ONLY THING I DON'T UNDER-STAND IS WHY THE TWO OF YOU WEREN'T KILLED...
...

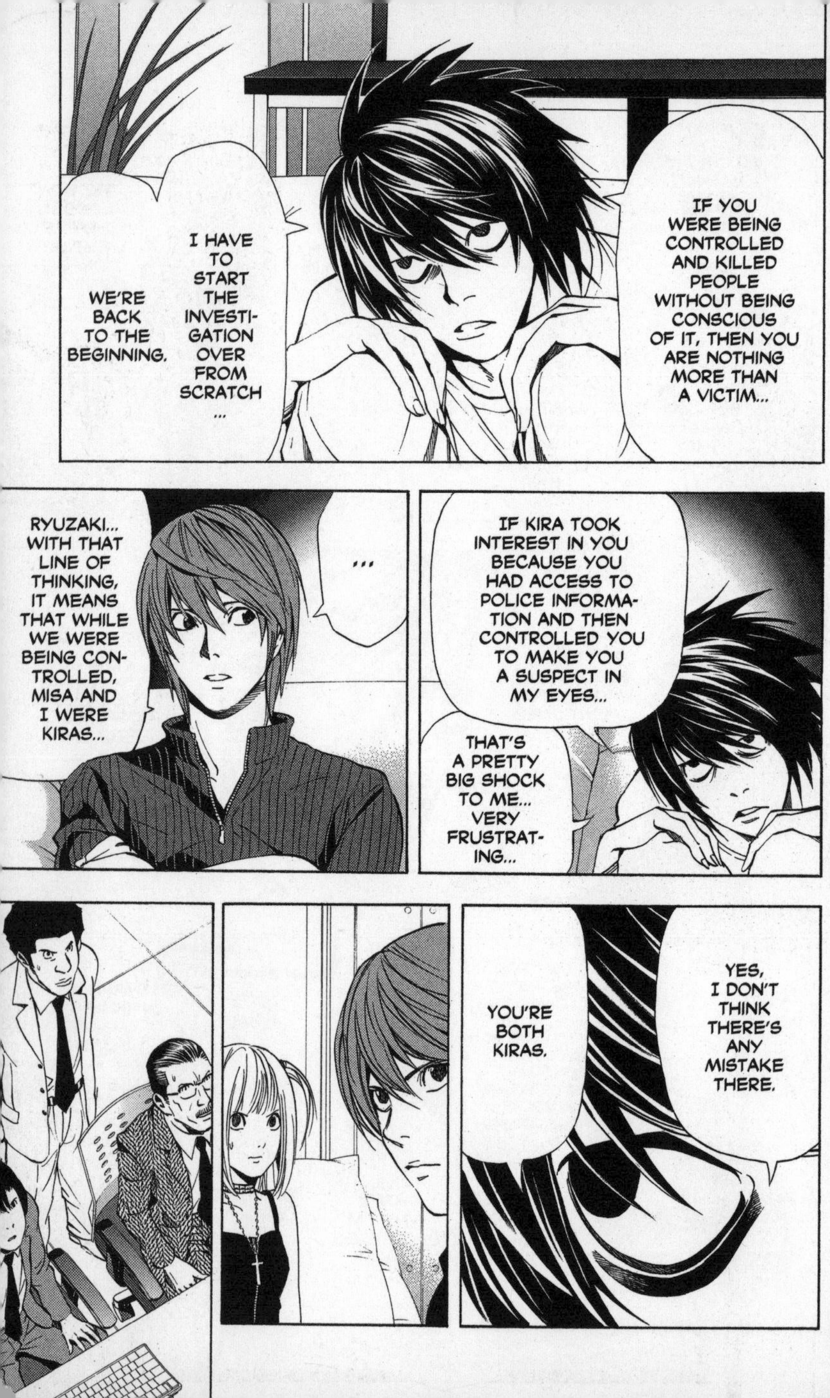
IF YOU WERE BEING CONTROLLED AND KILLED PEOPLE WITHOUT BEING CONSCIOUS OF IT, THEN YOU ARE NOTHING MORE THAN A VICTIM...
I HAVE TO START THE INVESTIGATION OVER FROM SCRATCH...
WE'RE BACK TO THE BEGINNING.
IF KIRA TOOK INTEREST IN YOU BECAUSE YOU HAD ACCESS TO POLICE INFORMATION AND THEN CONTROLLED YOU TO MAKE YOU A SUSPECT IN MY EYES...
THAT'S A PRETTY BIG SHOCK TO ME... VERY FRUSTRATING...
...
RYUZAKI... WITH THAT LINE OF THINKING, IT MEANS THAT WHILE WE WERE BEING CONTROLLED, MISA AND I WERE KIRAS...
YES, I DON'T THINK THERE'S ANY MISTAKE THERE.
YOU'RE BOTH KIRAS.

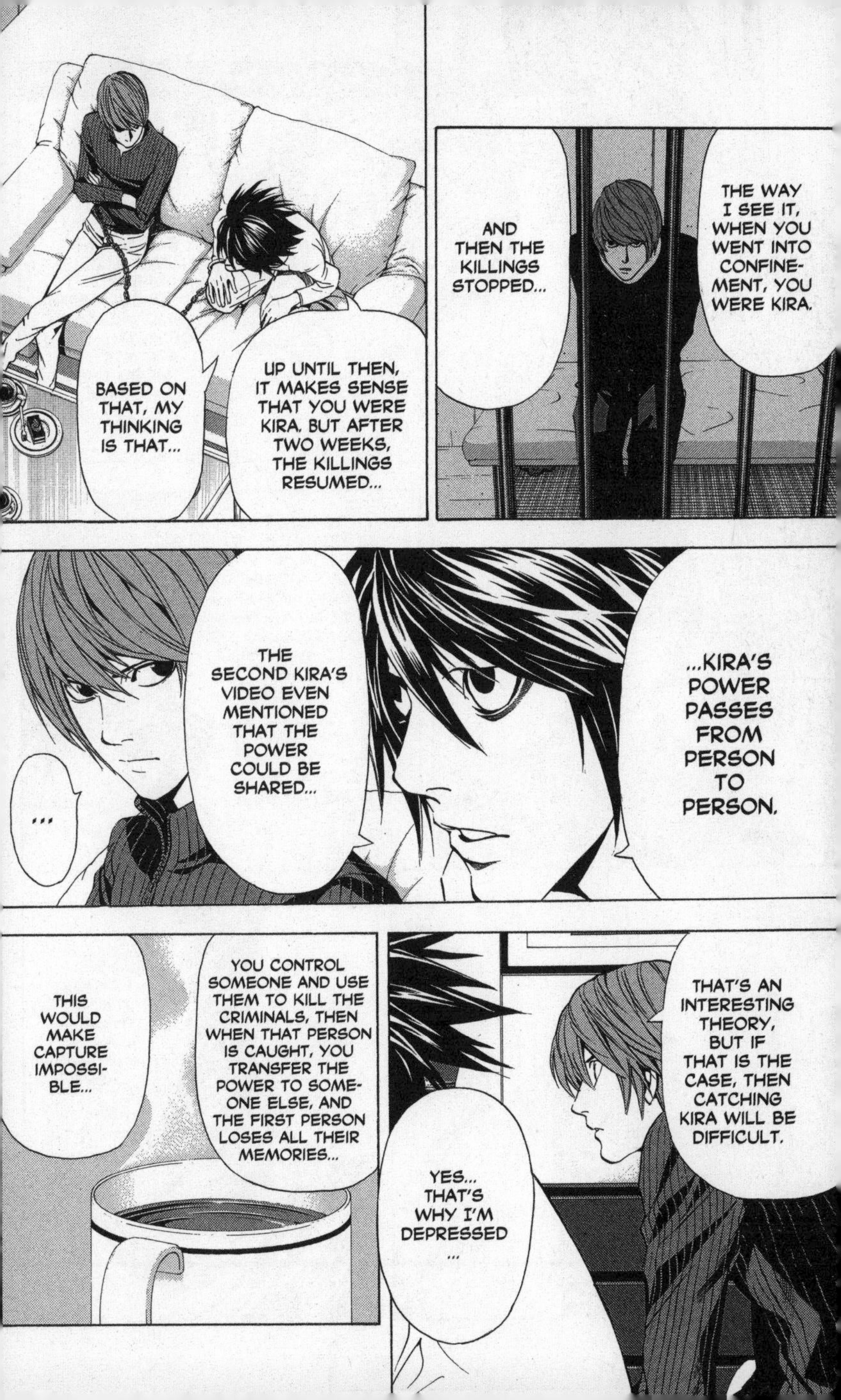
THE WAY I SEE IT, WHEN YOU WENT INTO CONFINE-MENT, YOU WERE KIRA.
AND THEN THE KILLINGS STOPPED...
UP UNTIL THEN, IT MAKES SENSE THAT YOU WERE KIRA. BUT AFTER TWO WEEKS, THE KILLINGS RESUMED...
BASED ON THAT, MY THINKING IS THAT...
...KIRA'S POWER PASSES FROM PERSON TO PERSON.
THE SECOND KIRA'S VIDEO EVEN MENTIONED THAT THE POWER COULD BE SHARED...
...
THAT'S AN INTERESTING THEORY, BUT IF THAT IS THE CASE, THEN CATCHING KIRA WILL BE DIFFICULT.
YES... THAT'S WHY I'M DEPRESSED ...
YOU CONTROL SOMEONE AND USE THEM TO KILL THE CRIMINALS, THEN WHEN THAT PERSON IS CAUGHT, YOU TRANSFER THE POWER TO SOME-ONE ELSE, AND THE FIRST PERSON LOSES ALL THEIR MEMORIES...
THIS WOULD MAKE CAPTURE IMPOSSI-BLE...

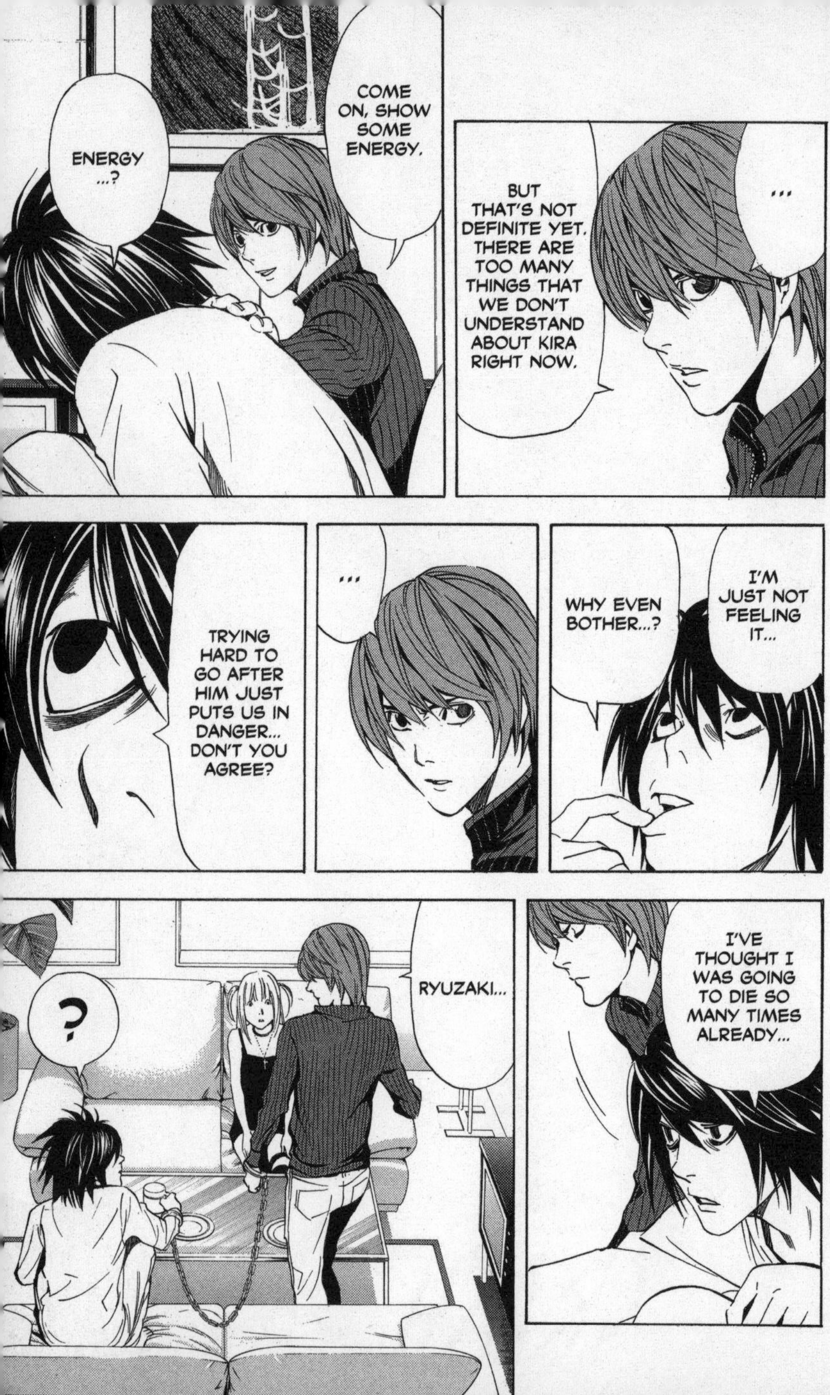
...
BUT THAT'S NOT DEFINITE YET. THERE ARE TOO MANY THINGS THAT WE DON'T UNDERSTAND ABOUT KIRA RIGHT NOW.
COME ON, SHOW SOME ENERGY.
ENERGY ...?
I'M JUST NOT FEELING IT...
WHY EVEN BOTHER...?
...
TRYING HARD TO GO AFTER HIM JUST PUTS US IN DANGER... DON'T YOU AGREE?
I'VE THOUGHT I WAS GOING TO DIE SO MANY TIMES ALREADY...
RYUZAKI...
?

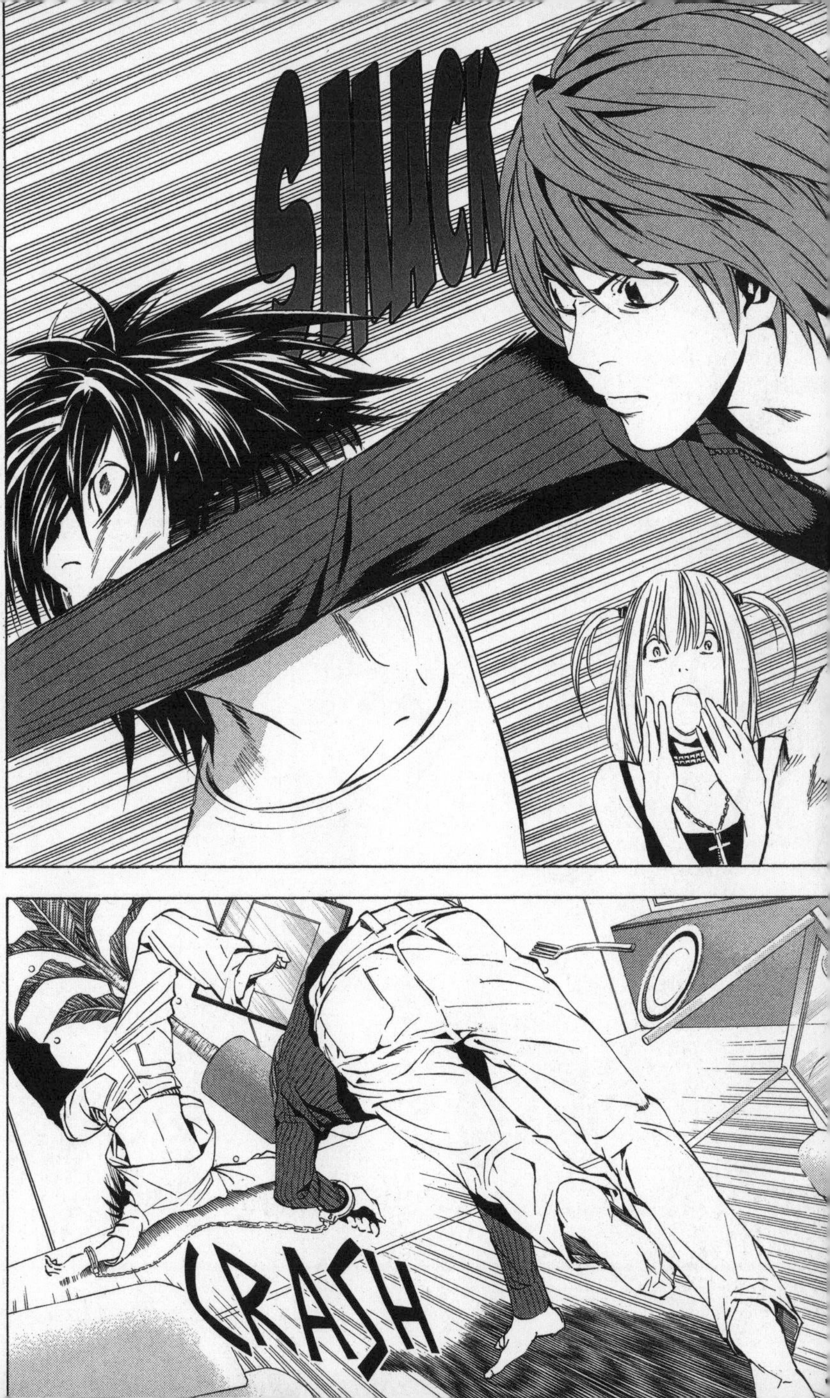
SMACK
CRASH

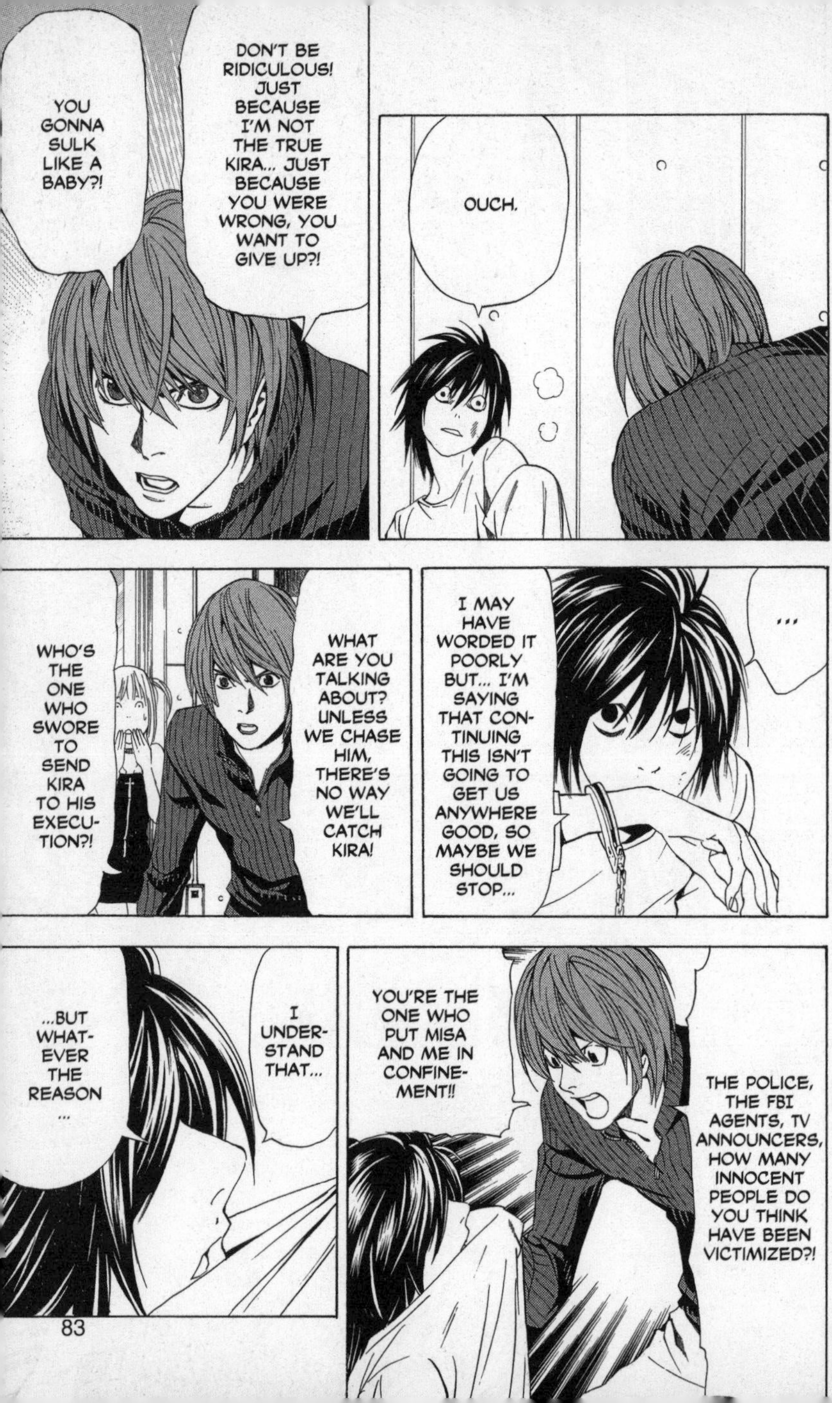
OUCH.
DON'T BE RIDICULOUS! JUST BECAUSE I'M NOT THE TRUE KIRA... JUST BECAUSE YOU WERE WRONG, YOU WANT TO GIVE UP?!
YOU GONNA SULK LIKE A BABY?!
...
I MAY HAVE WORDED IT POORLY BUT... I'M SAYING THAT CONTINUING THIS ISN'T GOING TO GET US ANYWHERE GOOD, SO MAYBE WE SHOULD STOP...
WHAT ARE YOU TALKING ABOUT? UNLESS WE CHASE HIM, THERE'S NO WAY WE'LL CATCH KIRA!
WHO'S THE ONE WHO SWORE TO SEND KIRA TO HIS EXECUTION?!
YOU'RE THE ONE WHO PUT MISA AND ME IN CONFINEMENT!!
THE POLICE, THE FBI AGENTS, TV ANNOUNCERS, HOW MANY INNOCENT PEOPLE DO YOU THINK HAVE BEEN VICTIMIZED?!
I UNDERSTAND THAT...
...BUT WHATEVER THE REASON ...

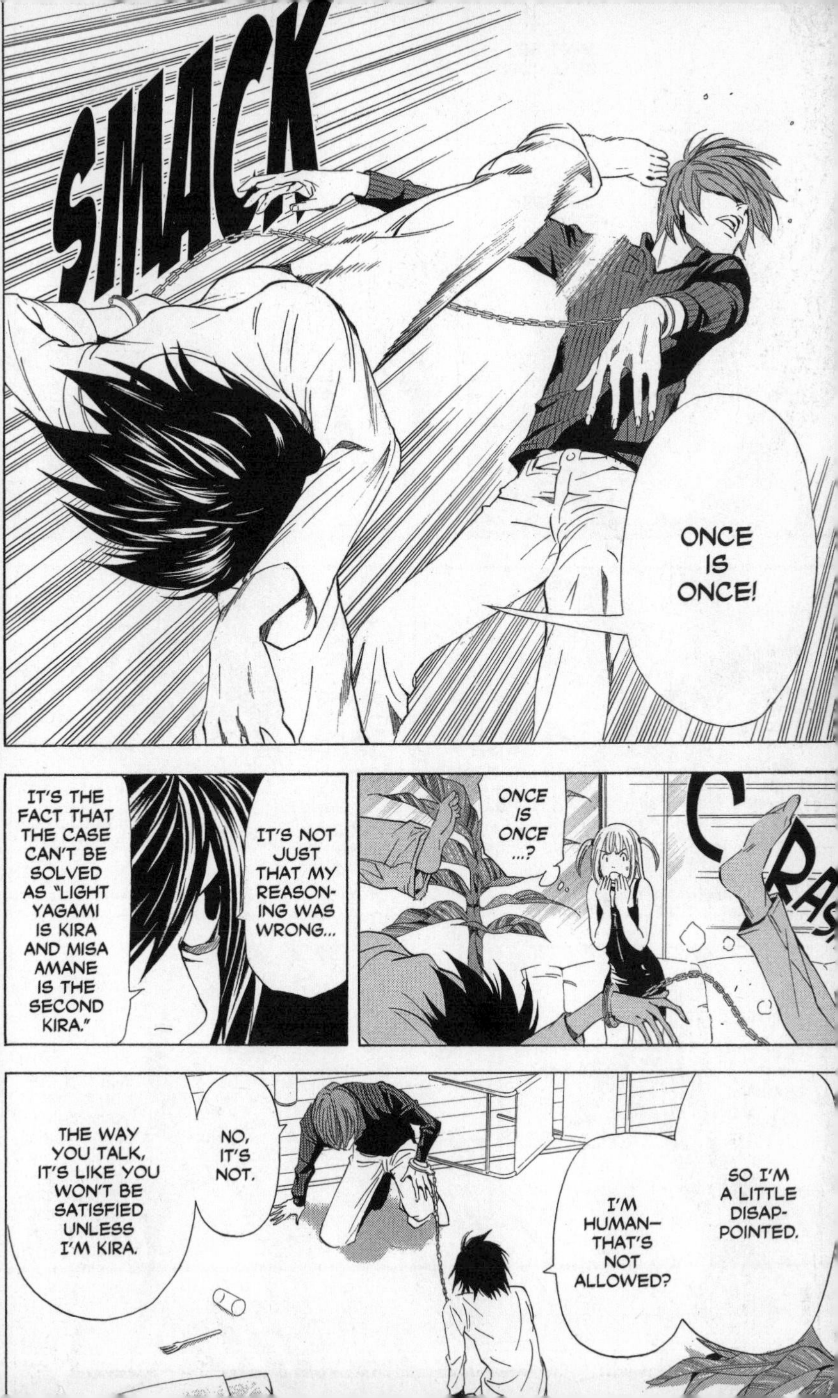
SMACK
ONCE IS ONCE!
CRAS
ONCE IS ONCE ...?
IT'S NOT JUST THAT MY REASONING WAS WRONG...
IT'S THE FACT THAT THE CASE CAN'T BE SOLVED AS "LIGHT YAGAMI IS KIRA AND MISA AMANE IS THE SECOND KIRA."
SO I'M A LITTLE DISAPPOINTED.
I'M HUMAN—THAT'S NOT ALLOWED?
NO, IT'S NOT.
THE WAY YOU TALK, IT'S LIKE YOU WON'T BE SATISFIED UNLESS I'M KIRA.

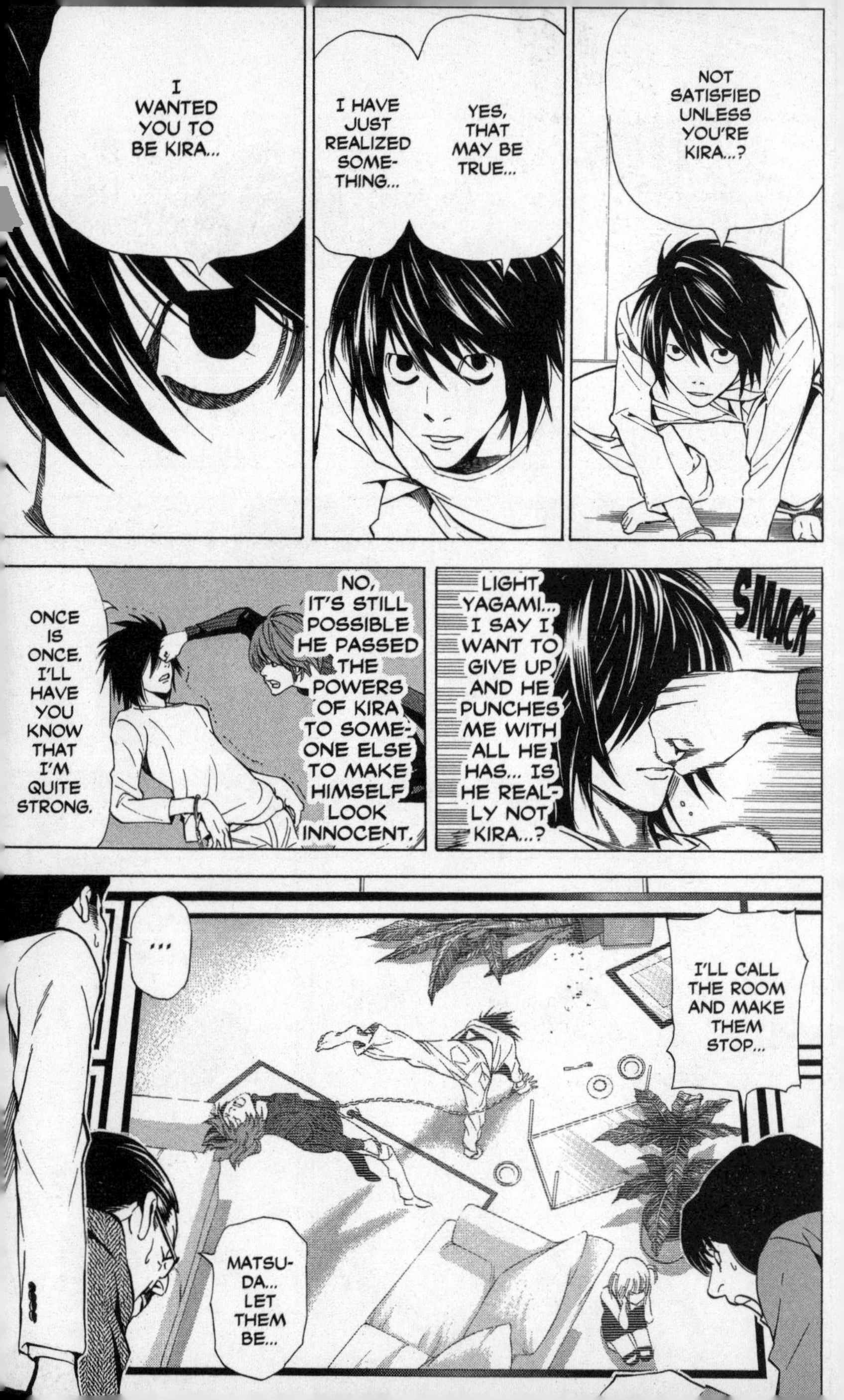
NOT SATISFIED UNLESS YOU'RE KIRA...?
YES, THAT MAY BE TRUE...
I HAVE JUST REALIZED SOMETHING...
I WANTED YOU TO BE KIRA...
SMACK
LIGHT YAGAMI... I SAY I WANT TO GIVE UP AND HE PUNCHES ME WITH ALL HE HAS... IS HE REALLY NOT KIRA...?
NO, IT'S STILL POSSIBLE HE PASSED THE POWERS OF KIRA TO SOMEONE ELSE TO MAKE HIMSELF LOOK INNOCENT.
ONCE IS ONCE. I'LL HAVE YOU KNOW THAT I'M QUITE STRONG.
I'LL CALL THE ROOM AND MAKE THEM STOP...
...
MATSUDA... LET THEM BE...

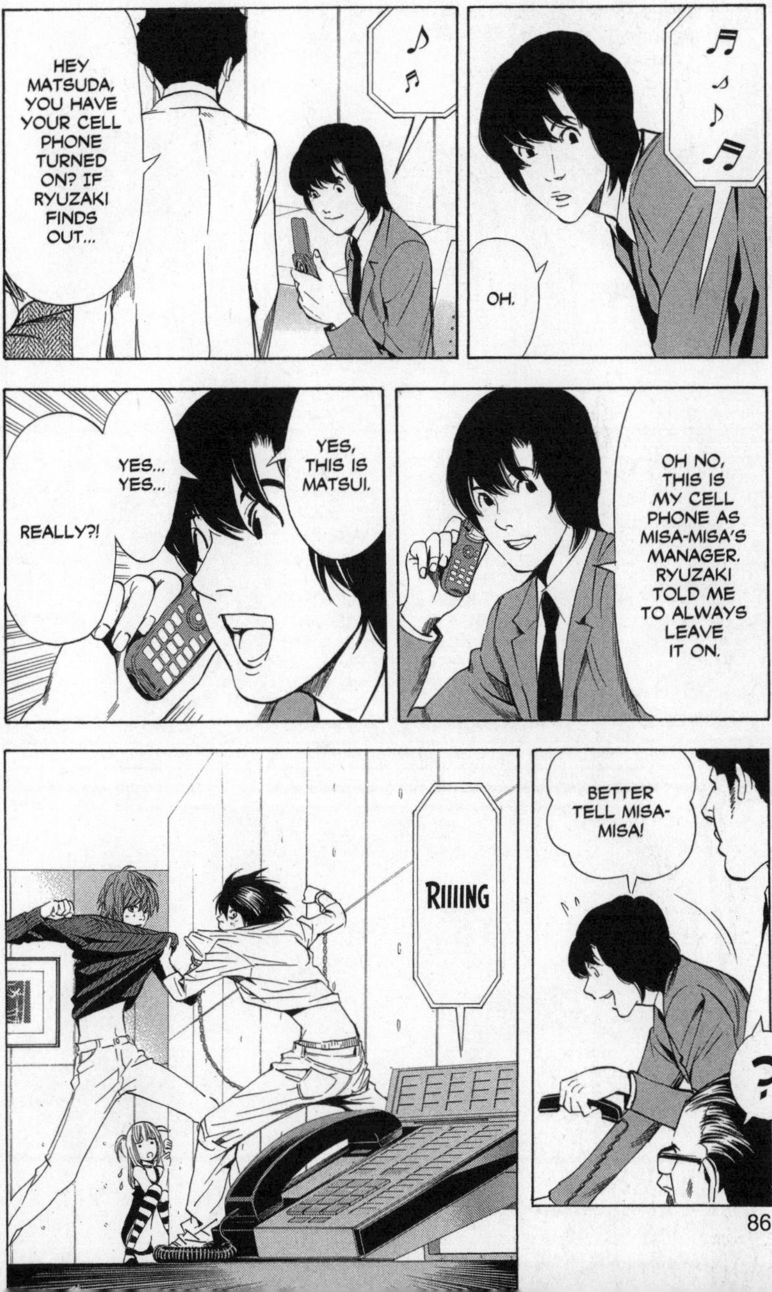
OH.
HEY MATSUDA, YOU HAVE YOUR CELL PHONE TURNED ON? IF RYUZAKI FINDS OUT...
OH NO, THIS IS MY CELL PHONE AS MISA-MISA'S MANAGER. RYUZAKI TOLD ME TO ALWAYS LEAVE IT ON.
YES, THIS IS MATSUI.
YES... YES...
REALLY?!
BETTER TELL MISA-MISA!
?
RIIIING

**READ THIS WAY**

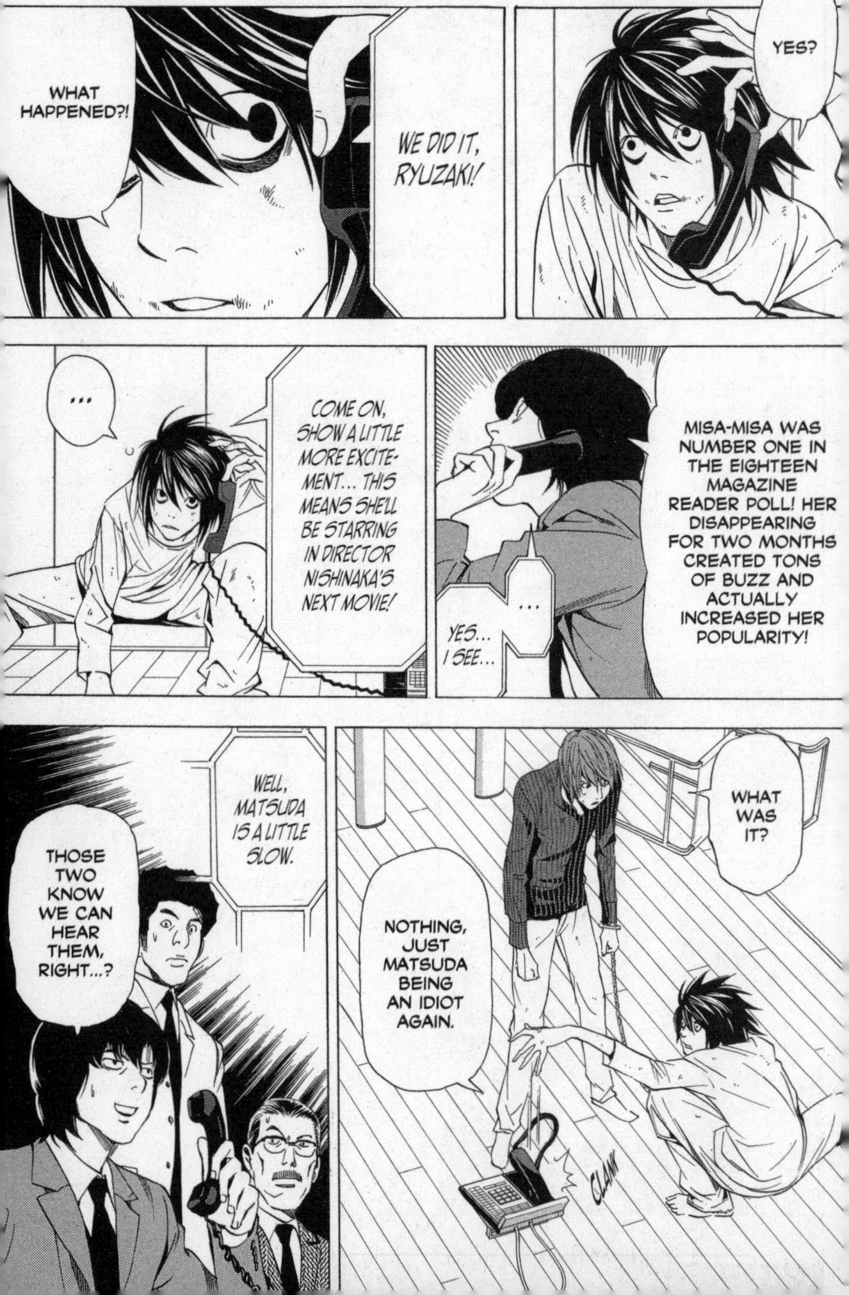
YES?
WE DID IT, RYUZAKI!
WHAT HAPPENED?!
MISA-MISA WAS NUMBER ONE IN THE EIGHTEEN MAGAZINE READER POLL! HER DISAPPEARING FOR TWO MONTHS CREATED TONS OF BUZZ AND ACTUALLY INCREASED HER POPULARITY!
...
YES... I SEE...
COME ON, SHOW A LITTLE MORE EXCITE-MENT... THIS MEANS SHE'LL BE STARRING IN DIRECTOR NISHINAKA'S NEXT MOVIE!
...
WHAT WAS IT?
NOTHING, JUST MATSUDA BEING AN IDIOT AGAIN.
CLANK
WELL, MATSUDA IS A LITTLE SLOW.
THOSE TWO KNOW WE CAN HEAR THEM, RIGHT...?

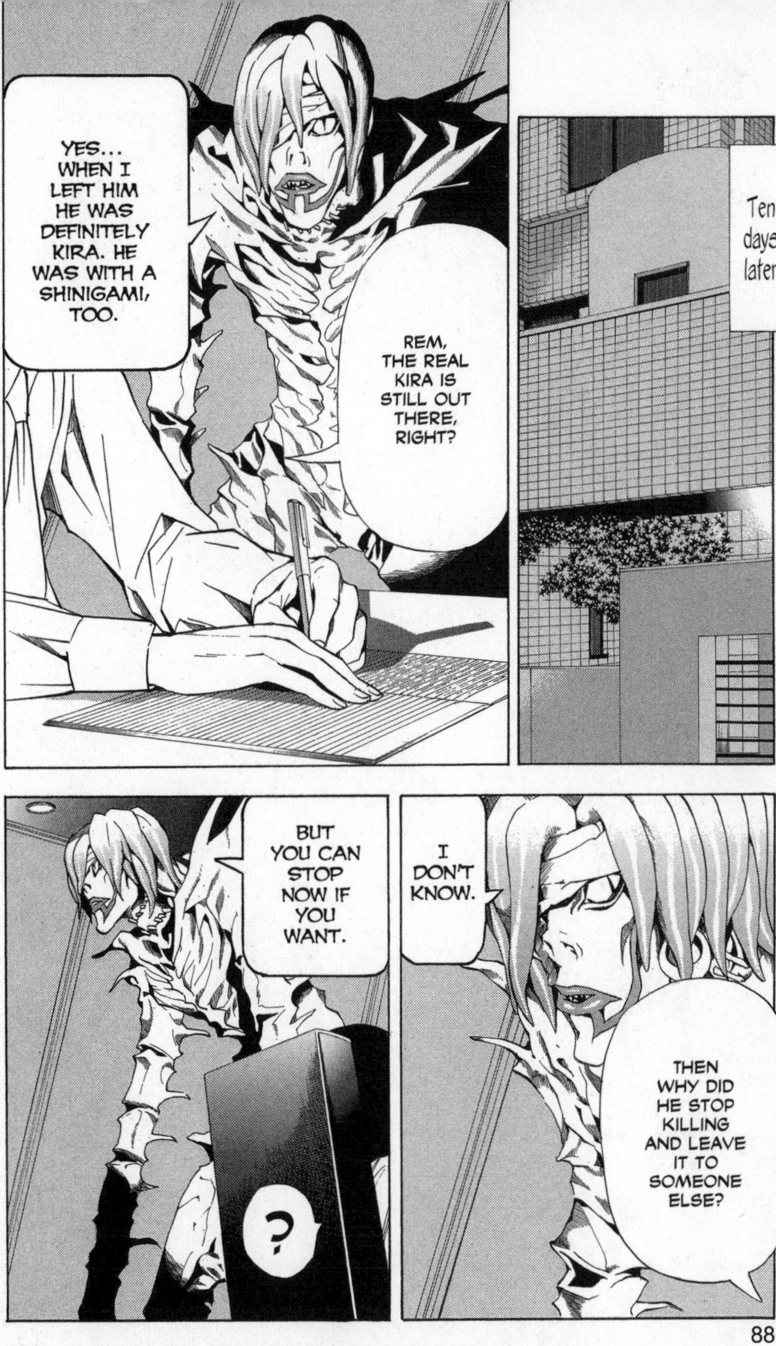

Ten days later
REM, THE REAL KIRA IS STILL OUT THERE, RIGHT?
YES... WHEN I LEFT HIM HE WAS DEFINITELY KIRA. HE WAS WITH A SHINIGAMI, TOO.
I DON'T KNOW.
THEN WHY DID HE STOP KILLING AND LEAVE IT TO SOMEONE ELSE?
BUT YOU CAN STOP NOW IF YOU WANT.
?

READ THIS WAY

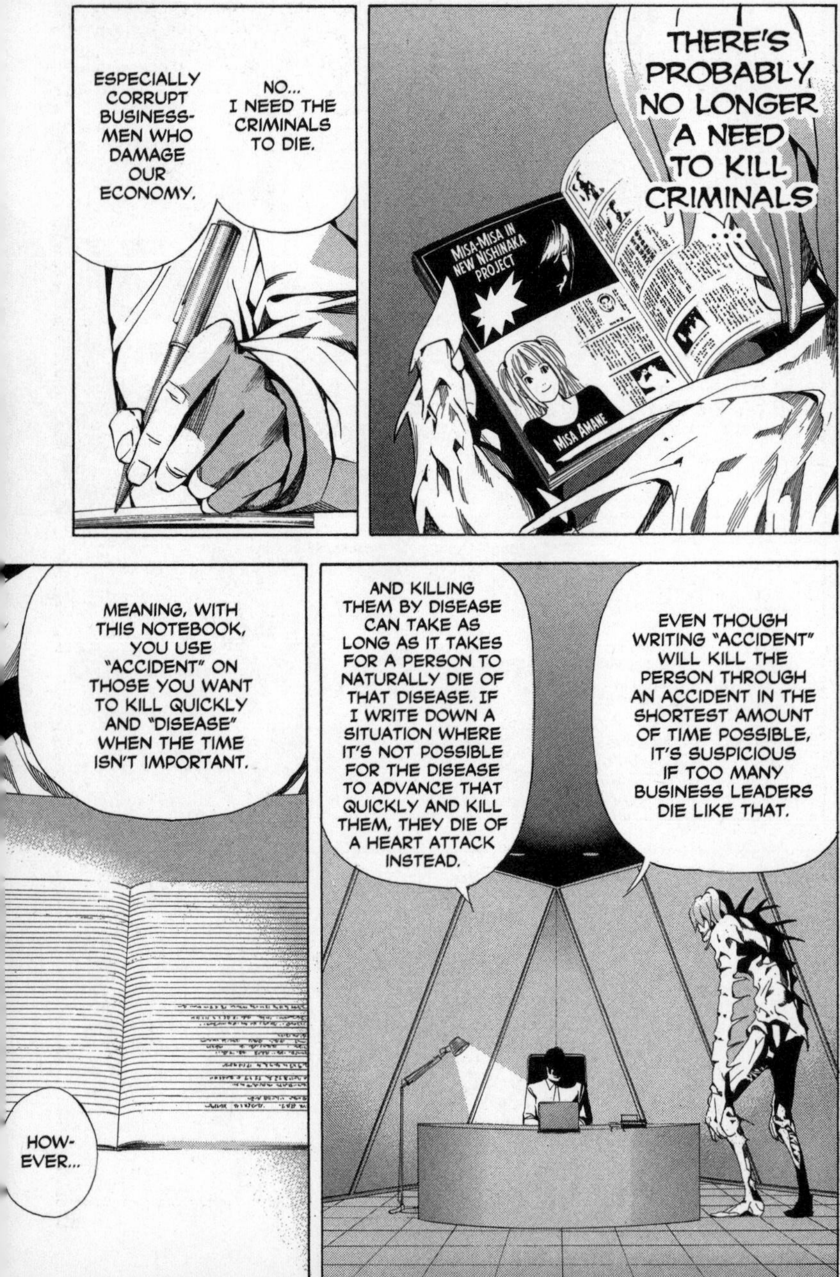
THERE'S PROBABLY NO LONGER A NEED TO KILL CRIMINALS
MISA-MISA IN NEW NISHINAKA PROJECT
MISA AMANE
NO... I NEED THE CRIMINALS TO DIE.
ESPECIALLY CORRUPT BUSINESS-MEN WHO DAMAGE OUR ECONOMY.
EVEN THOUGH WRITING "ACCIDENT" WILL KILL THE PERSON THROUGH AN ACCIDENT IN THE SHORTEST AMOUNT OF TIME POSSIBLE, IT'S SUSPICIOUS IF TOO MANY BUSINESS LEADERS DIE LIKE THAT.
AND KILLING THEM BY DISEASE CAN TAKE AS LONG AS IT TAKES FOR A PERSON TO NATURALLY DIE OF THAT DISEASE. IF I WRITE DOWN A SITUATION WHERE IT'S NOT POSSIBLE FOR THE DISEASE TO ADVANCE THAT QUICKLY AND KILL THEM, THEY DIE OF A HEART ATTACK INSTEAD.
MEANING, WITH THIS NOTEBOOK, YOU USE "ACCIDENT" ON THOSE YOU WANT TO KILL QUICKLY AND "DISEASE" WHEN THE TIME ISN'T IMPORTANT.
HOW-EVER...

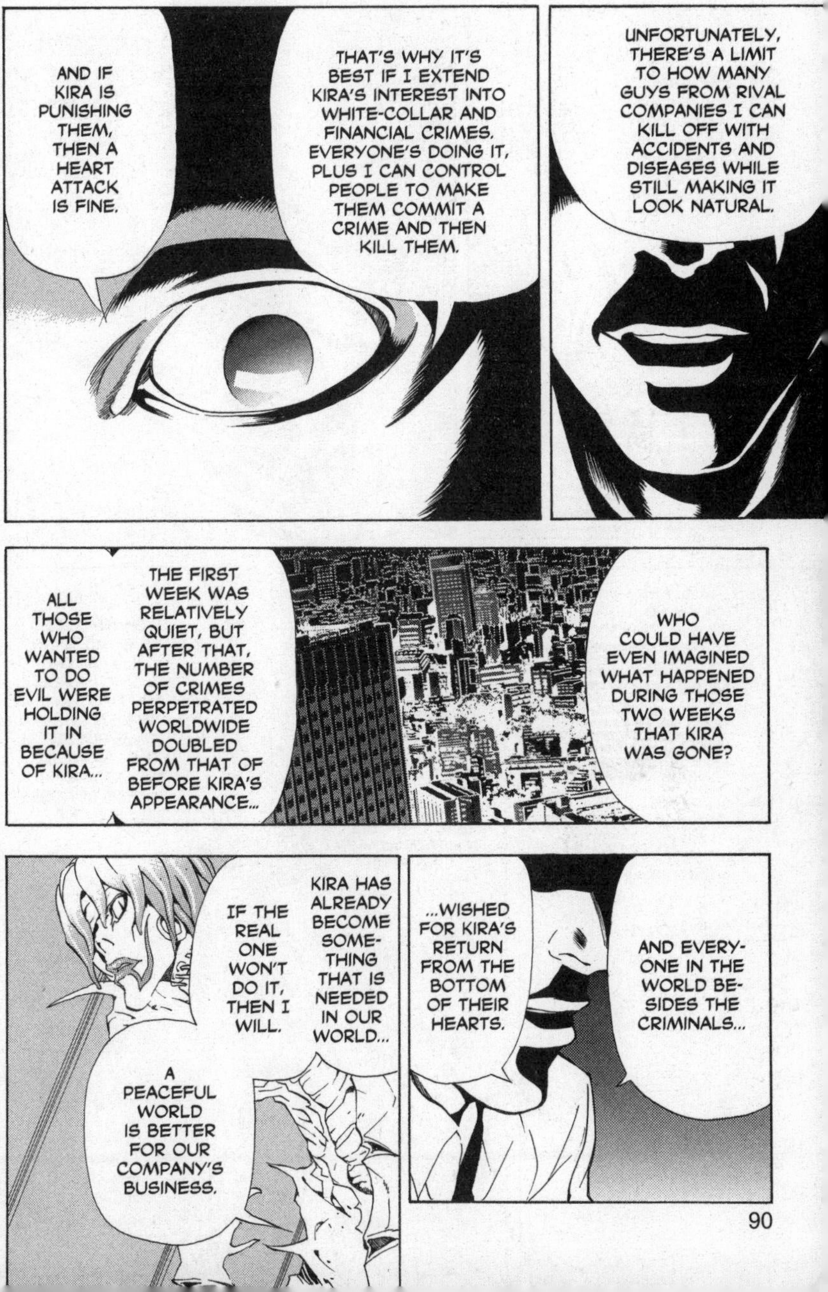
UNFORTUNATELY, THERE'S A LIMIT TO HOW MANY GUYS FROM RIVAL COMPANIES I CAN KILL OFF WITH ACCIDENTS AND DISEASES WHILE STILL MAKING IT LOOK NATURAL.
THAT'S WHY IT'S BEST IF I EXTEND KIRA'S INTEREST INTO WHITE-COLLAR AND FINANCIAL CRIMES. EVERYONE'S DOING IT, PLUS I CAN CONTROL PEOPLE TO MAKE THEM COMMIT A CRIME AND THEN KILL THEM.
AND IF KIRA IS PUNISHING THEM, THEN A HEART ATTACK IS FINE.
WHO COULD HAVE EVEN IMAGINED WHAT HAPPENED DURING THOSE TWO WEEKS THAT KIRA WAS GONE?
THE FIRST WEEK WAS RELATIVELY QUIET, BUT AFTER THAT, THE NUMBER OF CRIMES PERPETRATED WORLDWIDE DOUBLED FROM THAT OF BEFORE KIRA'S APPEARANCE...
ALL THOSE WHO WANTED TO DO EVIL WERE HOLDING IT IN BECAUSE OF KIRA...
AND EVERY-ONE IN THE WORLD BE-SIDES THE CRIMINALS...
...WISHED FOR KIRA'S RETURN FROM THE BOTTOM OF THEIR HEARTS.
KIRA HAS ALREADY BECOME SOME-THING THAT IS NEEDED IN OUR WORLD...
IF THE REAL ONE WON'T DO IT, THEN I WILL.
A PEACEFUL WORLD IS BETTER FOR OUR COMPANY'S BUSINESS.

READ THIS WAY

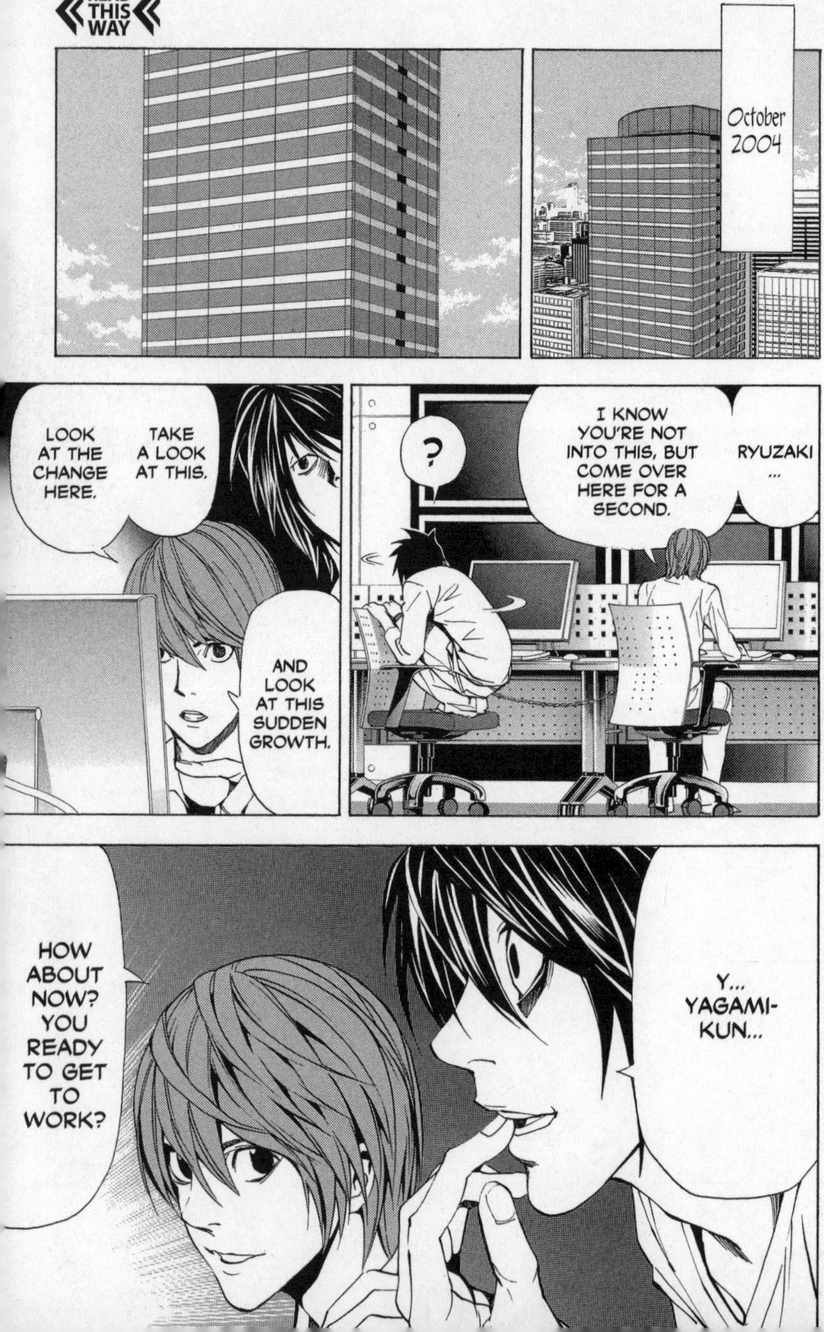
October 2004
RYUZAKI ...
I KNOW YOU'RE NOT INTO THIS, BUT COME OVER HERE FOR A SECOND.
?
TAKE A LOOK AT THIS.
LOOK AT THE CHANGE HERE.
AND LOOK AT THIS SUDDEN GROWTH.
Y... YAGAMI-KUN...
HOW ABOUT NOW? YOU READY TO GET TO WORK?

# DEATH NOTE
## How to use it
### XXVI

⊙ If you just write, "die of accident" for the cause of death, the victim will die from a natural accident after 6 minutes and 40 seconds from the time of writing it.

事故死とだけ書き死の状況を書かない場合は、
そこから6分40秒以後、最短で不自然でない事故に遭い、死亡する。

⊙ Even though only one name is written in the DEATH NOTE, if it influences and causes other humans that are not written in it to die, the victim's cause of death will be a heart attack.

事故死の死の状況は、たとえその時死亡する人間が名前を書かれた者
だけであっても、人間界の環境に多大な影響を与え
その事で後に死者が出るような物は「人を巻き込む」事になる為、
心臓麻痺となる。

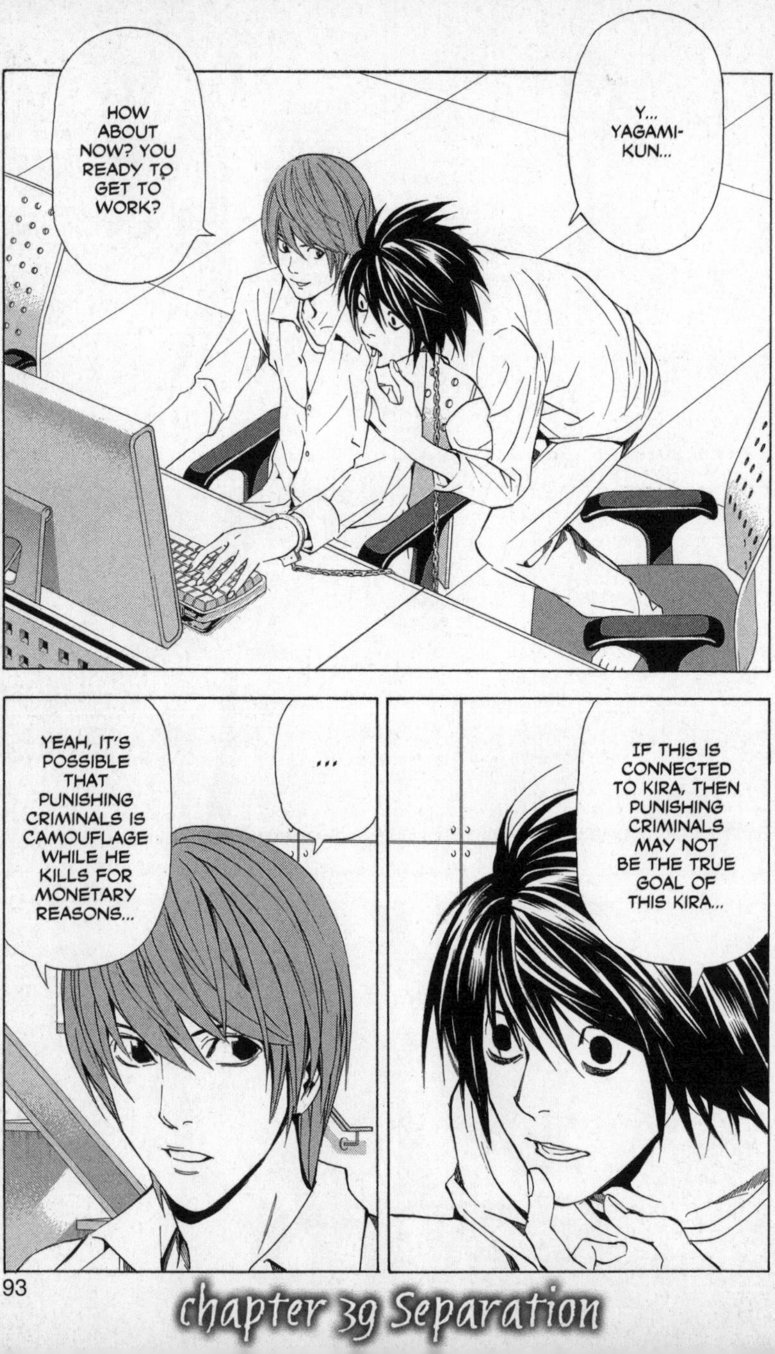
Y... YAGAMI-KUN...
HOW ABOUT NOW? YOU READY TO GET TO WORK?
IF THIS IS CONNECTED TO KIRA, THEN PUNISHING CRIMINALS MAY NOT BE THE TRUE GOAL OF THIS KIRA...
...
YEAH, IT'S POSSIBLE THAT PUNISHING CRIMINALS IS CAMOUFLAGE WHILE HE KILLS FOR MONETARY REASONS...

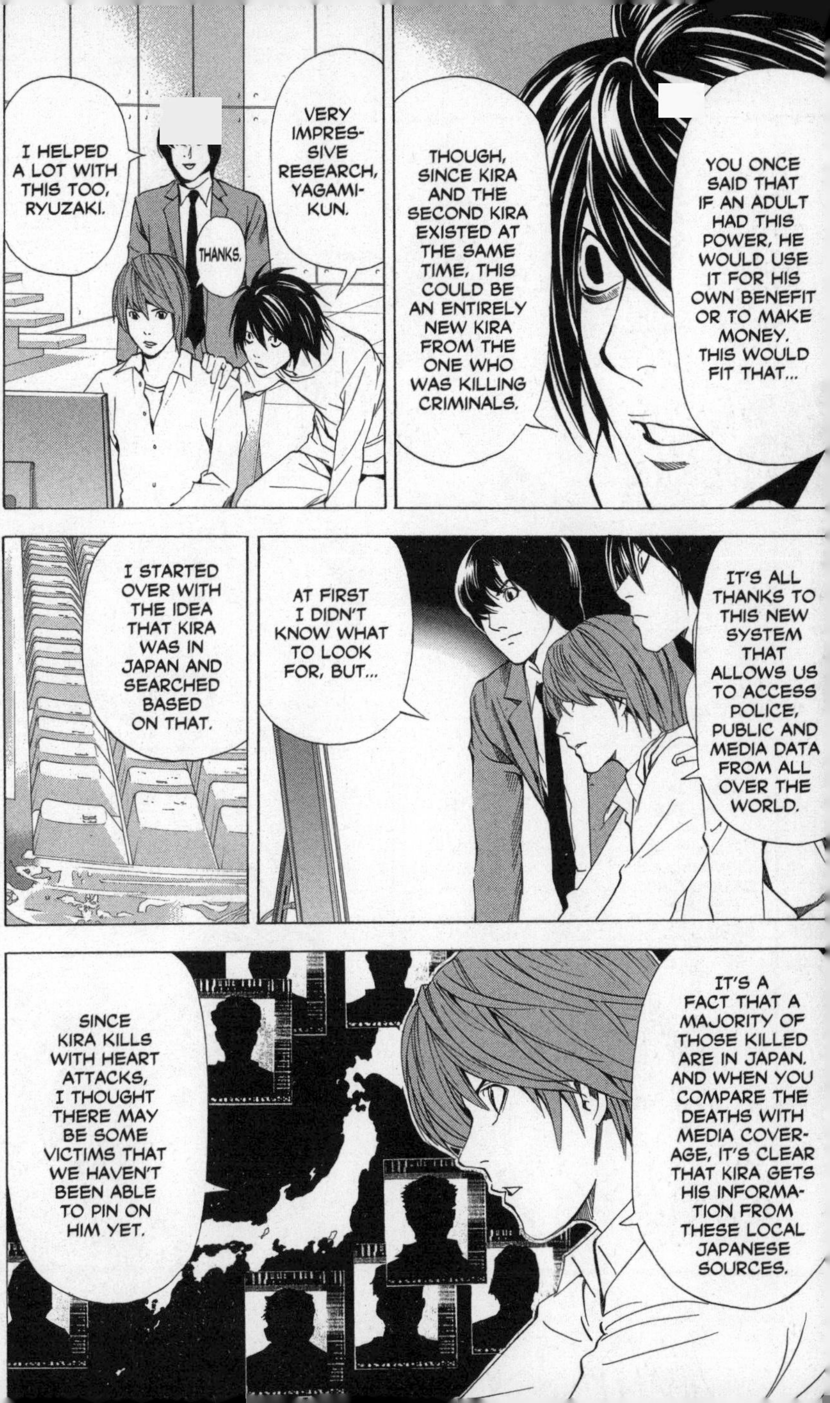
YOU ONCE SAID THAT IF AN ADULT HAD THIS POWER, HE WOULD USE IT FOR HIS OWN BENEFIT OR TO MAKE MONEY. THIS WOULD FIT THAT...
THOUGH, SINCE KIRA AND THE SECOND KIRA EXISTED AT THE SAME TIME, THIS COULD BE AN ENTIRELY NEW KIRA FROM THE ONE WHO WAS KILLING CRIMINALS.
VERY IMPRESSIVE RESEARCH, YAGAMI-KUN.
THANKS.
I HELPED A LOT WITH THIS TOO, RYUZAKI.
IT'S ALL THANKS TO THIS NEW SYSTEM THAT ALLOWS US TO ACCESS POLICE, PUBLIC AND MEDIA DATA FROM ALL OVER THE WORLD.
AT FIRST I DIDN'T KNOW WHAT TO LOOK FOR, BUT...
I STARTED OVER WITH THE IDEA THAT KIRA WAS IN JAPAN AND SEARCHED BASED ON THAT.
IT'S A FACT THAT A MAJORITY OF THOSE KILLED ARE IN JAPAN. AND WHEN YOU COMPARE THE DEATHS WITH MEDIA COVERAGE, IT'S CLEAR THAT KIRA GETS HIS INFORMATION FROM THESE LOCAL JAPANESE SOURCES.
SINCE KIRA KILLS WITH HEART ATTACKS, I THOUGHT THERE MAY BE SOME VICTIMS THAT WE HAVEN'T BEEN ABLE TO PIN ON HIM YET.

...I QUICKLY NOTICED THREE SUSPICIOUS CASES. TWO COULD BE COINCIDENCE, BUT NOT THREE.

I PLANNED TO CAREFULLY EXAMINE EVERY HEART ATTACK VICTIM OVER THE LAST FIVE MONTHS BUT...

I HELPED A LOT ON THIS, RYUZAKI.

THAT WOULD USUALLY BE AN INCREDIBLE AMOUNT OF WORK, BUT THIS SYSTEM MADE IT RELATIVELY FAST.

SO I SEARCHED FOR ALL THE PEOPLE WHO DIED OF HEART ATTACKS UP TO NOW, INCLUDING NON-CRIMINALS.

ALL THREE WERE IN IMPORTANT POSITIONS IN THE JAPANESE BUSINESS WORLD AND ALL DIED OF HEART ATTACKS.

SEKIMARU CORP'S VP OF DEVELOPMENT, ROPPEI TAMIYA. AOI INDUSTRIES' DIRECTOR OF INTEGRATED SYSTEMS, KOUJI AOI. FORMER YOTSUBA VICE-PRESIDENT, TAKEYOSHI MORIYA.

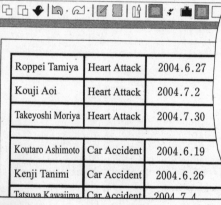

| Roppei Tamiya | Heart Attack | 2004.6.27 |
| Kouji Aoi | Heart Attack | 2004.7.2 |
| Takeyoshi Moriya | Heart Attack | 2004.7.30 |
| | | |
| Koutaro Ashimoto | Car Accident | 2004.6.19 |
| Kenji Tanimi | Car Accident | 2004.6.26 |
| Tatsuya Kawajima | Car Accident | 2004.7.4 |

YEAH, AND LOOK...

SO THEN YOU DID FURTHER RESEARCH INTO OTHER DEATHS INVOLVING PEOPLE IN THE BUSINESS WORLD...?

YOTSUBA'S STOCK HAS BEEN RISING STEADILY WHILE SEKIMARU AND AOI'S HAVE PLUMMETED.

SO THEN I RESEARCHED SEKIMARU, AOI, AND YOTSUBA.

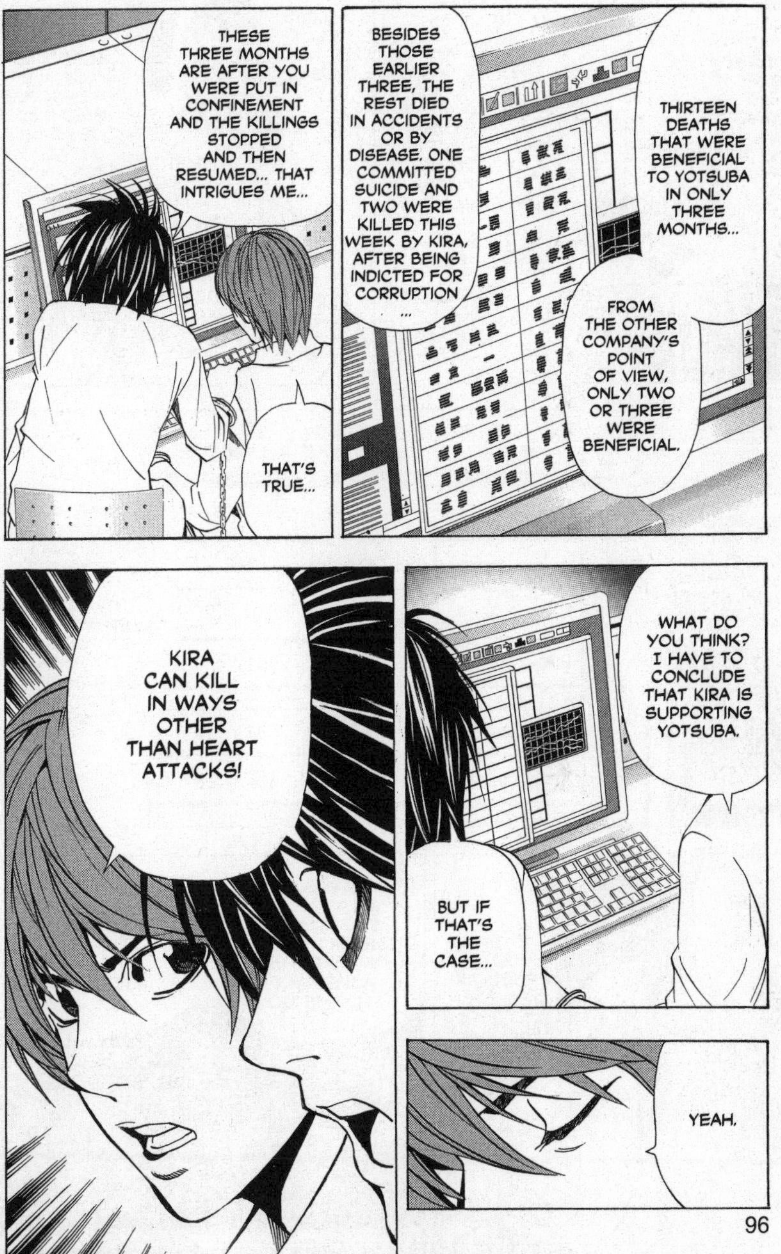
THIRTEEN DEATHS THAT WERE BENEFICIAL TO YOTSUBA IN ONLY THREE MONTHS...
BESIDES THOSE EARLIER THREE, THE REST DIED IN ACCIDENTS OR BY DISEASE. ONE COMMITTED SUICIDE AND TWO WERE KILLED THIS WEEK BY KIRA, AFTER BEING INDICTED FOR CORRUPTION ...
FROM THE OTHER COMPANY'S POINT OF VIEW, ONLY TWO OR THREE WERE BENEFICIAL.
THESE THREE MONTHS ARE AFTER YOU WERE PUT IN CONFINEMENT AND THE KILLINGS STOPPED AND THEN RESUMED... THAT INTRIGUES ME...
THAT'S TRUE...
WHAT DO YOU THINK? I HAVE TO CONCLUDE THAT KIRA IS SUPPORTING YOTSUBA.
BUT IF THAT'S THE CASE...
YEAH.
KIRA CAN KILL IN WAYS OTHER THAN HEART ATTACKS!

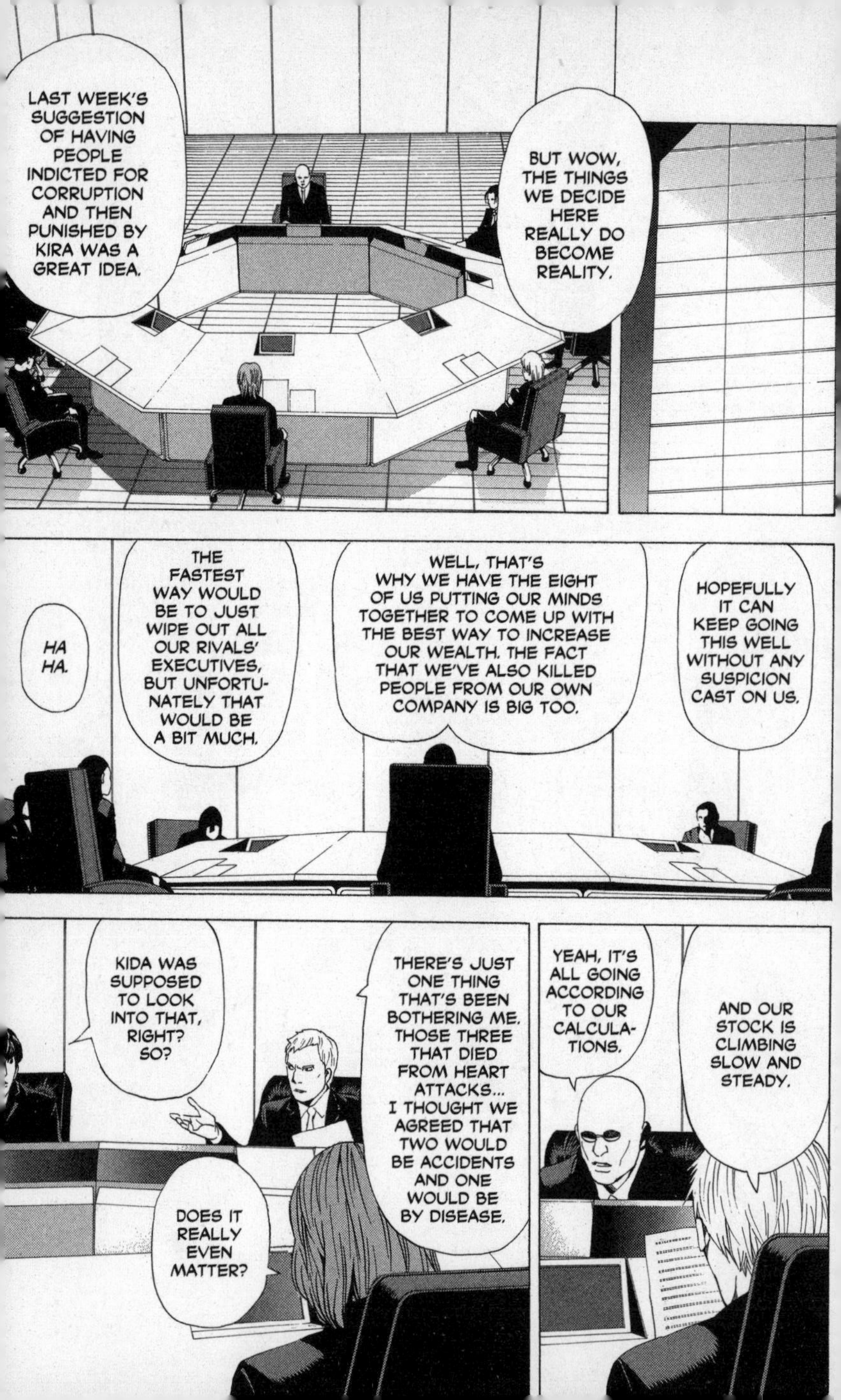
LAST WEEK'S SUGGESTION OF HAVING PEOPLE INDICTED FOR CORRUPTION AND THEN PUNISHED BY KIRA WAS A GREAT IDEA.
BUT WOW, THE THINGS WE DECIDE HERE REALLY DO BECOME REALITY.
HOPEFULLY IT CAN KEEP GOING THIS WELL WITHOUT ANY SUSPICION CAST ON US.
WELL, THAT'S WHY WE HAVE THE EIGHT OF US PUTTING OUR MINDS TOGETHER TO COME UP WITH THE BEST WAY TO INCREASE OUR WEALTH. THE FACT THAT WE'VE ALSO KILLED PEOPLE FROM OUR OWN COMPANY IS BIG TOO.
THE FASTEST WAY WOULD BE TO JUST WIPE OUT ALL OUR RIVALS' EXECUTIVES, BUT UNFORTUNATELY THAT WOULD BE A BIT MUCH.
HA HA.
AND OUR STOCK IS CLIMBING SLOW AND STEADY.
YEAH, IT'S ALL GOING ACCORDING TO OUR CALCULATIONS.
THERE'S JUST ONE THING THAT'S BEEN BOTHERING ME. THOSE THREE THAT DIED FROM HEART ATTACKS... I THOUGHT WE AGREED THAT TWO WOULD BE ACCIDENTS AND ONE WOULD BE BY DISEASE.
KIDA WAS SUPPOSED TO LOOK INTO THAT, RIGHT? SO?
DOES IT REALLY EVEN MATTER?

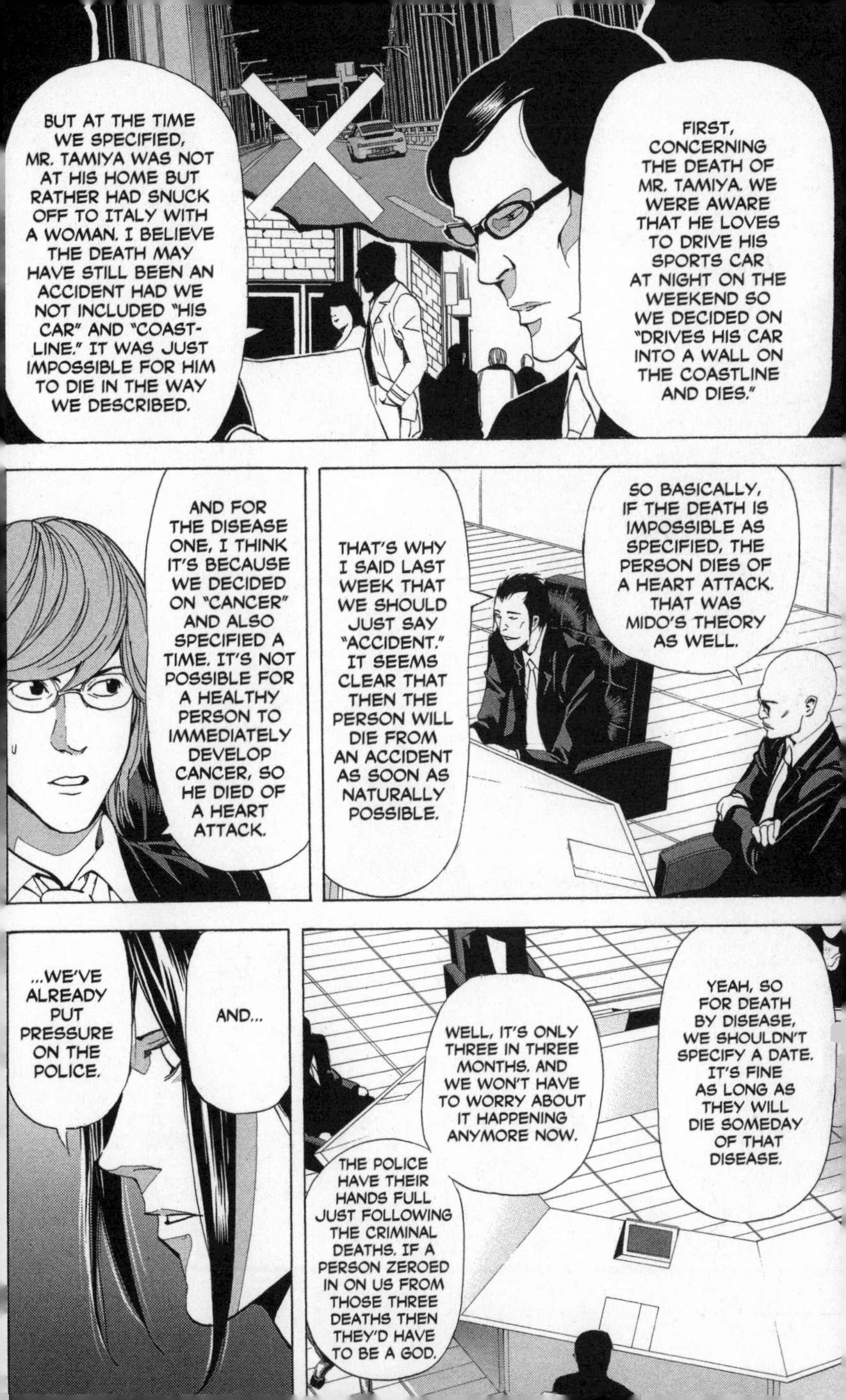
FIRST, CONCERNING THE DEATH OF MR. TAMIYA. WE WERE AWARE THAT HE LOVES TO DRIVE HIS SPORTS CAR AT NIGHT ON THE WEEKEND SO WE DECIDED ON "DRIVES HIS CAR INTO A WALL ON THE COASTLINE AND DIES."
BUT AT THE TIME WE SPECIFIED, MR. TAMIYA WAS NOT AT HIS HOME BUT RATHER HAD SNUCK OFF TO ITALY WITH A WOMAN. I BELIEVE THE DEATH MAY HAVE STILL BEEN AN ACCIDENT HAD WE NOT INCLUDED "HIS CAR" AND "COAST-LINE." IT WAS JUST IMPOSSIBLE FOR HIM TO DIE IN THE WAY WE DESCRIBED.
SO BASICALLY, IF THE DEATH IS IMPOSSIBLE AS SPECIFIED, THE PERSON DIES OF A HEART ATTACK. THAT WAS MIDO'S THEORY AS WELL.
THAT'S WHY I SAID LAST WEEK THAT WE SHOULD JUST SAY "ACCIDENT." IT SEEMS CLEAR THAT THEN THE PERSON WILL DIE FROM AN ACCIDENT AS SOON AS NATURALLY POSSIBLE.
AND FOR THE DISEASE ONE, I THINK IT'S BECAUSE WE DECIDED ON "CANCER" AND ALSO SPECIFIED A TIME. IT'S NOT POSSIBLE FOR A HEALTHY PERSON TO IMMEDIATELY DEVELOP CANCER, SO HE DIED OF A HEART ATTACK.
YEAH, SO FOR DEATH BY DISEASE, WE SHOULDN'T SPECIFY A DATE. IT'S FINE AS LONG AS THEY WILL DIE SOMEDAY OF THAT DISEASE.
WELL, IT'S ONLY THREE IN THREE MONTHS. AND WE WON'T HAVE TO WORRY ABOUT IT HAPPENING ANYMORE NOW.
THE POLICE HAVE THEIR HANDS FULL JUST FOLLOWING THE CRIMINAL DEATHS. IF A PERSON ZEROED IN ON US FROM THOSE THREE DEATHS THEN THEY'D HAVE TO BE A GOD.
AND...
...WE'VE ALREADY PUT PRESSURE ON THE POLICE.

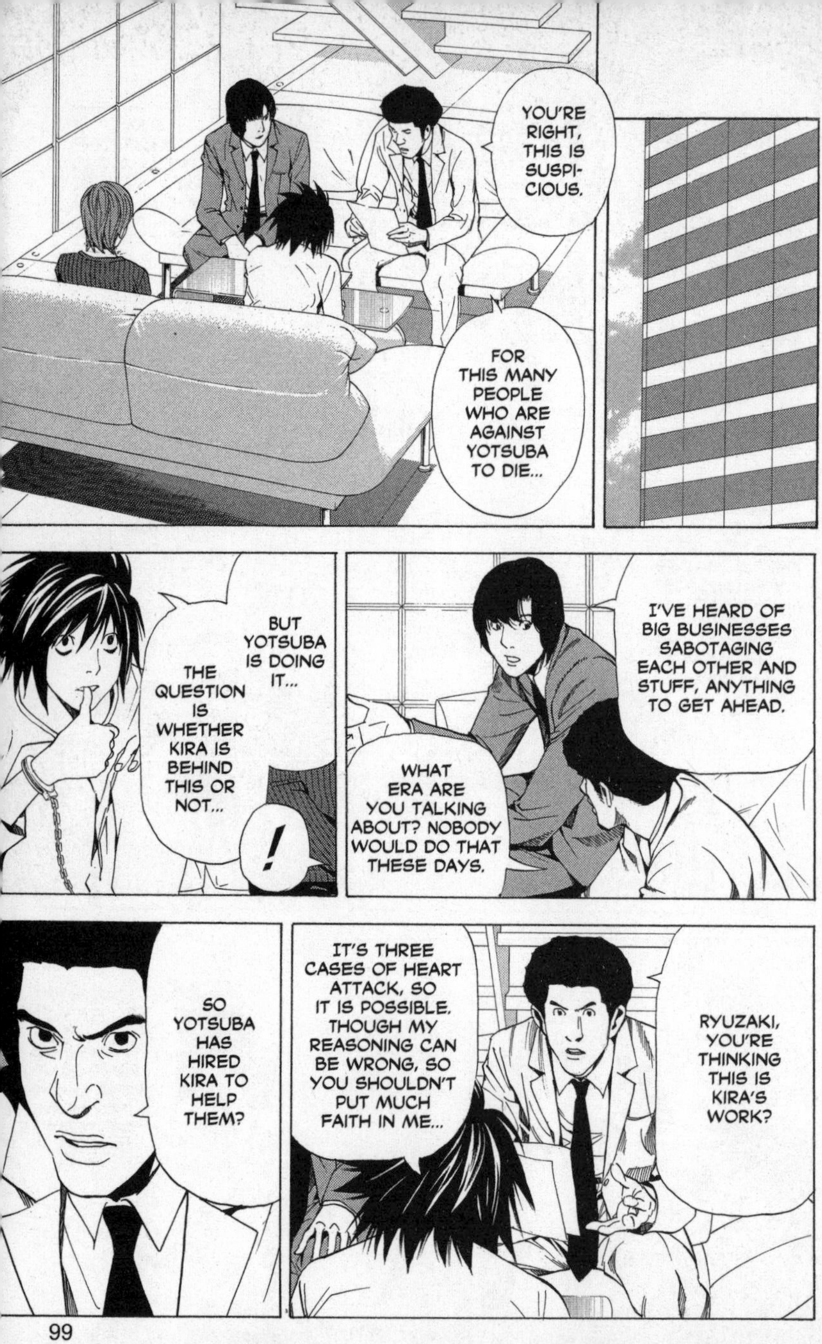
YOU'RE RIGHT, THIS IS SUSPICIOUS.
FOR THIS MANY PEOPLE WHO ARE AGAINST YOTSUBA TO DIE...
I'VE HEARD OF BIG BUSINESSES SABOTAGING EACH OTHER AND STUFF, ANYTHING TO GET AHEAD.
WHAT ERA ARE YOU TALKING ABOUT? NOBODY WOULD DO THAT THESE DAYS.
BUT YOTSUBA IS DOING IT...
THE QUESTION IS WHETHER KIRA IS BEHIND THIS OR NOT...
!
RYUZAKI, YOU'RE THINKING THIS IS KIRA'S WORK?
IT'S THREE CASES OF HEART ATTACK, SO IT IS POSSIBLE. THOUGH MY REASONING CAN BE WRONG, SO YOU SHOULDN'T PUT MUCH FAITH IN ME...
SO YOTSUBA HAS HIRED KIRA TO HELP THEM?

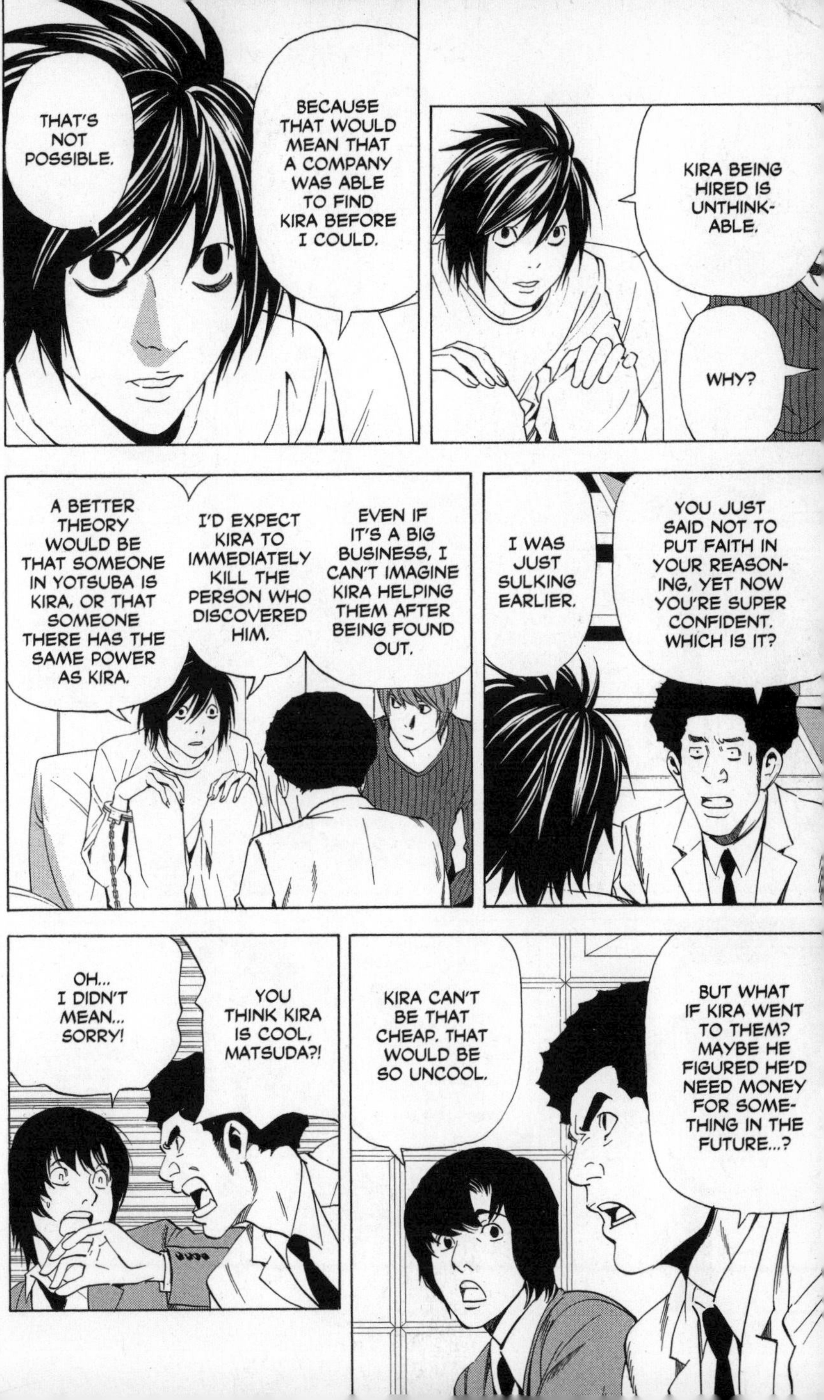
KIRA BEING HIRED IS UNTHINKABLE.
WHY?
THAT'S NOT POSSIBLE.
BECAUSE THAT WOULD MEAN THAT A COMPANY WAS ABLE TO FIND KIRA BEFORE I COULD.
YOU JUST SAID NOT TO PUT FAITH IN YOUR REASONING, YET NOW YOU'RE SUPER CONFIDENT. WHICH IS IT?
I WAS JUST SULKING EARLIER.
EVEN IF IT'S A BIG BUSINESS, I CAN'T IMAGINE KIRA HELPING THEM AFTER BEING FOUND OUT.
I'D EXPECT KIRA TO IMMEDIATELY KILL THE PERSON WHO DISCOVERED HIM.
A BETTER THEORY WOULD BE THAT SOMEONE IN YOTSUBA IS KIRA, OR THAT SOMEONE THERE HAS THE SAME POWER AS KIRA.
BUT WHAT IF KIRA WENT TO THEM? MAYBE HE FIGURED HE'D NEED MONEY FOR SOMETHING IN THE FUTURE...?
KIRA CAN'T BE THAT CHEAP. THAT WOULD BE SO UNCOOL.
YOU THINK KIRA IS COOL, MATSUDA?!
OH... I DIDN'T MEAN... SORRY!

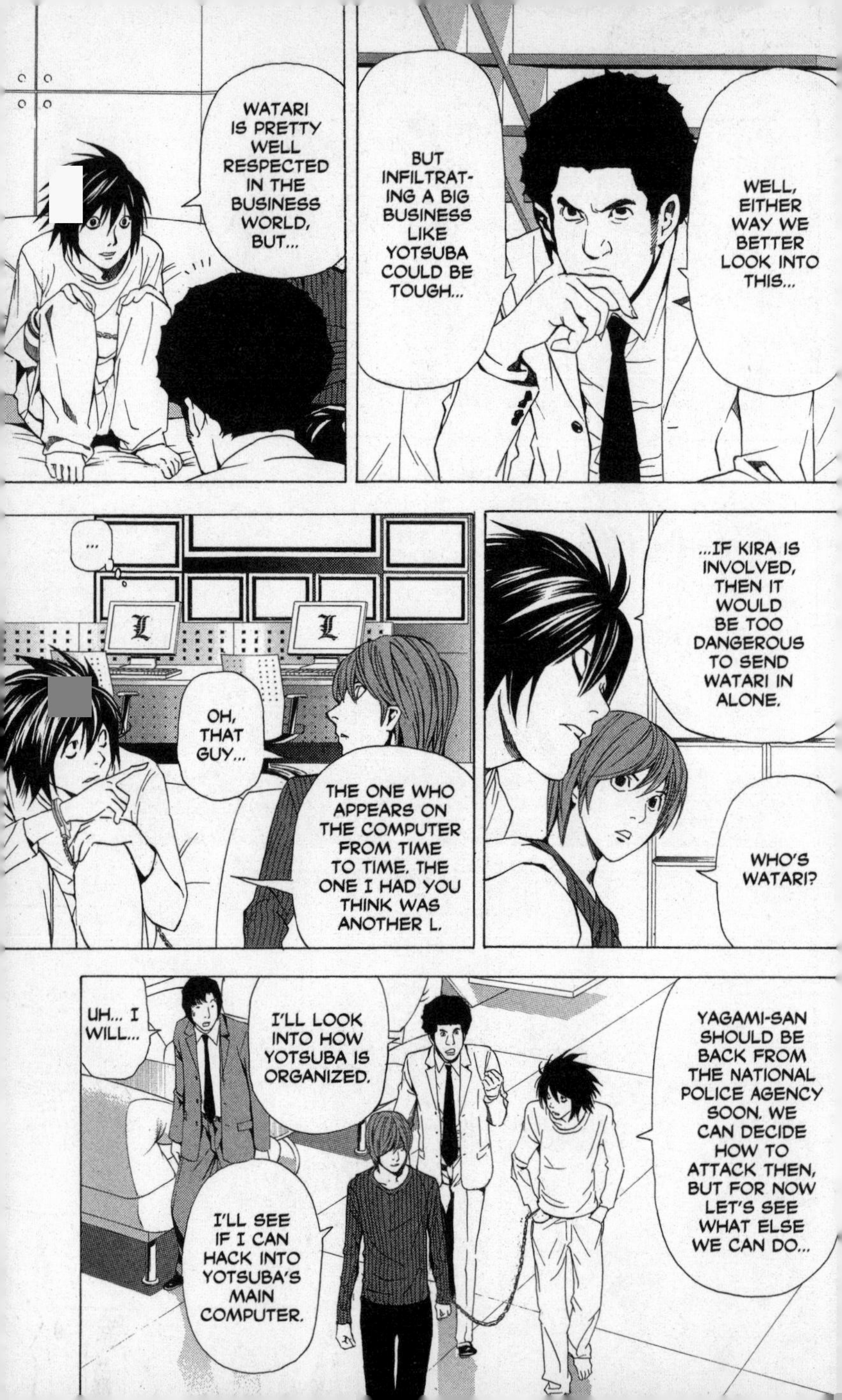
WELL, EITHER WAY WE BETTER LOOK INTO THIS...
BUT INFILTRAT-ING A BIG BUSINESS LIKE YOTSUBA COULD BE TOUGH...
WATARI IS PRETTY WELL RESPECTED IN THE BUSINESS WORLD, BUT...
...IF KIRA IS INVOLVED, THEN IT WOULD BE TOO DANGEROUS TO SEND WATARI IN ALONE.
WHO'S WATARI?
...
OH, THAT GUY...
THE ONE WHO APPEARS ON THE COMPUTER FROM TIME TO TIME. THE ONE I HAD YOU THINK WAS ANOTHER L.
YAGAMI-SAN SHOULD BE BACK FROM THE NATIONAL POLICE AGENCY SOON. WE CAN DECIDE HOW TO ATTACK THEN, BUT FOR NOW LET'S SEE WHAT ELSE WE CAN DO...
I'LL LOOK INTO HOW YOTSUBA IS ORGANIZED.
I'LL SEE IF I CAN HACK INTO YOTSUBA'S MAIN COMPUTER.
UH... I WILL...

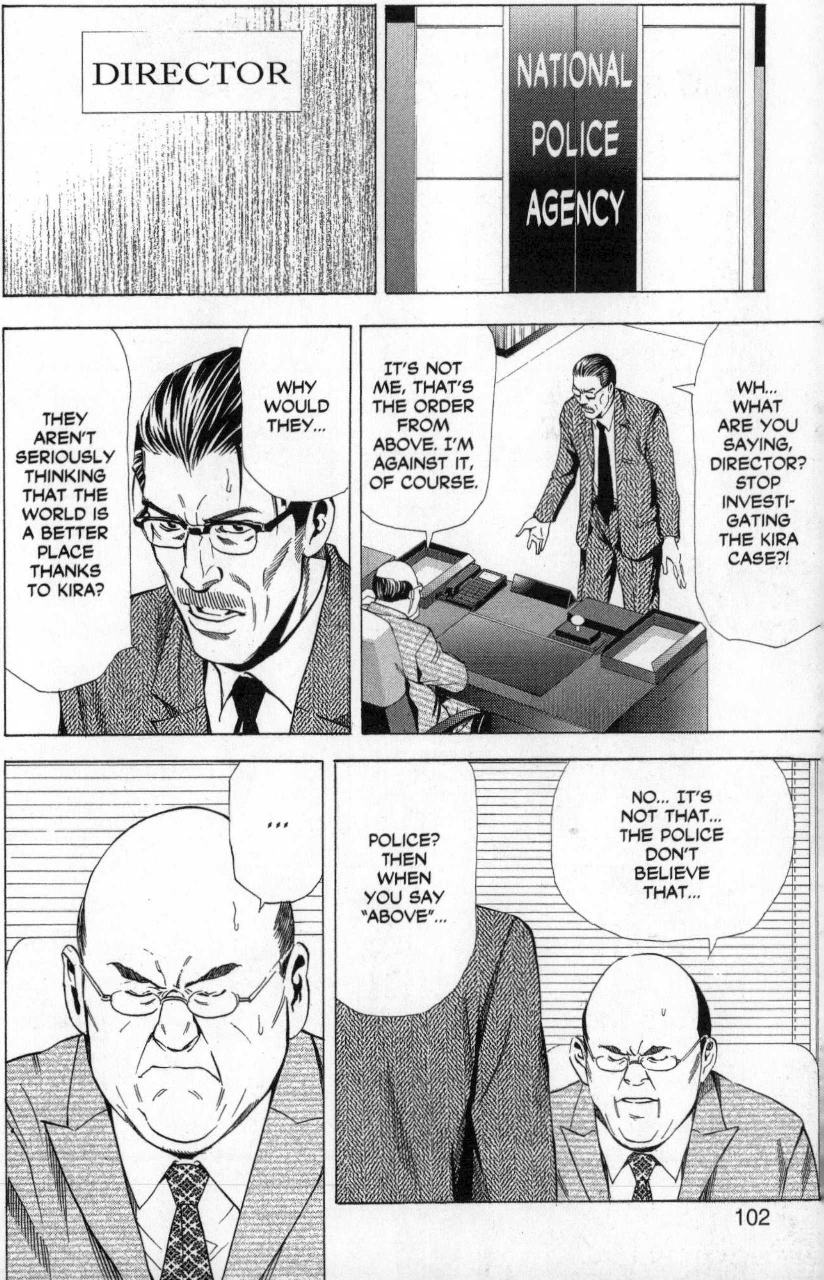
NATIONAL POLICE AGENCY
DIRECTOR
WH... WHAT ARE YOU SAYING, DIRECTOR? STOP INVESTI-GATING THE KIRA CASE?!
IT'S NOT ME, THAT'S THE ORDER FROM ABOVE. I'M AGAINST IT, OF COURSE.
WHY WOULD THEY...
THEY AREN'T SERIOUSLY THINKING THAT THE WORLD IS A BETTER PLACE THANKS TO KIRA?
NO... IT'S NOT THAT... THE POLICE DON'T BELIEVE THAT...
POLICE? THEN WHEN YOU SAY "ABOVE"...
...

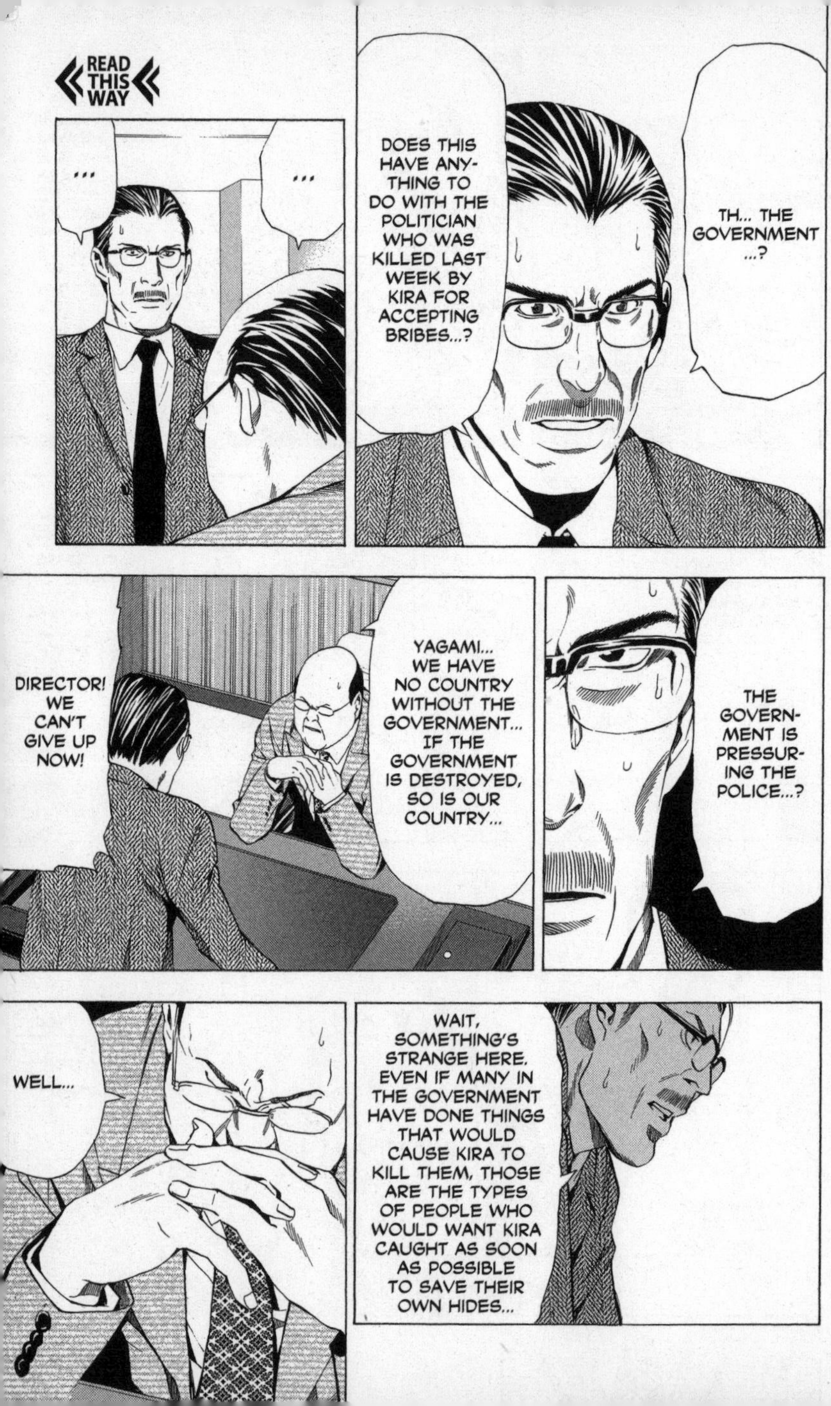
READ THIS WAY
TH... THE GOVERNMENT ...?
DOES THIS HAVE ANY-THING TO DO WITH THE POLITICIAN WHO WAS KILLED LAST WEEK BY KIRA FOR ACCEPTING BRIBES...?
...
...
THE GOVERN-MENT IS PRESSUR-ING THE POLICE...?
YAGAMI... WE HAVE NO COUNTRY WITHOUT THE GOVERNMENT... IF THE GOVERNMENT IS DESTROYED, SO IS OUR COUNTRY...
DIRECTOR! WE CAN'T GIVE UP NOW!
WAIT, SOMETHING'S STRANGE HERE. EVEN IF MANY IN THE GOVERNMENT HAVE DONE THINGS THAT WOULD CAUSE KIRA TO KILL THEM, THOSE ARE THE TYPES OF PEOPLE WHO WOULD WANT KIRA CAUGHT AS SOON AS POSSIBLE TO SAVE THEIR OWN HIDES...
WELL...

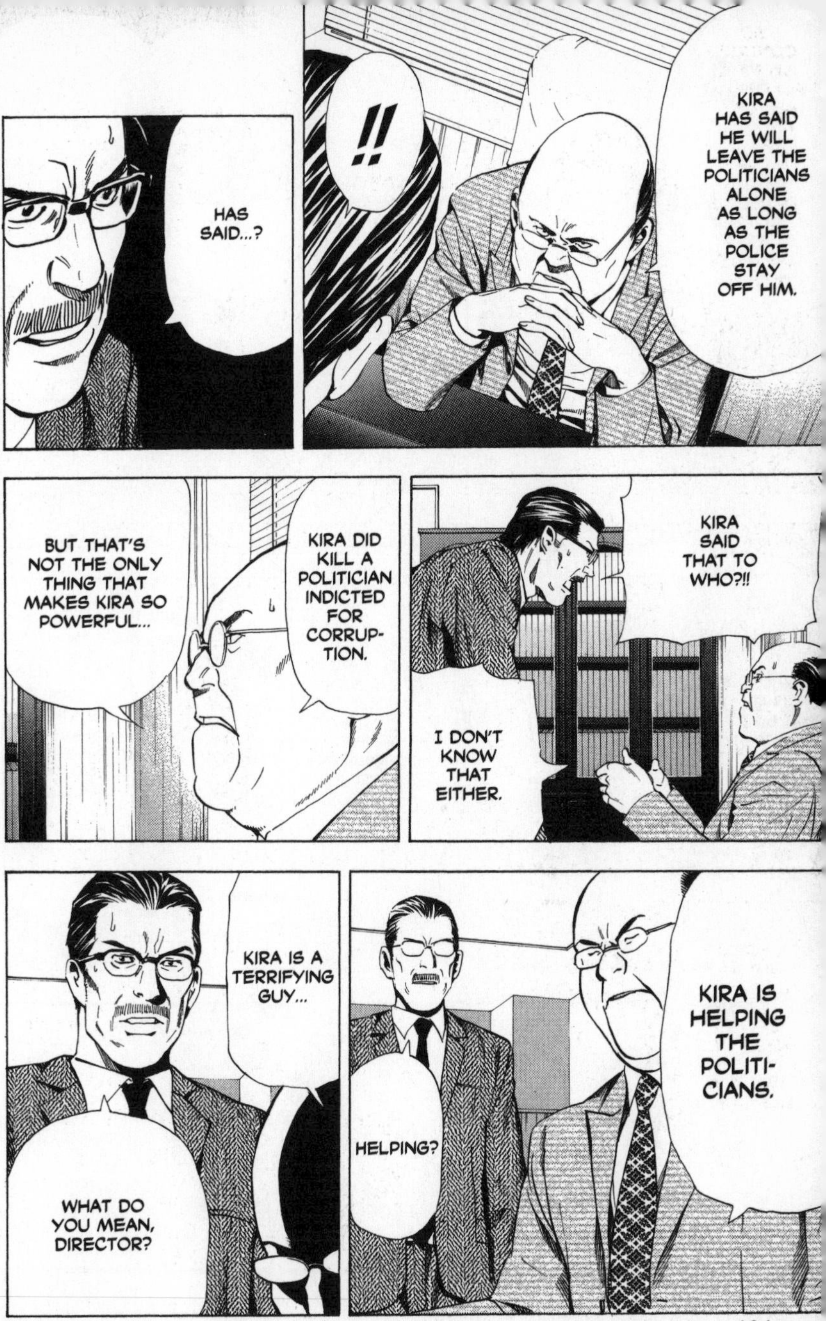
KIRA HAS SAID HE WILL LEAVE THE POLITICIANS ALONE AS LONG AS THE POLICE STAY OFF HIM.
!!
HAS SAID...?
KIRA SAID THAT TO WHO?!!
I DON'T KNOW THAT EITHER.
KIRA DID KILL A POLITICIAN INDICTED FOR CORRUP-TION.
BUT THAT'S NOT THE ONLY THING THAT MAKES KIRA SO POWERFUL...
KIRA IS HELPING THE POLITI-CIANS.
HELPING?
KIRA IS A TERRIFYING GUY...
WHAT DO YOU MEAN, DIRECTOR?

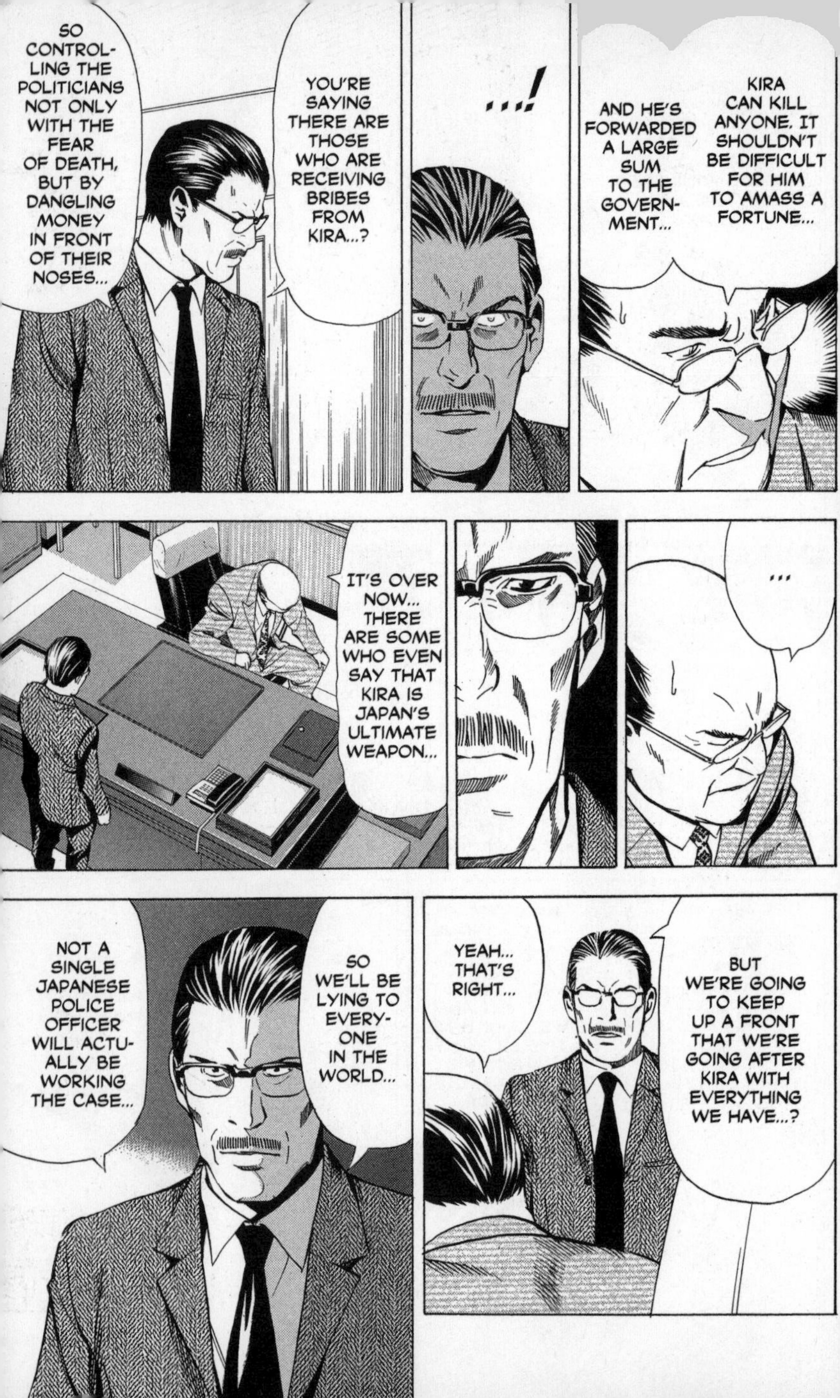
KIRA CAN KILL ANYONE. IT SHOULDN'T BE DIFFICULT FOR HIM TO AMASS A FORTUNE...
AND HE'S FORWARDED A LARGE SUM TO THE GOVERNMENT...
...!
YOU'RE SAYING THERE ARE THOSE WHO ARE RECEIVING BRIBES FROM KIRA...?
SO CONTROLLING THE POLITICIANS NOT ONLY WITH THE FEAR OF DEATH, BUT BY DANGLING MONEY IN FRONT OF THEIR NOSES...
...
IT'S OVER NOW... THERE ARE SOME WHO EVEN SAY THAT KIRA IS JAPAN'S ULTIMATE WEAPON...
BUT WE'RE GOING TO KEEP UP A FRONT THAT WE'RE GOING AFTER KIRA WITH EVERYTHING WE HAVE...?
YEAH... THAT'S RIGHT...
SO WE'LL BE LYING TO EVERYONE IN THE WORLD...
NOT A SINGLE JAPANESE POLICE OFFICER WILL ACTUALLY BE WORKING THE CASE...

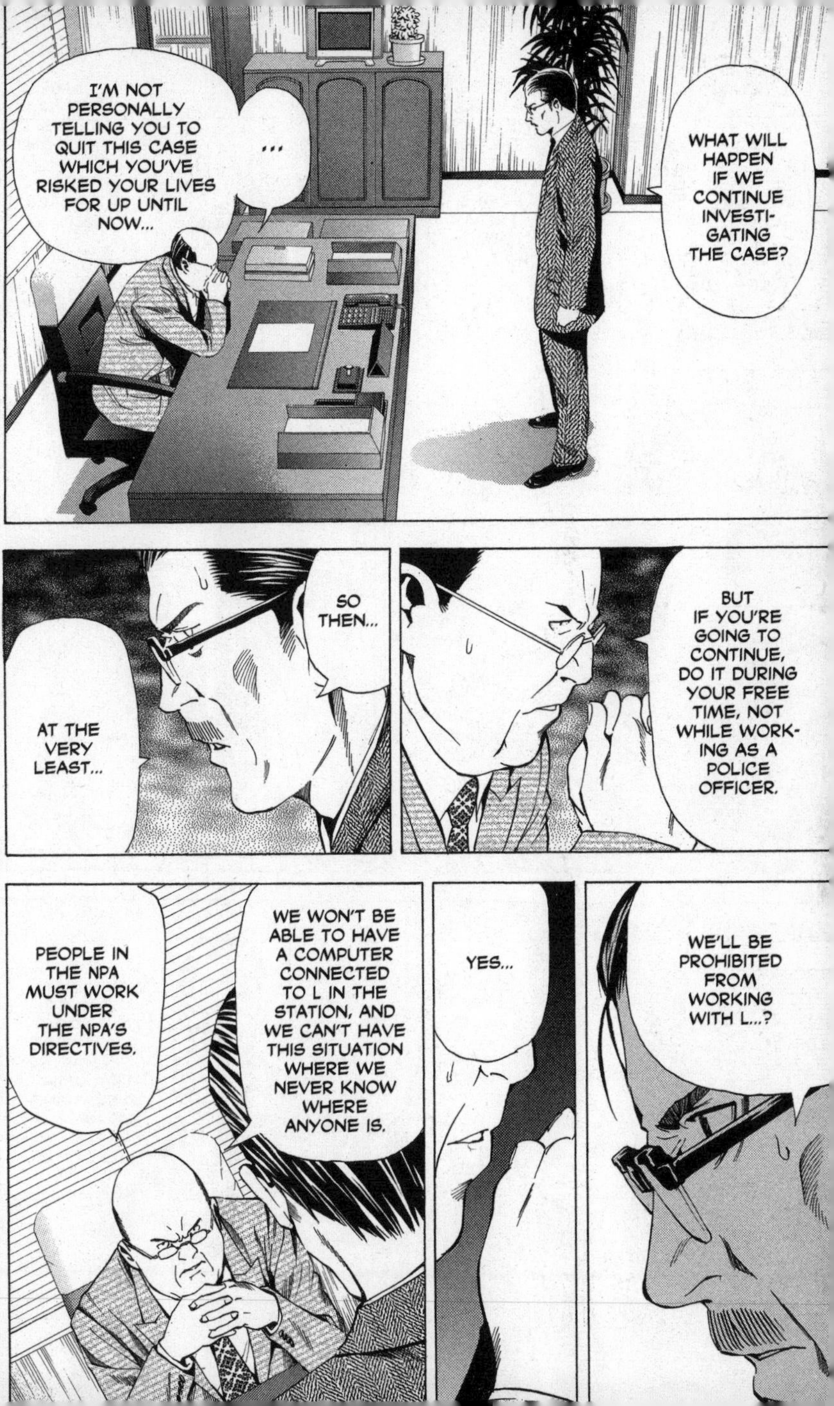
WHAT WILL HAPPEN IF WE CONTINUE INVESTIGATING THE CASE?
...
I'M NOT PERSONALLY TELLING YOU TO QUIT THIS CASE WHICH YOU'VE RISKED YOUR LIVES FOR UP UNTIL NOW...
BUT IF YOU'RE GOING TO CONTINUE, DO IT DURING YOUR FREE TIME, NOT WHILE WORKING AS A POLICE OFFICER.
SO THEN...
AT THE VERY LEAST...
WE'LL BE PROHIBITED FROM WORKING WITH L...?
YES...
WE WON'T BE ABLE TO HAVE A COMPUTER CONNECTED TO L IN THE STATION, AND WE CAN'T HAVE THIS SITUATION WHERE WE NEVER KNOW WHERE ANYONE IS.
PEOPLE IN THE NPA MUST WORK UNDER THE NPA'S DIRECTIVES.

READ THIS WAY

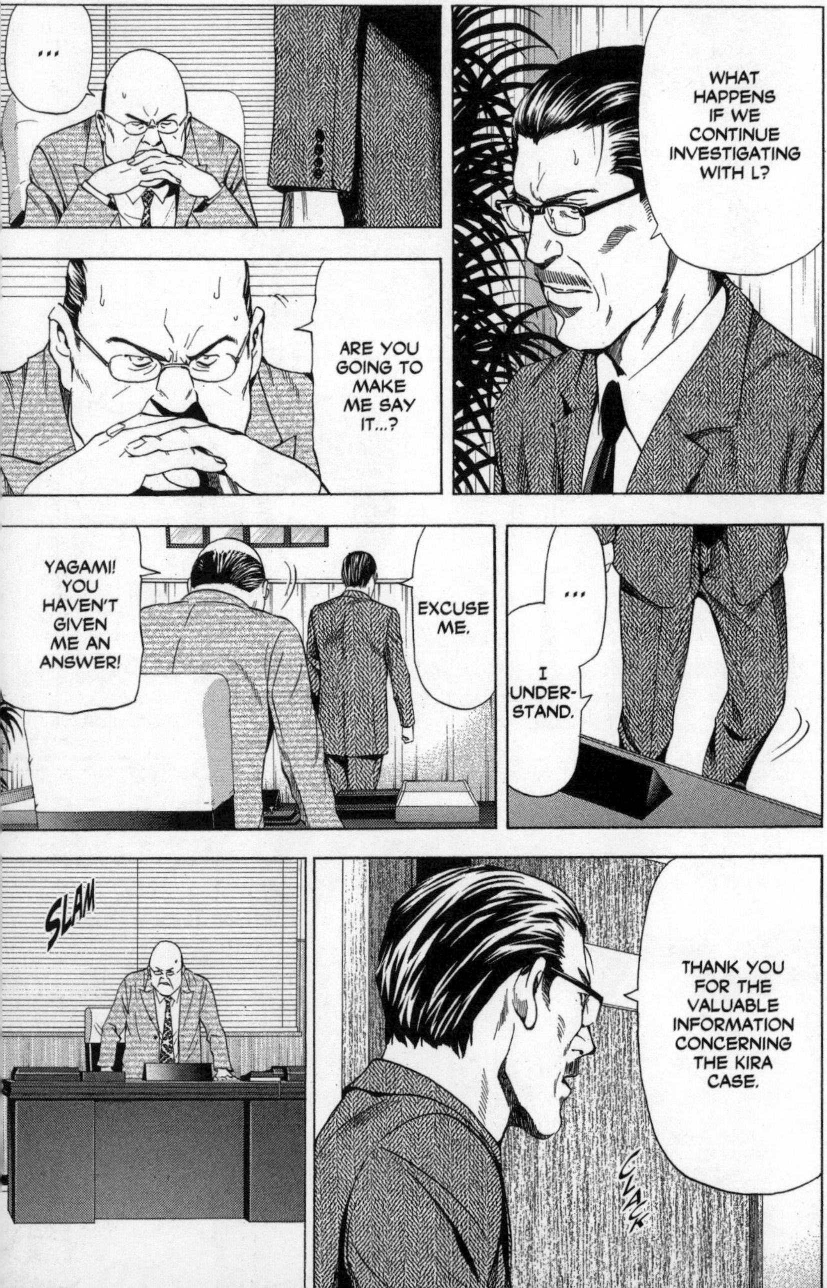
WHAT HAPPENS IF WE CONTINUE INVESTIGATING WITH L?
...
ARE YOU GOING TO MAKE ME SAY IT...?
...
I UNDER-STAND.
EXCUSE ME.
YAGAMI! YOU HAVEN'T GIVEN ME AN ANSWER!
THANK YOU FOR THE VALUABLE INFORMATION CONCERNING THE KIRA CASE.
CLACK
SLAM

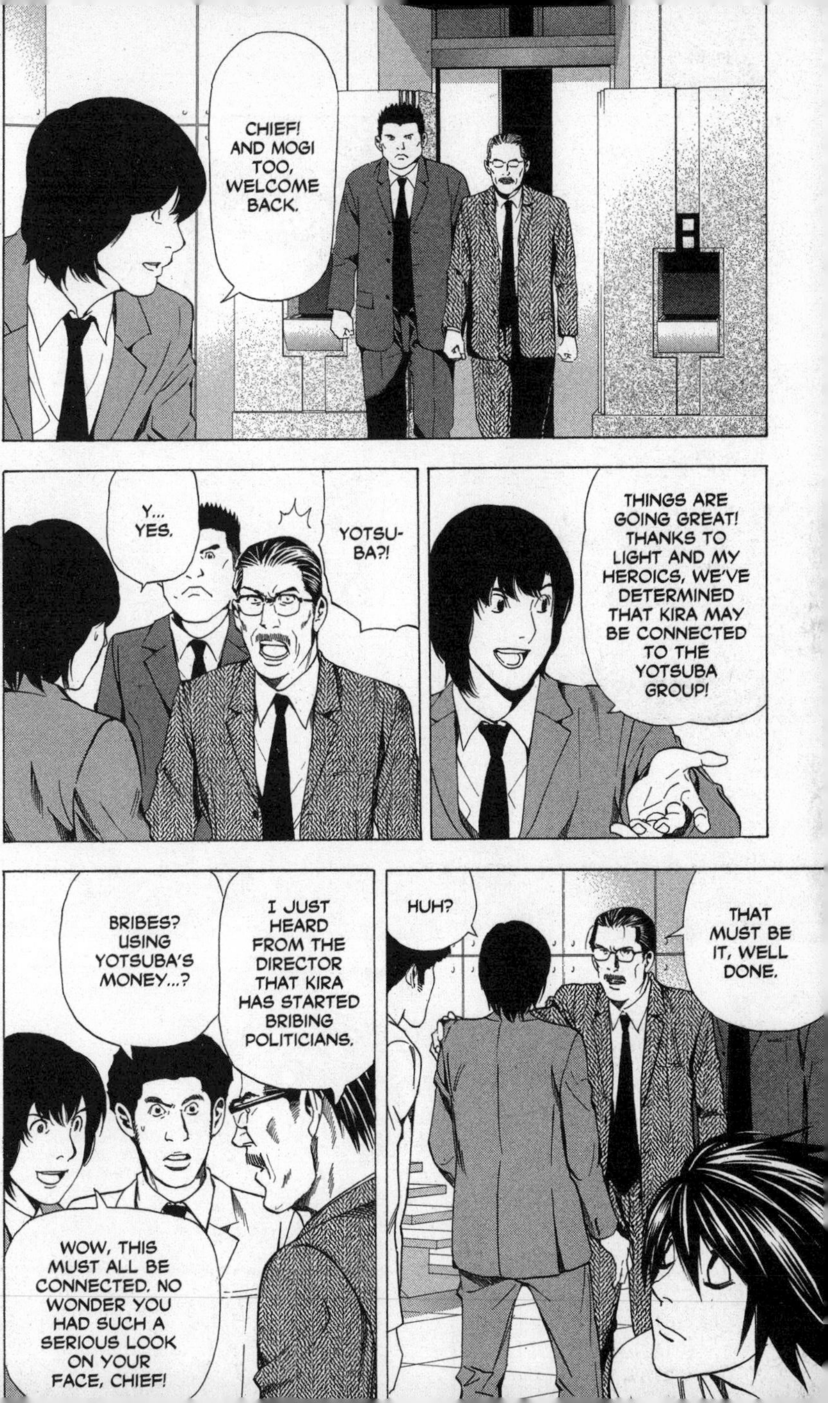
CHIEF! AND MOGI TOO, WELCOME BACK.
THINGS ARE GOING GREAT! THANKS TO LIGHT AND MY HEROICS, WE'VE DETERMINED THAT KIRA MAY BE CONNECTED TO THE YOTSUBA GROUP!
YOTSU-BA?!
Y... YES.
THAT MUST BE IT, WELL DONE.
HUH?
I JUST HEARD FROM THE DIRECTOR THAT KIRA HAS STARTED BRIBING POLITICIANS.
BRIBES? USING YOTSUBA'S MONEY...?
WOW, THIS MUST ALL BE CONNECTED. NO WONDER YOU HAD SUCH A SERIOUS LOOK ON YOUR FACE, CHIEF!

READ THIS WAY

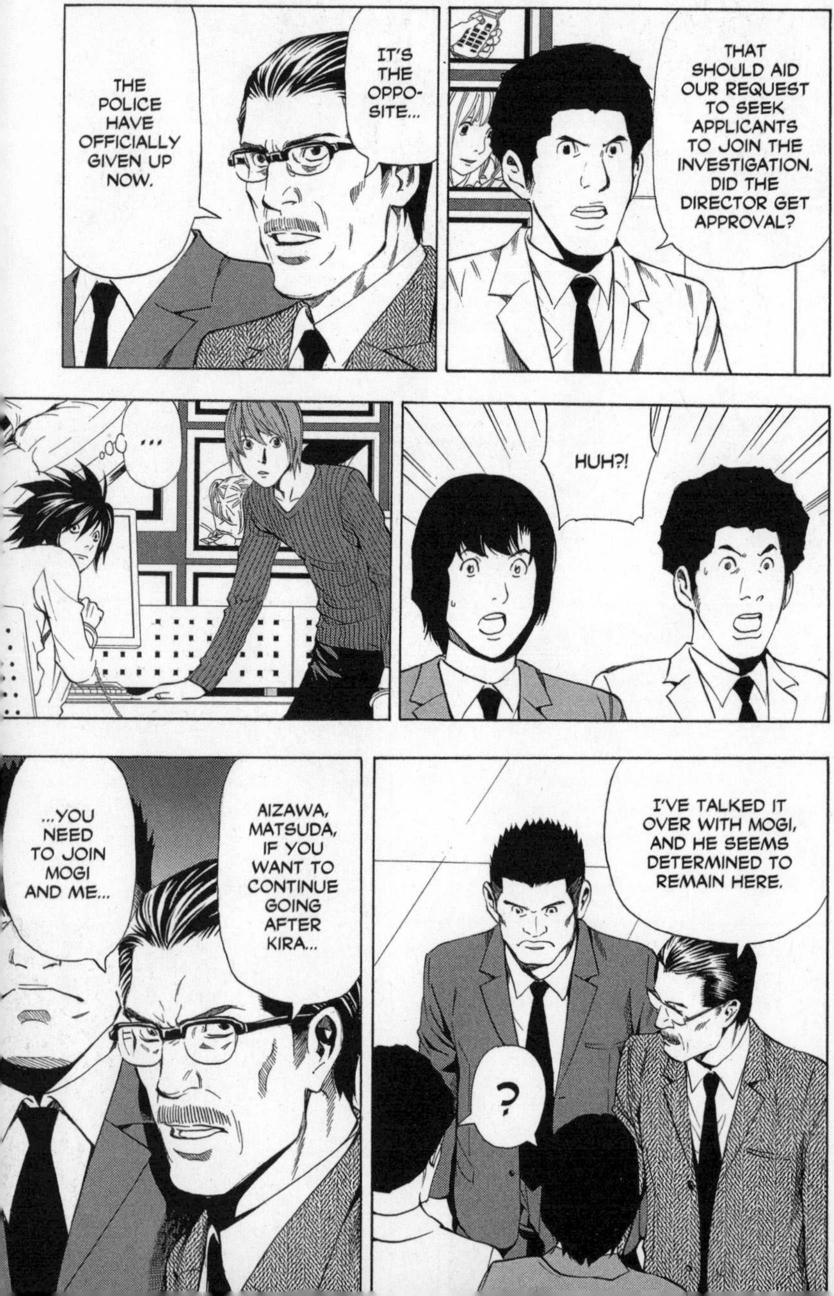
THAT SHOULD AID OUR REQUEST TO SEEK APPLICANTS TO JOIN THE INVESTIGATION. DID THE DIRECTOR GET APPROVAL?
IT'S THE OPPO-SITE...
THE POLICE HAVE OFFICIALLY GIVEN UP NOW.
HUH?!
...
I'VE TALKED IT OVER WITH MOGI, AND HE SEEMS DETERMINED TO REMAIN HERE.
?
AIZAWA, MATSUDA, IF YOU WANT TO CONTINUE GOING AFTER KIRA...
...YOU NEED TO JOIN MOGI AND ME...

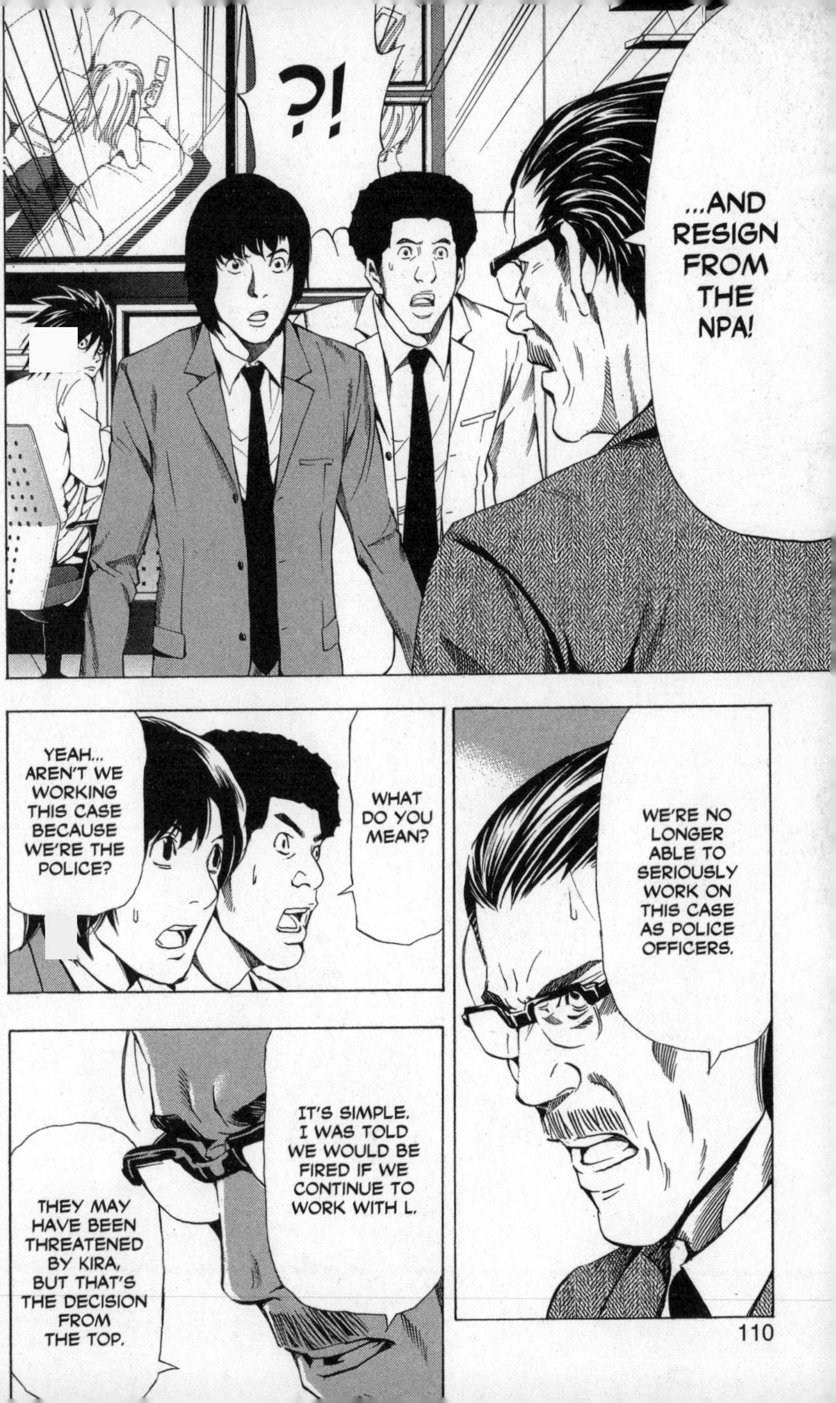
...AND RESIGN FROM THE NPA!
?!
WE'RE NO LONGER ABLE TO SERIOUSLY WORK ON THIS CASE AS POLICE OFFICERS.
WHAT DO YOU MEAN?
YEAH... AREN'T WE WORKING THIS CASE BECAUSE WE'RE THE POLICE?
IT'S SIMPLE. I WAS TOLD WE WOULD BE FIRED IF WE CONTINUE TO WORK WITH L.
THEY MAY HAVE BEEN THREATENED BY KIRA, BUT THAT'S THE DECISION FROM THE TOP.

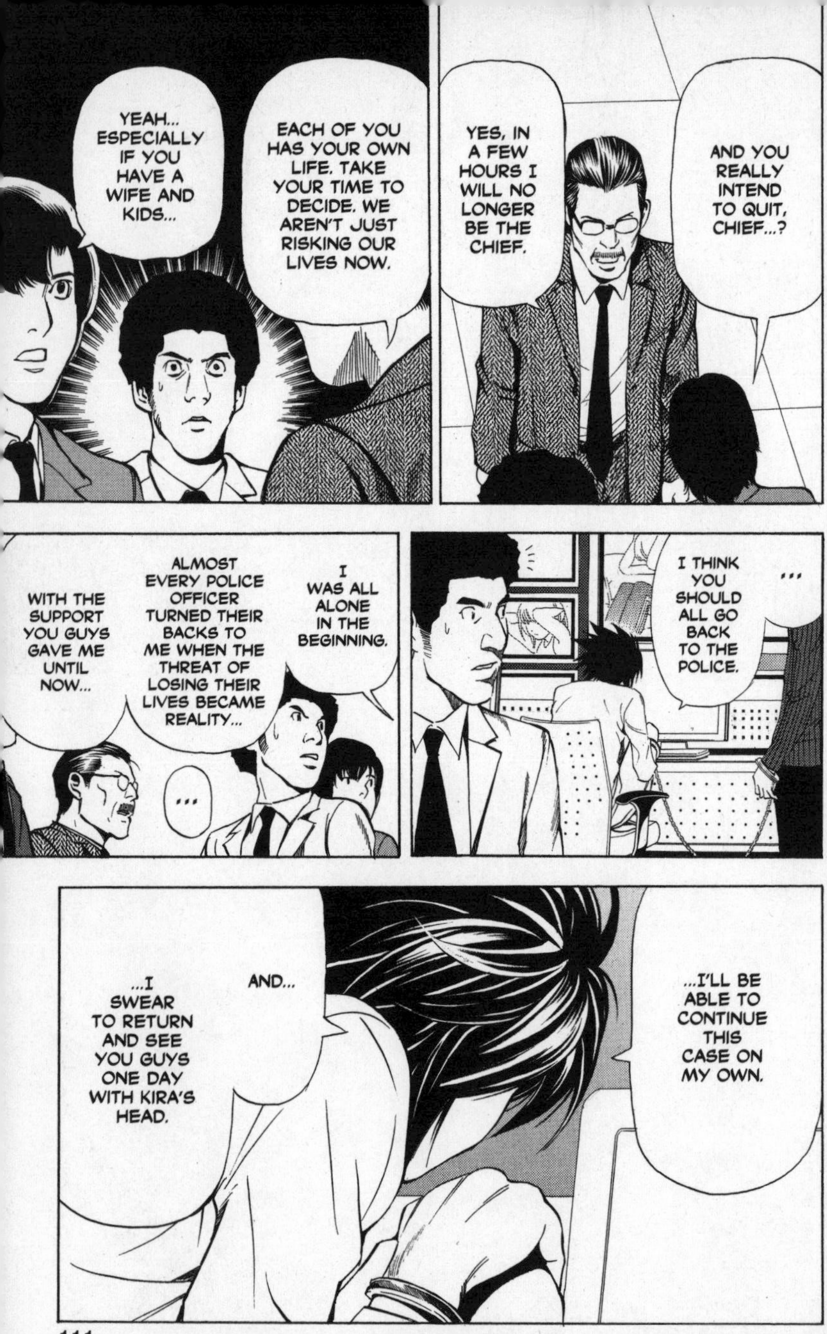
AND YOU REALLY INTEND TO QUIT, CHIEF...?
YES, IN A FEW HOURS I WILL NO LONGER BE THE CHIEF.
EACH OF YOU HAS YOUR OWN LIFE. TAKE YOUR TIME TO DECIDE. WE AREN'T JUST RISKING OUR LIVES NOW.
YEAH... ESPECIALLY IF YOU HAVE A WIFE AND KIDS...
...
I THINK YOU SHOULD ALL GO BACK TO THE POLICE.
I WAS ALL ALONE IN THE BEGINNING.
ALMOST EVERY POLICE OFFICER TURNED THEIR BACKS TO ME WHEN THE THREAT OF LOSING THEIR LIVES BECAME REALITY...
WITH THE SUPPORT YOU GUYS GAVE ME UNTIL NOW...
...
...I'LL BE ABLE TO CONTINUE THIS CASE ON MY OWN.
AND...
...I SWEAR TO RETURN AND SEE YOU GUYS ONE DAY WITH KIRA'S HEAD.

# DEATH NOTE
## How to use it
### XXVII

○ If you write, "die of disease" with a specific disease's name and the person's time of death, there must be a sufficient amount of time for the disease to progress. If the set time is too tight, the victim will die of a heart attack after 6 minutes and 40 seconds after completing the DEATH NOTE.

デスノートに病死と書き、病名と時間を指定をした場合、
その病気の進行に必要なだけの時間指定がされておらず
無理が生じると、書き終えてから40秒後に心臓麻痺となる。

○ If you write, "die of disease" for the cause of death, but only write a specific time of death without the actual name of disease, the human will die from an adequate disease. But the DEATH NOTE can only operate within 23 days (in the human calendar).

This is called the 23-day rule.

病死と書いた場合、病名を書かず時間指定をすれば、
その時間通りに適した病気で死ぬ。
ただし、デスノートで操れる死の時間は人間界単位で23日間以内である。

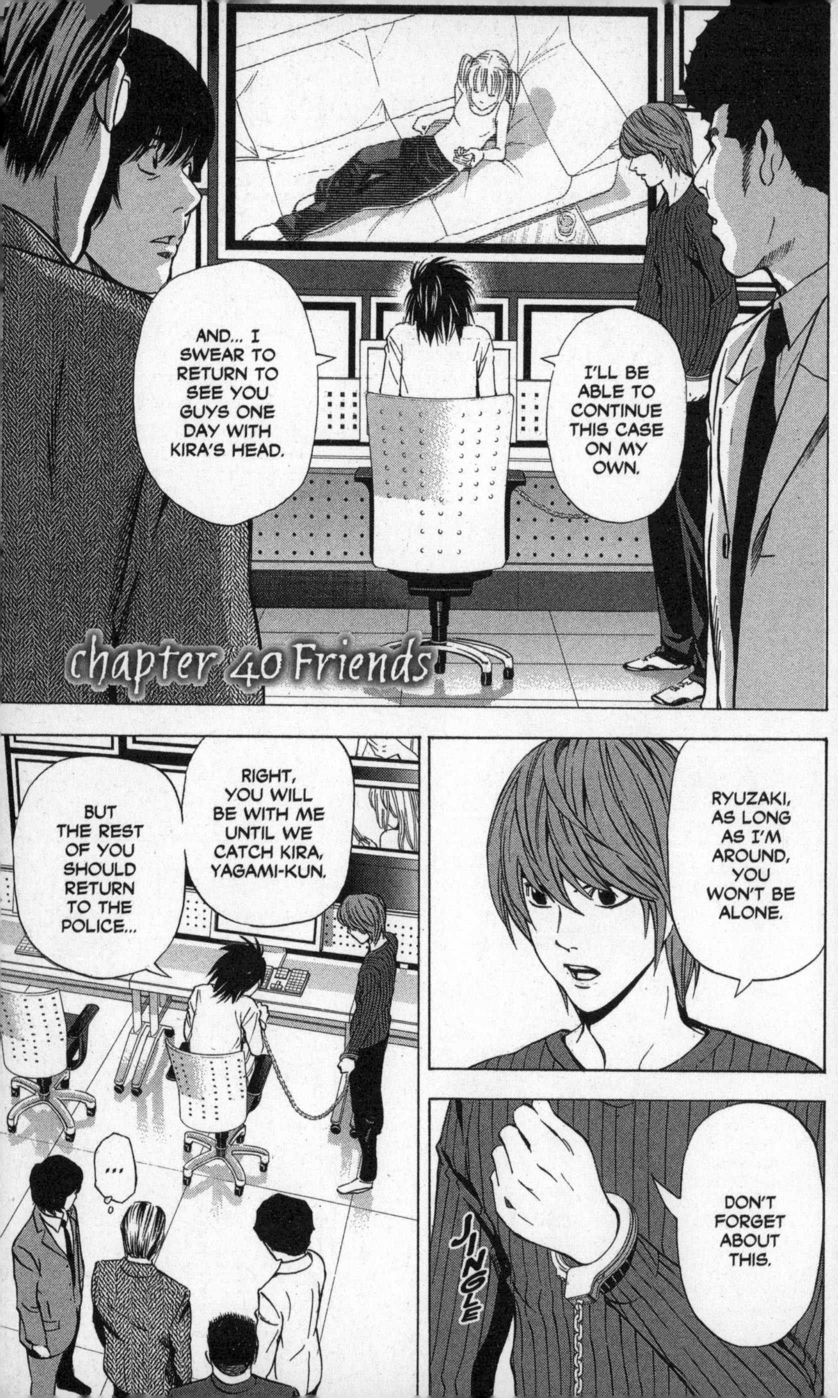
I'LL BE ABLE TO CONTINUE THIS CASE ON MY OWN.
AND... I SWEAR TO RETURN TO SEE YOU GUYS ONE DAY WITH KIRA'S HEAD.
chapter 40 Friends
RYUZAKI, AS LONG AS I'M AROUND, YOU WON'T BE ALONE.
DON'T FORGET ABOUT THIS.
JINGLE
RIGHT, YOU WILL BE WITH ME UNTIL WE CATCH KIRA, YAGAMI-KUN.
BUT THE REST OF YOU SHOULD RETURN TO THE POLICE...
...

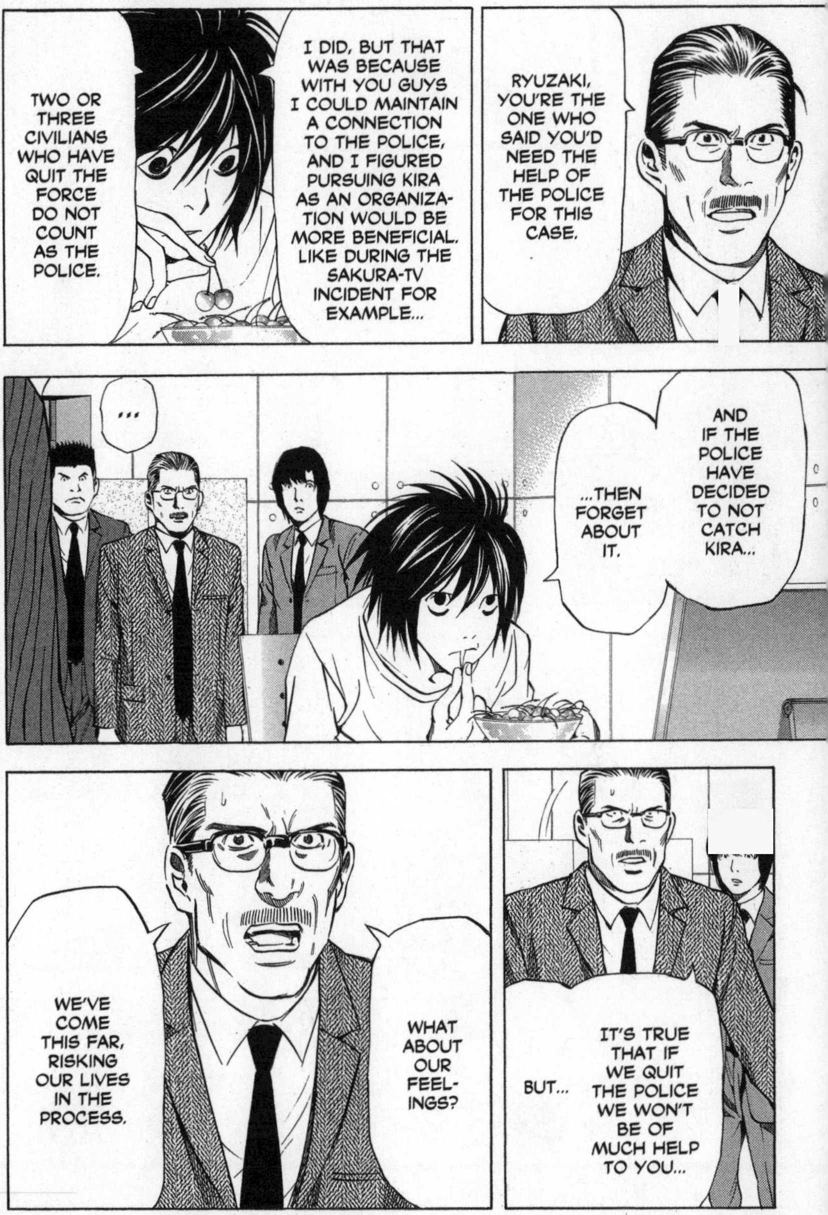
RYUZAKI, YOU'RE THE ONE WHO SAID YOU'D NEED THE HELP OF THE POLICE FOR THIS CASE.
I DID, BUT THAT WAS BECAUSE WITH YOU GUYS I COULD MAINTAIN A CONNECTION TO THE POLICE, AND I FIGURED PURSUING KIRA AS AN ORGANIZATION WOULD BE MORE BENEFICIAL. LIKE DURING THE SAKURA-TV INCIDENT FOR EXAMPLE...
TWO OR THREE CIVILIANS WHO HAVE QUIT THE FORCE DO NOT COUNT AS THE POLICE.
AND IF THE POLICE HAVE DECIDED TO NOT CATCH KIRA...
...THEN FORGET ABOUT IT.
...
IT'S TRUE THAT IF WE QUIT THE POLICE WE WON'T BE OF MUCH HELP TO YOU...
BUT...
WHAT ABOUT OUR FEELINGS?
WE'VE COME THIS FAR, RISKING OUR LIVES IN THE PROCESS.

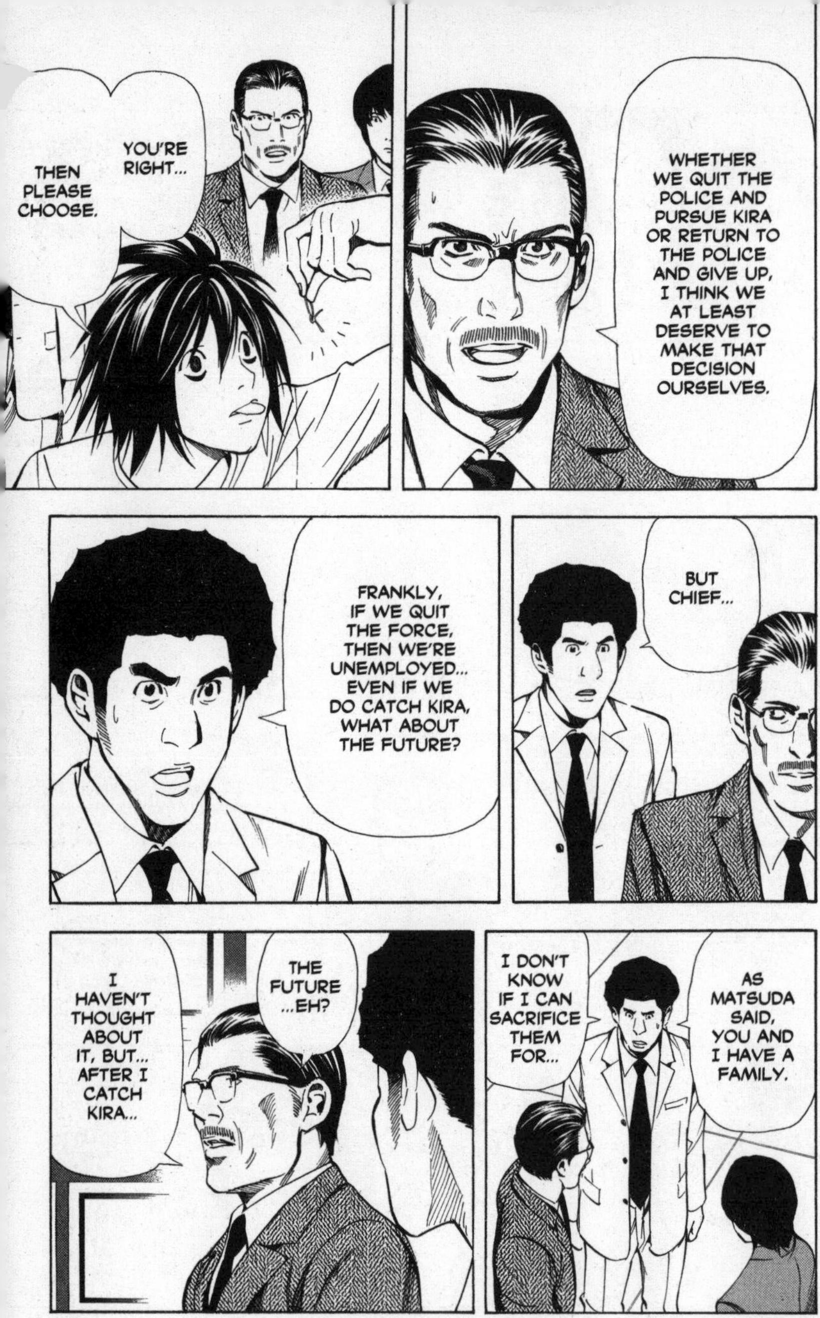
WHETHER WE QUIT THE POLICE AND PURSUE KIRA OR RETURN TO THE POLICE AND GIVE UP, I THINK WE AT LEAST DESERVE TO MAKE THAT DECISION OURSELVES.
YOU'RE RIGHT...
THEN PLEASE CHOOSE.
BUT CHIEF...
FRANKLY, IF WE QUIT THE FORCE, THEN WE'RE UNEMPLOYED... EVEN IF WE DO CATCH KIRA, WHAT ABOUT THE FUTURE?
AS MATSUDA SAID, YOU AND I HAVE A FAMILY.
I DON'T KNOW IF I CAN SACRIFICE THEM FOR...
THE FUTURE ...EH?
I HAVEN'T THOUGHT ABOUT IT, BUT... AFTER I CATCH KIRA...

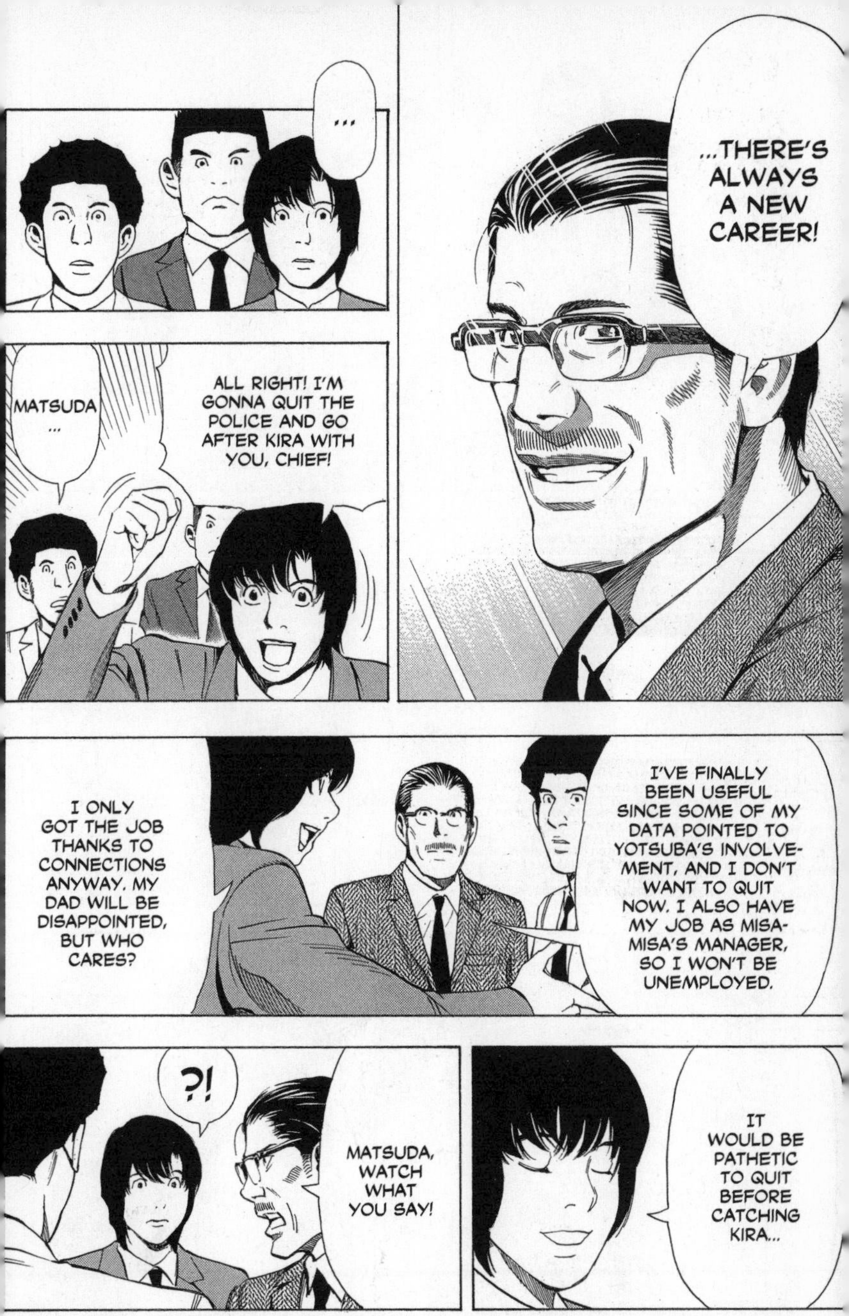
...THERE'S ALWAYS A NEW CAREER!
...
ALL RIGHT! I'M GONNA QUIT THE POLICE AND GO AFTER KIRA WITH YOU, CHIEF!
MATSUDA ...
I'VE FINALLY BEEN USEFUL SINCE SOME OF MY DATA POINTED TO YOTSUBA'S INVOLVEMENT, AND I DON'T WANT TO QUIT NOW. I ALSO HAVE MY JOB AS MISA-MISA'S MANAGER, SO I WON'T BE UNEMPLOYED.
I ONLY GOT THE JOB THANKS TO CONNECTIONS ANYWAY. MY DAD WILL BE DISAPPOINTED, BUT WHO CARES?
IT WOULD BE PATHETIC TO QUIT BEFORE CATCHING KIRA...
MATSUDA, WATCH WHAT YOU SAY!
?!

READ THIS WAY

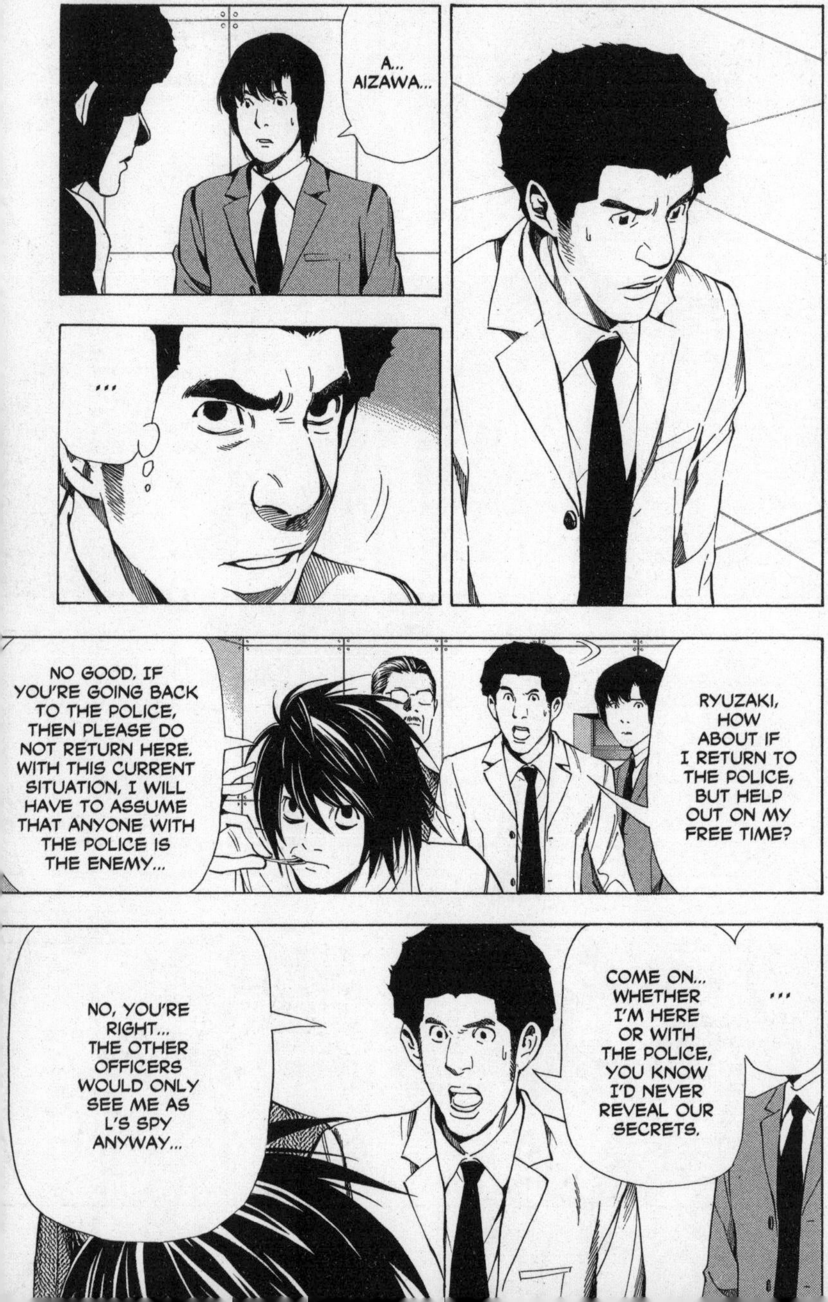
A... AIZAWA...
...
RYUZAKI, HOW ABOUT IF I RETURN TO THE POLICE, BUT HELP OUT ON MY FREE TIME?
NO GOOD. IF YOU'RE GOING BACK TO THE POLICE, THEN PLEASE DO NOT RETURN HERE. WITH THIS CURRENT SITUATION, I WILL HAVE TO ASSUME THAT ANYONE WITH THE POLICE IS THE ENEMY...
...
COME ON... WHETHER I'M HERE OR WITH THE POLICE, YOU KNOW I'D NEVER REVEAL OUR SECRETS.
NO, YOU'RE RIGHT... THE OTHER OFFICERS WOULD ONLY SEE ME AS L'S SPY ANYWAY...

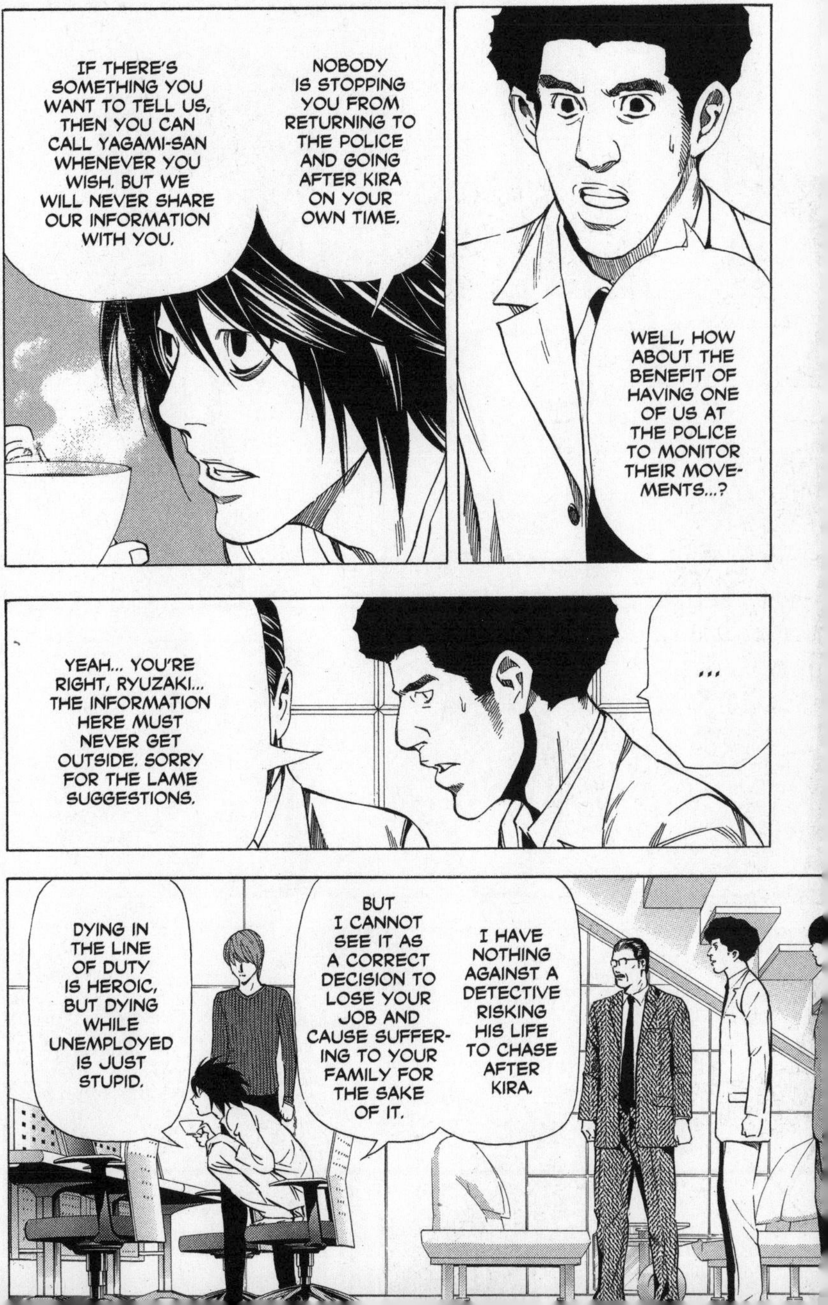
WELL, HOW ABOUT THE BENEFIT OF HAVING ONE OF US AT THE POLICE TO MONITOR THEIR MOVEMENTS...?
NOBODY IS STOPPING YOU FROM RETURNING TO THE POLICE AND GOING AFTER KIRA ON YOUR OWN TIME.
IF THERE'S SOMETHING YOU WANT TO TELL US, THEN YOU CAN CALL YAGAMI-SAN WHENEVER YOU WISH. BUT WE WILL NEVER SHARE OUR INFORMATION WITH YOU.
...
YEAH... YOU'RE RIGHT, RYUZAKI... THE INFORMATION HERE MUST NEVER GET OUTSIDE. SORRY FOR THE LAME SUGGESTIONS.
I HAVE NOTHING AGAINST A DETECTIVE RISKING HIS LIFE TO CHASE AFTER KIRA.
BUT I CANNOT SEE IT AS A CORRECT DECISION TO LOSE YOUR JOB AND CAUSE SUFFERING TO YOUR FAMILY FOR THE SAKE OF IT.
DYING IN THE LINE OF DUTY IS HEROIC, BUT DYING WHILE UNEMPLOYED IS JUST STUPID.

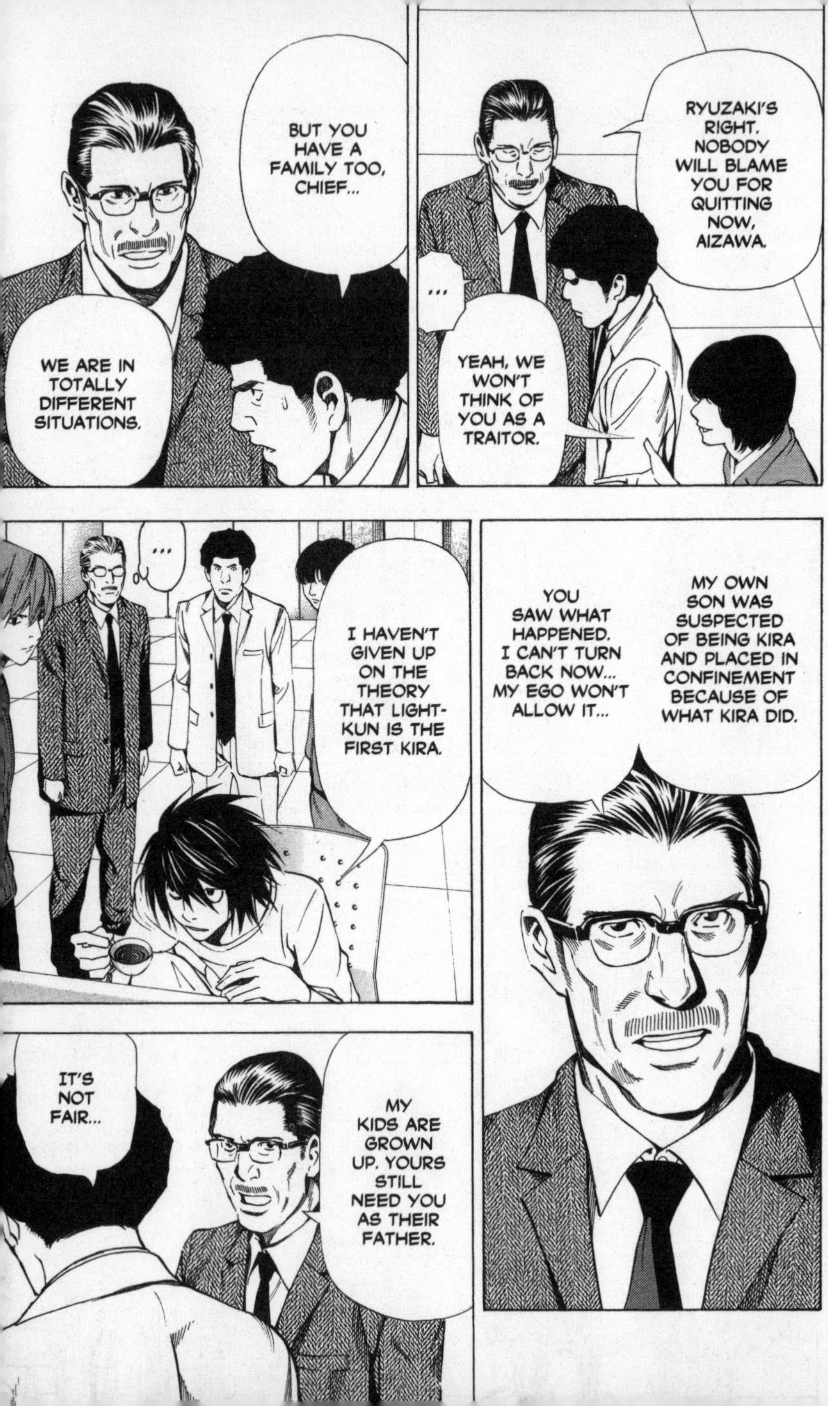
RYUZAKI'S RIGHT. NOBODY WILL BLAME YOU FOR QUITTING NOW, AIZAWA.
YEAH, WE WON'T THINK OF YOU AS A TRAITOR.
...
BUT YOU HAVE A FAMILY TOO, CHIEF...
WE ARE IN TOTALLY DIFFERENT SITUATIONS.
MY OWN SON WAS SUSPECTED OF BEING KIRA AND PLACED IN CONFINEMENT BECAUSE OF WHAT KIRA DID.
YOU SAW WHAT HAPPENED. I CAN'T TURN BACK NOW... MY EGO WON'T ALLOW IT...
I HAVEN'T GIVEN UP ON THE THEORY THAT LIGHT-KUN IS THE FIRST KIRA.
...
MY KIDS ARE GROWN UP. YOURS STILL NEED YOU AS THEIR FATHER.
IT'S NOT FAIR...

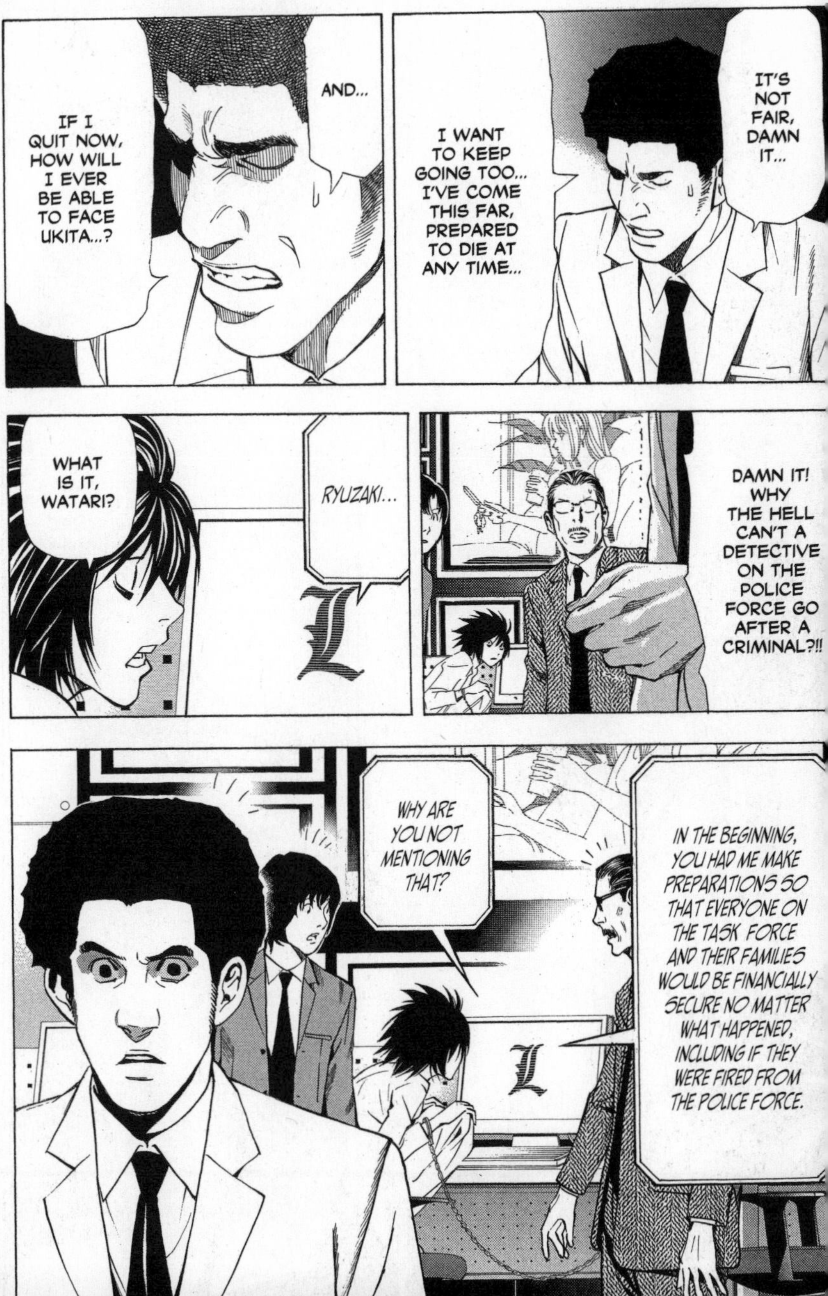
IT'S NOT FAIR, DAMN IT...
I WANT TO KEEP GOING TOO... I'VE COME THIS FAR, PREPARED TO DIE AT ANY TIME...
AND...
IF I QUIT NOW, HOW WILL I EVER BE ABLE TO FACE UKITA...?
DAMN IT! WHY THE HELL CAN'T A DETECTIVE ON THE POLICE FORCE GO AFTER A CRIMINAL?!!
RYUZAKI...
WHAT IS IT, WATARI?
IN THE BEGINNING, YOU HAD ME MAKE PREPARATIONS SO THAT EVERYONE ON THE TASK FORCE AND THEIR FAMILIES WOULD BE FINANCIALLY SECURE NO MATTER WHAT HAPPENED, INCLUDING IF THEY WERE FIRED FROM THE POLICE FORCE.
WHY ARE YOU NOT MENTIONING THAT?

READ THIS WAY

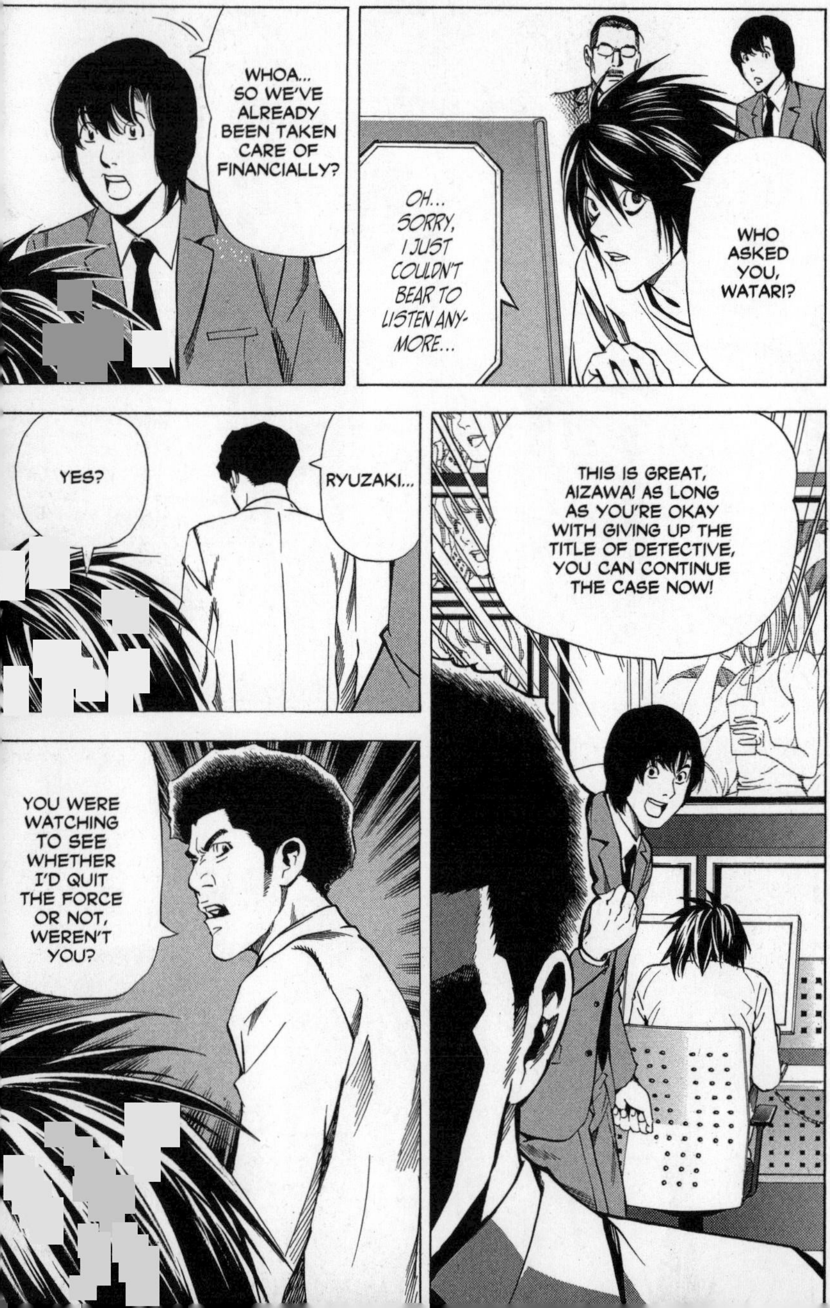
OH... SORRY, I JUST COULDN'T BEAR TO LISTEN ANY-MORE...
WHO ASKED YOU, WATARI?
WHOA... SO WE'VE ALREADY BEEN TAKEN CARE OF FINANCIALLY?
THIS IS GREAT, AIZAWA! AS LONG AS YOU'RE OKAY WITH GIVING UP THE TITLE OF DETECTIVE, YOU CAN CONTINUE THE CASE NOW!
RYUZAKI...
YES?
YOU WERE WATCHING TO SEE WHETHER I'D QUIT THE FORCE OR NOT, WEREN'T YOU?

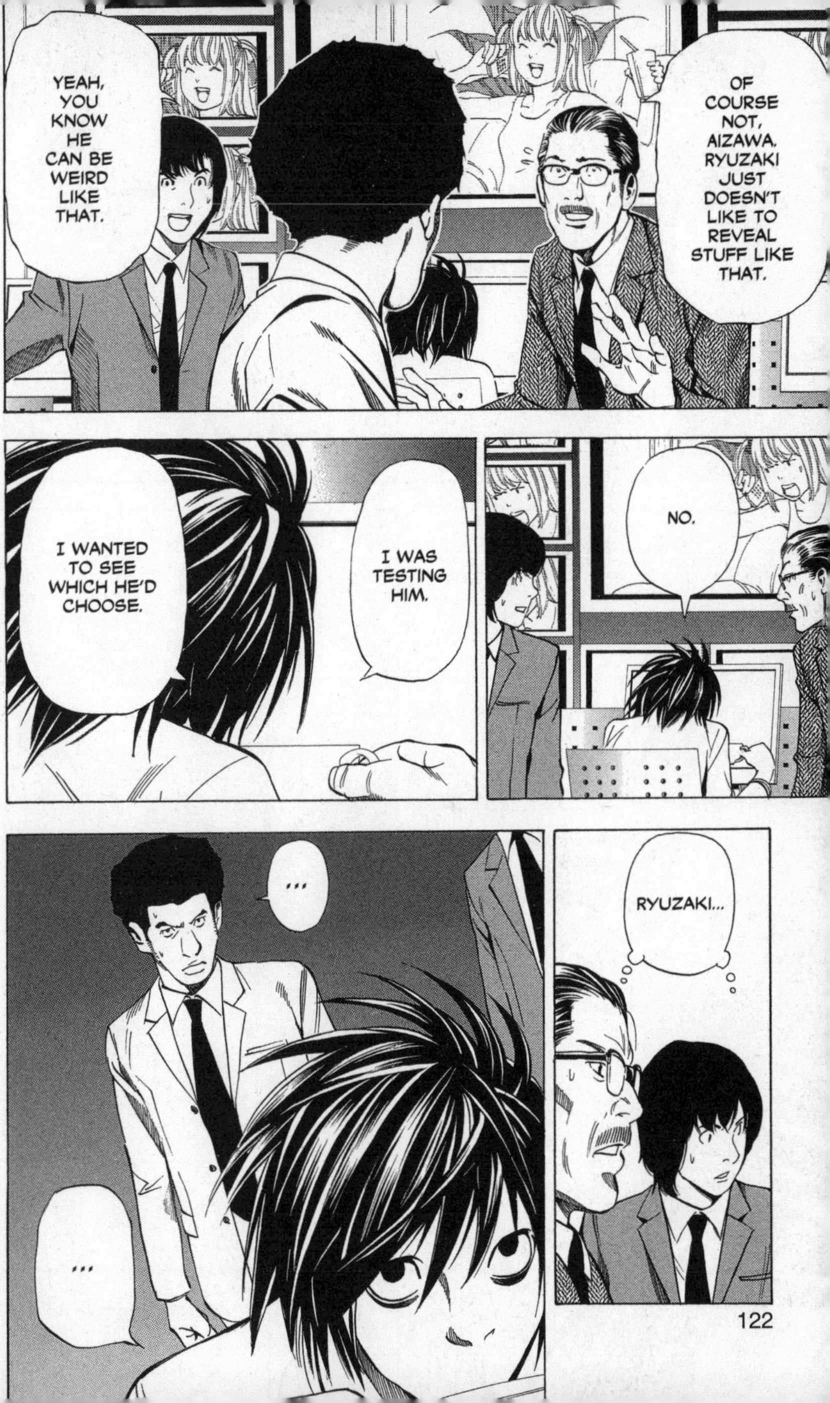
OF COURSE NOT, AIZAWA. RYUZAKI JUST DOESN'T LIKE TO REVEAL STUFF LIKE THAT.
YEAH, YOU KNOW HE CAN BE WEIRD LIKE THAT.
NO.
I WAS TESTING HIM.
I WANTED TO SEE WHICH HE'D CHOOSE.
RYUZAKI...
...
...

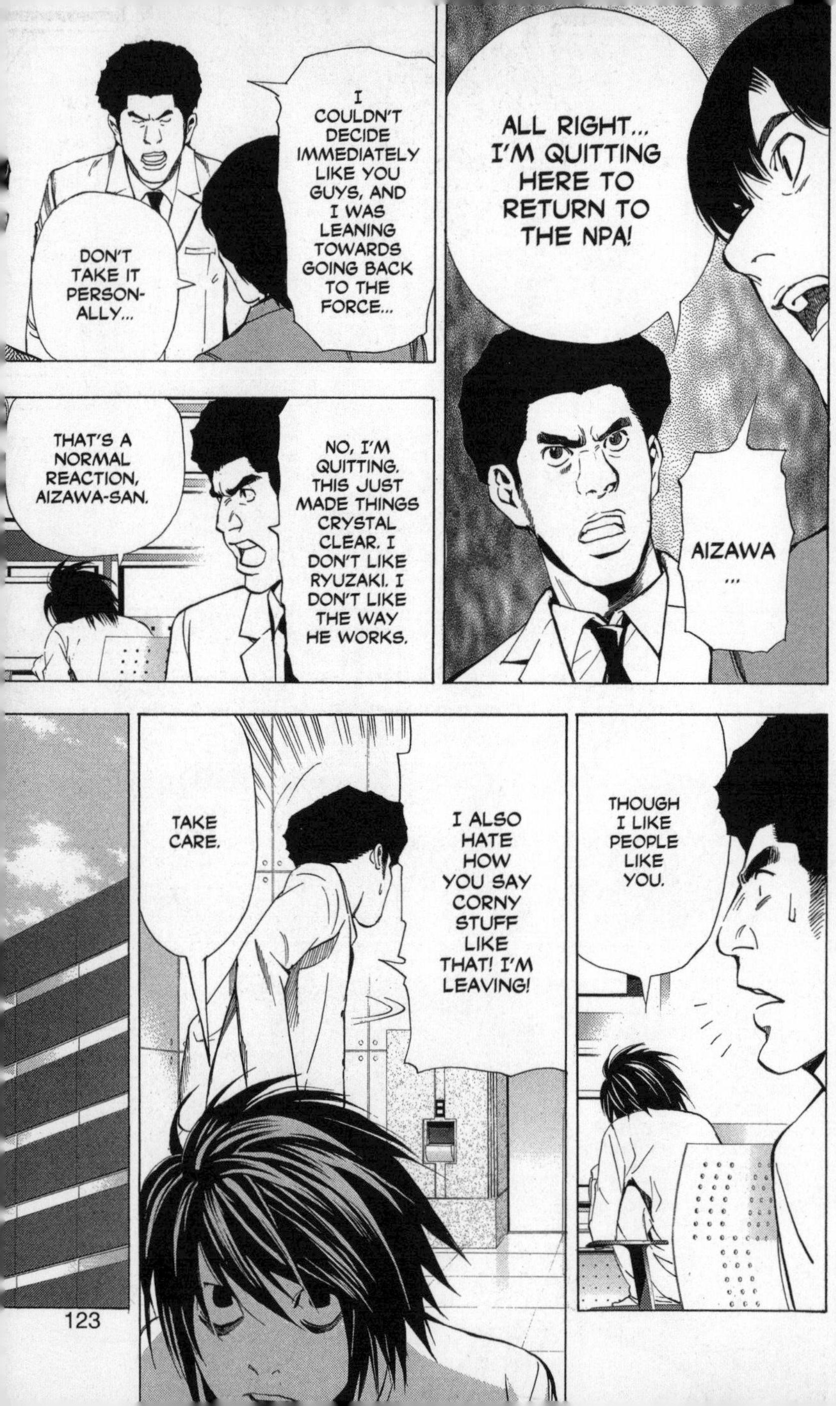
ALL RIGHT... I'M QUITTING HERE TO RETURN TO THE NPA!
AIZAWA ...
I COULDN'T DECIDE IMMEDIATELY LIKE YOU GUYS, AND I WAS LEANING TOWARDS GOING BACK TO THE FORCE...
DON'T TAKE IT PERSON-ALLY...
NO, I'M QUITTING. THIS JUST MADE THINGS CRYSTAL CLEAR. I DON'T LIKE RYUZAKI. I DON'T LIKE THE WAY HE WORKS.
THAT'S A NORMAL REACTION, AIZAWA-SAN.
THOUGH I LIKE PEOPLE LIKE YOU.
I ALSO HATE HOW YOU SAY CORNY STUFF LIKE THAT! I'M LEAVING!
TAKE CARE.

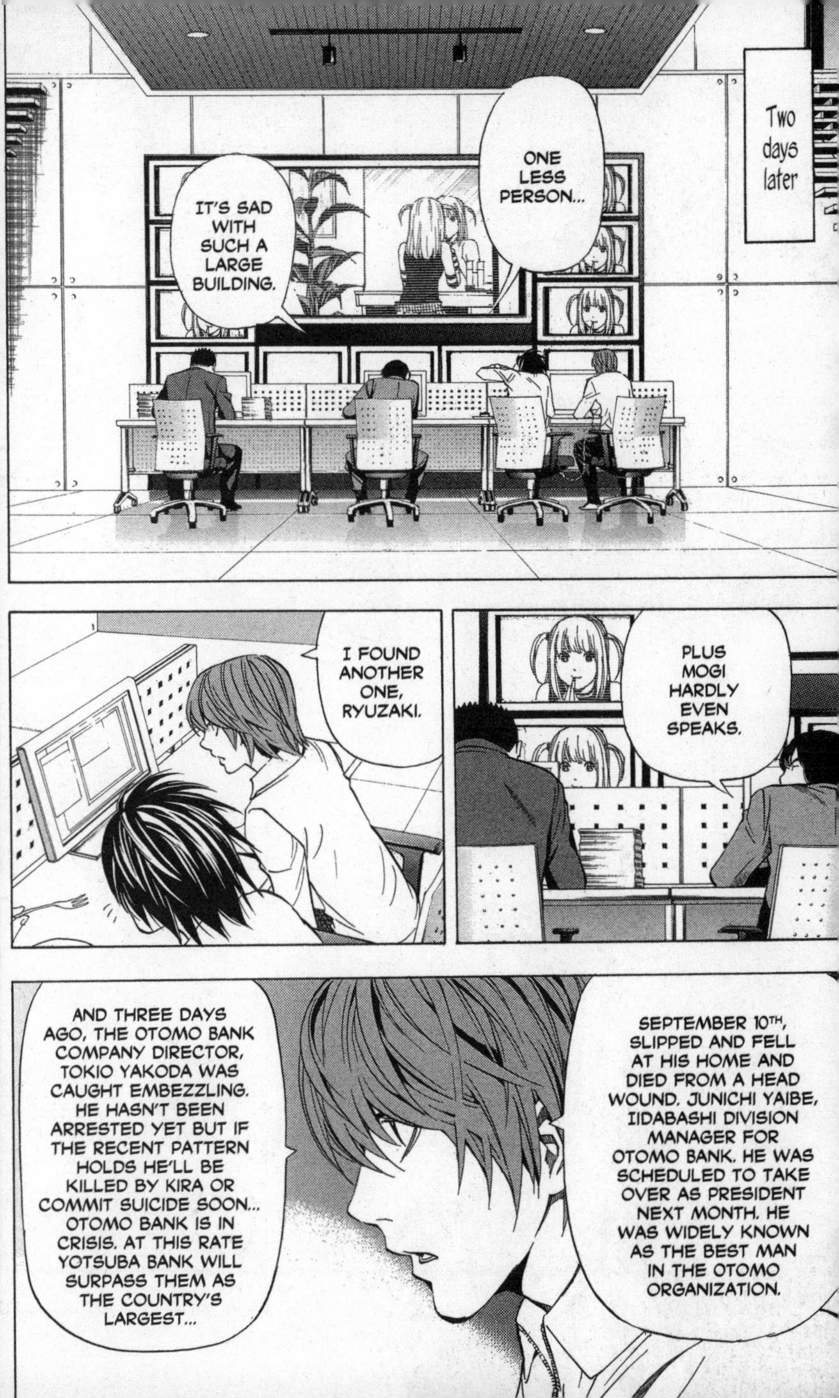
Two days later
ONE LESS PERSON...
IT'S SAD WITH SUCH A LARGE BUILDING.
PLUS MOGI HARDLY EVEN SPEAKS.
I FOUND ANOTHER ONE, RYUZAKI.
SEPTEMBER 10TH, SLIPPED AND FELL AT HIS HOME AND DIED FROM A HEAD WOUND. JUNICHI YAIBE, IIDABASHI DIVISION MANAGER FOR OTOMO BANK. HE WAS SCHEDULED TO TAKE OVER AS PRESIDENT NEXT MONTH. HE WAS WIDELY KNOWN AS THE BEST MAN IN THE OTOMO ORGANIZATION.
AND THREE DAYS AGO, THE OTOMO BANK COMPANY DIRECTOR, TOKIO YAKODA WAS CAUGHT EMBEZZLING. HE HASN'T BEEN ARRESTED YET BUT IF THE RECENT PATTERN HOLDS HE'LL BE KILLED BY KIRA OR COMMIT SUICIDE SOON... OTOMO BANK IS IN CRISIS. AT THIS RATE YOTSUBA BANK WILL SURPASS THEM AS THE COUNTRY'S LARGEST...

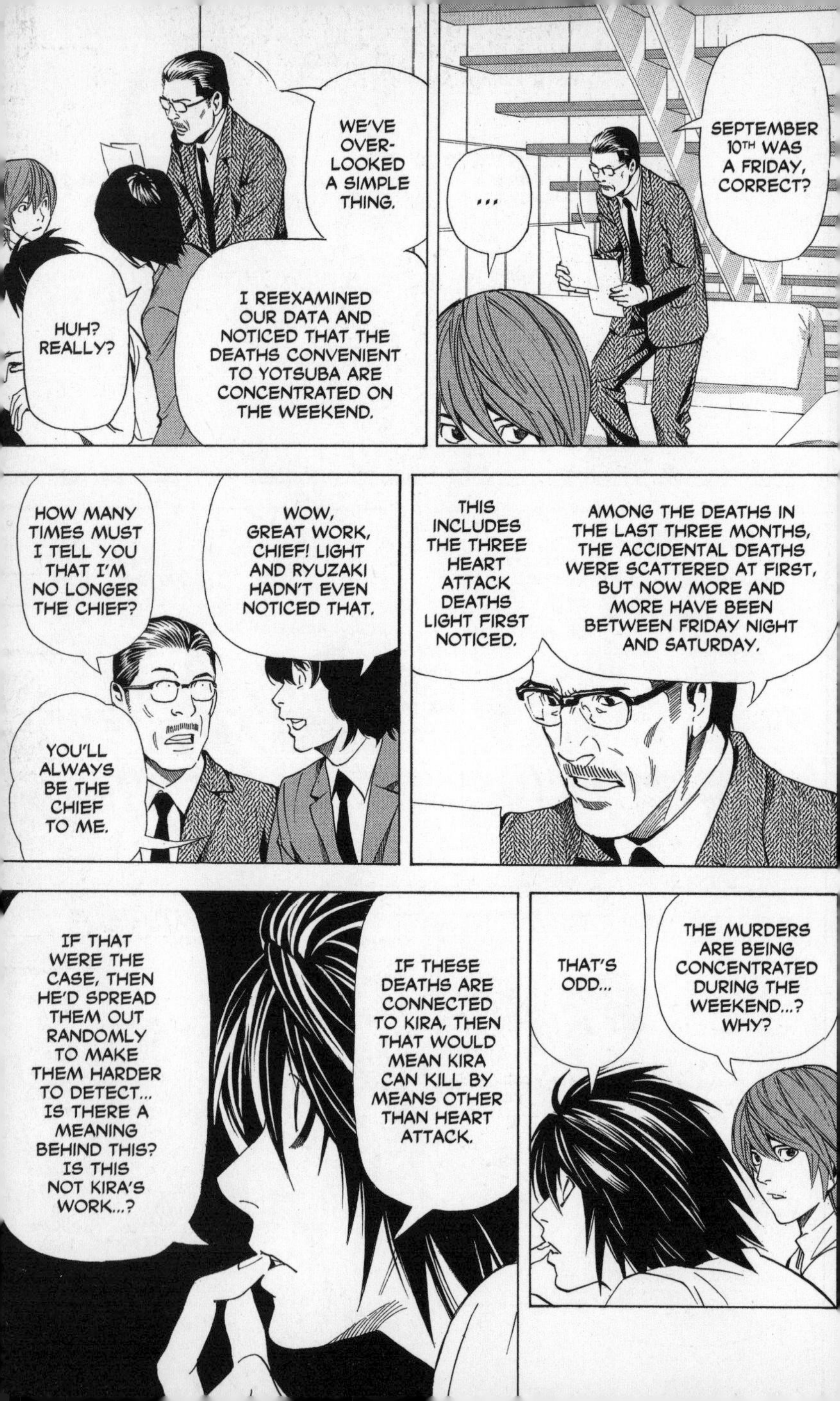
SEPTEMBER 10TH WAS A FRIDAY, CORRECT?
...
WE'VE OVER-LOOKED A SIMPLE THING.
I REEXAMINED OUR DATA AND NOTICED THAT THE DEATHS CONVENIENT TO YOTSUBA ARE CONCENTRATED ON THE WEEKEND.
HUH? REALLY?
AMONG THE DEATHS IN THE LAST THREE MONTHS, THE ACCIDENTAL DEATHS WERE SCATTERED AT FIRST, BUT NOW MORE AND MORE HAVE BEEN BETWEEN FRIDAY NIGHT AND SATURDAY.
THIS INCLUDES THE THREE HEART ATTACK DEATHS LIGHT FIRST NOTICED.
WOW, GREAT WORK, CHIEF! LIGHT AND RYUZAKI HADN'T EVEN NOTICED THAT.
HOW MANY TIMES MUST I TELL YOU THAT I'M NO LONGER THE CHIEF?
YOU'LL ALWAYS BE THE CHIEF TO ME.
THE MURDERS ARE BEING CONCENTRATED DURING THE WEEKEND...? WHY?
THAT'S ODD...
IF THESE DEATHS ARE CONNECTED TO KIRA, THEN THAT WOULD MEAN KIRA CAN KILL BY MEANS OTHER THAN HEART ATTACK.
IF THAT WERE THE CASE, THEN HE'D SPREAD THEM OUT RANDOMLY TO MAKE THEM HARDER TO DETECT... IS THERE A MEANING BEHIND THIS? IS THIS NOT KIRA'S WORK...?

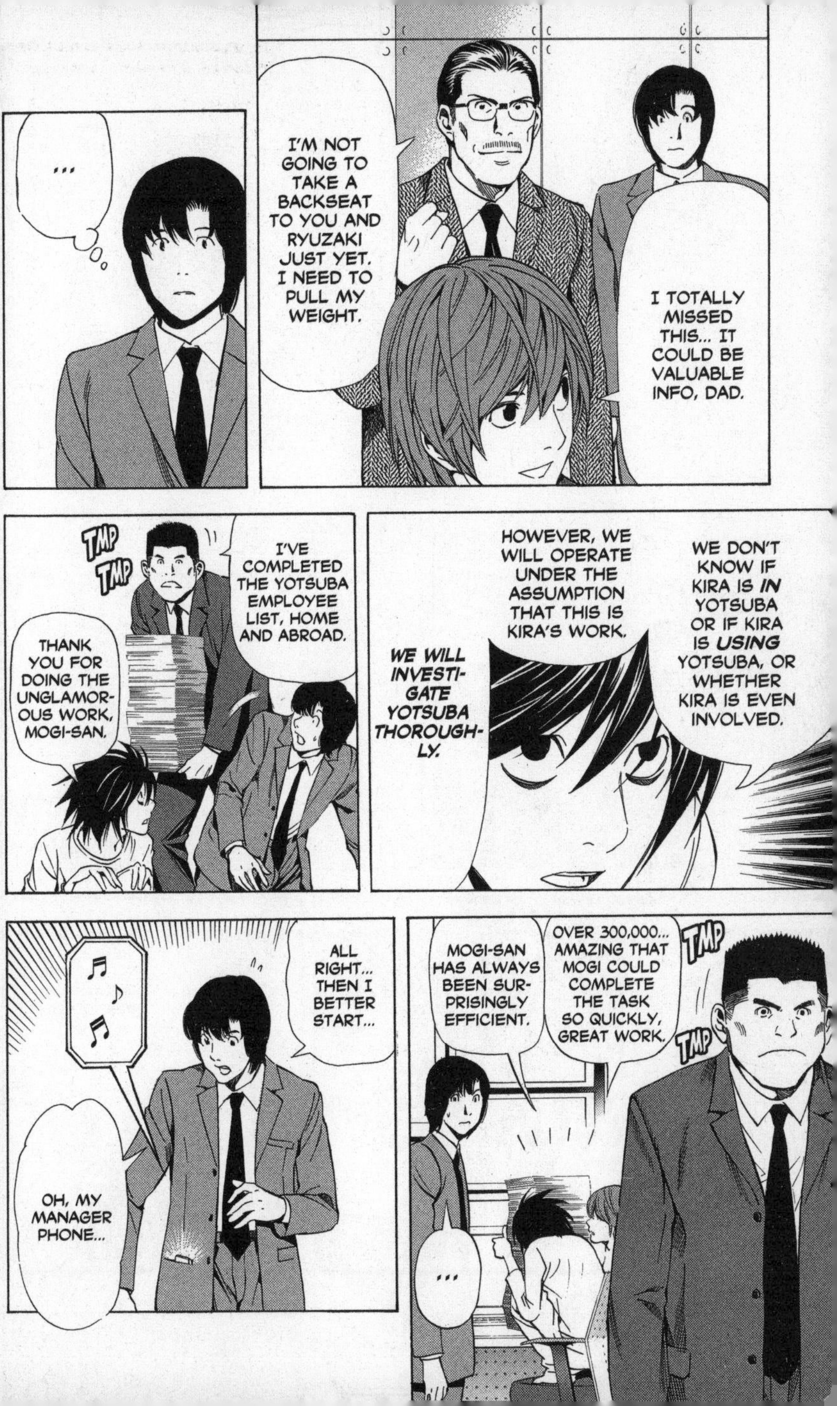
I TOTALLY MISSED THIS... IT COULD BE VALUABLE INFO, DAD.
I'M NOT GOING TO TAKE A BACKSEAT TO YOU AND RYUZAKI JUST YET. I NEED TO PULL MY WEIGHT.
...
WE DON'T KNOW IF KIRA IS *IN* YOTSUBA OR IF KIRA IS *USING* YOTSUBA, OR WHETHER KIRA IS EVEN INVOLVED.
HOWEVER, WE WILL OPERATE UNDER THE ASSUMPTION THAT THIS IS KIRA'S WORK.
WE WILL INVESTIGATE YOTSUBA THOROUGHLY.
TMP
TMP
I'VE COMPLETED THE YOTSUBA EMPLOYEE LIST, HOME AND ABROAD.
THANK YOU FOR DOING THE UNGLAMOROUS WORK, MOGI-SAN.
TMP
OVER 300,000... AMAZING THAT MOGI COULD COMPLETE THE TASK SO QUICKLY, GREAT WORK.
MOGI-SAN HAS ALWAYS BEEN SURPRISINGLY EFFICIENT.
TMP
...
ALL RIGHT... THEN I BETTER START...
OH, MY MANAGER PHONE...

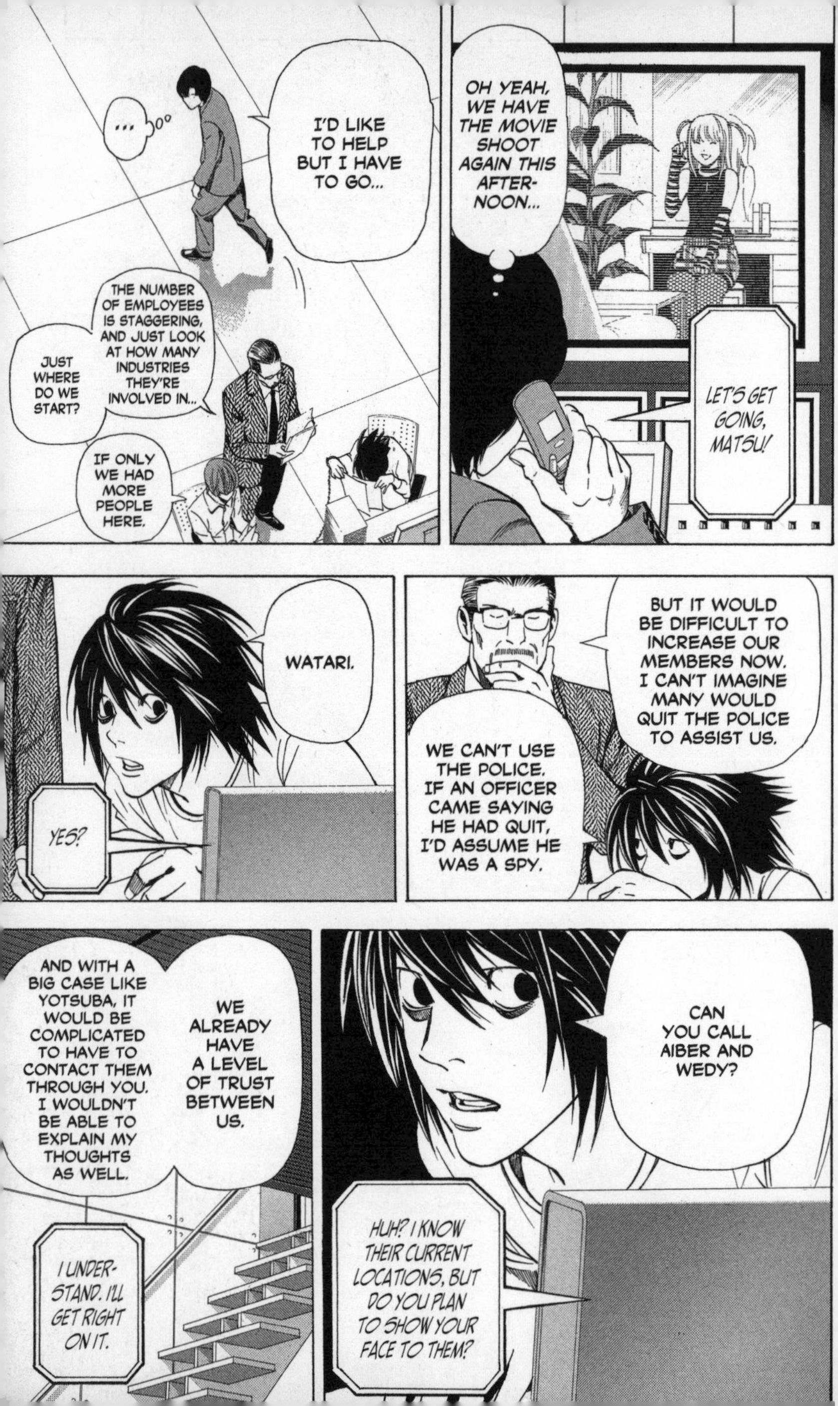
OH YEAH, WE HAVE THE MOVIE SHOOT AGAIN THIS AFTERNOON...
LET'S GET GOING, MATSU!
I'D LIKE TO HELP BUT I HAVE TO GO...
...
THE NUMBER OF EMPLOYEES IS STAGGERING, AND JUST LOOK AT HOW MANY INDUSTRIES THEY'RE INVOLVED IN...
JUST WHERE DO WE START?
IF ONLY WE HAD MORE PEOPLE HERE.
BUT IT WOULD BE DIFFICULT TO INCREASE OUR MEMBERS NOW. I CAN'T IMAGINE MANY WOULD QUIT THE POLICE TO ASSIST US.
WE CAN'T USE THE POLICE. IF AN OFFICER CAME SAYING HE HAD QUIT, I'D ASSUME HE WAS A SPY.
WATARI.
YES?
CAN YOU CALL AIBER AND WEDY?
HUH? I KNOW THEIR CURRENT LOCATIONS, BUT DO YOU PLAN TO SHOW YOUR FACE TO THEM?
WE ALREADY HAVE A LEVEL OF TRUST BETWEEN US.
AND WITH A BIG CASE LIKE YOTSUBA, IT WOULD BE COMPLICATED TO HAVE TO CONTACT THEM THROUGH YOU. I WOULDN'T BE ABLE TO EXPLAIN MY THOUGHTS AS WELL.
I UNDERSTAND. I'LL GET RIGHT ON IT.

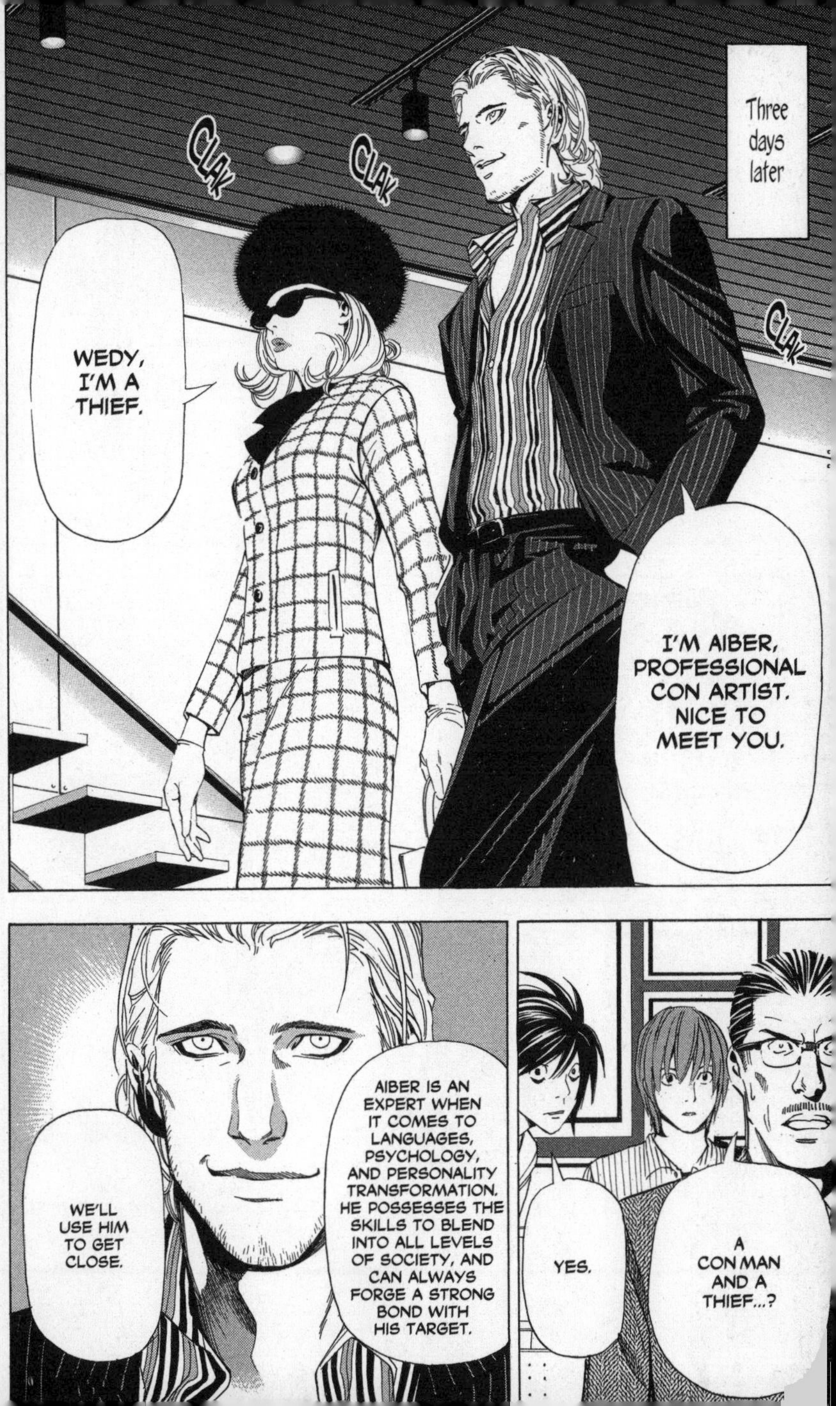
Three days later
CLAK
CLAK
CLAK
I'M AIBER, PROFESSIONAL CON ARTIST. NICE TO MEET YOU.
WEDY, I'M A THIEF.
A CON MAN AND A THIEF...?
YES.
AIBER IS AN EXPERT WHEN IT COMES TO LANGUAGES, PSYCHOLOGY, AND PERSONALITY TRANSFORMATION. HE POSSESSES THE SKILLS TO BLEND INTO ALL LEVELS OF SOCIETY, AND CAN ALWAYS FORGE A STRONG BOND WITH HIS TARGET.
WE'LL USE HIM TO GET CLOSE.

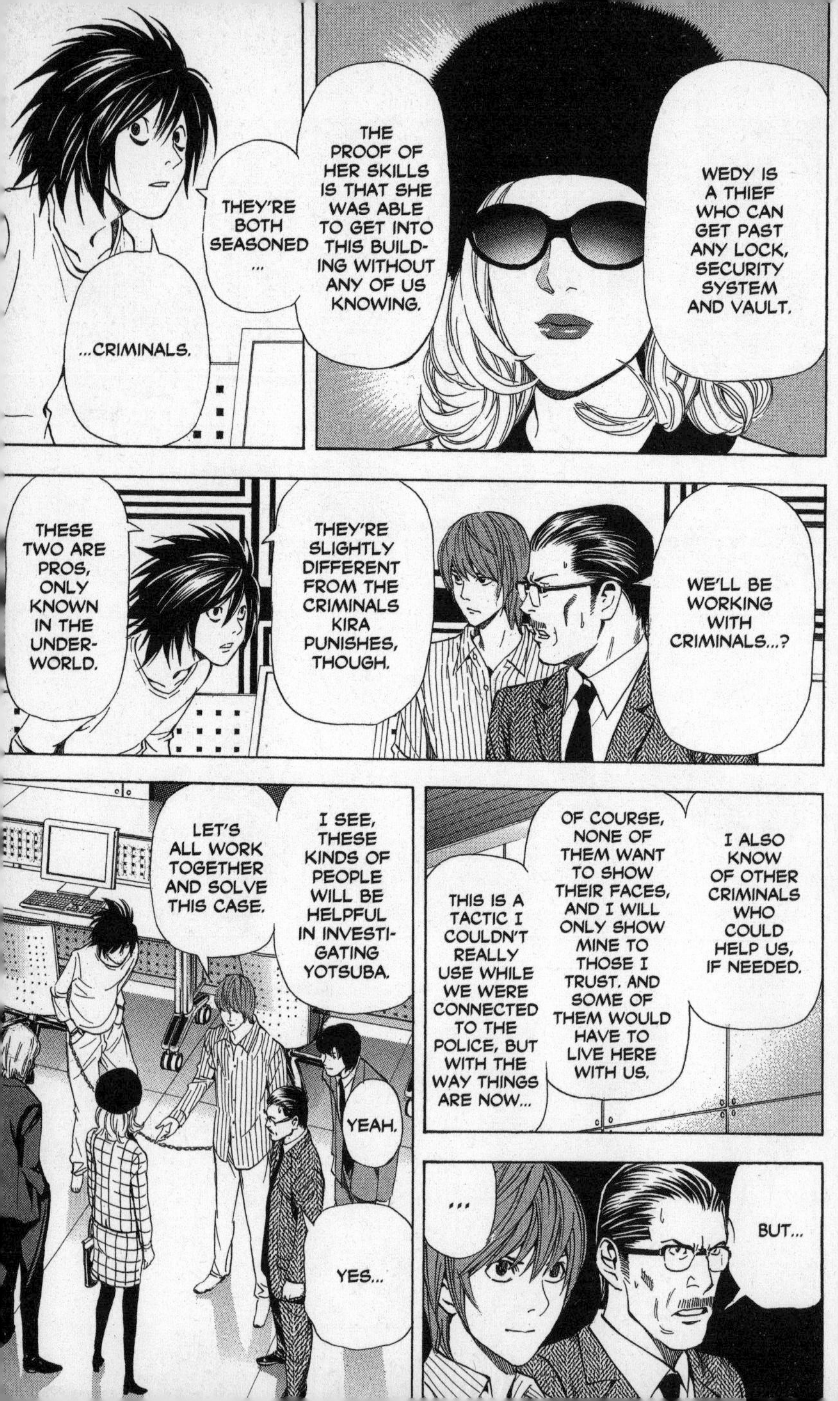

WEDY IS A THIEF WHO CAN GET PAST ANY LOCK, SECURITY SYSTEM AND VAULT.
THE PROOF OF HER SKILLS IS THAT SHE WAS ABLE TO GET INTO THIS BUILDING WITHOUT ANY OF US KNOWING.
THEY'RE BOTH SEASONED ...
...CRIMINALS.
WE'LL BE WORKING WITH CRIMINALS...?
THEY'RE SLIGHTLY DIFFERENT FROM THE CRIMINALS KIRA PUNISHES, THOUGH.
THESE TWO ARE PROS, ONLY KNOWN IN THE UNDERWORLD.
I ALSO KNOW OF OTHER CRIMINALS WHO COULD HELP US, IF NEEDED.
OF COURSE, NONE OF THEM WANT TO SHOW THEIR FACES, AND I WILL ONLY SHOW MINE TO THOSE I TRUST. AND SOME OF THEM WOULD HAVE TO LIVE HERE WITH US.
THIS IS A TACTIC I COULDN'T REALLY USE WHILE WE WERE CONNECTED TO THE POLICE, BUT WITH THE WAY THINGS ARE NOW...
BUT...
...
I SEE, THESE KINDS OF PEOPLE WILL BE HELPFUL IN INVESTIGATING YOTSUBA.
LET'S ALL WORK TOGETHER AND SOLVE THIS CASE.
YEAH.
YES...

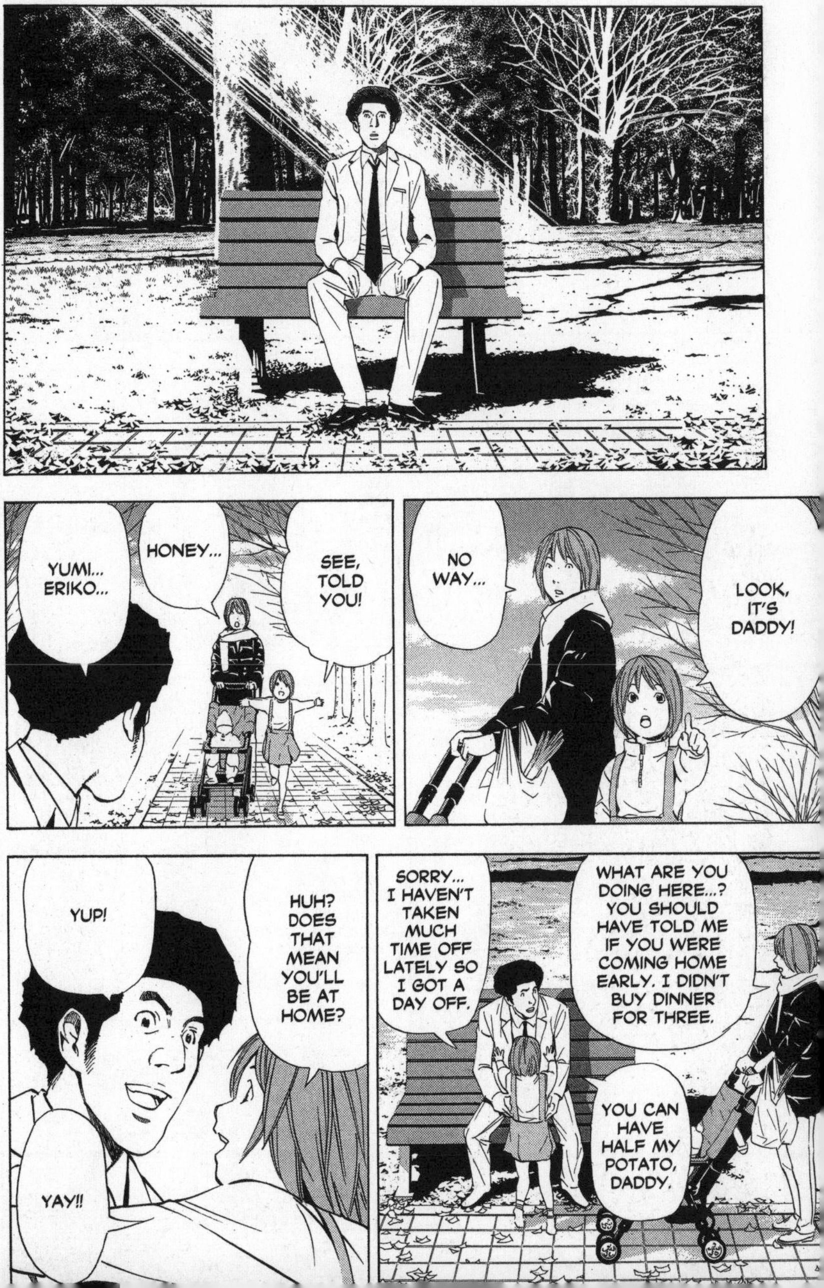
LOOK, IT'S DADDY!
NO WAY...
SEE, TOLD YOU!
HONEY...
YUMI... ERIKO...
WHAT ARE YOU DOING HERE...? YOU SHOULD HAVE TOLD ME IF YOU WERE COMING HOME EARLY. I DIDN'T BUY DINNER FOR THREE.
SORRY... I HAVEN'T TAKEN MUCH TIME OFF LATELY SO I GOT A DAY OFF.
YOU CAN HAVE HALF MY POTATO, DADDY.
HUH? DOES THAT MEAN YOU'LL BE AT HOME?
YUP!
YAY!!

READ THIS WAY

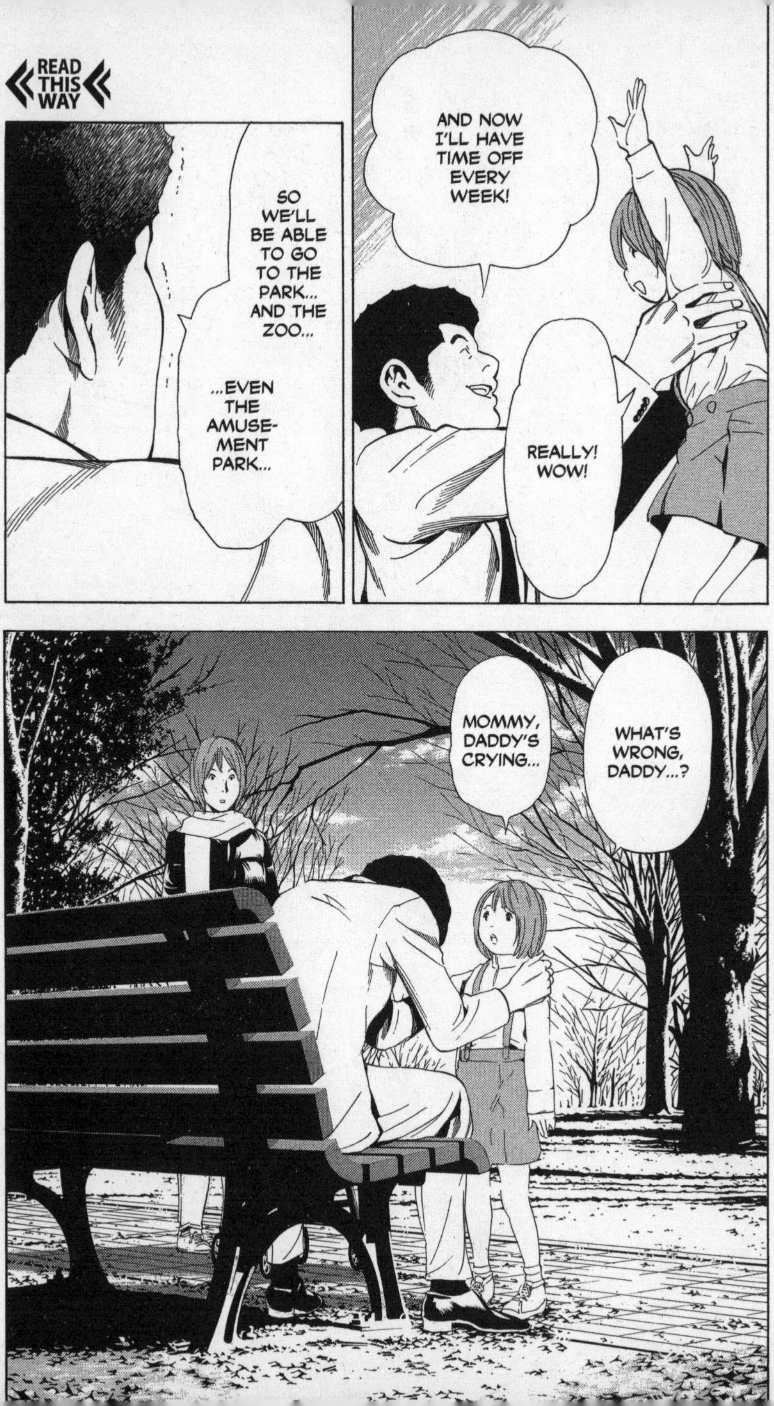
AND NOW I'LL HAVE TIME OFF EVERY WEEK!
REALLY! WOW!
SO WE'LL BE ABLE TO GO TO THE PARK... AND THE ZOO...
...EVEN THE AMUSEMENT PARK...
WHAT'S WRONG, DADDY...?
MOMMY, DADDY'S CRYING...

# DEATH NOTE

## How to Use It

## XXVIII

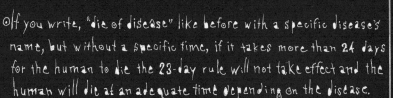

○ If you write, "die of disease" like before with a specific disease's name, but without a specific time, if it takes more than 24 days for the human to die the 23-day rule will not take effect and the human will die at an adequate time depending on the disease.

病死とし、病名は書き死の時間指定をしない場合、
その病気で死ぬのに24日間以上かかる時は
「死の時間を操れるのは23日間」は適用されず、
その病気で死ぬのに適した時に死ぬ。

○ When rewriting the cause and/or details of death it must be done within 6 minutes and 40 seconds. You cannot change the victim's time of death, however soon it may be.

上記の場合でも、死因や死の状況等を書き直せるのは6分40秒以内であり、
どんなに先の死であろうとその死の時間を動かす事はできない。

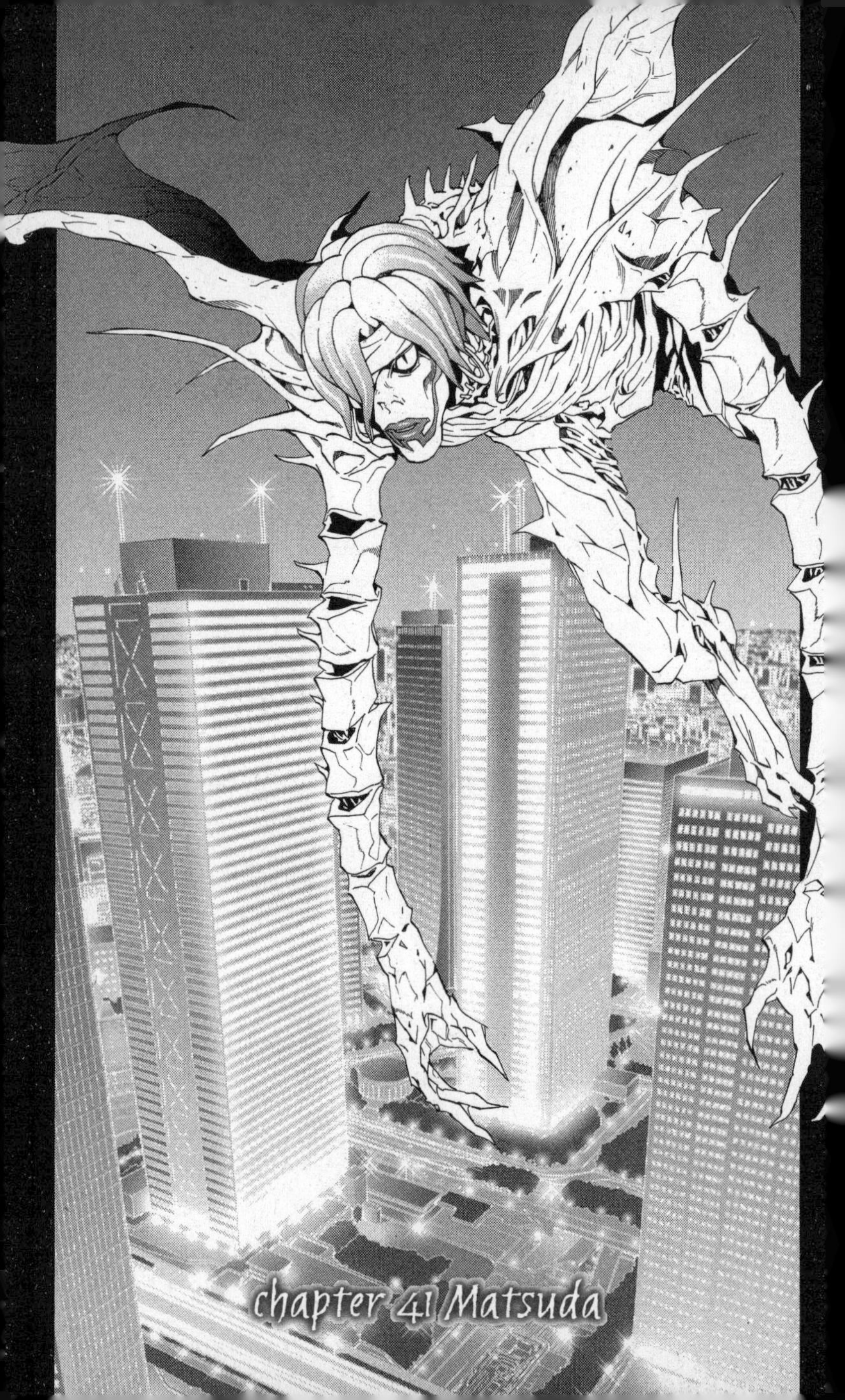
chapter 41 Matsuda

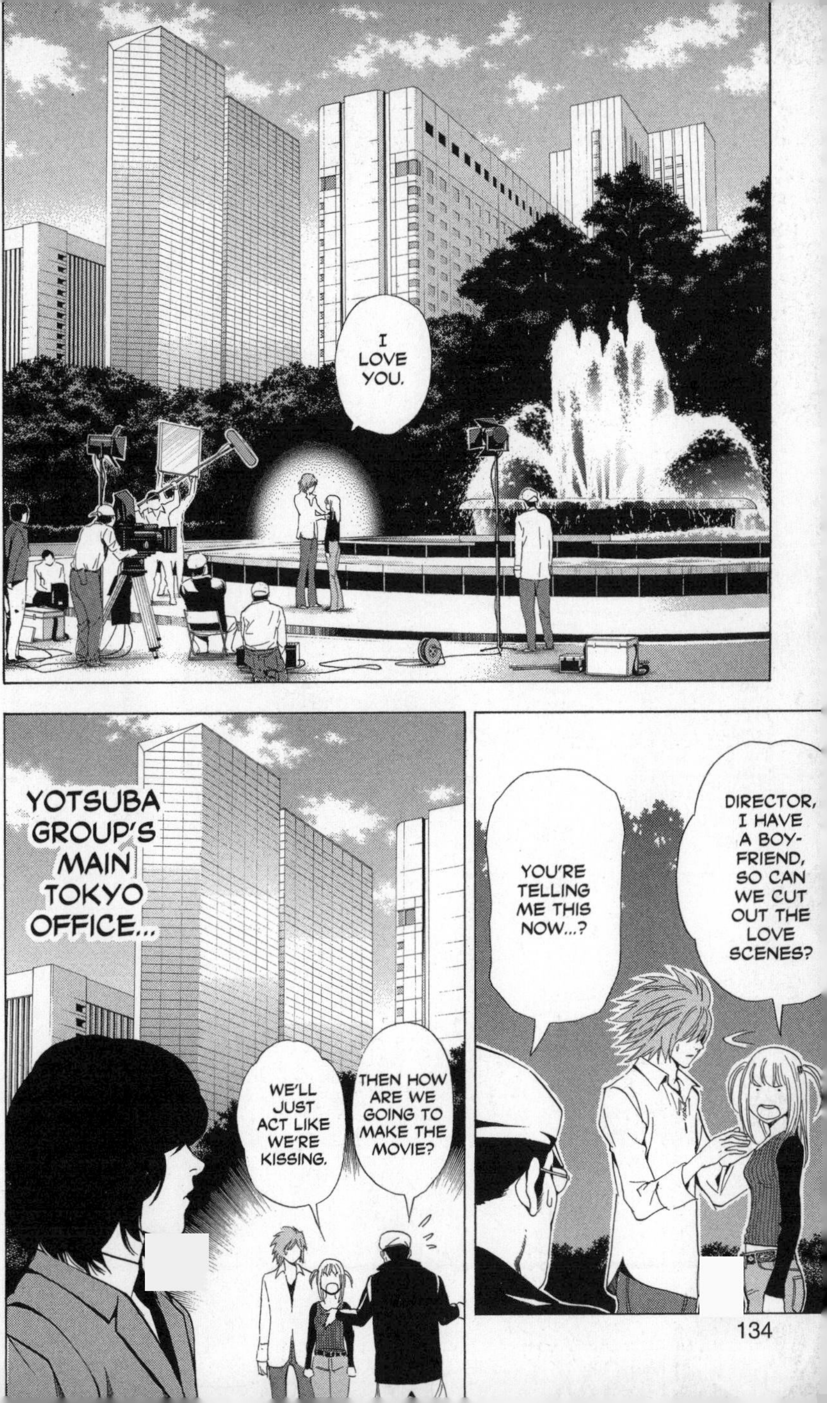
I LOVE YOU.
DIRECTOR, I HAVE A BOY-FRIEND, SO CAN WE CUT OUT THE LOVE SCENES?
YOU'RE TELLING ME THIS NOW...?
YOTSUBA GROUP'S MAIN TOKYO OFFICE...
THEN HOW ARE WE GOING TO MAKE THE MOVIE?
WE'LL JUST ACT LIKE WE'RE KISSING.

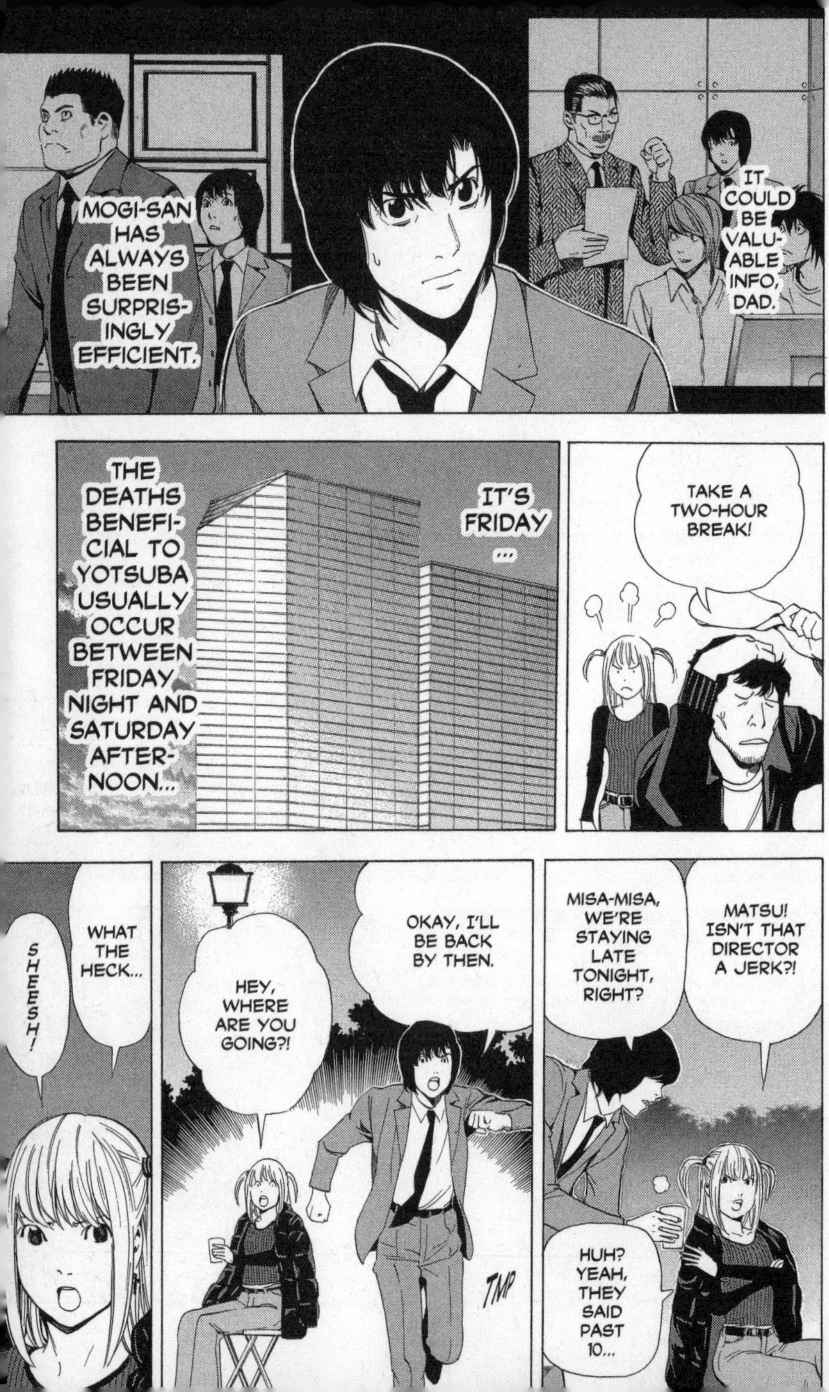
IT COULD BE VALUABLE INFO, DAD.
MOGI-SAN HAS ALWAYS BEEN SURPRISINGLY EFFICIENT.
TAKE A TWO-HOUR BREAK!
IT'S FRIDAY ...
THE DEATHS BENEFICIAL TO YOTSUBA USUALLY OCCUR BETWEEN FRIDAY NIGHT AND SATURDAY AFTERNOON...
MATSU! ISN'T THAT DIRECTOR A JERK?!
MISA-MISA, WE'RE STAYING LATE TONIGHT, RIGHT?
HUH? YEAH, THEY SAID PAST 10...
OKAY, I'LL BE BACK BY THEN.
HEY, WHERE ARE YOU GOING?!
TMP
WHAT THE HECK...
SHEESH!

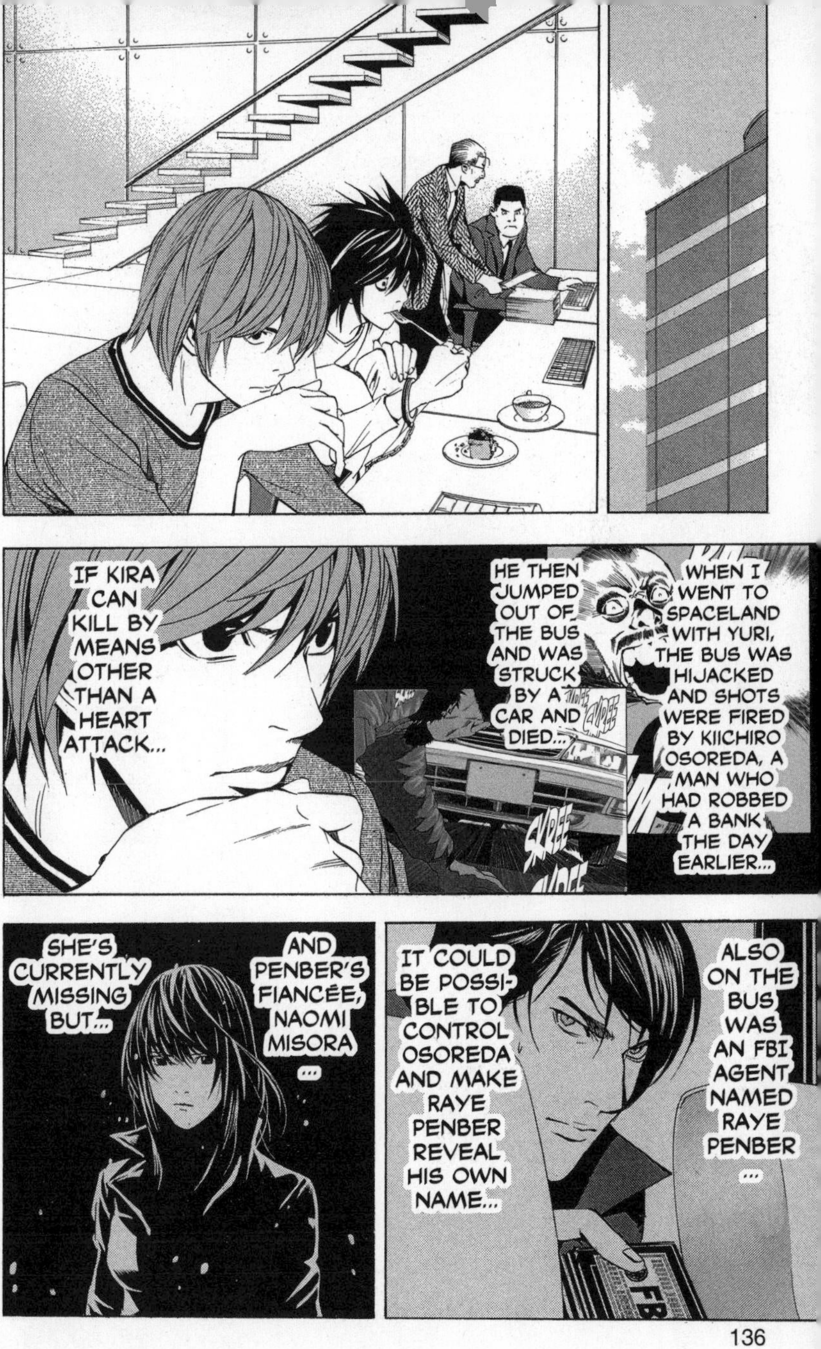
WHEN I WENT TO SPACELAND WITH YURI, THE BUS WAS HIJACKED AND SHOTS WERE FIRED BY KIICHIRO OSOREDA, A MAN WHO HAD ROBBED A BANK THE DAY EARLIER...
HE THEN JUMPED OUT OF THE BUS AND WAS STRUCK BY A CAR AND DIED...
IF KIRA CAN KILL BY MEANS OTHER THAN A HEART ATTACK...
ALSO ON THE BUS WAS AN FBI AGENT NAMED RAYE PENBER ...
IT COULD BE POSSI-BLE TO CONTROL OSOREDA AND MAKE RAYE PENBER REVEAL HIS OWN NAME...
AND PENBER'S FIANCÉE, NAOMI MISORA ...
SHE'S CURRENTLY MISSING BUT...
FBI

READ THIS WAY

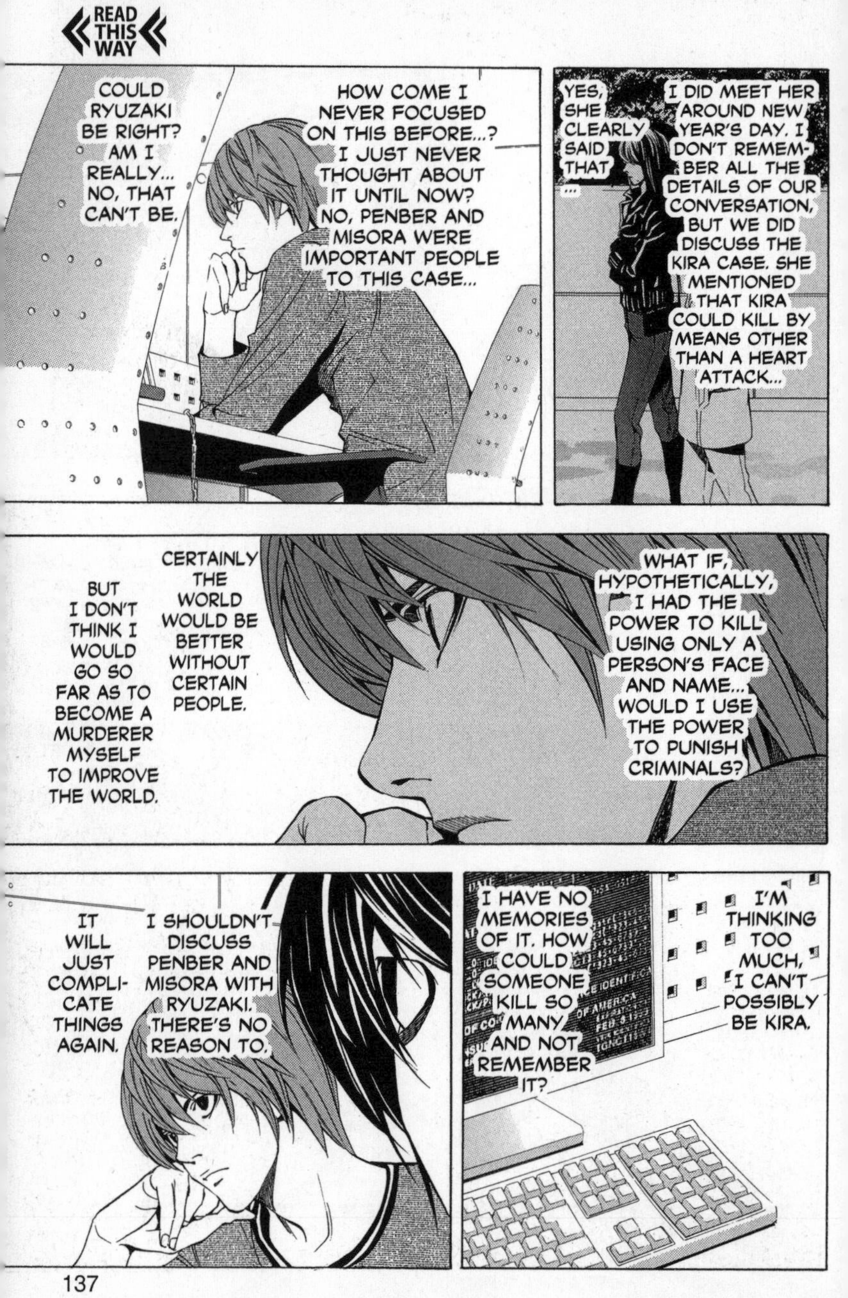

I DID MEET HER AROUND NEW YEAR'S DAY. I DON'T REMEMBER ALL THE DETAILS OF OUR CONVERSATION, BUT WE DID DISCUSS THE KIRA CASE. SHE MENTIONED THAT KIRA COULD KILL BY MEANS OTHER THAN A HEART ATTACK...
YES, SHE CLEARLY SAID THAT...
HOW COME I NEVER FOCUSED ON THIS BEFORE...? I JUST NEVER THOUGHT ABOUT IT UNTIL NOW? NO, PENBER AND MISORA WERE IMPORTANT PEOPLE TO THIS CASE...
COULD RYUZAKI BE RIGHT? AM I REALLY... NO, THAT CAN'T BE.
WHAT IF, HYPOTHETICALLY, I HAD THE POWER TO KILL USING ONLY A PERSON'S FACE AND NAME... WOULD I USE THE POWER TO PUNISH CRIMINALS?
CERTAINLY THE WORLD WOULD BE BETTER WITHOUT CERTAIN PEOPLE.
BUT I DON'T THINK I WOULD GO SO FAR AS TO BECOME A MURDERER MYSELF TO IMPROVE THE WORLD.
I'M THINKING TOO MUCH, I CAN'T POSSIBLY BE KIRA.
I HAVE NO MEMORIES OF IT. HOW COULD SOMEONE KILL SO MANY AND NOT REMEMBER IT?
I SHOULDN'T DISCUSS PENBER AND MISORA WITH RYUZAKI. THERE'S NO REASON TO.
IT WILL JUST COMPLICATE THINGS AGAIN.

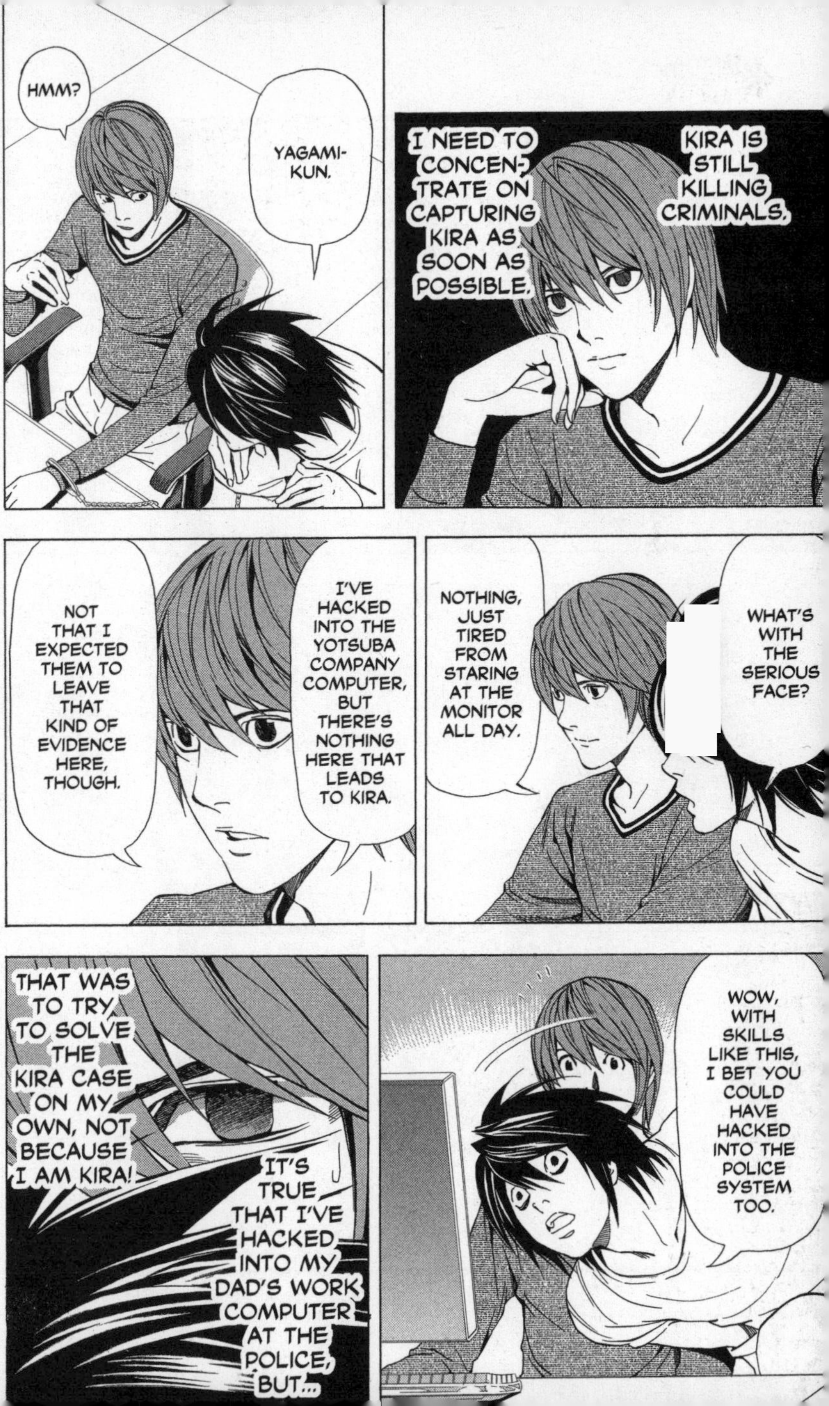
KIRA IS STILL KILLING CRIMINALS.
I NEED TO CONCEN-TRATE ON CAPTURING KIRA AS SOON AS POSSIBLE.
YAGAMI-KUN.
HMM?
WHAT'S WITH THE SERIOUS FACE?
NOTHING, JUST TIRED FROM STARING AT THE MONITOR ALL DAY.
I'VE HACKED INTO THE YOTSUBA COMPANY COMPUTER, BUT THERE'S NOTHING HERE THAT LEADS TO KIRA.
NOT THAT I EXPECTED THEM TO LEAVE THAT KIND OF EVIDENCE HERE, THOUGH.
WOW, WITH SKILLS LIKE THIS, I BET YOU COULD HAVE HACKED INTO THE POLICE SYSTEM TOO.
IT'S TRUE THAT I'VE HACKED INTO MY DAD'S WORK COMPUTER AT THE POLICE, BUT...
THAT WAS TO TRY TO SOLVE THE KIRA CASE ON MY OWN, NOT BECAUSE I AM KIRA!

READ THIS WAY

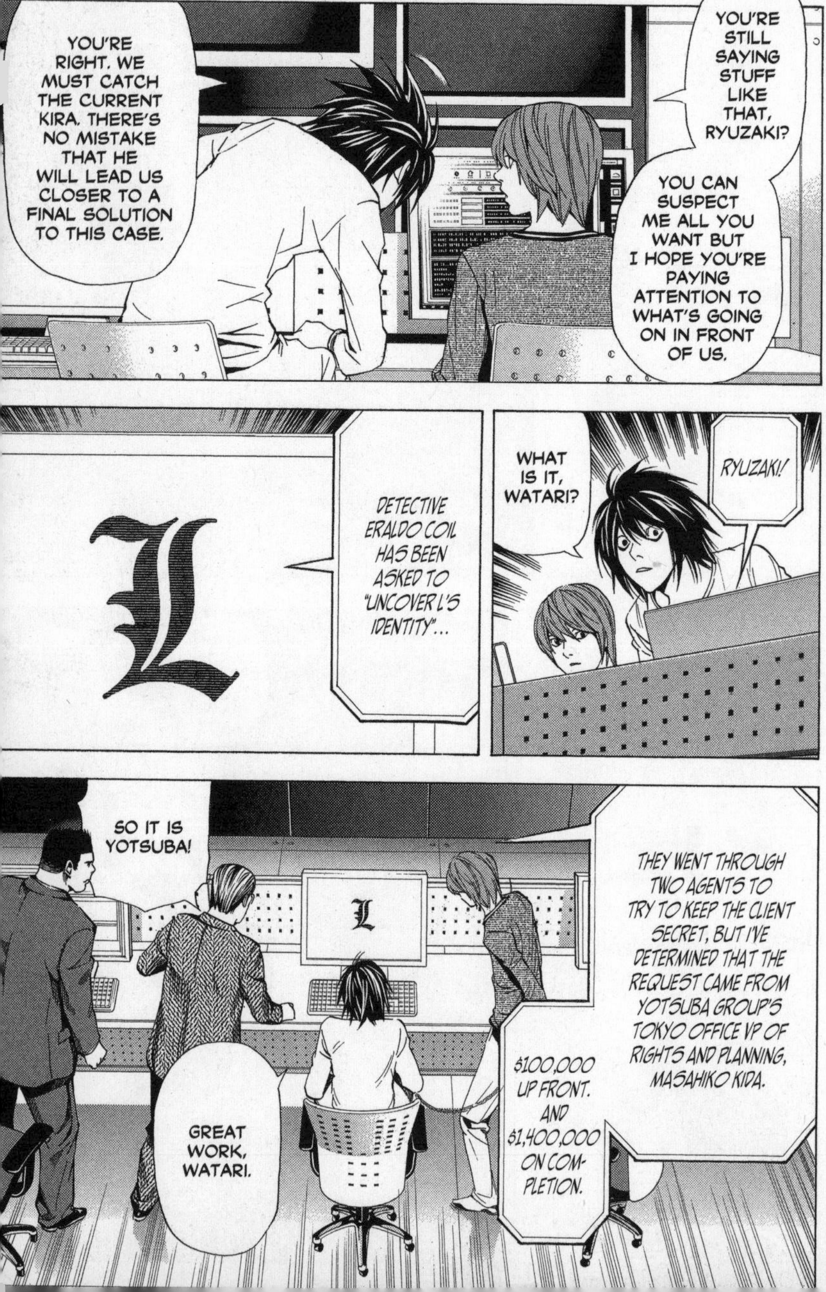
YOU'RE STILL SAYING STUFF LIKE THAT, RYUZAKI?
YOU CAN SUSPECT ME ALL YOU WANT BUT I HOPE YOU'RE PAYING ATTENTION TO WHAT'S GOING ON IN FRONT OF US.
YOU'RE RIGHT. WE MUST CATCH THE CURRENT KIRA. THERE'S NO MISTAKE THAT HE WILL LEAD US CLOSER TO A FINAL SOLUTION TO THIS CASE.
RYUZAKI!
WHAT IS IT, WATARI?
L
DETECTIVE ERALDO COIL HAS BEEN ASKED TO "UNCOVER L'S IDENTITY"...
THEY WENT THROUGH TWO AGENTS TO TRY TO KEEP THE CLIENT SECRET, BUT I'VE DETERMINED THAT THE REQUEST CAME FROM YOTSUBA GROUP'S TOKYO OFFICE VP OF RIGHTS AND PLANNING, MASAHIKO KIDA.
$100,000 UP FRONT. AND $1,400,000 ON COMPLETION.
SO IT IS YOTSUBA!
L
GREAT WORK, WATARI.

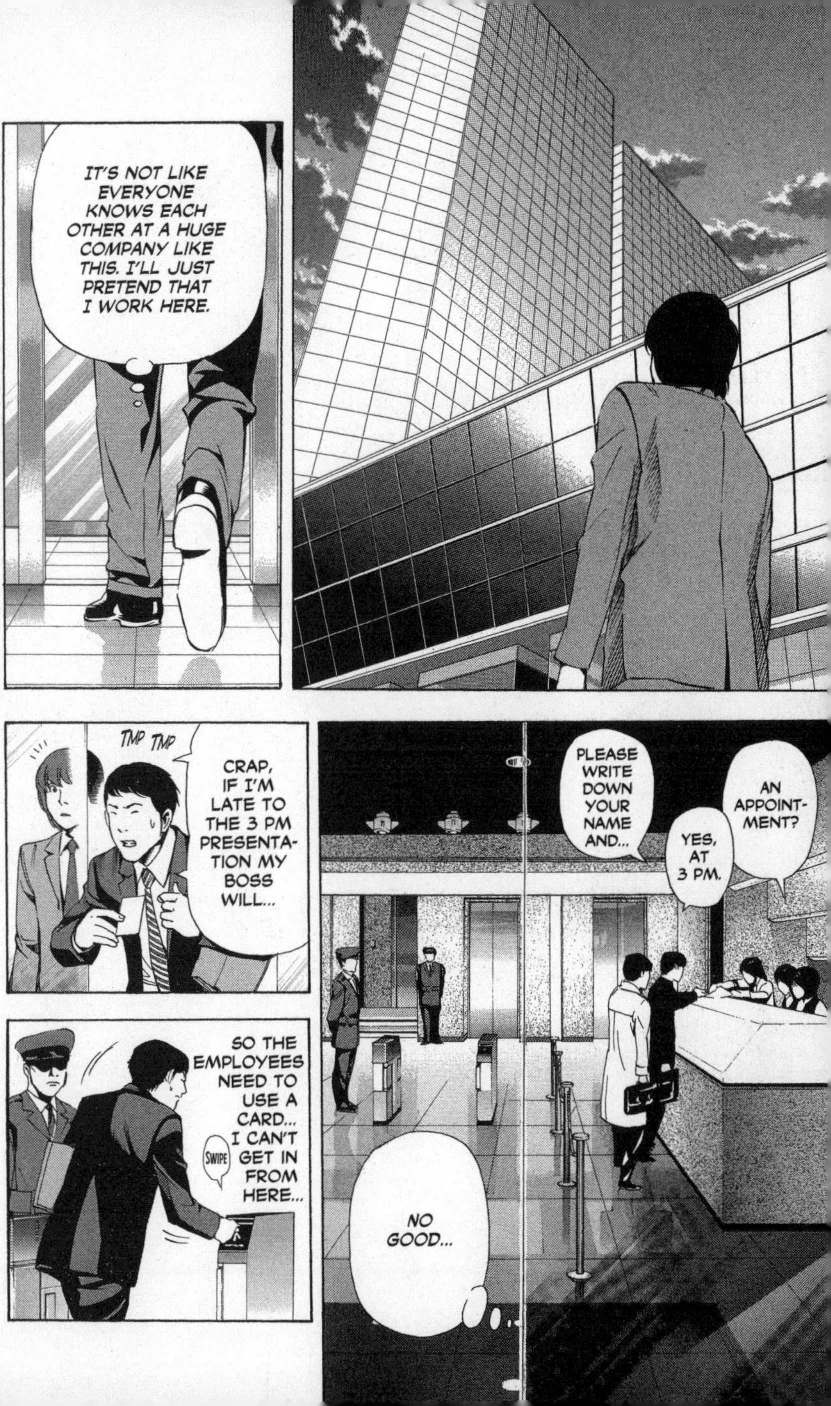
IT'S NOT LIKE EVERYONE KNOWS EACH OTHER AT A HUGE COMPANY LIKE THIS. I'LL JUST PRETEND THAT I WORK HERE.
AN APPOINTMENT?
YES, AT 3 PM.
PLEASE WRITE DOWN YOUR NAME AND...
NO GOOD...
TMP TMP
CRAP, IF I'M LATE TO THE 3 PM PRESENTATION MY BOSS WILL...
SO THE EMPLOYEES NEED TO USE A CARD... I CAN'T GET IN FROM HERE...
SWIPE

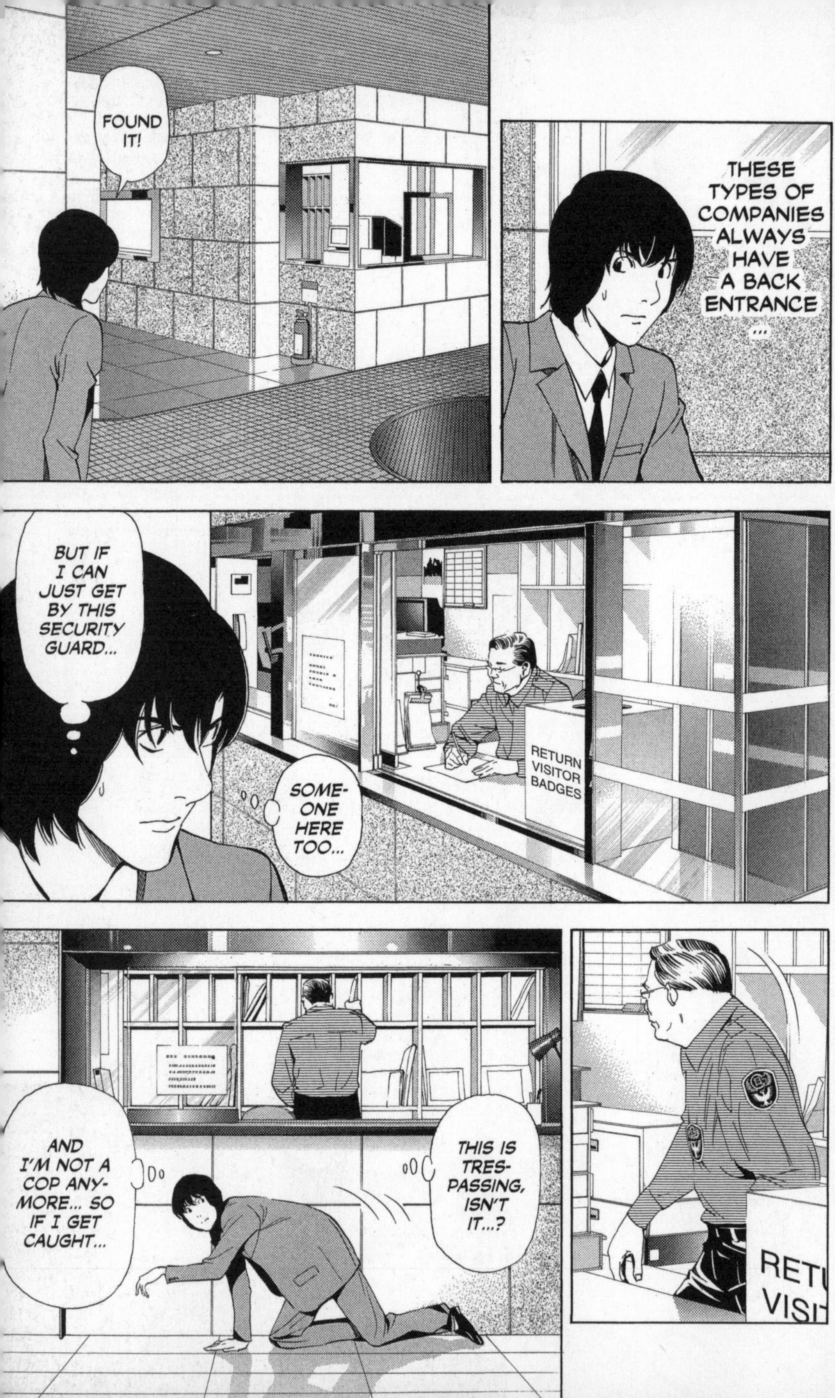
THESE TYPES OF COMPANIES ALWAYS HAVE A BACK ENTRANCE...
FOUND IT!
SOME-ONE HERE TOO...
BUT IF I CAN JUST GET BY THIS SECURITY GUARD...
RETURN VISITOR BADGES
THIS IS TRES-PASSING, ISN'T IT...?
AND I'M NOT A COP ANY-MORE... SO IF I GET CAUGHT...

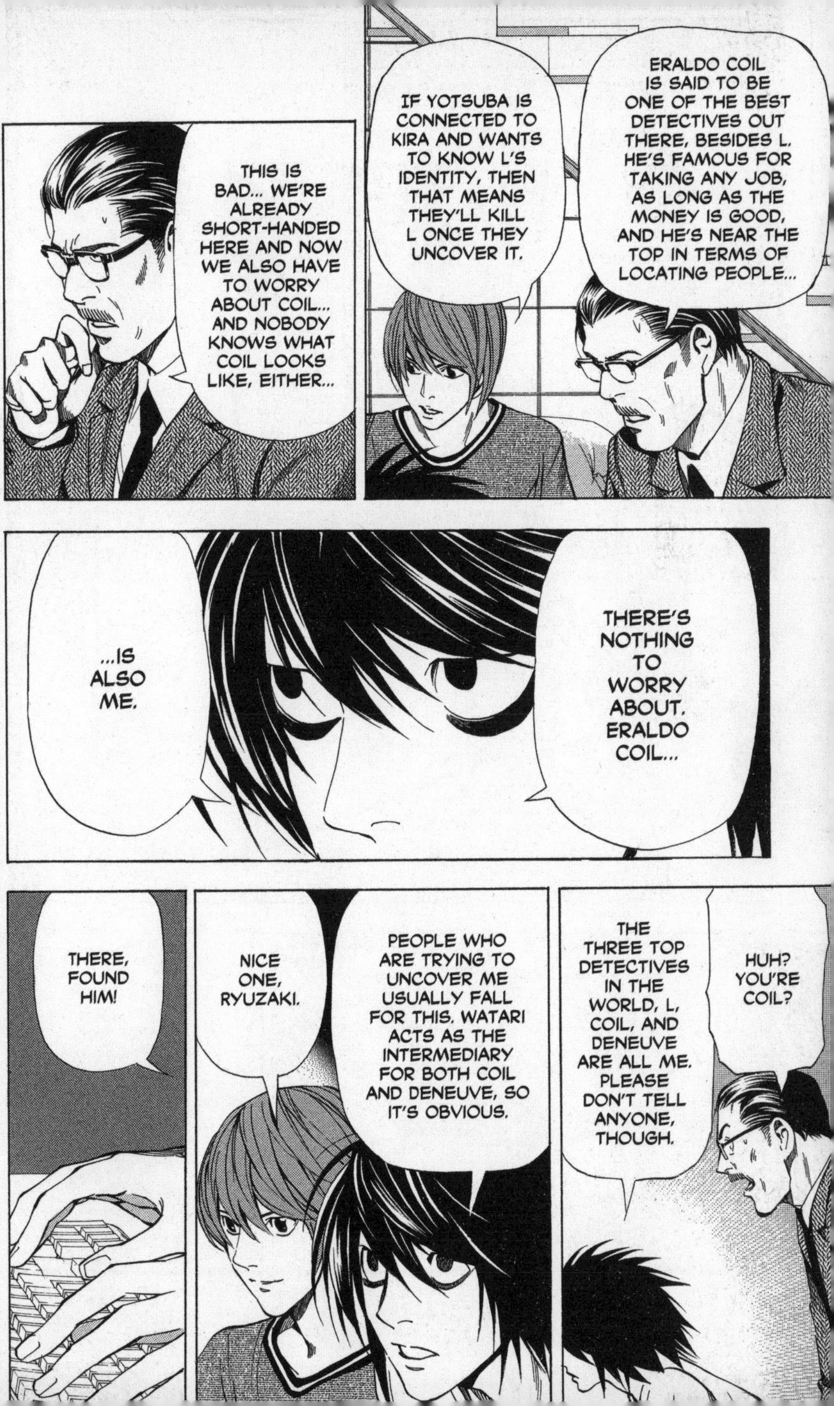
ERALDO COIL IS SAID TO BE ONE OF THE BEST DETECTIVES OUT THERE, BESIDES L. HE'S FAMOUS FOR TAKING ANY JOB, AS LONG AS THE MONEY IS GOOD, AND HE'S NEAR THE TOP IN TERMS OF LOCATING PEOPLE...
IF YOTSUBA IS CONNECTED TO KIRA AND WANTS TO KNOW L'S IDENTITY, THEN THAT MEANS THEY'LL KILL L ONCE THEY UNCOVER IT.
THIS IS BAD... WE'RE ALREADY SHORT-HANDED HERE AND NOW WE ALSO HAVE TO WORRY ABOUT COIL... AND NOBODY KNOWS WHAT COIL LOOKS LIKE, EITHER...
THERE'S NOTHING TO WORRY ABOUT. ERALDO COIL...
...IS ALSO ME.
HUH? YOU'RE COIL?
THE THREE TOP DETECTIVES IN THE WORLD, L, COIL, AND DENEUVE ARE ALL ME. PLEASE DON'T TELL ANYONE, THOUGH.
PEOPLE WHO ARE TRYING TO UNCOVER ME USUALLY FALL FOR THIS. WATARI ACTS AS THE INTERMEDIARY FOR BOTH COIL AND DENEUVE, SO IT'S OBVIOUS.
NICE ONE, RYUZAKI.
THERE, FOUND HIM!

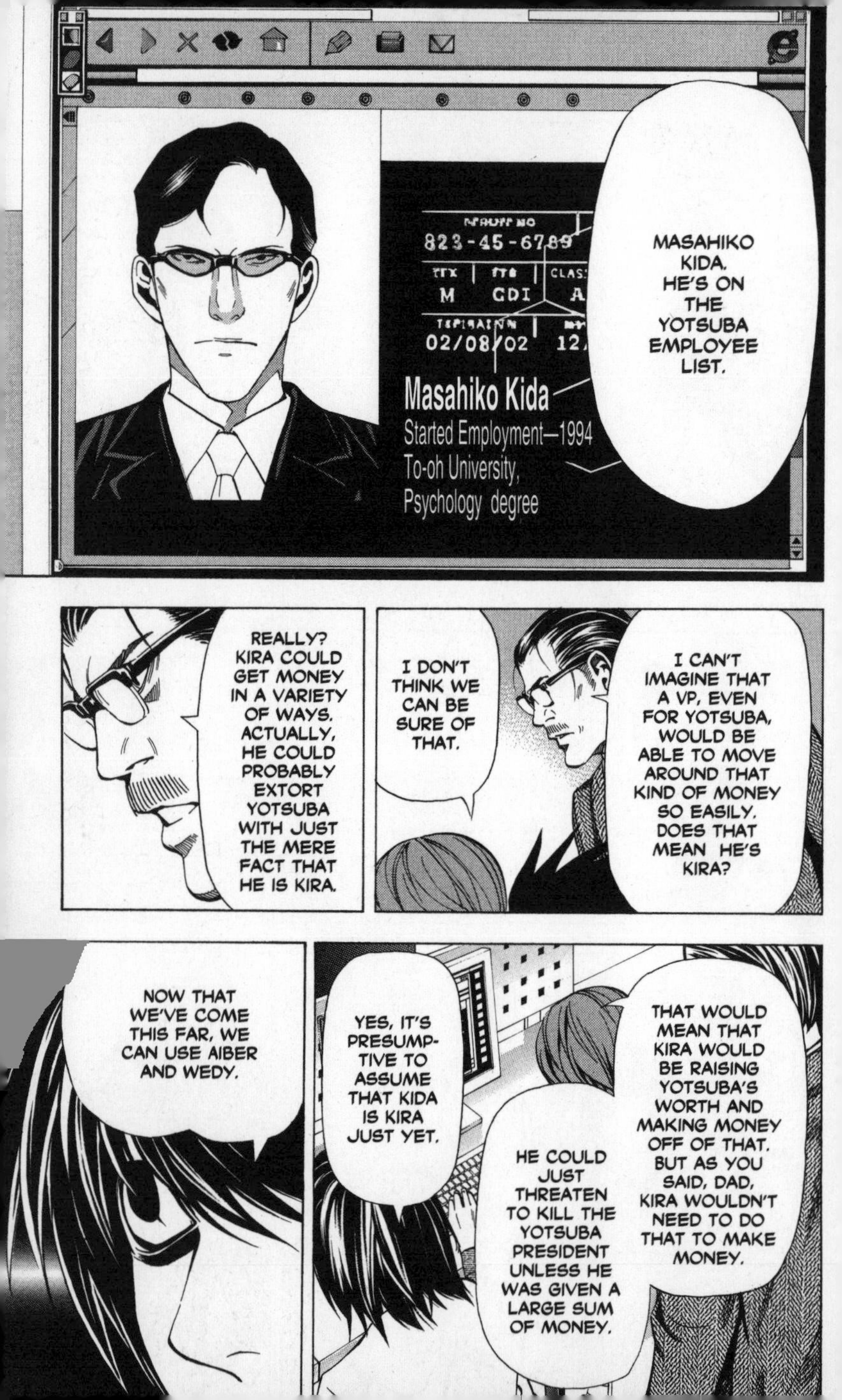

MASAHIKO KIDA. HE'S ON THE YOTSUBA EMPLOYEE LIST.
823-45-6789
M
CDI
A
02/08/02
Masahiko Kida
Started Employment—1994
To-oh University,
Psychology degree
I CAN'T IMAGINE THAT A VP, EVEN FOR YOTSUBA, WOULD BE ABLE TO MOVE AROUND THAT KIND OF MONEY SO EASILY. DOES THAT MEAN HE'S KIRA?
I DON'T THINK WE CAN BE SURE OF THAT.
REALLY? KIRA COULD GET MONEY IN A VARIETY OF WAYS. ACTUALLY, HE COULD PROBABLY EXTORT YOTSUBA WITH JUST THE MERE FACT THAT HE IS KIRA.
THAT WOULD MEAN THAT KIRA WOULD BE RAISING YOTSUBA'S WORTH AND MAKING MONEY OFF OF THAT. BUT AS YOU SAID, DAD, KIRA WOULDN'T NEED TO DO THAT TO MAKE MONEY.
HE COULD JUST THREATEN TO KILL THE YOTSUBA PRESIDENT UNLESS HE WAS GIVEN A LARGE SUM OF MONEY.
YES, IT'S PRESUMP-TIVE TO ASSUME THAT KIDA IS KIRA JUST YET.
NOW THAT WE'VE COME THIS FAR, WE CAN USE AIBER AND WEDY.

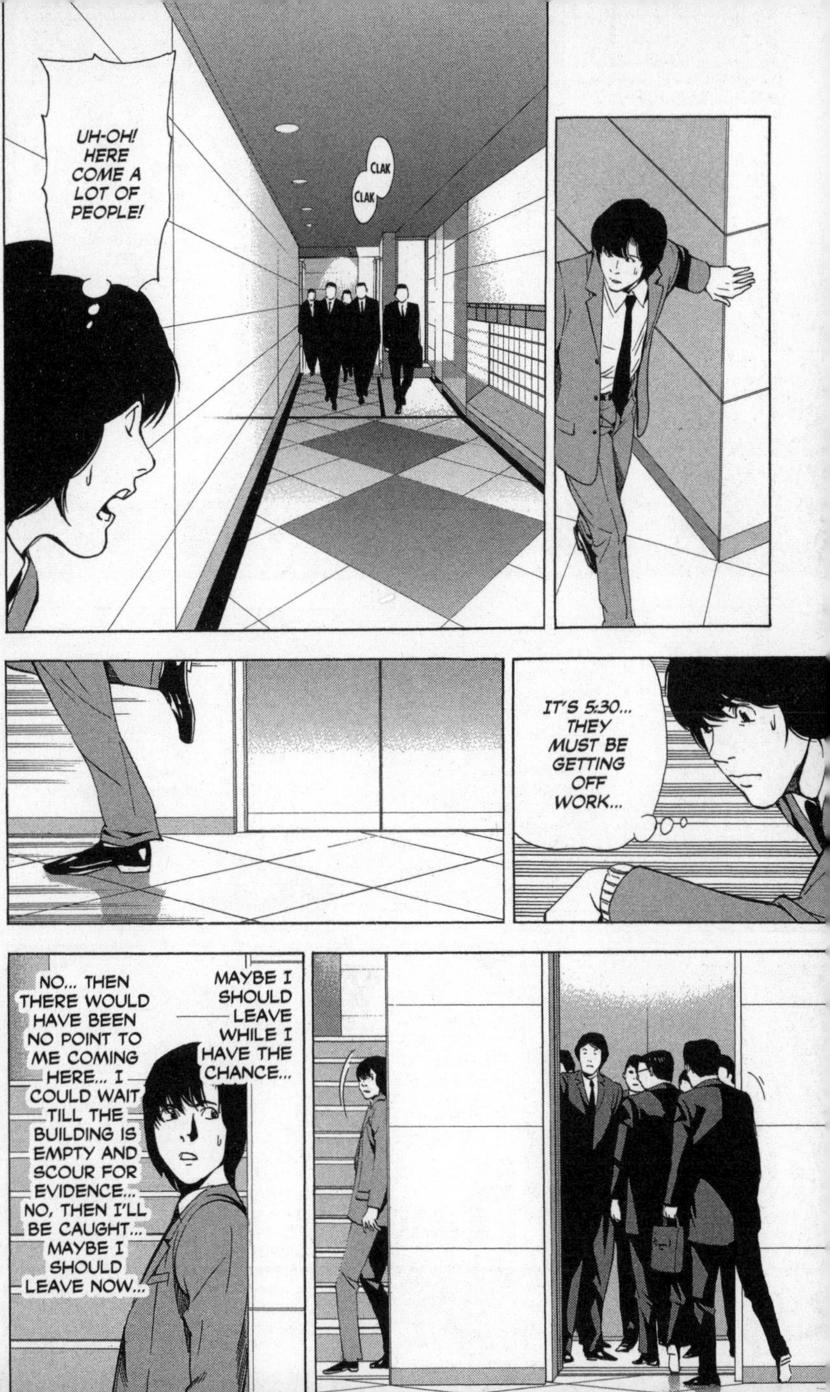
UH-OH! HERE COME A LOT OF PEOPLE!
CLAK
CLAK
IT'S 5:30... THEY MUST BE GETTING OFF WORK...
MAYBE I SHOULD LEAVE WHILE I HAVE THE CHANCE...
NO... THEN THERE WOULD HAVE BEEN NO POINT TO ME COMING HERE... I COULD WAIT TILL THE BUILDING IS EMPTY AND SCOUR FOR EVIDENCE... NO, THEN I'LL BE CAUGHT... MAYBE I SHOULD LEAVE NOW...

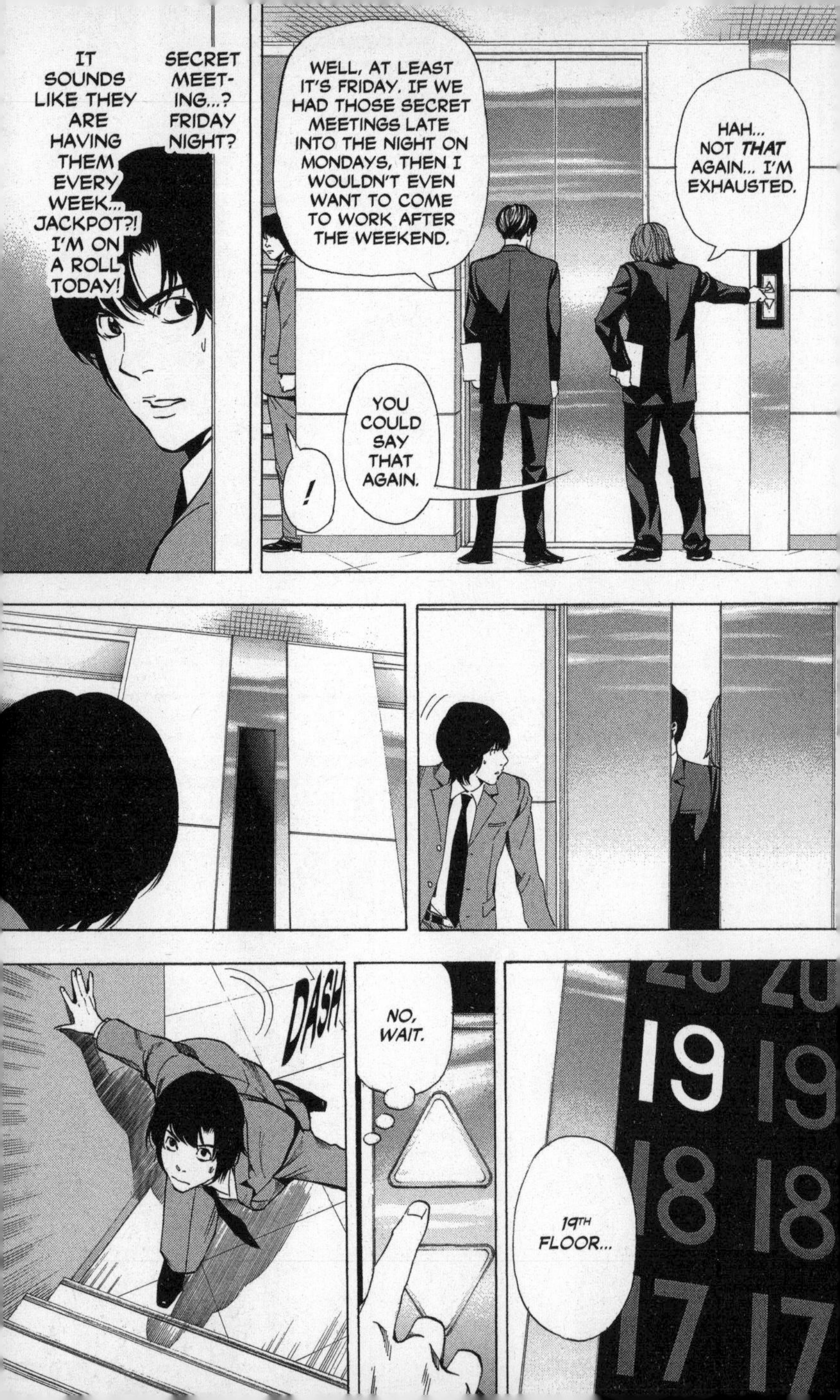
HAH... NOT *THAT* AGAIN... I'M EXHAUSTED.
WELL, AT LEAST IT'S FRIDAY. IF WE HAD THOSE SECRET MEETINGS LATE INTO THE NIGHT ON MONDAYS, THEN I WOULDN'T EVEN WANT TO COME TO WORK AFTER THE WEEKEND.
YOU COULD SAY THAT AGAIN.
!
SECRET MEETING...? FRIDAY NIGHT?
IT SOUNDS LIKE THEY ARE HAVING THEM EVERY WEEK... JACKPOT?! I'M ON A ROLL TODAY!
19 19
18 18
17 17
19TH FLOOR...
NO, WAIT.
DASH

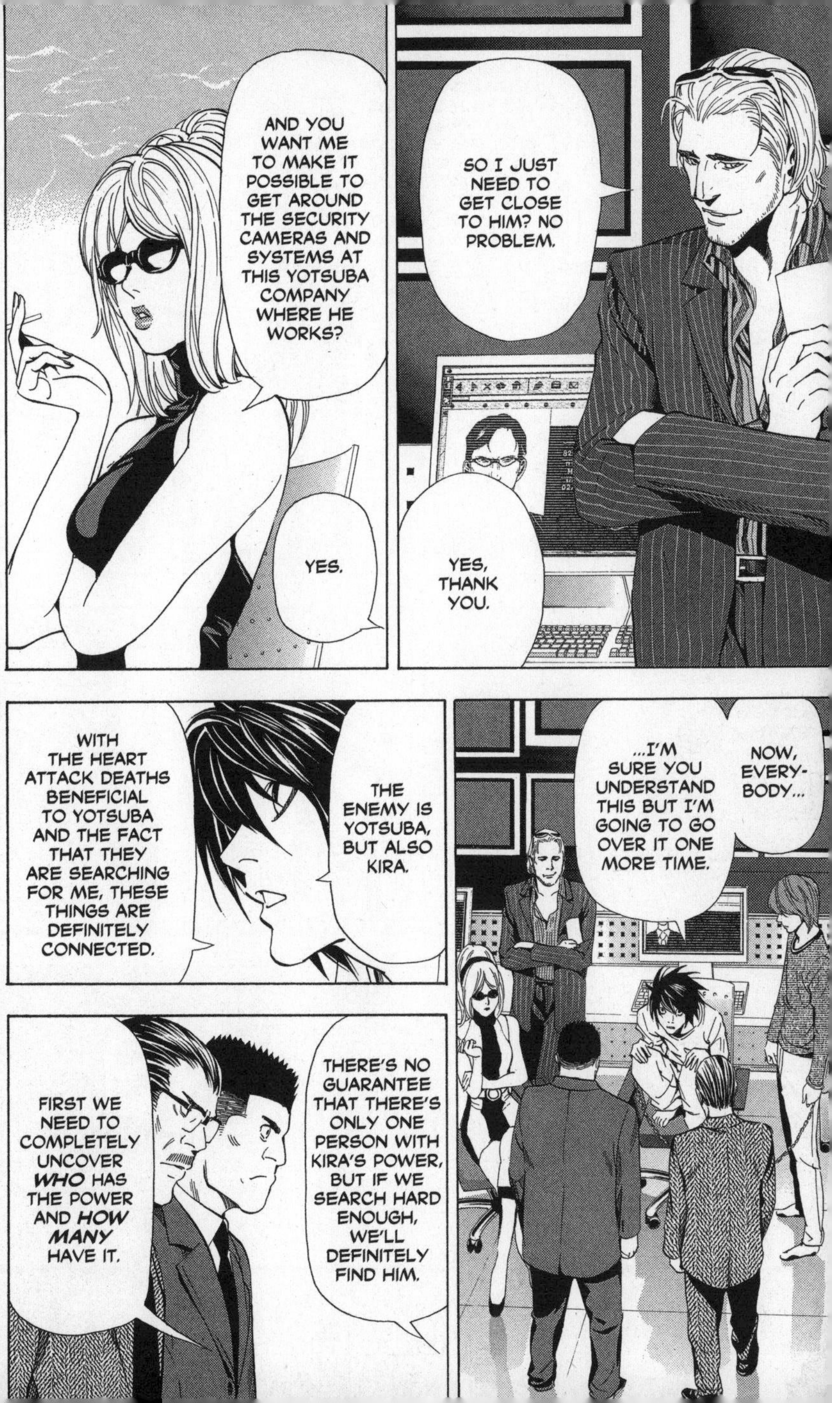
SO I JUST NEED TO GET CLOSE TO HIM? NO PROBLEM.
YES, THANK YOU.
AND YOU WANT ME TO MAKE IT POSSIBLE TO GET AROUND THE SECURITY CAMERAS AND SYSTEMS AT THIS YOTSUBA COMPANY WHERE HE WORKS?
YES.
NOW, EVERYBODY...
...I'M SURE YOU UNDERSTAND THIS BUT I'M GOING TO GO OVER IT ONE MORE TIME.
THE ENEMY IS YOTSUBA, BUT ALSO KIRA.
WITH THE HEART ATTACK DEATHS BENEFICIAL TO YOTSUBA AND THE FACT THAT THEY ARE SEARCHING FOR ME, THESE THINGS ARE DEFINITELY CONNECTED.
THERE'S NO GUARANTEE THAT THERE'S ONLY ONE PERSON WITH KIRA'S POWER, BUT IF WE SEARCH HARD ENOUGH, WE'LL DEFINITELY FIND HIM.
FIRST WE NEED TO COMPLETELY UNCOVER *WHO* HAS THE POWER AND *HOW MANY* HAVE IT.

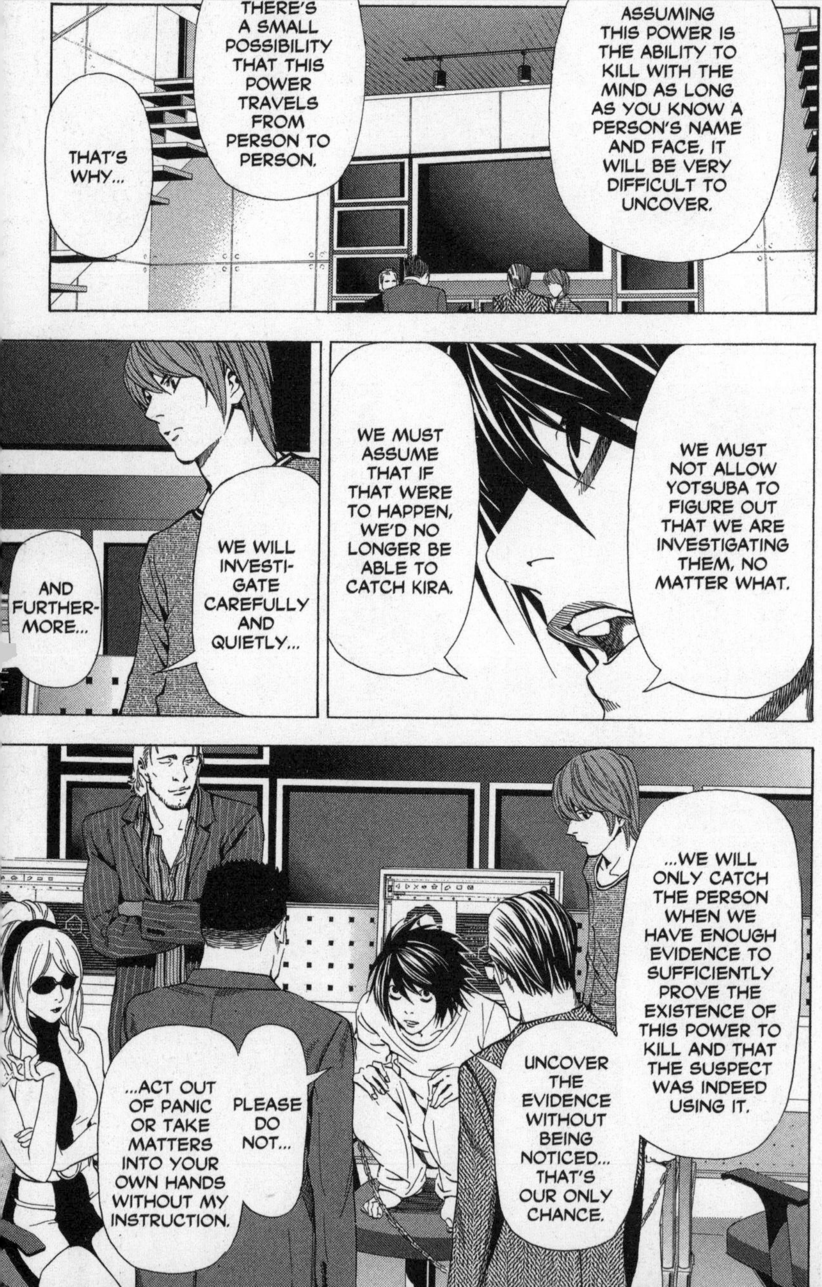
ASSUMING THIS POWER IS THE ABILITY TO KILL WITH THE MIND AS LONG AS YOU KNOW A PERSON'S NAME AND FACE, IT WILL BE VERY DIFFICULT TO UNCOVER.
AND THERE'S A SMALL POSSIBILITY THAT THIS POWER TRAVELS FROM PERSON TO PERSON.
THAT'S WHY...
WE MUST NOT ALLOW YOTSUBA TO FIGURE OUT THAT WE ARE INVESTIGATING THEM, NO MATTER WHAT.
WE MUST ASSUME THAT IF THAT WERE TO HAPPEN, WE'D NO LONGER BE ABLE TO CATCH KIRA.
WE WILL INVESTI-GATE CAREFULLY AND QUIETLY...
AND FURTHER-MORE...
...WE WILL ONLY CATCH THE PERSON WHEN WE HAVE ENOUGH EVIDENCE TO SUFFICIENTLY PROVE THE EXISTENCE OF THIS POWER TO KILL AND THAT THE SUSPECT WAS INDEED USING IT.
UNCOVER THE EVIDENCE WITHOUT BEING NOTICED... THAT'S OUR ONLY CHANCE.
PLEASE DO NOT...
...ACT OUT OF PANIC OR TAKE MATTERS INTO YOUR OWN HANDS WITHOUT MY INSTRUCTION.

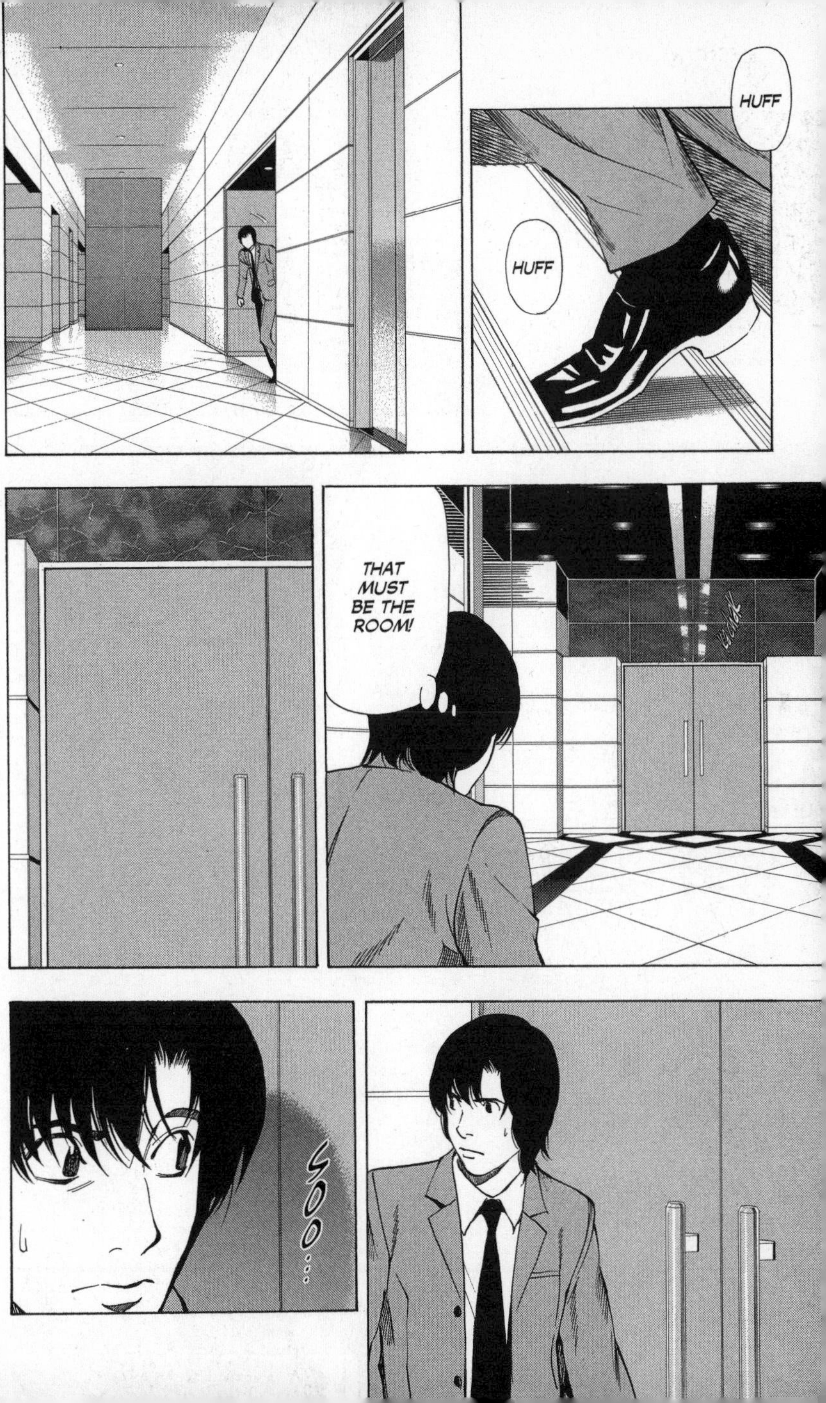
HUFF
HUFF
THAT MUST BE THE ROOM!
SOO...

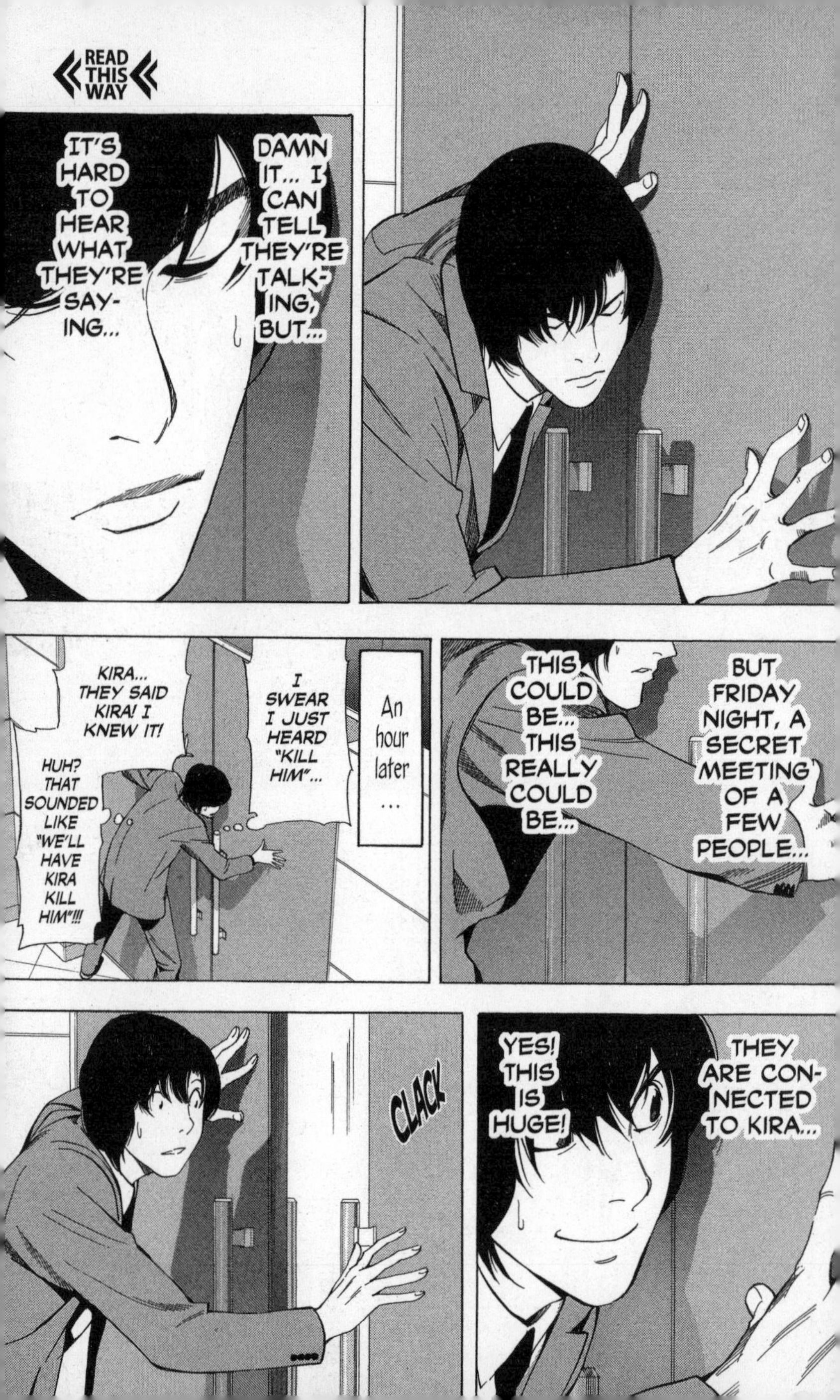
READ THIS WAY
DAMN IT... I CAN TELL THEY'RE TALKING, BUT...
IT'S HARD TO HEAR WHAT THEY'RE SAYING...
BUT FRIDAY NIGHT, A SECRET MEETING OF A FEW PEOPLE...
THIS COULD BE... THIS REALLY COULD BE...
An hour later...
I SWEAR I JUST HEARD "KILL HIM"...
KIRA... THEY SAID KIRA! I KNEW IT!
HUH? THAT SOUNDED LIKE "WE'LL HAVE KIRA KILL HIM"!!!
THEY ARE CONNECTED TO KIRA...
YES! THIS IS HUGE!
CLACK

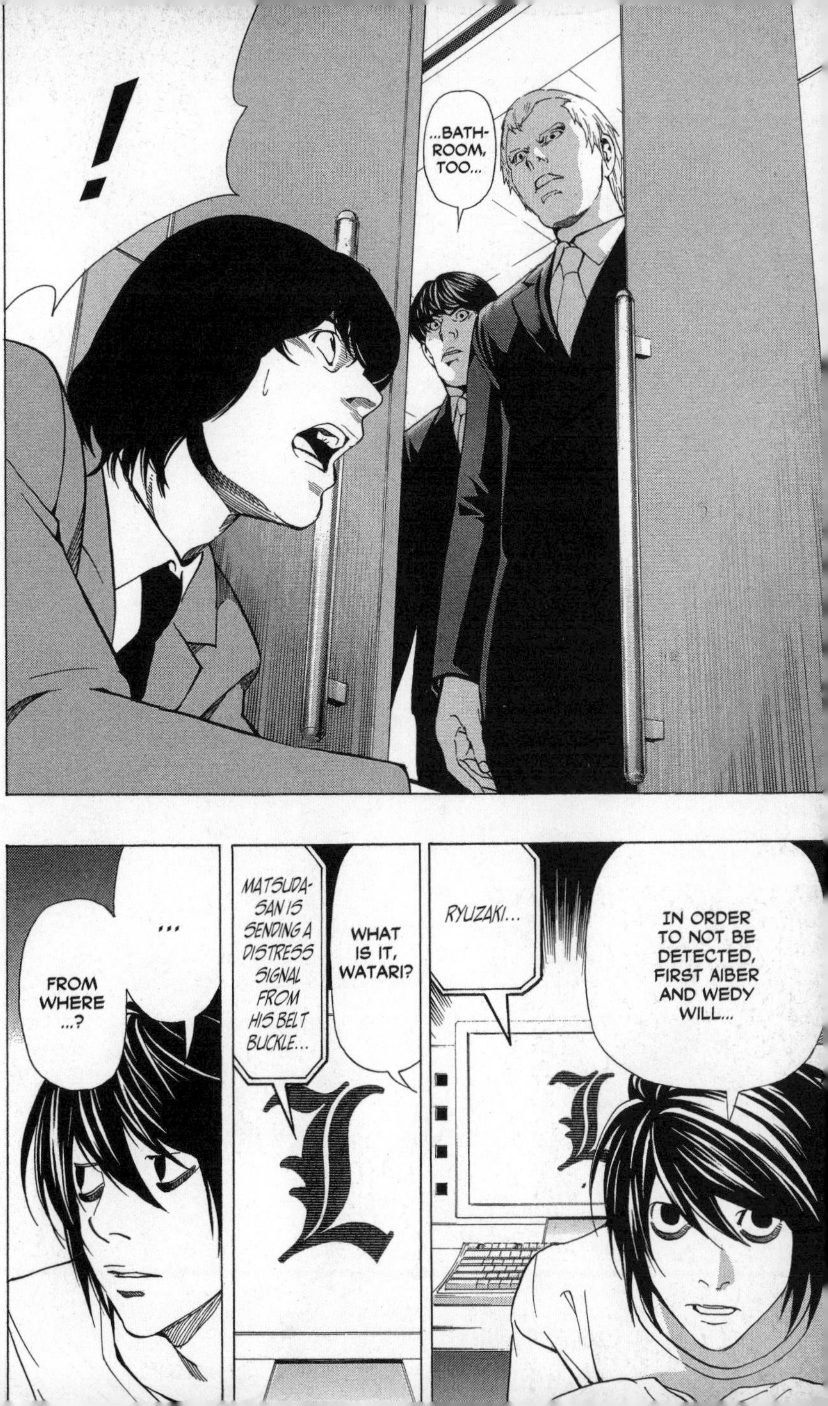
...BATH-ROOM, TOO...
!
IN ORDER TO NOT BE DETECTED, FIRST AIBER AND WEDY WILL...
RYUZAKI...
WHAT IS IT, WATARI?
MATSUDA-SAN IS SENDING A DISTRESS SIGNAL FROM HIS BELT BUCKLE...
...
FROM WHERE ...?

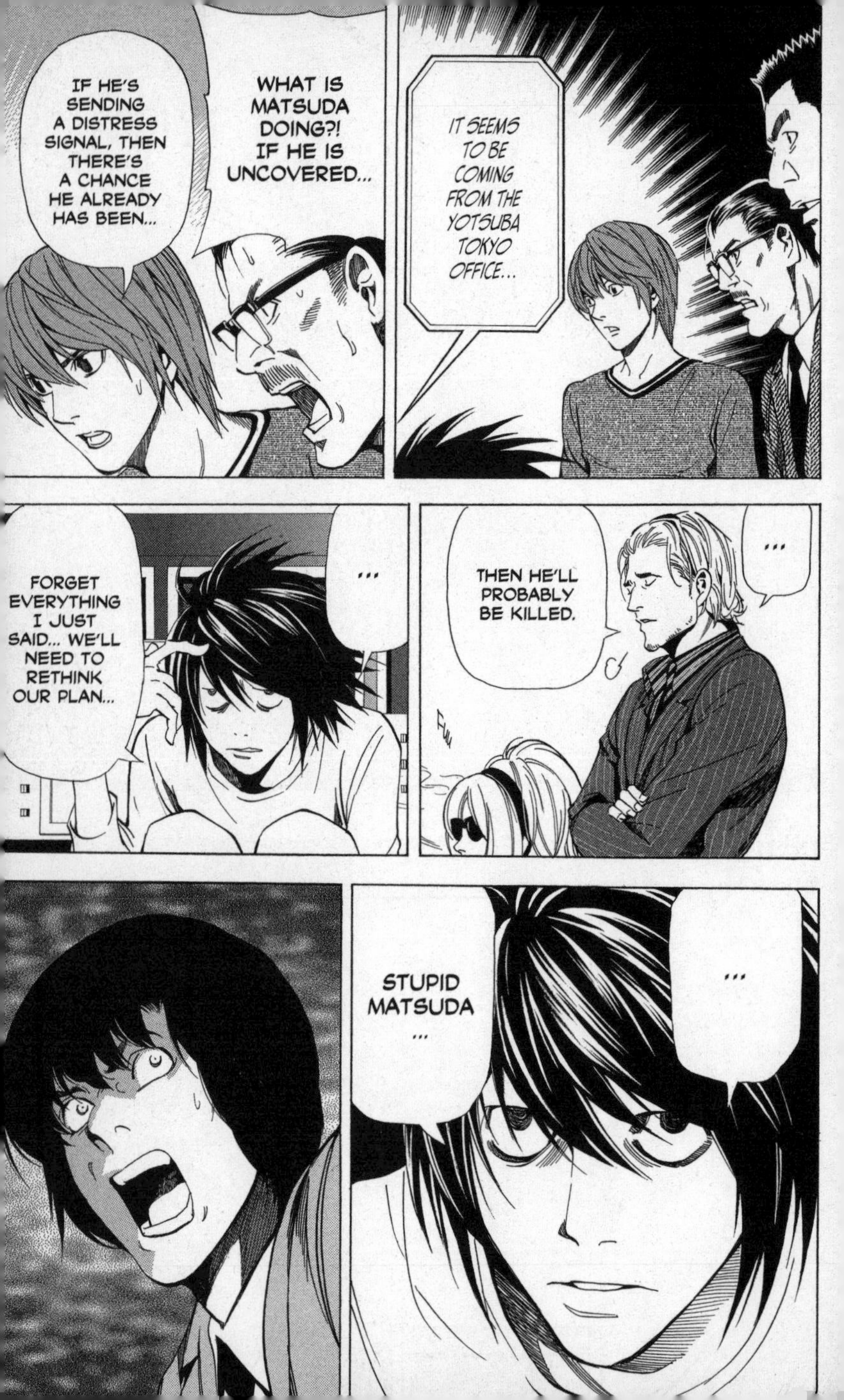
IT SEEMS TO BE COMING FROM THE YOTSUBA TOKYO OFFICE...
WHAT IS MATSUDA DOING?! IF HE IS UNCOVERED...
IF HE'S SENDING A DISTRESS SIGNAL, THEN THERE'S A CHANCE HE ALREADY HAS BEEN...
...
THEN HE'LL PROBABLY BE KILLED.
FUU
...
FORGET EVERYTHING I JUST SAID... WE'LL NEED TO RETHINK OUR PLAN...
...
STUPID MATSUDA ...

# DEATH NOTE
## How to use it
### XXIX

o You cannot kill humans at the age of 124 and over with the DEATH NOTE.

人間界単位で124歳以上の人間をデスノートで殺す事はできない。

o You cannot kill humans with less than 12 minutes of life left
  (in human calculations).

残りの寿命が人間界単位で12分以下の人間はデスノートで殺す事はできない。

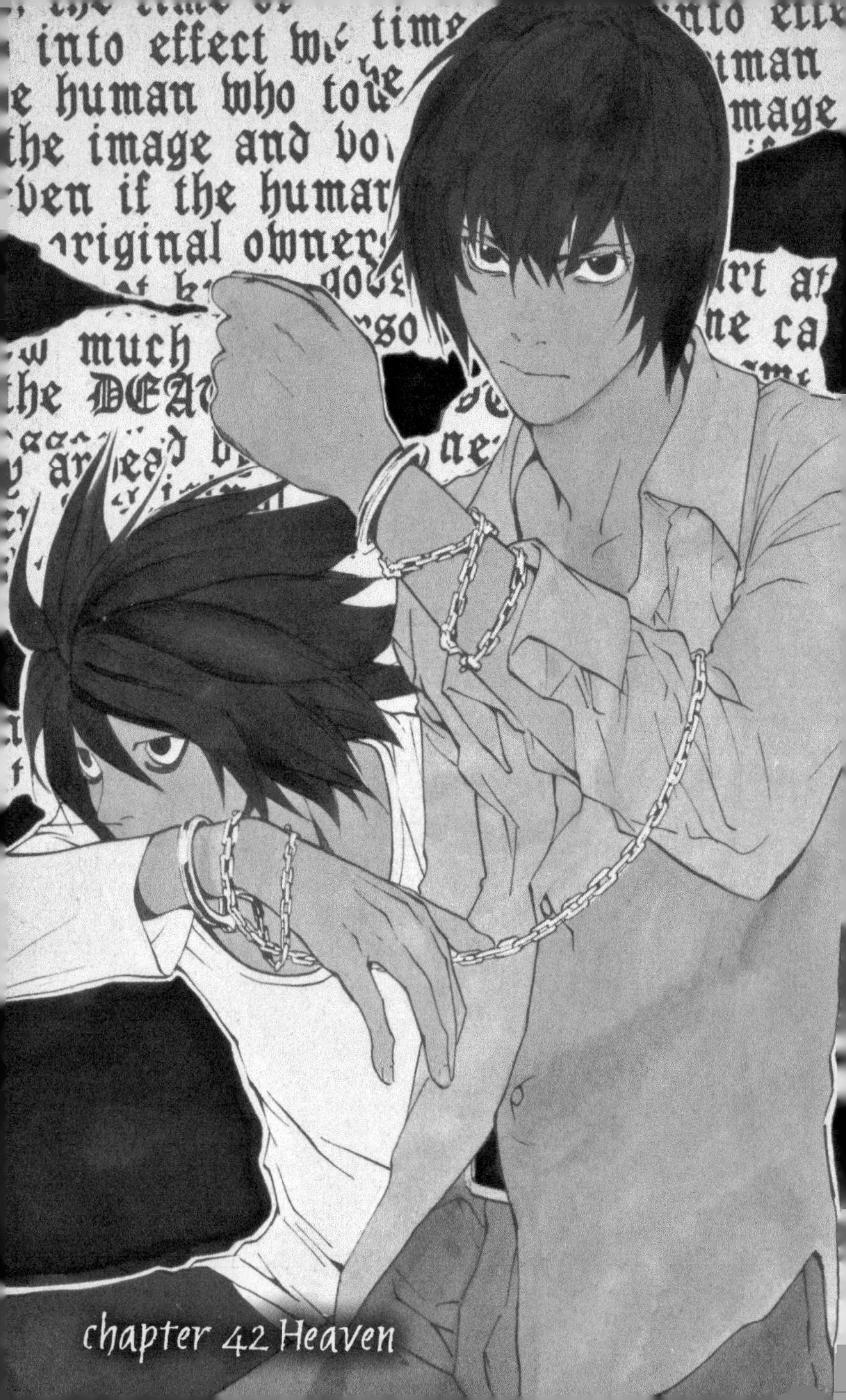
into effect w
time
e human who tou
the image and vo
ven if the huma
riginal owner
much
the DEA
uman
mage
rt at
ne ca

# chapter 42 Heaven

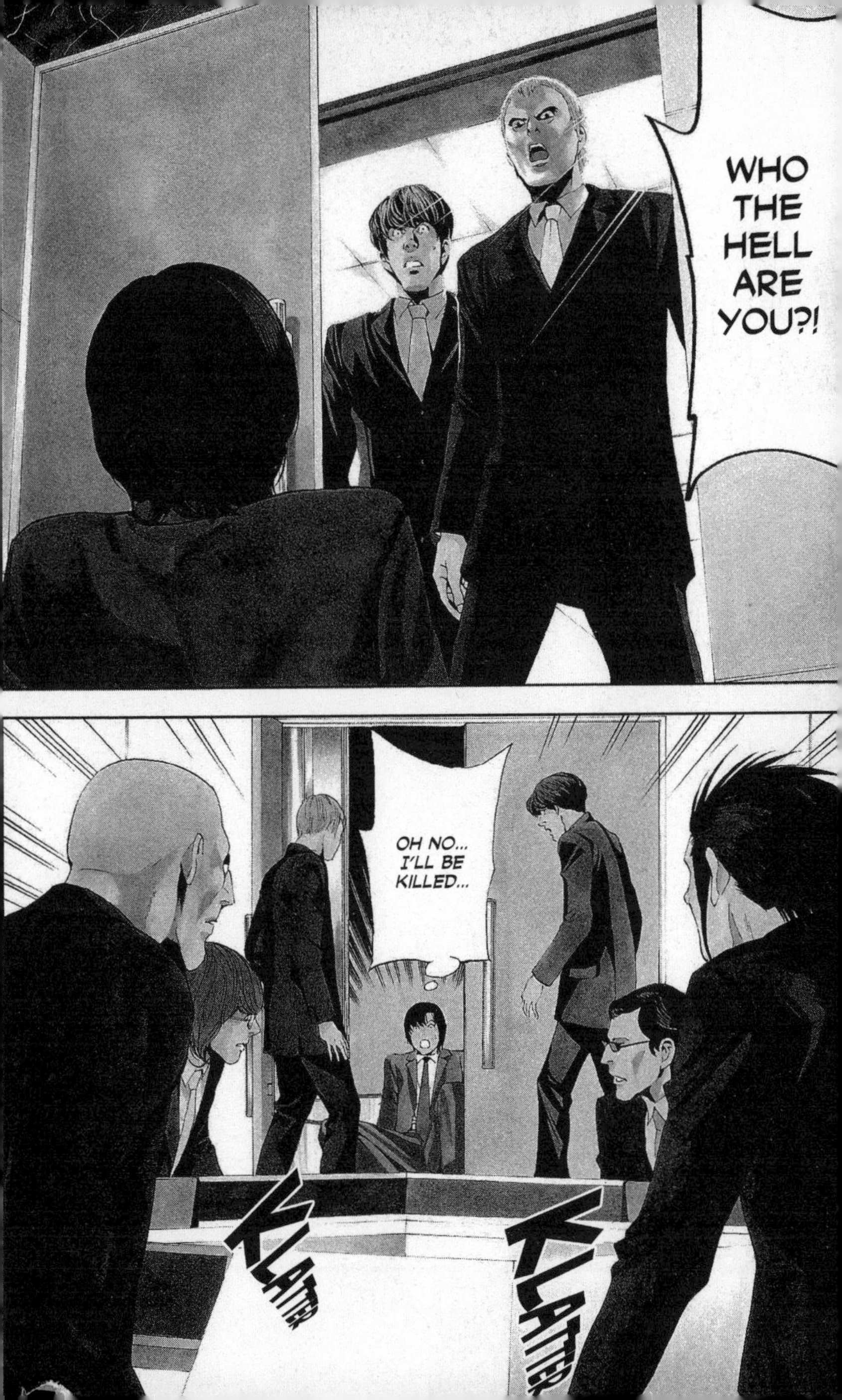
WHO THE HELL ARE YOU?!
OH NO... I'LL BE KILLED...
KLATTER
KLATTER

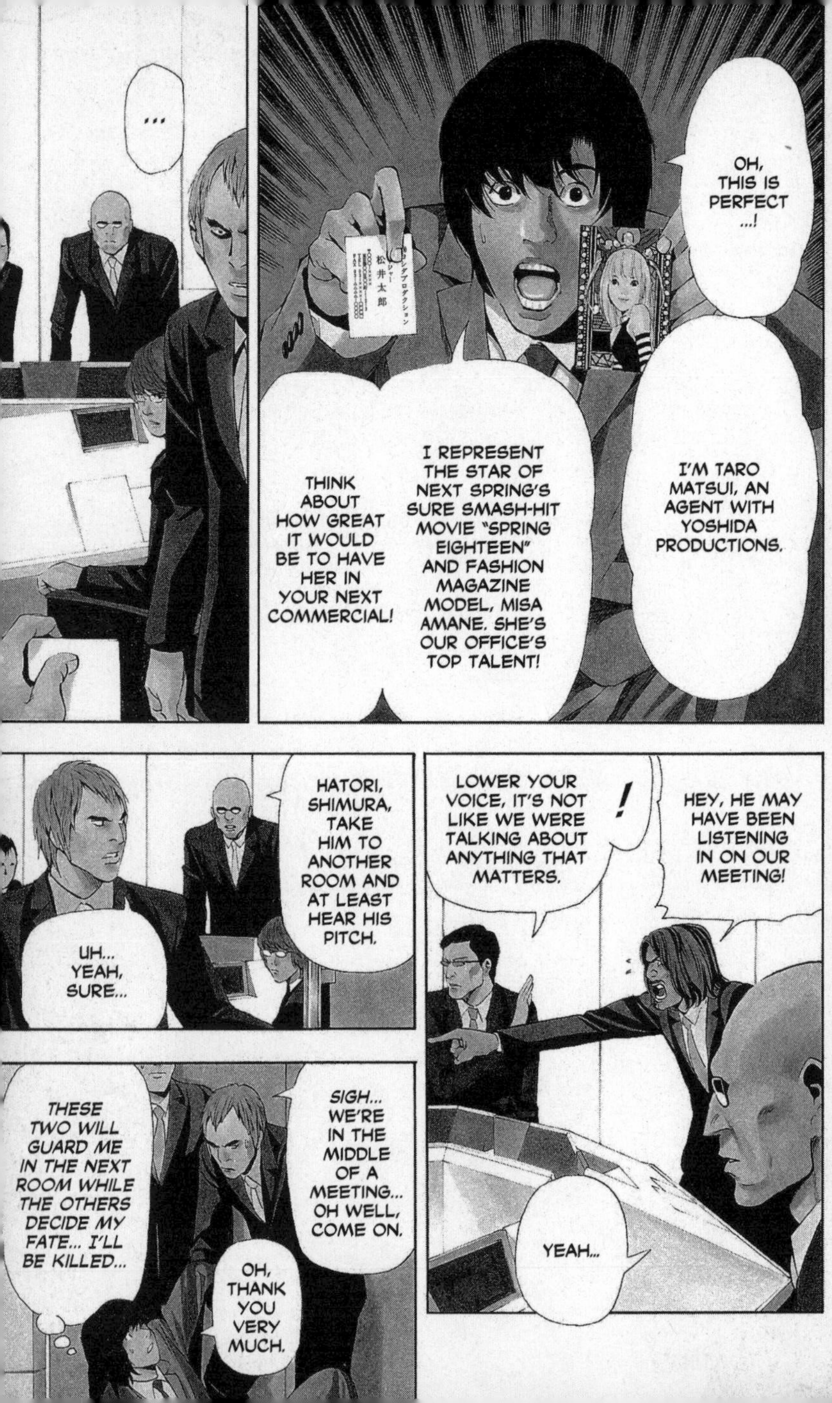
OH, THIS IS PERFECT...!
I'M TARO MATSUI, AN AGENT WITH YOSHIDA PRODUCTIONS.
松井太郎
I REPRESENT THE STAR OF NEXT SPRING'S SURE SMASH-HIT MOVIE "SPRING EIGHTEEN" AND FASHION MAGAZINE MODEL, MISA AMANE. SHE'S OUR OFFICE'S TOP TALENT!
THINK ABOUT HOW GREAT IT WOULD BE TO HAVE HER IN YOUR NEXT COMMERCIAL!
...
HEY, HE MAY HAVE BEEN LISTENING IN ON OUR MEETING!
!
LOWER YOUR VOICE, IT'S NOT LIKE WE WERE TALKING ABOUT ANYTHING THAT MATTERS.
YEAH...
HATORI, SHIMURA, TAKE HIM TO ANOTHER ROOM AND AT LEAST HEAR HIS PITCH.
UH... YEAH, SURE...
SIGH... WE'RE IN THE MIDDLE OF A MEETING... OH WELL, COME ON.
THESE TWO WILL GUARD ME IN THE NEXT ROOM WHILE THE OTHERS DECIDE MY FATE... I'LL BE KILLED...
OH, THANK YOU VERY MUCH.

READ THIS WAY

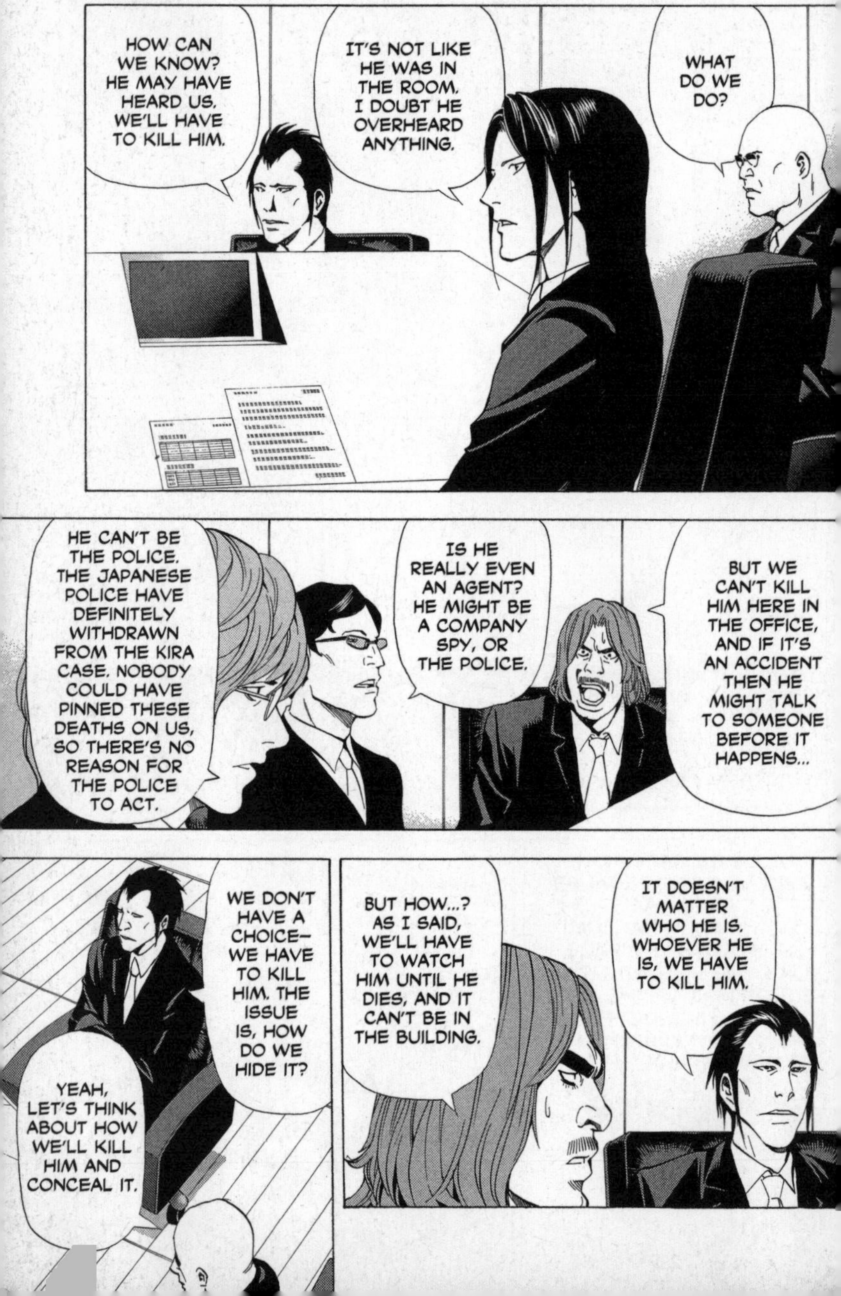
WHAT DO WE DO?
IT'S NOT LIKE HE WAS IN THE ROOM. I DOUBT HE OVERHEARD ANYTHING.
HOW CAN WE KNOW? HE MAY HAVE HEARD US. WE'LL HAVE TO KILL HIM.
BUT WE CAN'T KILL HIM HERE IN THE OFFICE, AND IF IT'S AN ACCIDENT THEN HE MIGHT TALK TO SOMEONE BEFORE IT HAPPENS...
IS HE REALLY EVEN AN AGENT? HE MIGHT BE A COMPANY SPY, OR THE POLICE.
HE CAN'T BE THE POLICE. THE JAPANESE POLICE HAVE DEFINITELY WITHDRAWN FROM THE KIRA CASE. NOBODY COULD HAVE PINNED THESE DEATHS ON US, SO THERE'S NO REASON FOR THE POLICE TO ACT.
IT DOESN'T MATTER WHO HE IS. WHOEVER HE IS, WE HAVE TO KILL HIM.
BUT HOW...? AS I SAID, WE'LL HAVE TO WATCH HIM UNTIL HE DIES, AND IT CAN'T BE IN THE BUILDING.
WE DON'T HAVE A CHOICE— WE HAVE TO KILL HIM. THE ISSUE IS, HOW DO WE HIDE IT?
YEAH, LET'S THINK ABOUT HOW WE'LL KILL HIM AND CONCEAL IT.

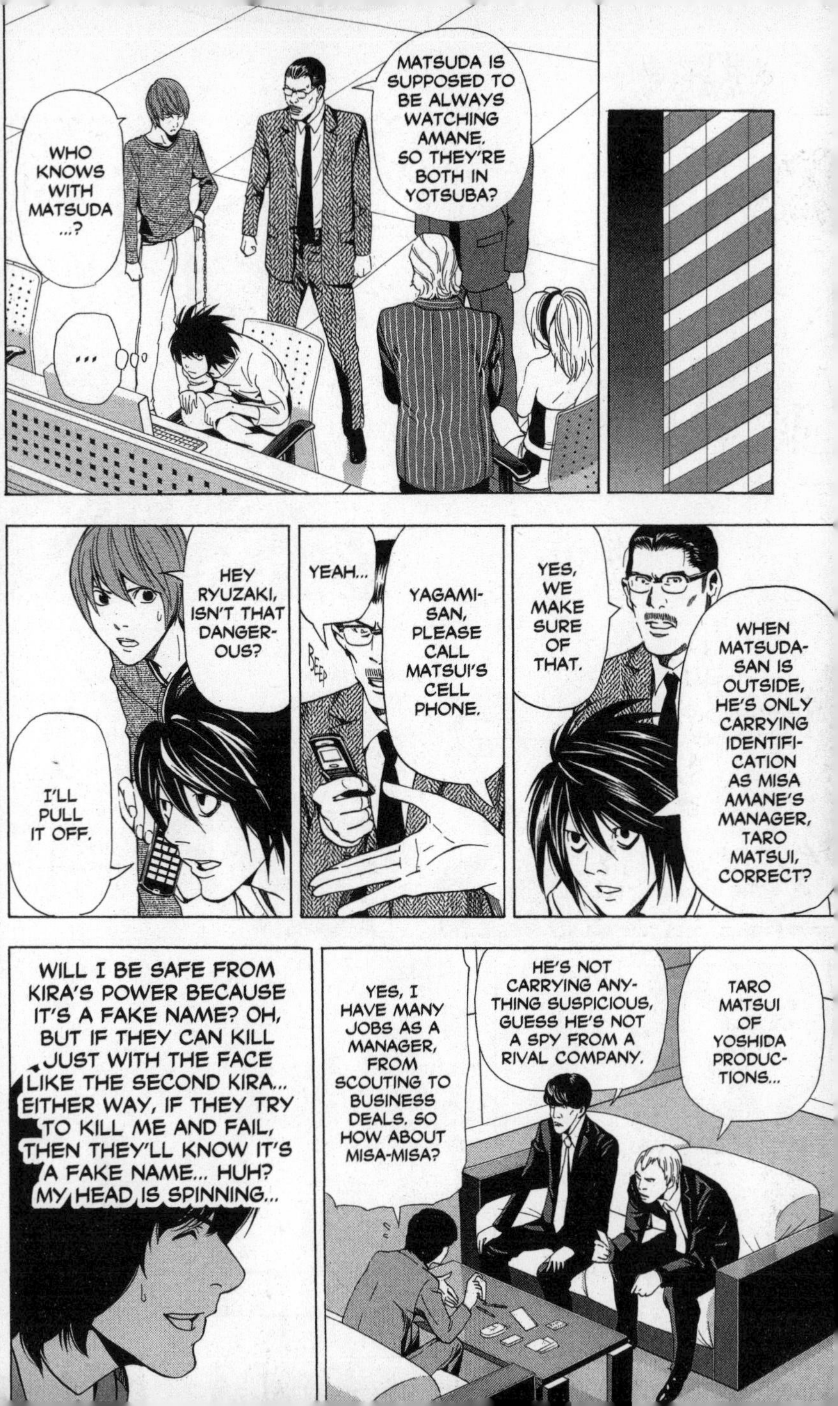
MATSUDA IS SUPPOSED TO BE ALWAYS WATCHING AMANE, SO THEY'RE BOTH IN YOTSUBA?
WHO KNOWS WITH MATSUDA ...?
...
WHEN MATSUDA-SAN IS OUTSIDE, HE'S ONLY CARRYING IDENTIFICATION AS MISA AMANE'S MANAGER, TARO MATSUI, CORRECT?
YES, WE MAKE SURE OF THAT.
YAGAMI-SAN, PLEASE CALL MATSUI'S CELL PHONE.
YEAH...
BEEP
HEY RYUZAKI, ISN'T THAT DANGEROUS?
I'LL PULL IT OFF.
TARO MATSUI OF YOSHIDA PRODUCTIONS...
HE'S NOT CARRYING ANYTHING SUSPICIOUS, GUESS HE'S NOT A SPY FROM A RIVAL COMPANY.
YES, I HAVE MANY JOBS AS A MANAGER, FROM SCOUTING TO BUSINESS DEALS. SO HOW ABOUT MISA-MISA?
WILL I BE SAFE FROM KIRA'S POWER BECAUSE IT'S A FAKE NAME? OH, BUT IF THEY CAN KILL JUST WITH THE FACE LIKE THE SECOND KIRA... EITHER WAY, IF THEY TRY TO KILL ME AND FAIL, THEN THEY'LL KNOW IT'S A FAKE NAME... HUH? MY HEAD IS SPINNING...

READ THIS WAY

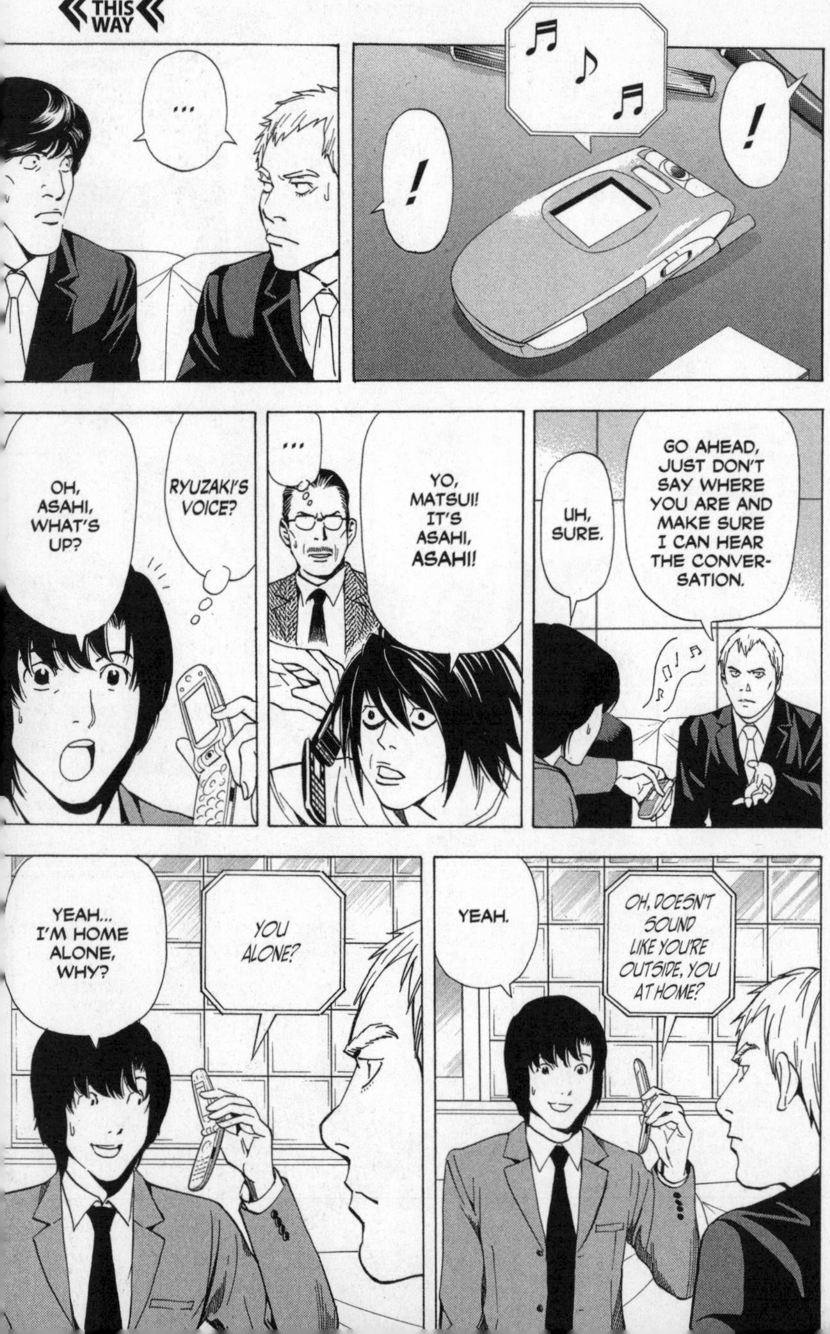

!
!
...
GO AHEAD, JUST DON'T SAY WHERE YOU ARE AND MAKE SURE I CAN HEAR THE CONVERSATION.
UH, SURE.
YO, MATSUI! IT'S ASAHI, ASAHI!
...
RYUZAKI'S VOICE?
OH, ASAHI, WHAT'S UP?
OH, DOESN'T SOUND LIKE YOU'RE OUTSIDE, YOU AT HOME?
YEAH.
YOU ALONE?
YEAH... I'M HOME ALONE, WHY?

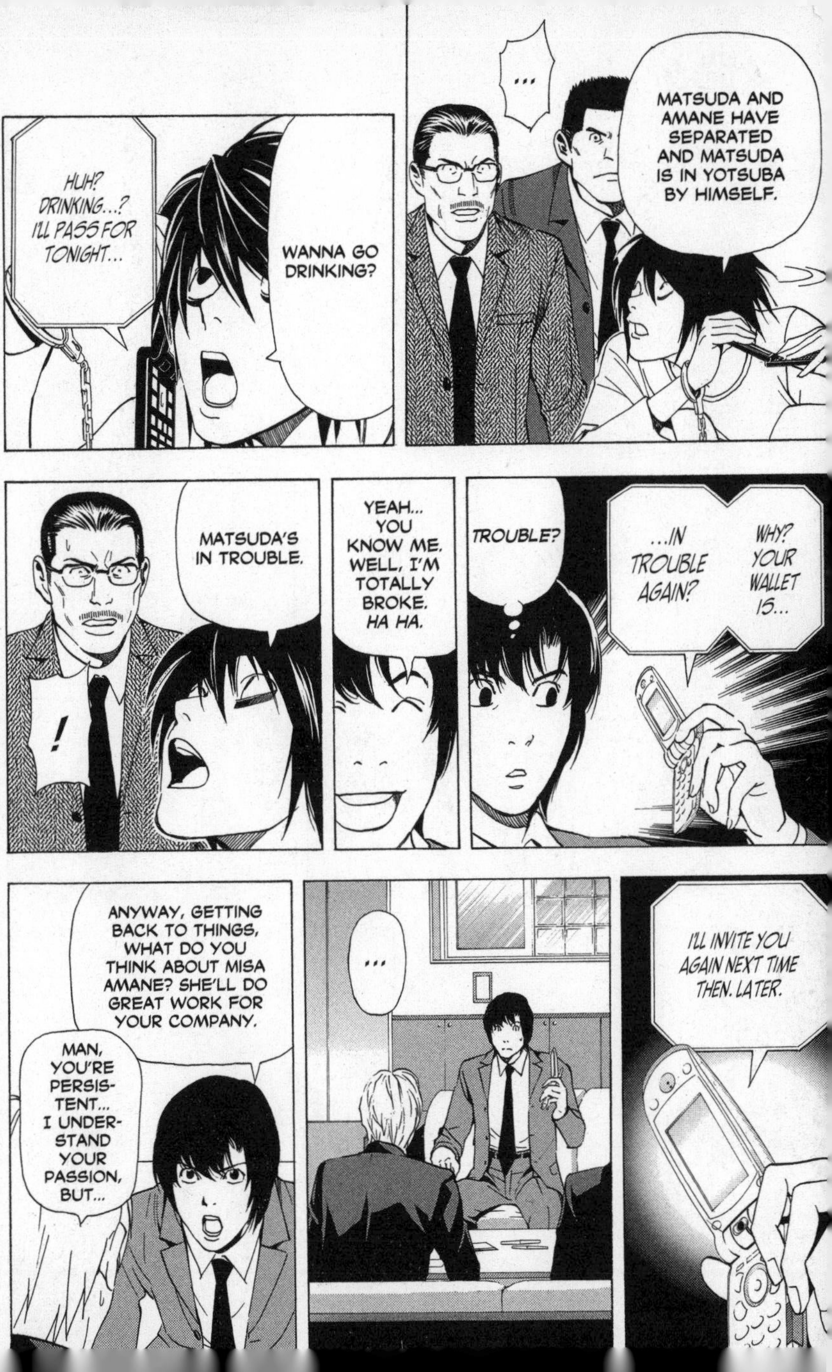
MATSUDA AND AMANE HAVE SEPARATED AND MATSUDA IS IN YOTSUBA BY HIMSELF.
...
WANNA GO DRINKING?
HUH? DRINKING...? I'LL PASS FOR TONIGHT...
WHY? YOUR WALLET IS...
...IN TROUBLE AGAIN?
TROUBLE?
YEAH... YOU KNOW ME. WELL, I'M TOTALLY BROKE. HA HA.
MATSUDA'S IN TROUBLE.
!
I'LL INVITE YOU AGAIN NEXT TIME THEN. LATER.
...
ANYWAY, GETTING BACK TO THINGS, WHAT DO YOU THINK ABOUT MISA AMANE? SHE'LL DO GREAT WORK FOR YOUR COMPANY.
MAN, YOU'RE PERSIS-TENT... I UNDER-STAND YOUR PASSION, BUT...

READ THIS WAY

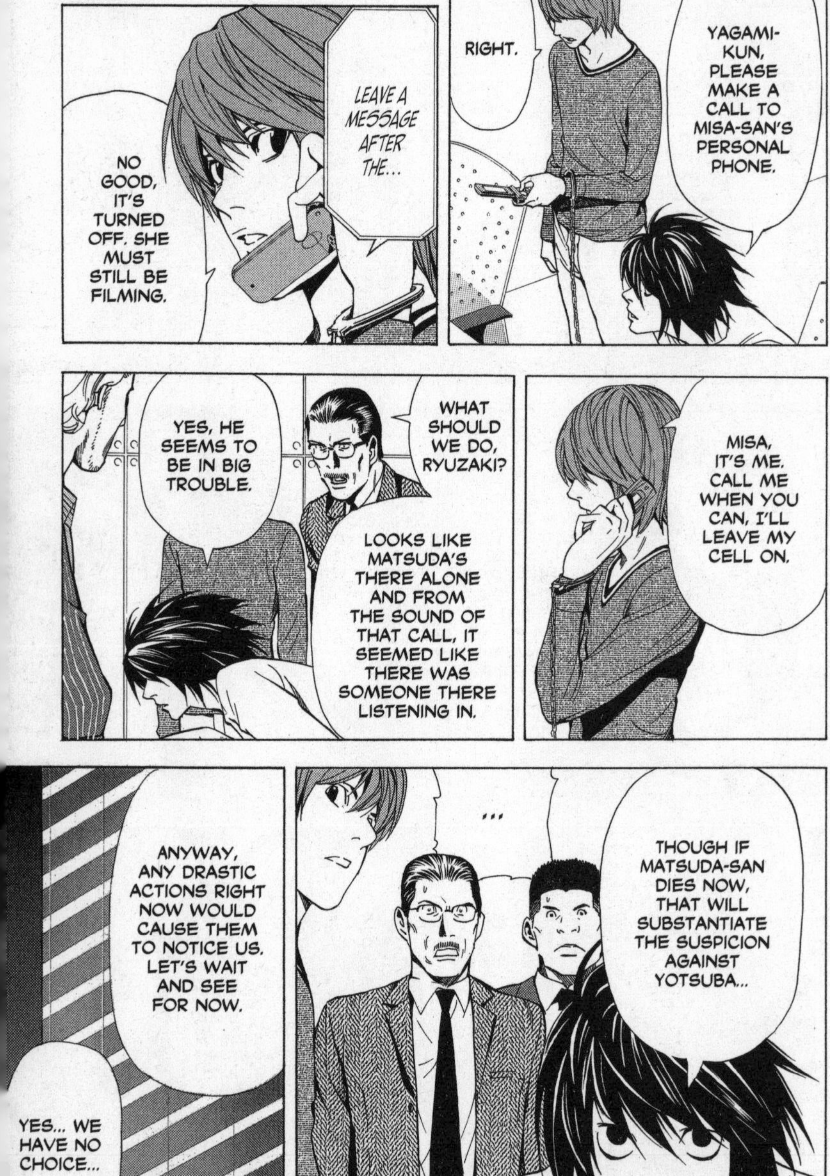
YAGAMI-KUN, PLEASE MAKE A CALL TO MISA-SAN'S PERSONAL PHONE.
RIGHT.
LEAVE A MESSAGE AFTER THE...
NO GOOD, IT'S TURNED OFF. SHE MUST STILL BE FILMING.
MISA, IT'S ME. CALL ME WHEN YOU CAN, I'LL LEAVE MY CELL ON.
WHAT SHOULD WE DO, RYUZAKI?
YES, HE SEEMS TO BE IN BIG TROUBLE.
LOOKS LIKE MATSUDA'S THERE ALONE AND FROM THE SOUND OF THAT CALL, IT SEEMED LIKE THERE WAS SOMEONE THERE LISTENING IN.
THOUGH IF MATSUDA-SAN DIES NOW, THAT WILL SUBSTANTIATE THE SUSPICION AGAINST YOTSUBA...
...
ANYWAY, ANY DRASTIC ACTIONS RIGHT NOW WOULD CAUSE THEM TO NOTICE US. LET'S WAIT AND SEE FOR NOW.
YES... WE HAVE NO CHOICE...

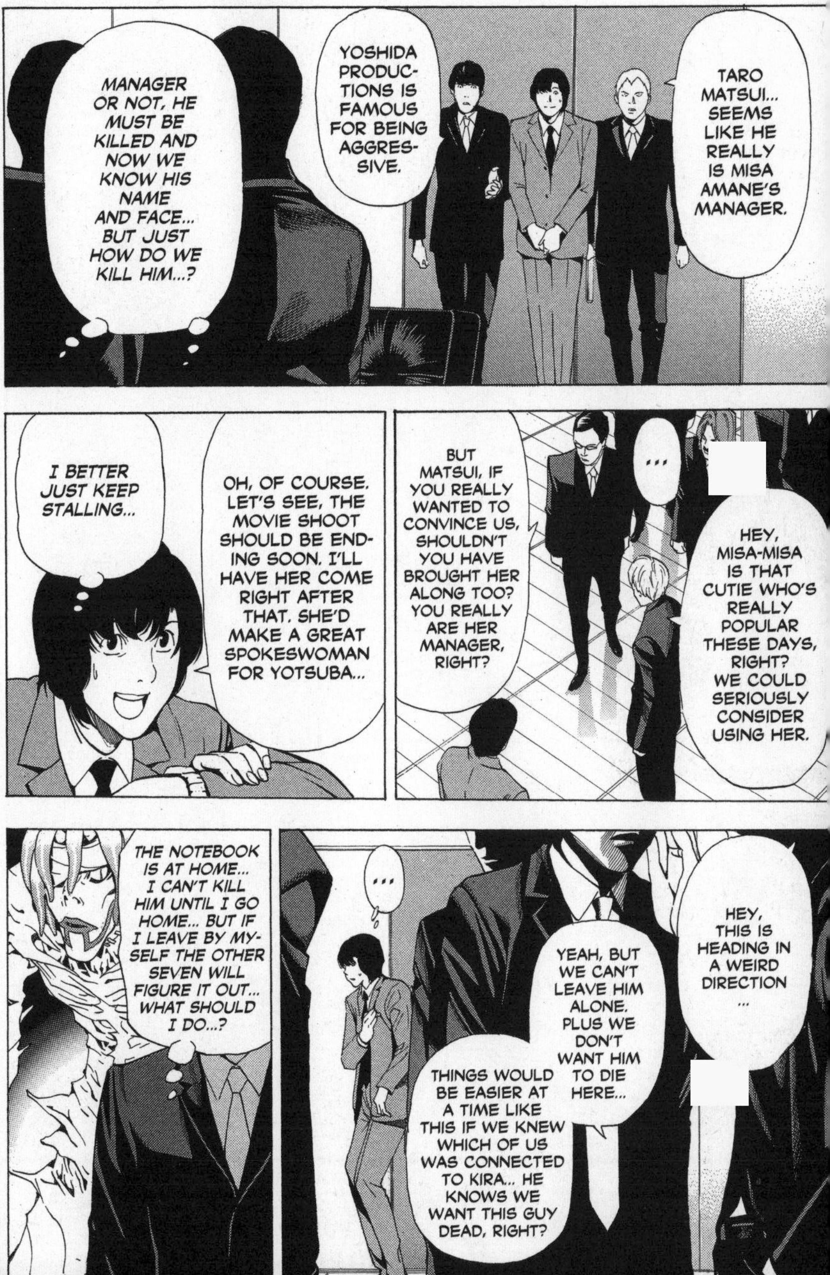
TARO MATSUI... SEEMS LIKE HE REALLY IS MISA AMANE'S MANAGER.
YOSHIDA PRODUCTIONS IS FAMOUS FOR BEING AGGRESSIVE.
MANAGER OR NOT, HE MUST BE KILLED AND NOW WE KNOW HIS NAME AND FACE... BUT JUST HOW DO WE KILL HIM...?
HEY, MISA-MISA IS THAT CUTIE WHO'S REALLY POPULAR THESE DAYS, RIGHT? WE COULD SERIOUSLY CONSIDER USING HER.
...
BUT MATSUI, IF YOU REALLY WANTED TO CONVINCE US, SHOULDN'T YOU HAVE BROUGHT HER ALONG TOO? YOU REALLY ARE HER MANAGER, RIGHT?
OH, OF COURSE. LET'S SEE, THE MOVIE SHOOT SHOULD BE ENDING SOON. I'LL HAVE HER COME RIGHT AFTER THAT. SHE'D MAKE A GREAT SPOKESWOMAN FOR YOTSUBA...
I BETTER JUST KEEP STALLING...
HEY, THIS IS HEADING IN A WEIRD DIRECTION ...
YEAH, BUT WE CAN'T LEAVE HIM ALONE. PLUS WE DON'T WANT HIM TO DIE HERE...
THINGS WOULD BE EASIER AT A TIME LIKE THIS IF WE KNEW WHICH OF US WAS CONNECTED TO KIRA... HE KNOWS WE WANT THIS GUY DEAD, RIGHT?
...
THE NOTEBOOK IS AT HOME... I CAN'T KILL HIM UNTIL I GO HOME... BUT IF I LEAVE BY MYSELF THE OTHER SEVEN WILL FIGURE IT OUT... WHAT SHOULD I DO...?

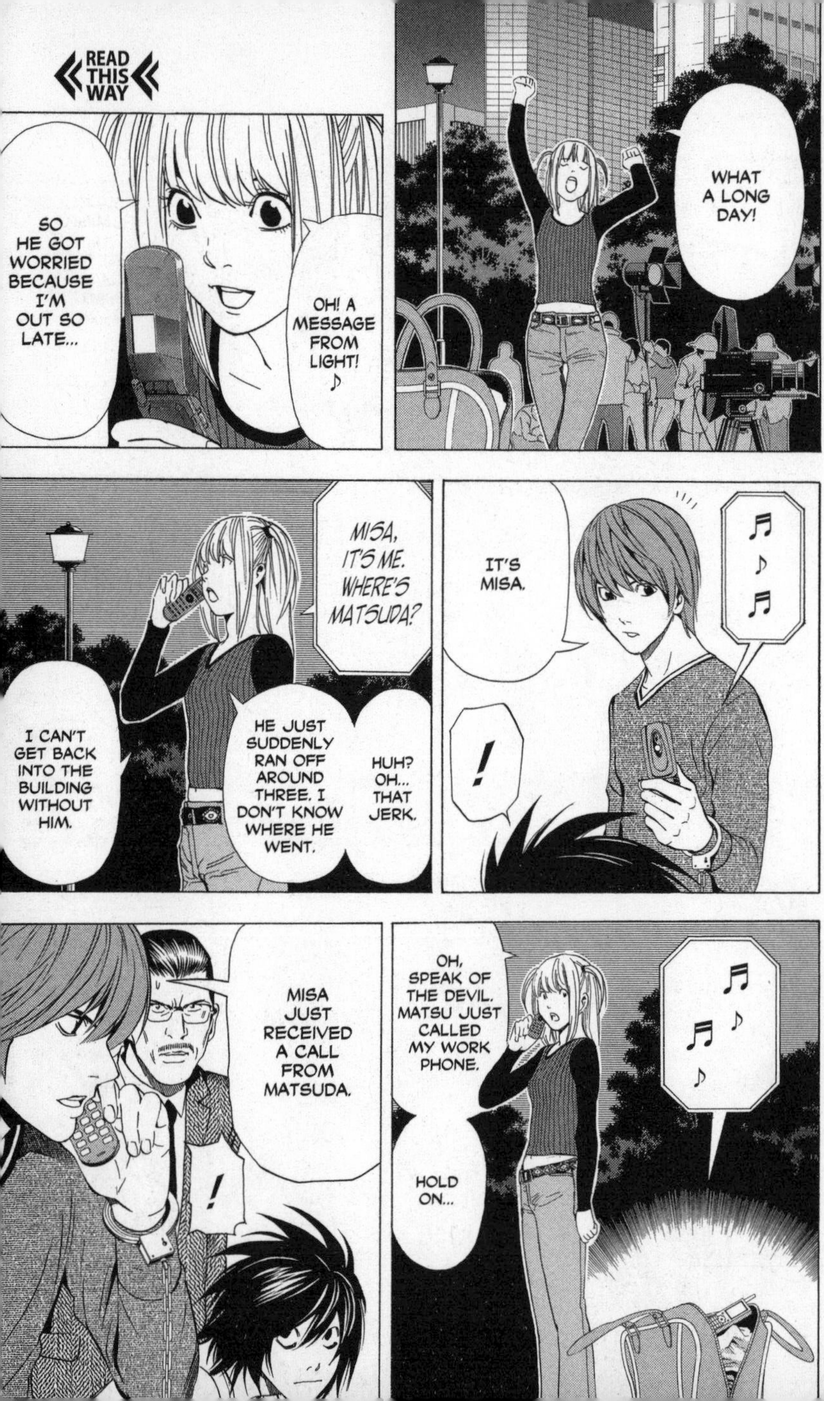
READ THIS WAY
WHAT A LONG DAY!
OH! A MESSAGE FROM LIGHT! ♪
SO HE GOT WORRIED BECAUSE I'M OUT SO LATE...
♬ ♪ ♬
IT'S MISA.
!
MISA, IT'S ME. WHERE'S MATSUDA?
HUH? OH... THAT JERK.
HE JUST SUDDENLY RAN OFF AROUND THREE. I DON'T KNOW WHERE HE WENT.
I CAN'T GET BACK INTO THE BUILDING WITHOUT HIM.
♬ ♪ ♬ ♪
OH, SPEAK OF THE DEVIL. MATSU JUST CALLED MY WORK PHONE.
HOLD ON...
MISA JUST RECEIVED A CALL FROM MATSUDA.
!

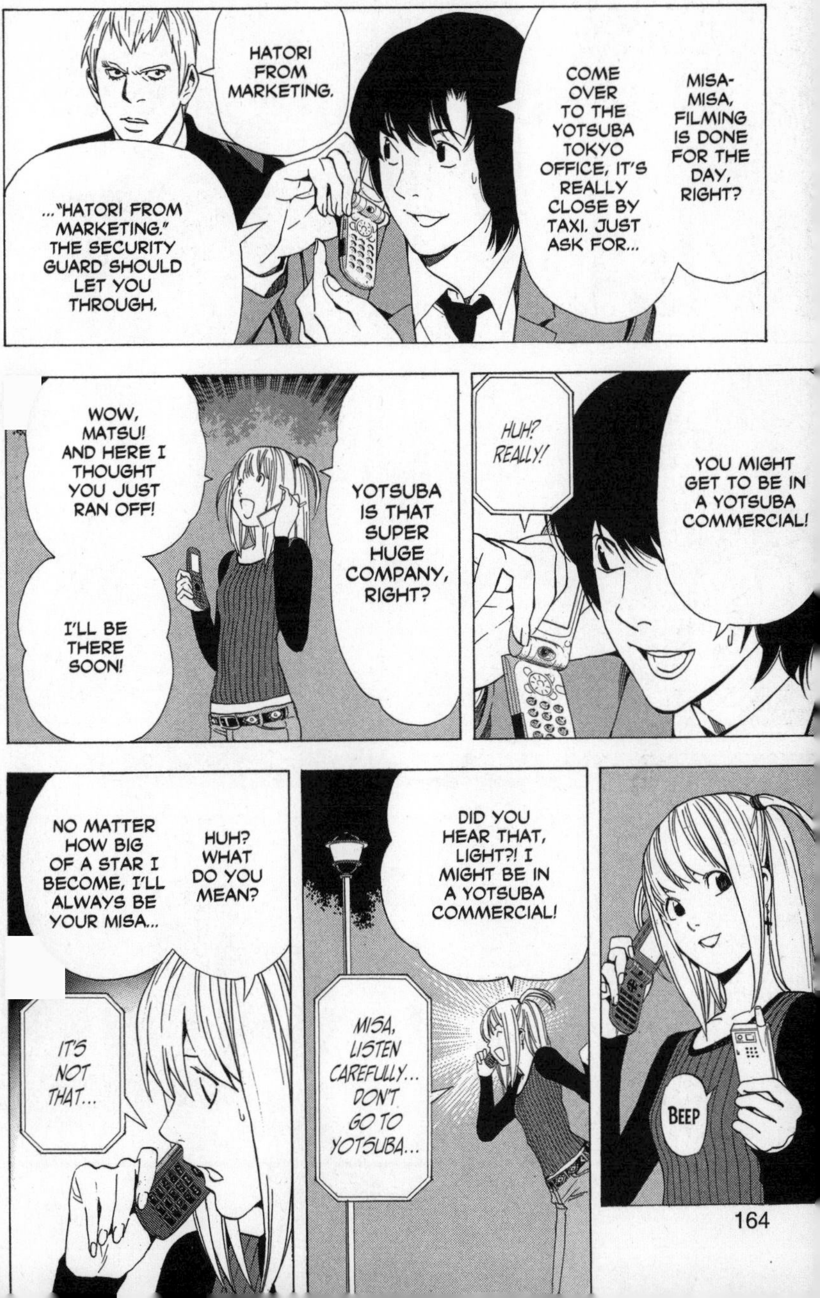
MISA-MISA, FILMING IS DONE FOR THE DAY, RIGHT?
COME OVER TO THE YOTSUBA TOKYO OFFICE, IT'S REALLY CLOSE BY TAXI. JUST ASK FOR...
HATORI FROM MARKETING.
..."HATORI FROM MARKETING." THE SECURITY GUARD SHOULD LET YOU THROUGH.
YOU MIGHT GET TO BE IN A YOTSUBA COMMERCIAL!
HUH? REALLY!
YOTSUBA IS THAT SUPER HUGE COMPANY, RIGHT?
WOW, MATSU! AND HERE I THOUGHT YOU JUST RAN OFF!
I'LL BE THERE SOON!
BEEP
DID YOU HEAR THAT, LIGHT?! I MIGHT BE IN A YOTSUBA COMMERCIAL!
MISA, LISTEN CAREFULLY... DON'T GO TO YOTSUBA...
HUH? WHAT DO YOU MEAN?
NO MATTER HOW BIG OF A STAR I BECOME, I'LL ALWAYS BE YOUR MISA...
IT'S NOT THAT...

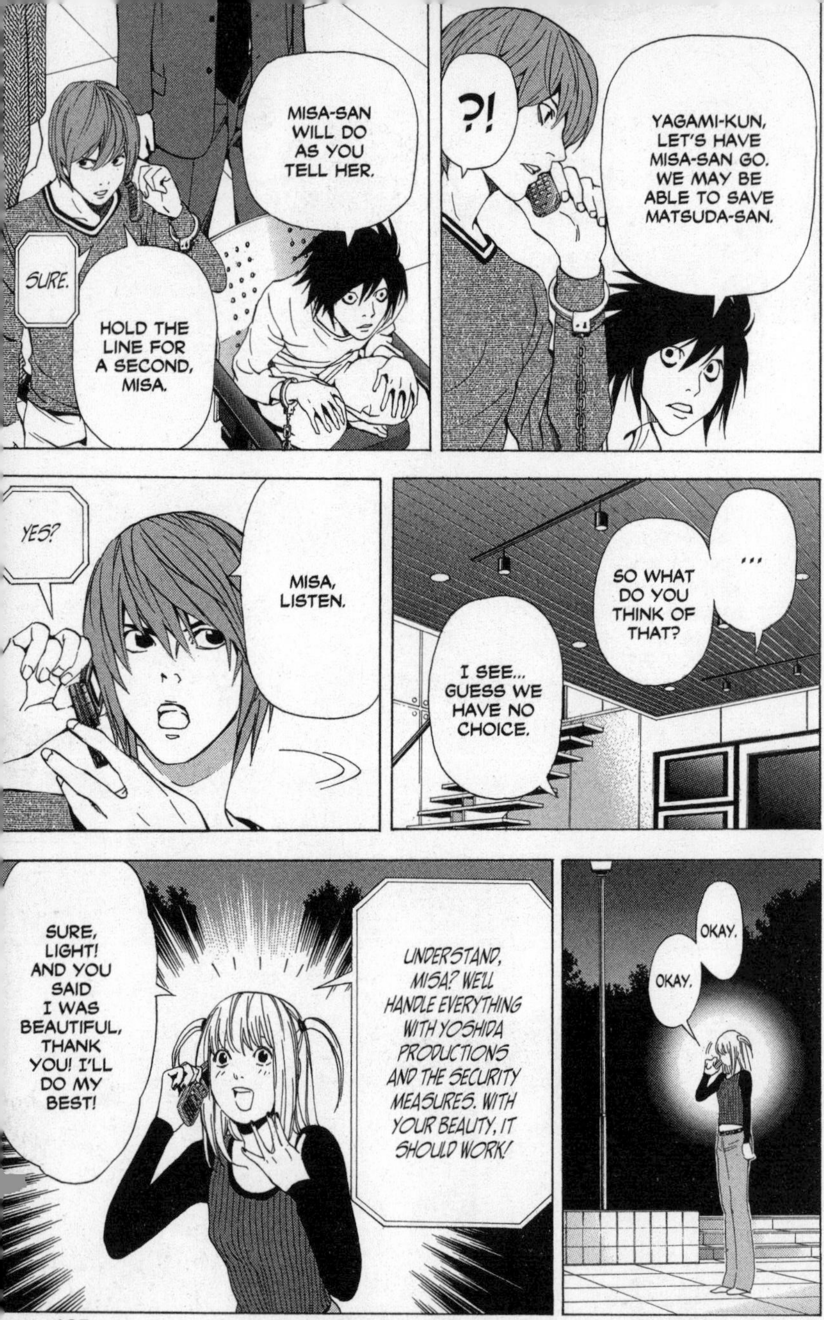
YAGAMI-KUN, LET'S HAVE MISA-SAN GO. WE MAY BE ABLE TO SAVE MATSUDA-SAN.
?!
MISA-SAN WILL DO AS YOU TELL HER.
SURE.
HOLD THE LINE FOR A SECOND, MISA.
...
SO WHAT DO YOU THINK OF THAT?
I SEE... GUESS WE HAVE NO CHOICE.
MISA, LISTEN.
YES?
OKAY.
OKAY.
UNDERSTAND, MISA? WE'LL HANDLE EVERYTHING WITH YOSHIDA PRODUCTIONS AND THE SECURITY MEASURES. WITH YOUR BEAUTY, IT SHOULD WORK!
SURE, LIGHT! AND YOU SAID I WAS BEAUTIFUL, THANK YOU! I'LL DO MY BEST!

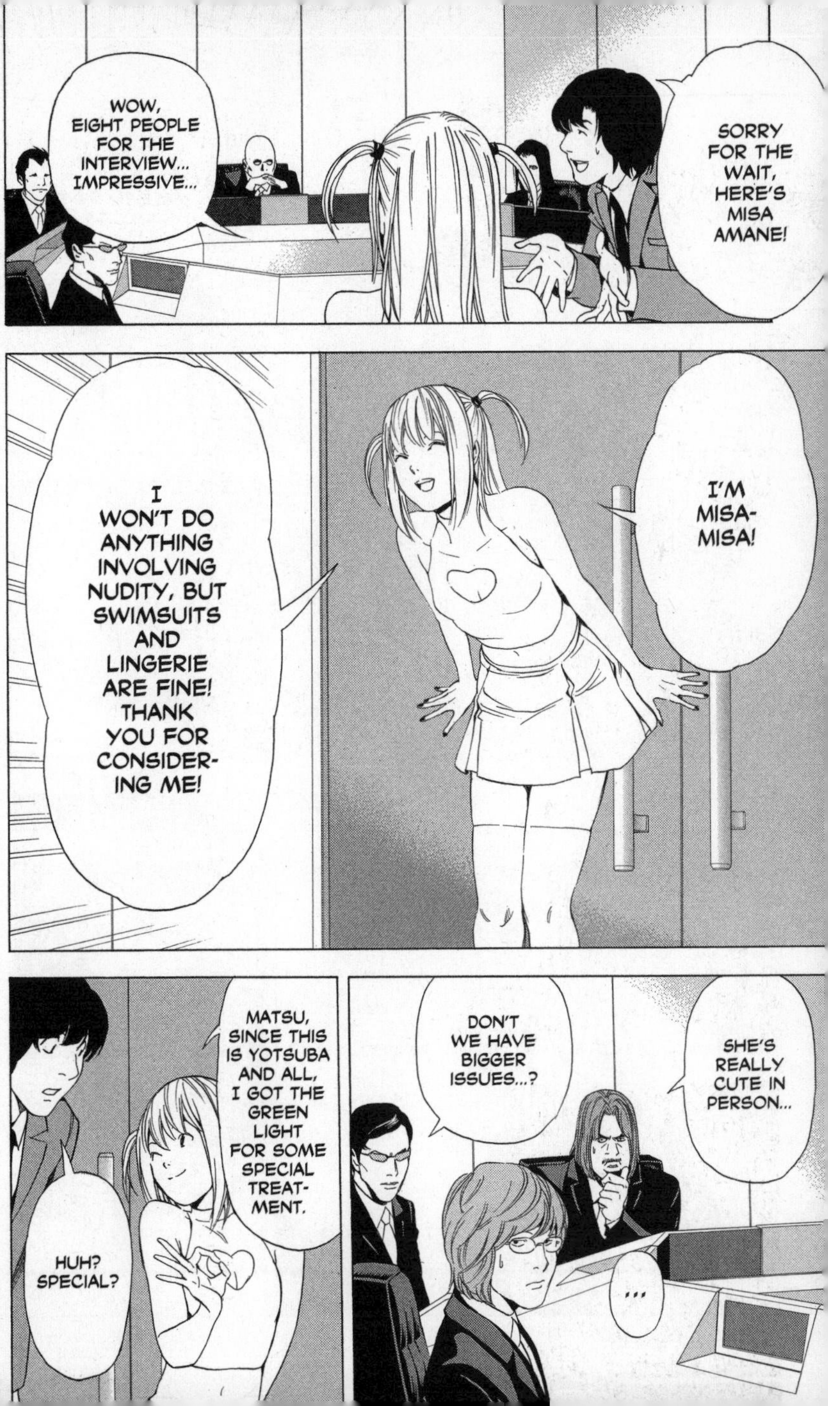
SORRY FOR THE WAIT, HERE'S MISA AMANE!
WOW, EIGHT PEOPLE FOR THE INTERVIEW... IMPRESSIVE...
I'M MISA-MISA!
I WON'T DO ANYTHING INVOLVING NUDITY, BUT SWIMSUITS AND LINGERIE ARE FINE! THANK YOU FOR CONSIDER-ING ME!
SHE'S REALLY CUTE IN PERSON...
DON'T WE HAVE BIGGER ISSUES...?
...
MATSU, SINCE THIS IS YOTSUBA AND ALL, I GOT THE GREEN LIGHT FOR SOME SPECIAL TREAT-MENT.
HUH? SPECIAL?

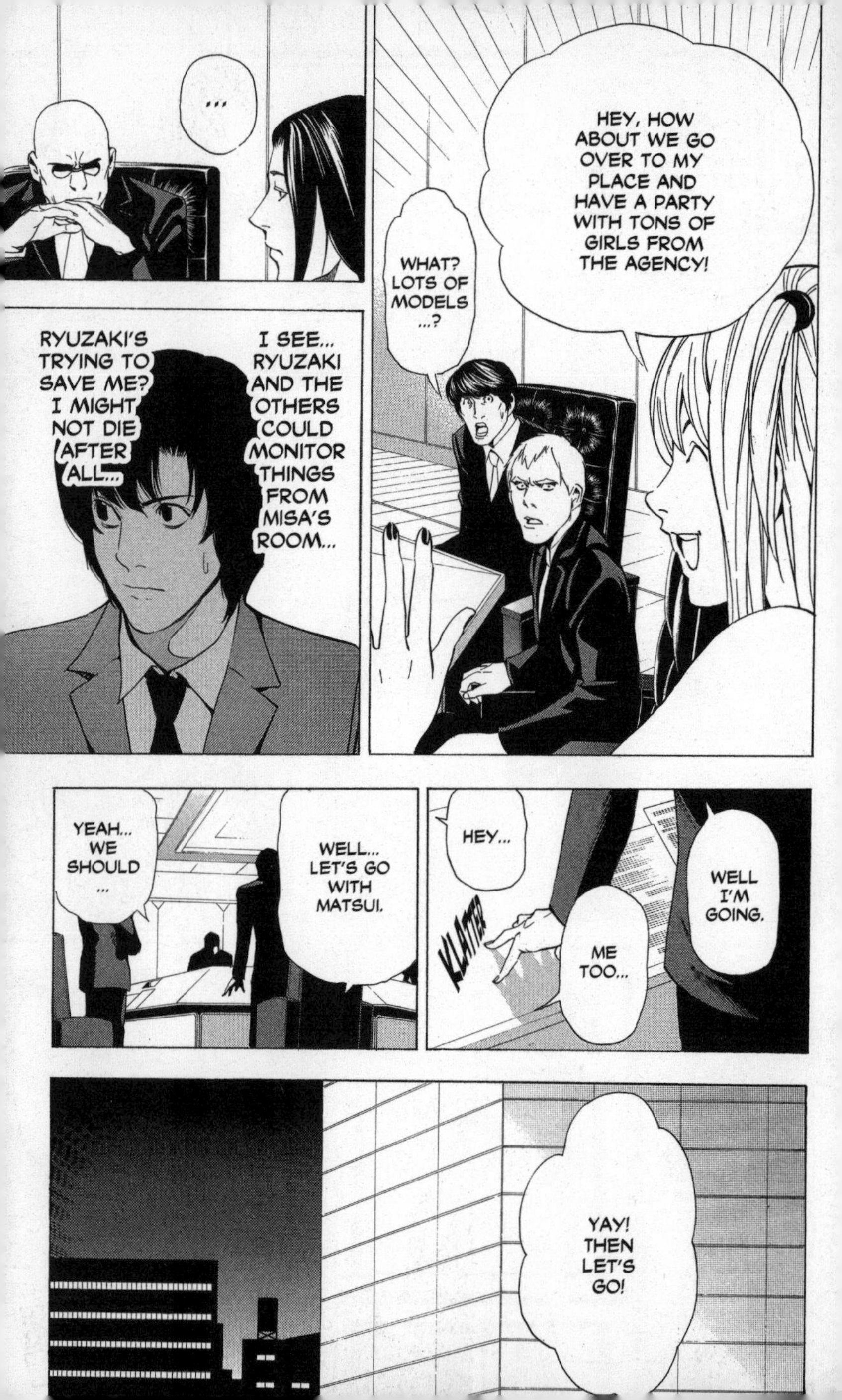
HEY, HOW ABOUT WE GO OVER TO MY PLACE AND HAVE A PARTY WITH TONS OF GIRLS FROM THE AGENCY!
WHAT? LOTS OF MODELS ...?
...
I SEE... RYUZAKI AND THE OTHERS COULD MONITOR THINGS FROM MISA'S ROOM...
RYUZAKI'S TRYING TO SAVE ME? I MIGHT NOT DIE AFTER ALL...
WELL I'M GOING.
HEY...
ME TOO...
KLATTER
WELL... LET'S GO WITH MATSUI.
YEAH... WE SHOULD ...
YAY! THEN LET'S GO!

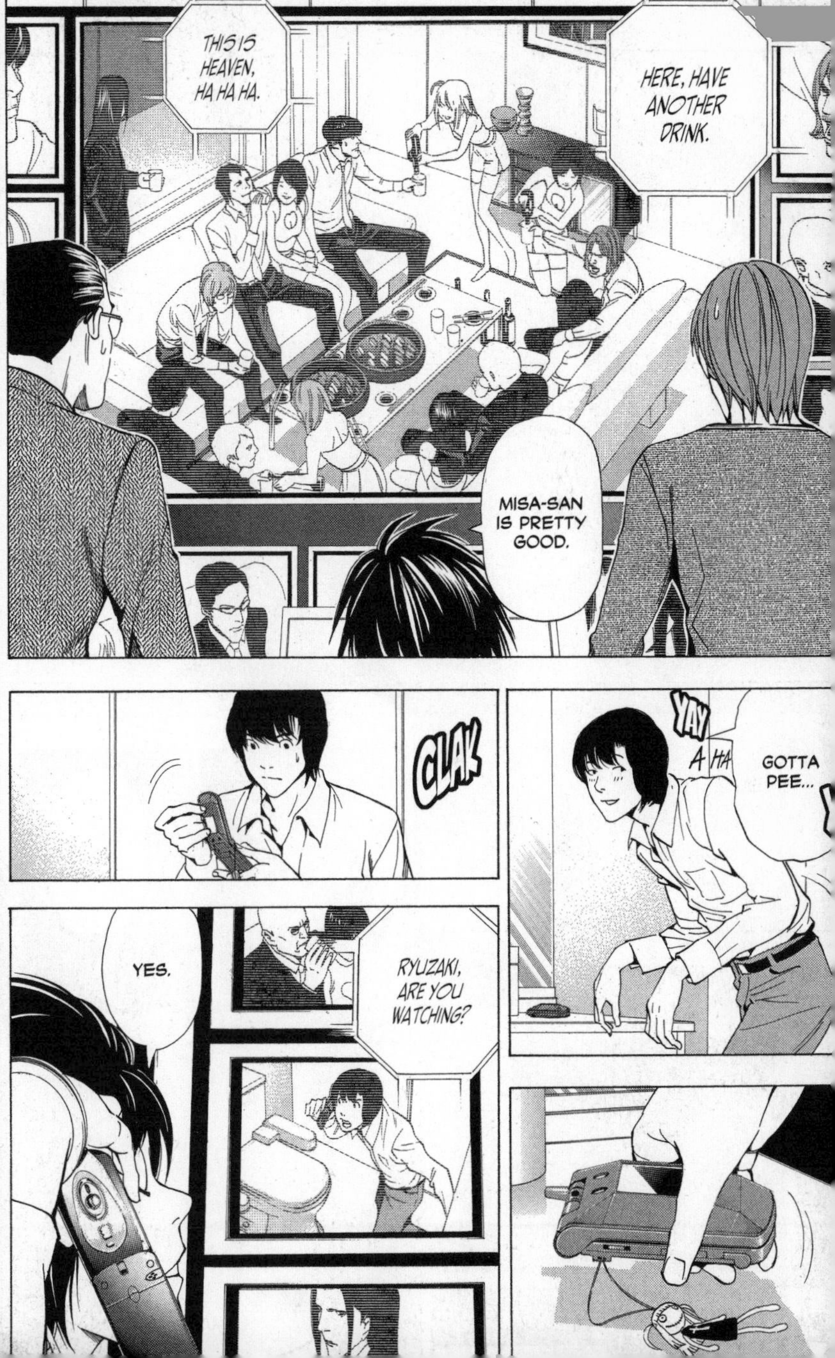
HERE, HAVE ANOTHER DRINK.
THIS IS HEAVEN, HA HA HA.
MISA-SAN IS PRETTY GOOD.
YAY
A HA
GOTTA PEE...
CLAK
RYUZAKI, ARE YOU WATCHING?
YES.

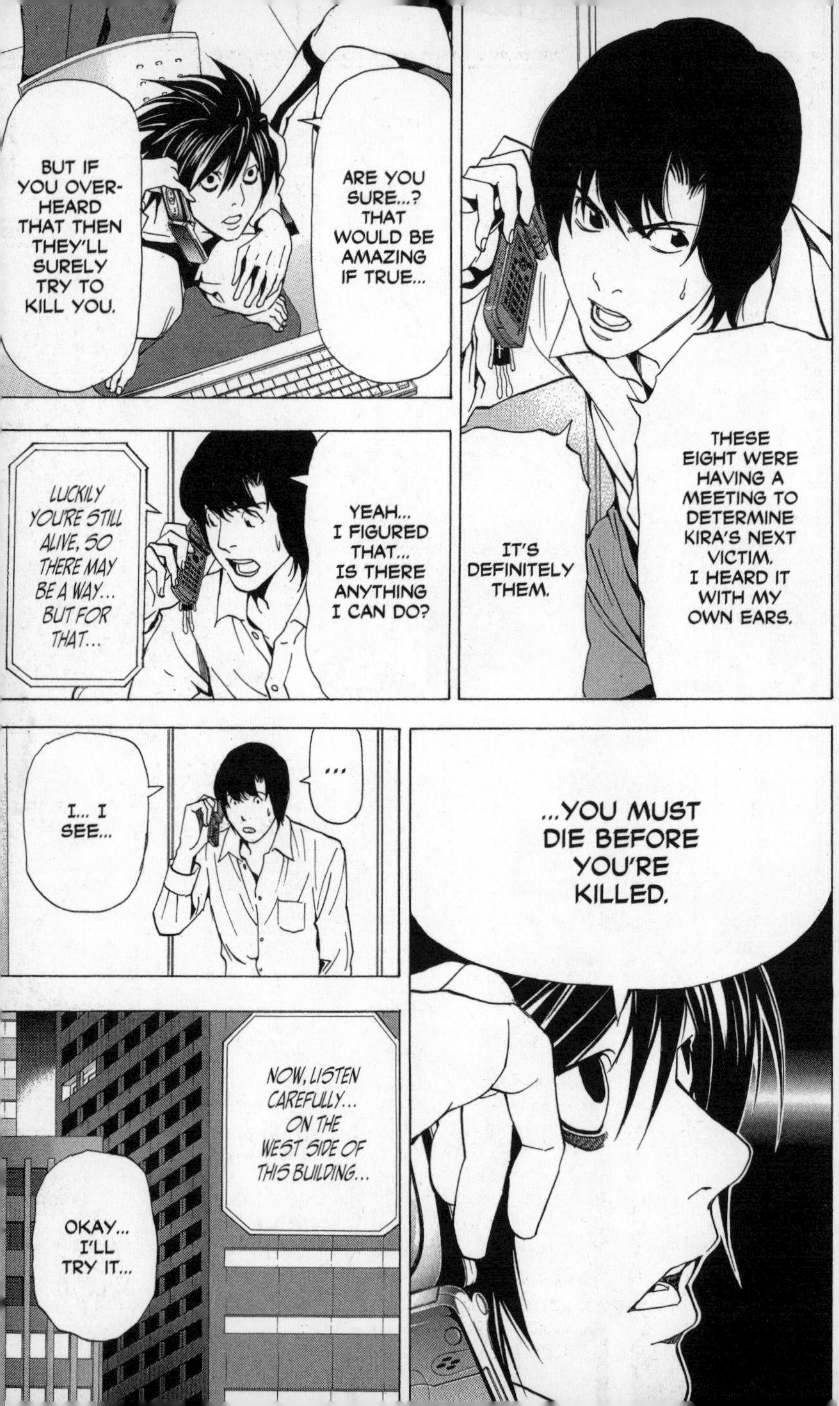
THESE EIGHT WERE HAVING A MEETING TO DETERMINE KIRA'S NEXT VICTIM. I HEARD IT WITH MY OWN EARS.
IT'S DEFINITELY THEM.
ARE YOU SURE...? THAT WOULD BE AMAZING IF TRUE...
BUT IF YOU OVER-HEARD THAT THEN THEY'LL SURELY TRY TO KILL YOU.
YEAH... I FIGURED THAT... IS THERE ANYTHING I CAN DO?
LUCKILY YOU'RE STILL ALIVE, SO THERE MAY BE A WAY... BUT FOR THAT...
...YOU MUST DIE BEFORE YOU'RE KILLED.
...
I... I SEE...
NOW, LISTEN CAREFULLY... ON THE WEST SIDE OF THIS BUILDING...
OKAY... I'LL TRY IT...

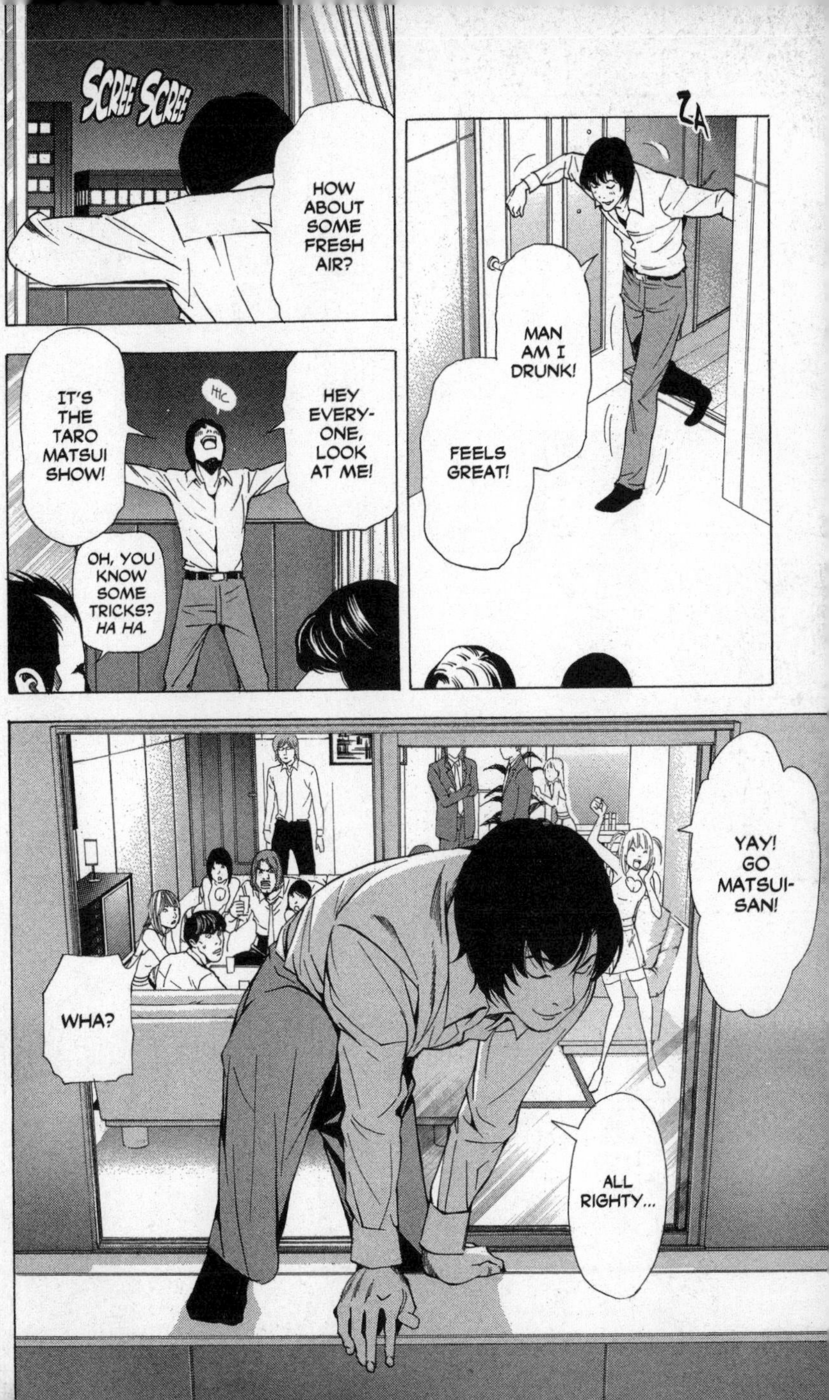
ZA
MAN AM I DRUNK!
FEELS GREAT!
SCREE SCREE
HOW ABOUT SOME FRESH AIR?
HIC
HEY EVERY-ONE, LOOK AT ME!
IT'S THE TARO MATSUI SHOW!
OH, YOU KNOW SOME TRICKS? HA HA.
YAY! GO MATSUI-SAN!
ALL RIGHTY...
WHA?

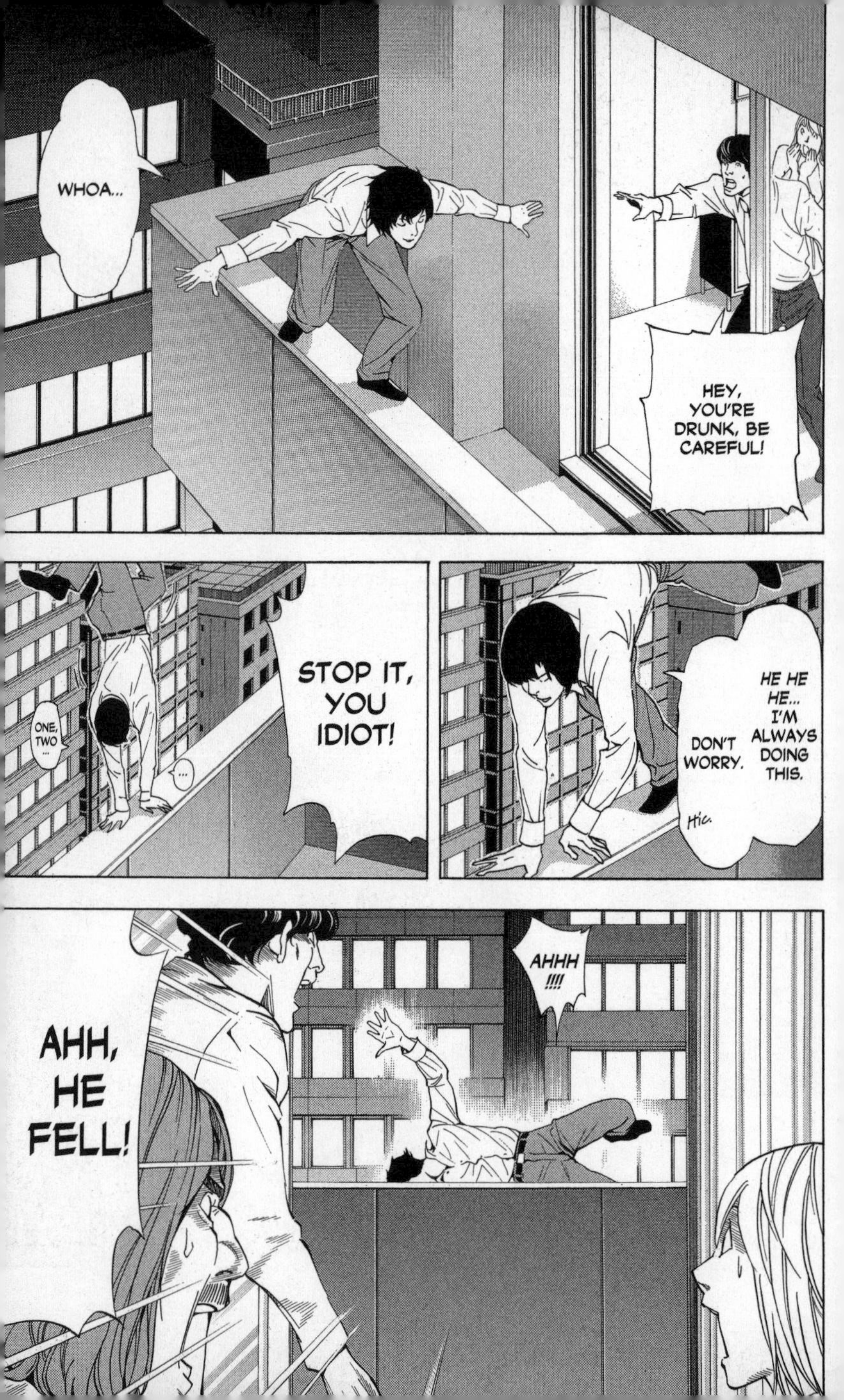
HEY, YOU'RE DRUNK, BE CAREFUL!
WHOA...
HE HE HE... I'M ALWAYS DOING THIS.
DON'T WORRY.
Hic.
STOP IT, YOU IDIOT!
ONE, TWO ...
...
AHHH !!!!
AHH, HE FELL!

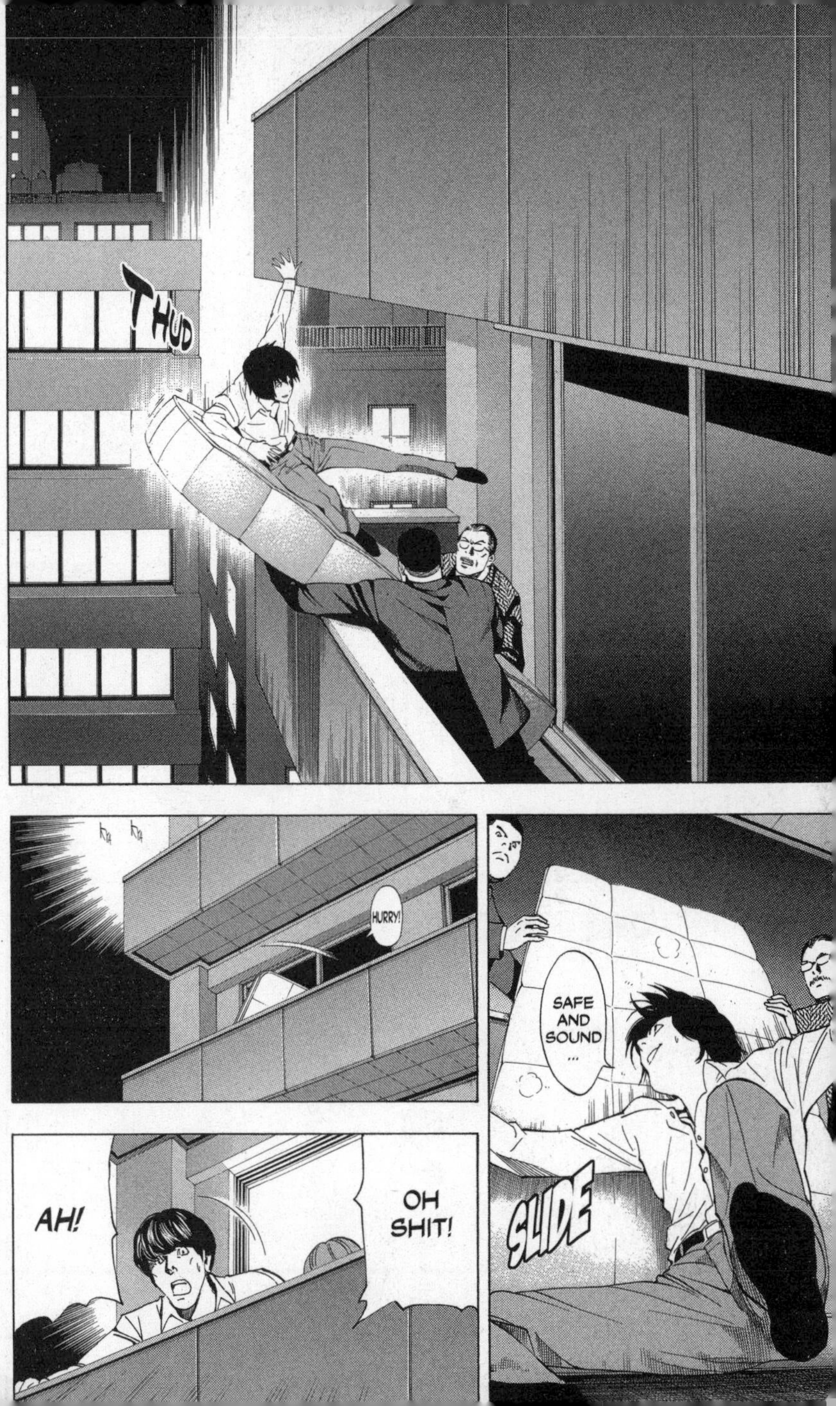
THUD
SAFE AND SOUND ...
SLIDE
HURRY!
OH SHIT!
AH!

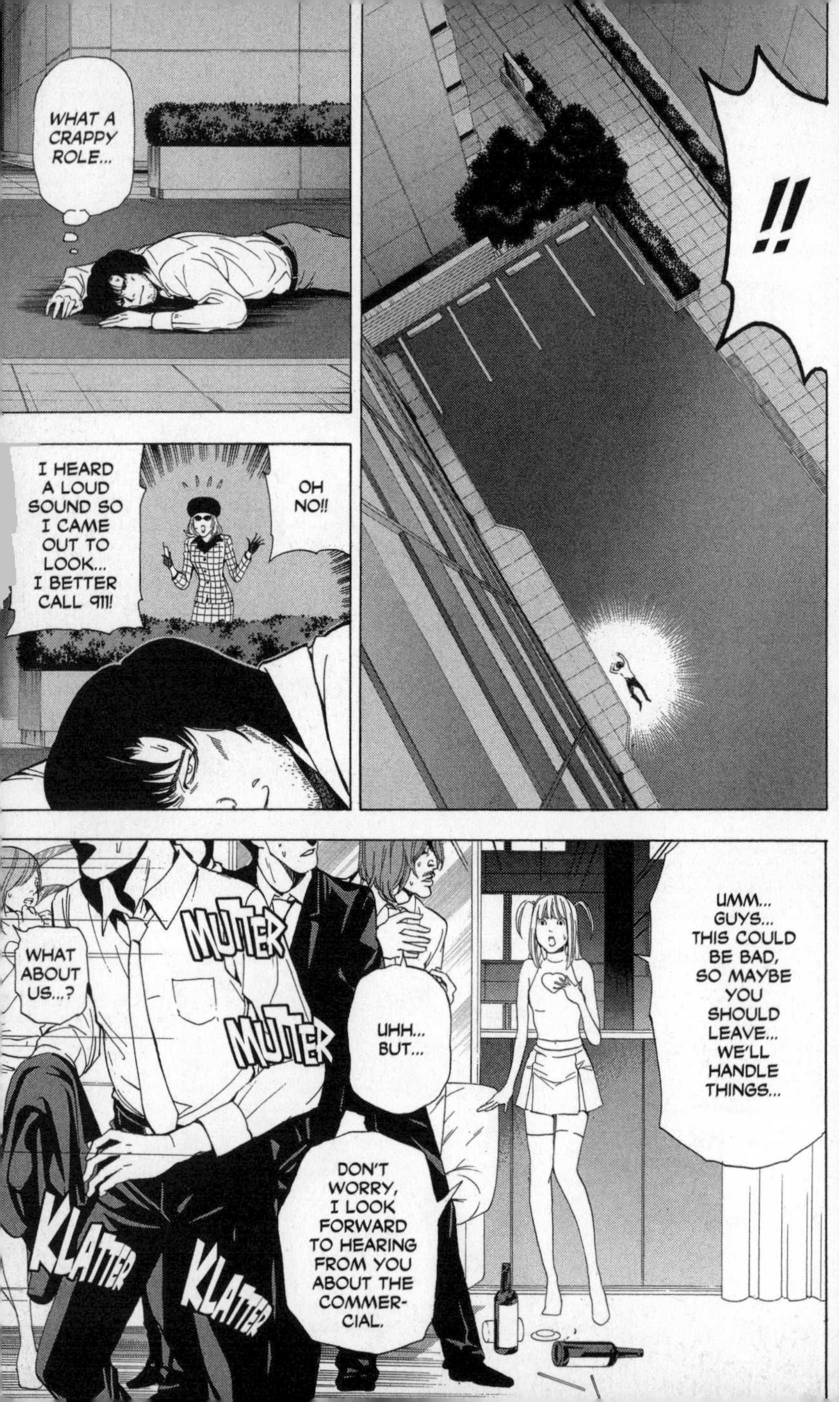
!!
WHAT A CRAPPY ROLE...
OH NO!!
I HEARD A LOUD SOUND SO I CAME OUT TO LOOK... I BETTER CALL 911!
UMM... GUYS... THIS COULD BE BAD, SO MAYBE YOU SHOULD LEAVE... WE'LL HANDLE THINGS...
UHH... BUT...
MUTTER
WHAT ABOUT US...?
MUTTER
DON'T WORRY, I LOOK FORWARD TO HEARING FROM YOU ABOUT THE COMMER-CIAL.
KLATTER
KLATTER

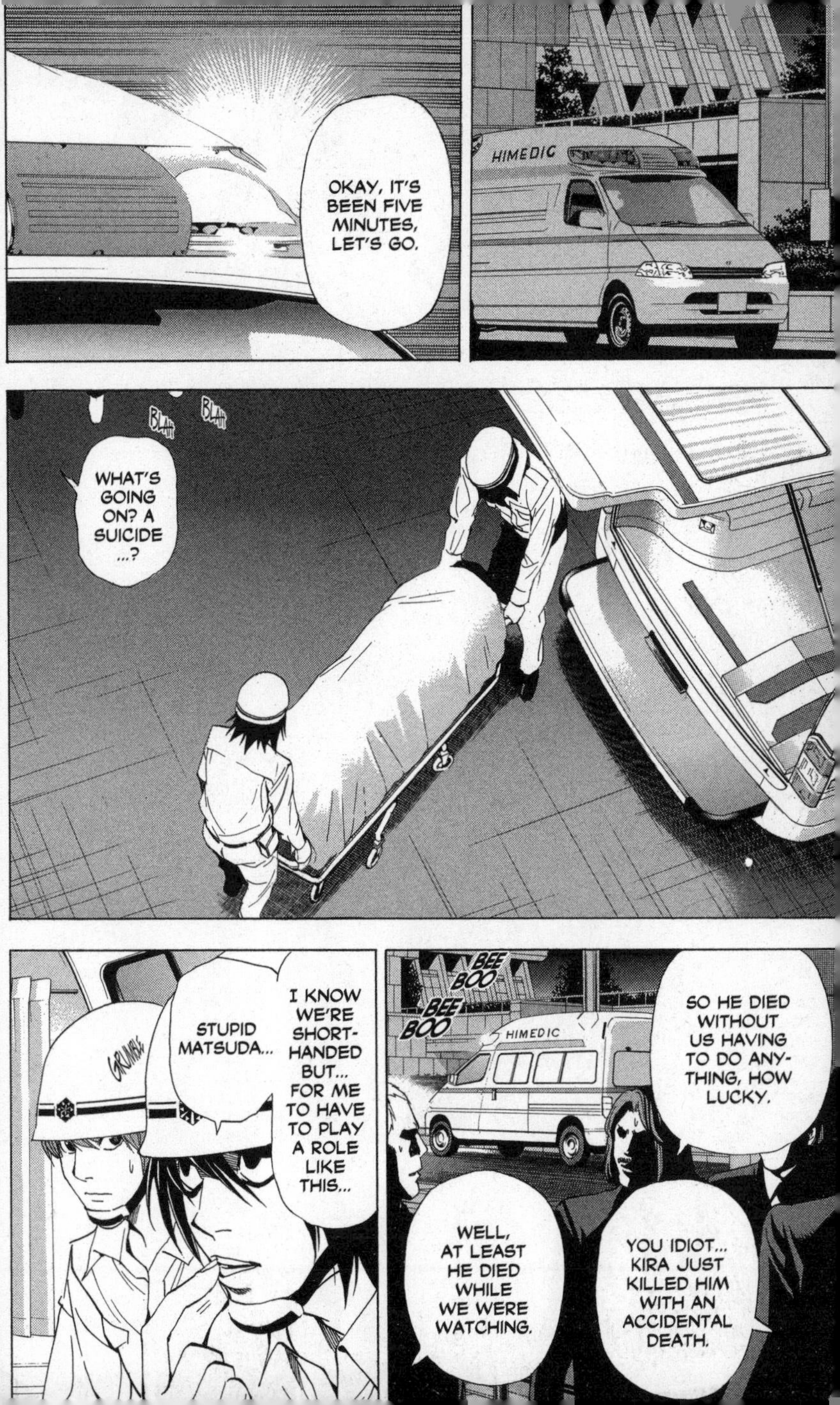
OKAY, IT'S BEEN FIVE MINUTES, LET'S GO.
HIMEDIC
BLAH BLAH
WHAT'S GOING ON? A SUICIDE ...?
BEE BOO BEE BOO
HIMEDIC
SO HE DIED WITHOUT US HAVING TO DO ANY-THING, HOW LUCKY.
YOU IDIOT... KIRA JUST KILLED HIM WITH AN ACCIDENTAL DEATH.
WELL, AT LEAST HE DIED WHILE WE WERE WATCHING.
I KNOW WE'RE SHORT-HANDED BUT... FOR ME TO HAVE TO PLAY A ROLE LIKE THIS...
STUPID MATSUDA...
GRUMBLE

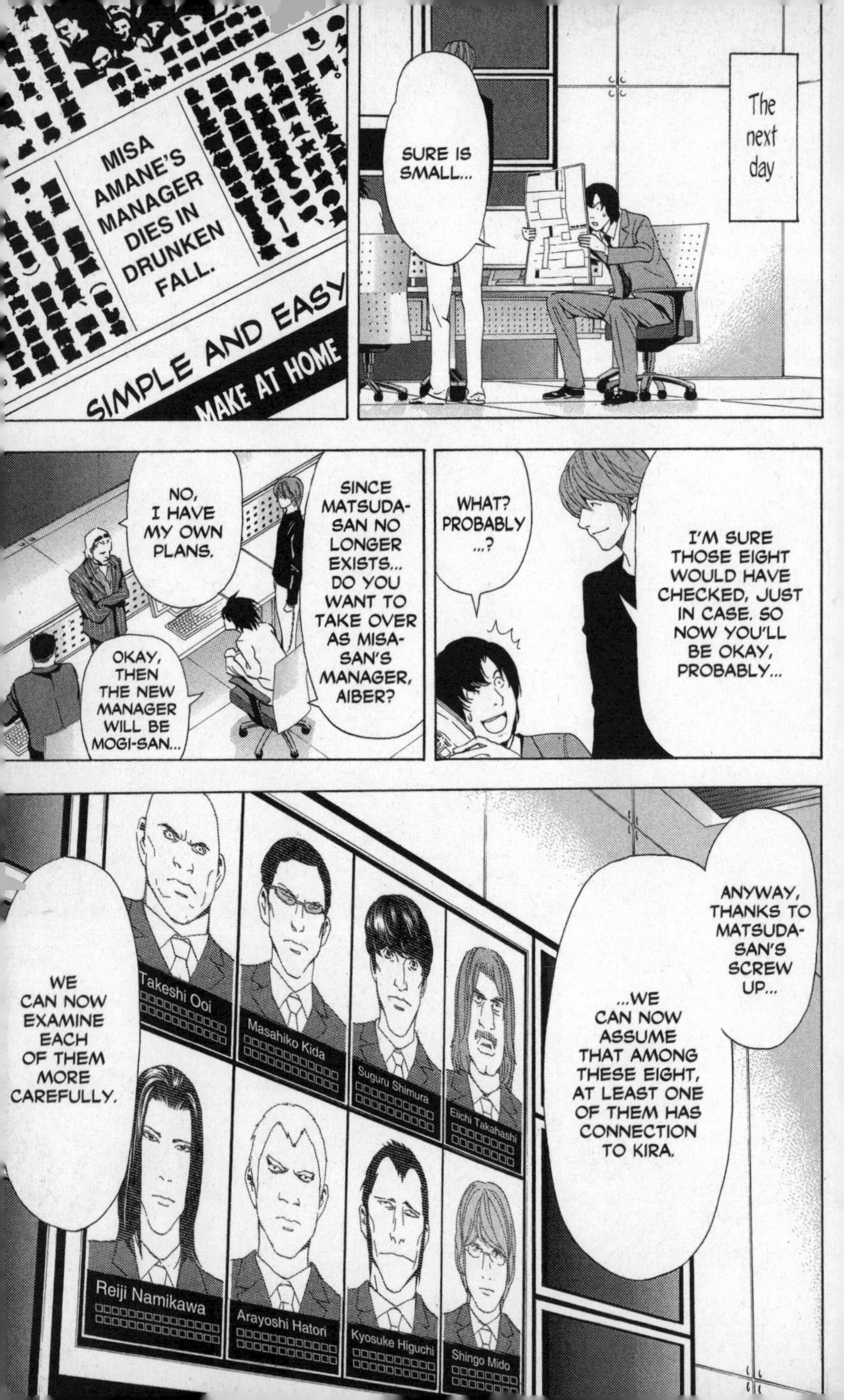
The next day
SURE IS SMALL...
MISA AMANE'S MANAGER DIES IN DRUNKEN FALL.
SIMPLE AND EASY
MAKE AT HOME
I'M SURE THOSE EIGHT WOULD HAVE CHECKED, JUST IN CASE. SO NOW YOU'LL BE OKAY, PROBABLY...
WHAT? PROBABLY ...?
SINCE MATSUDA-SAN NO LONGER EXISTS... DO YOU WANT TO TAKE OVER AS MISA-SAN'S MANAGER, AIBER?
NO, I HAVE MY OWN PLANS.
OKAY, THEN THE NEW MANAGER WILL BE MOGI-SAN...
ANYWAY, THANKS TO MATSUDA-SAN'S SCREW UP...
...WE CAN NOW ASSUME THAT AMONG THESE EIGHT, AT LEAST ONE OF THEM HAS CONNECTION TO KIRA.
WE CAN NOW EXAMINE EACH OF THEM MORE CAREFULLY.
Takeshi Ooi
Masahiko Kida
Suguru Shimura
Eiichi Takahashi
Reiji Namikawa
Arayoshi Hatori
Kyosuke Higuchi
Shingo Mido

# DEATH NOTE
## How to use it
## XXX

○ If you have traded the eye power of a god of death, you will see a person's primary life span in the human world.

死神と眼球の取引をし、その目で見える人間の寿命は
人間界にあるデスノートに関わっていない人間界での本来の寿命である。

○ The names you see with the eye power of a god of death are the names needed to kill that person. You will be able to see the names even if that person isn't registered in the family registration.

また、死神の目で見る事のできる人間の名前は
「その人間を殺すのに必要な名前」であり、たとえ戸籍等に
名前がなくとも殺すのに必要な名前は見える。

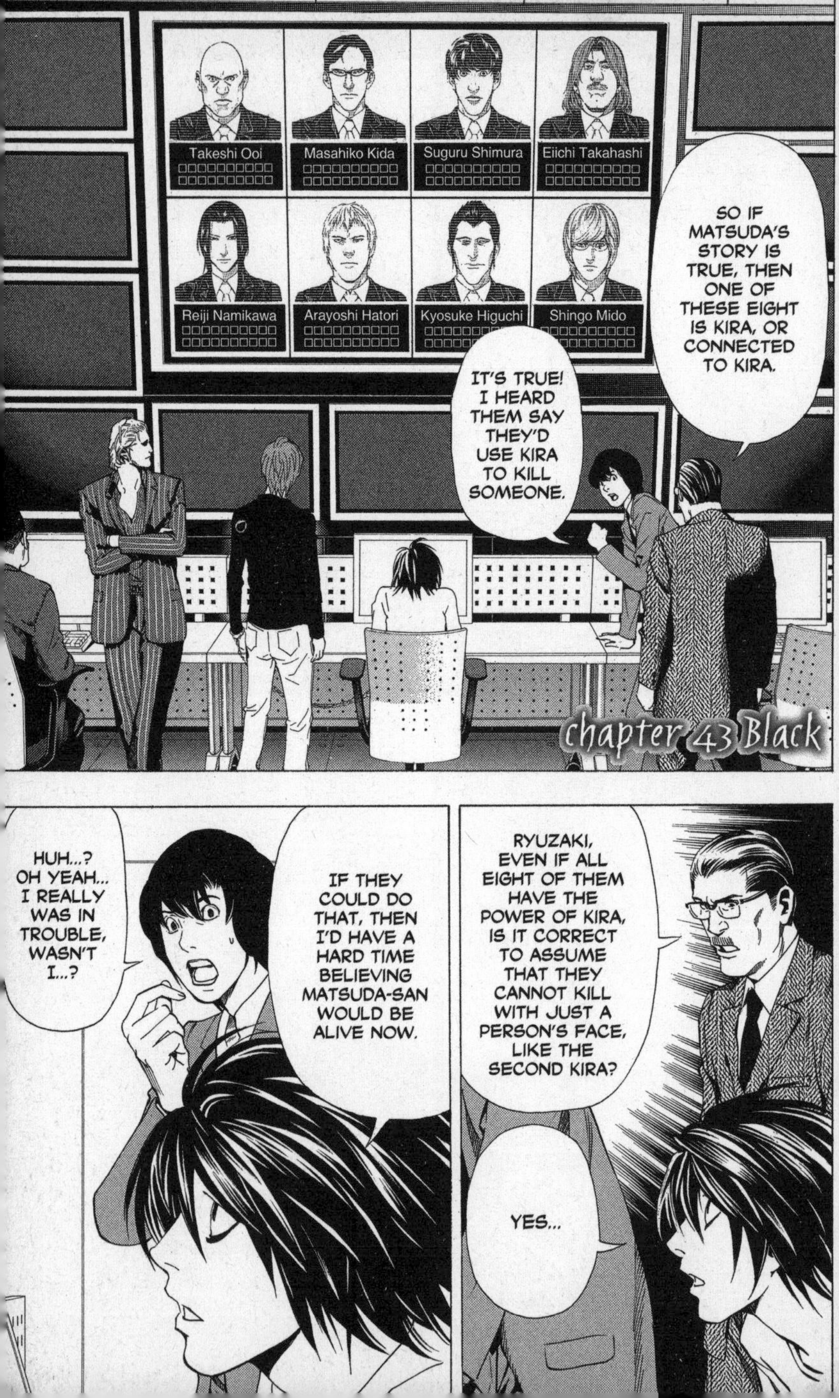
SO IF MATSUDA'S STORY IS TRUE, THEN ONE OF THESE EIGHT IS KIRA, OR CONNECTED TO KIRA.
IT'S TRUE! I HEARD THEM SAY THEY'D USE KIRA TO KILL SOMEONE.
Takeshi Ooi
Masahiko Kida
Suguru Shimura
Eiichi Takahashi
Reiji Namikawa
Arayoshi Hatori
Kyosuke Higuchi
Shingo Mido
chapter 43 Black
RYUZAKI, EVEN IF ALL EIGHT OF THEM HAVE THE POWER OF KIRA, IS IT CORRECT TO ASSUME THAT THEY CANNOT KILL WITH JUST A PERSON'S FACE, LIKE THE SECOND KIRA?
YES...
IF THEY COULD DO THAT, THEN I'D HAVE A HARD TIME BELIEVING MATSUDA-SAN WOULD BE ALIVE NOW.
HUH...? OH YEAH... I REALLY WAS IN TROUBLE, WASN'T I...?

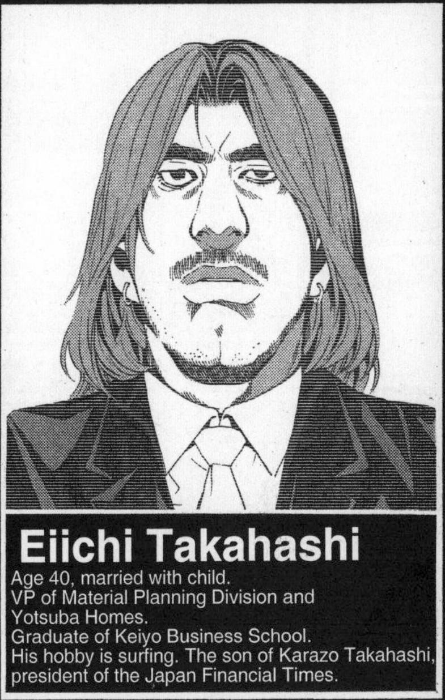
Eiichi Takahashi
Age 40, married with child.
VP of Material Planning Division and
Yotsuba Homes.
Graduate of Keiyo Business School.
His hobby is surfing. The son of Karazo Takahashi,
president of the Japan Financial Times.

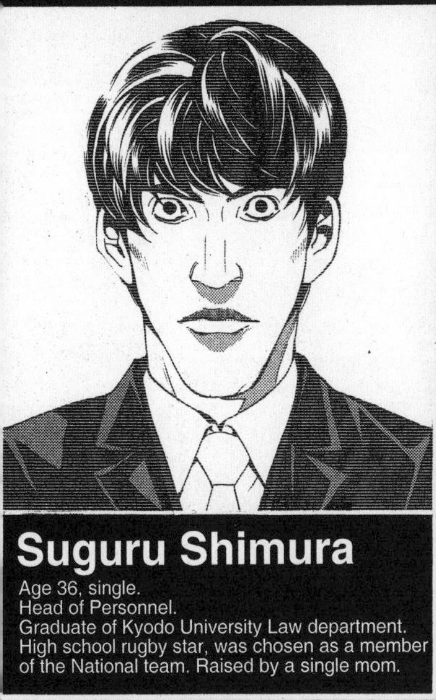
Suguru Shimura
Age 36, single.
Head of Personnel.
Graduate of Kyodo University Law department.
High school rugby star, was chosen as a member
of the National team. Raised by a single mom.

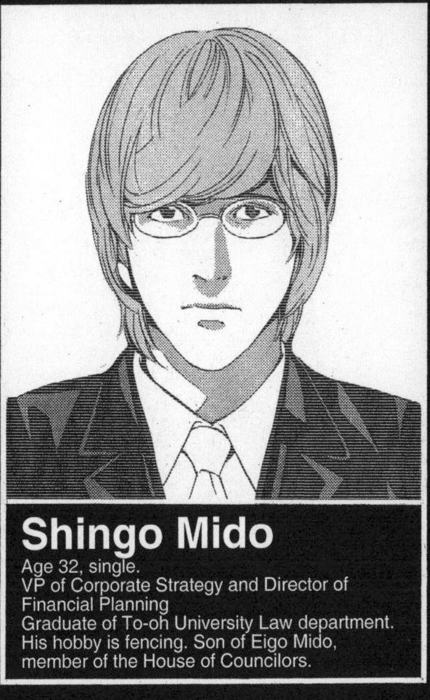
Shingo Mido
Age 32, single.
VP of Corporate Strategy and Director of
Financial Planning
Graduate of To-oh University Law department.
His hobby is fencing. Son of Eigo Mido,
member of the House of Councilors.

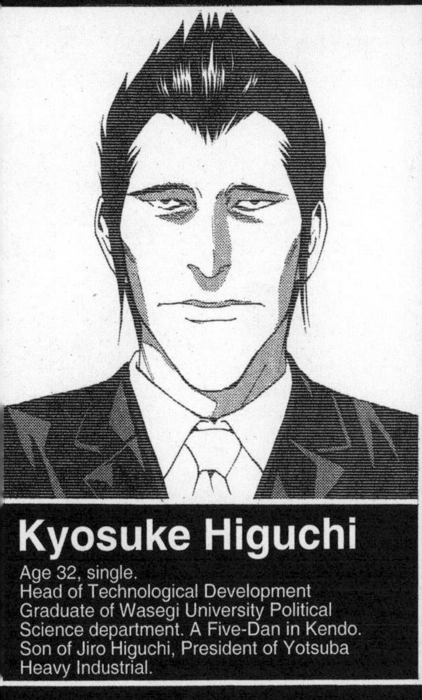
Kyosuke Higuchi
Age 32, single.
Head of Technological Development
Graduate of Wasegi University Political
Science department. A Five-Dan in Kendo.
Son of Jiro Higuchi, President of Yotsuba
Heavy Industrial.

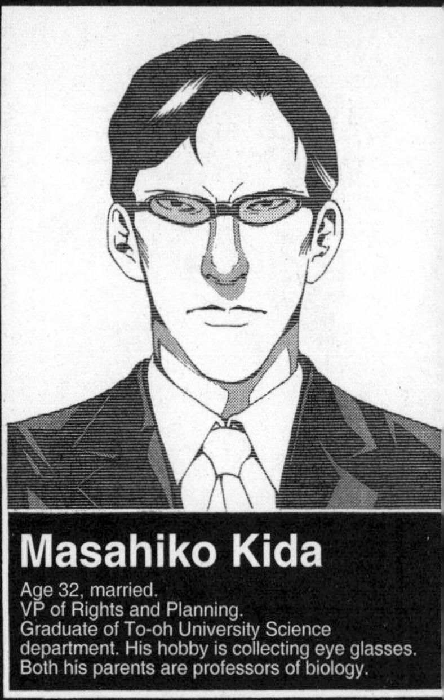
Masahiko Kida
Age 32, married.
VP of Rights and Planning.
Graduate of To-oh University Science department. His hobby is collecting eye glasses.
Both his parents are professors of biology.

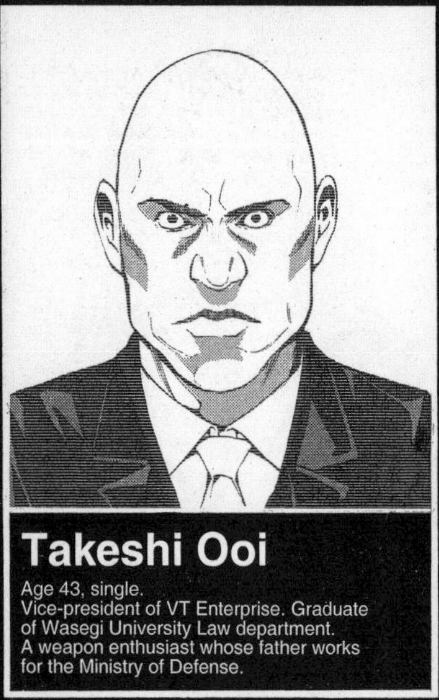
Takeshi Ooi
Age 43, single.
Vice-president of VT Enterprise. Graduate of Wasegi University Law department.
A weapon enthusiast whose father works for the Ministry of Defense.

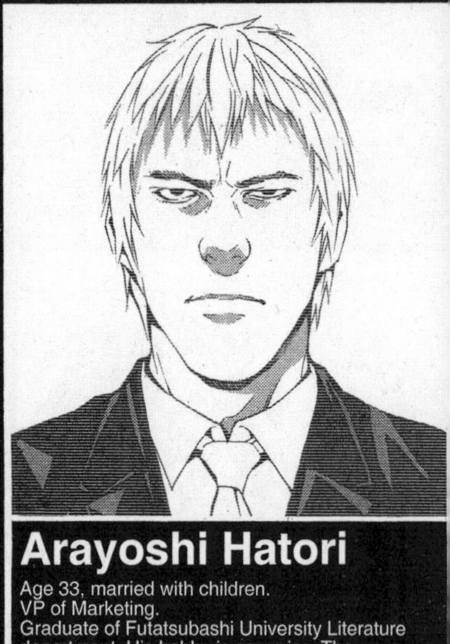
Arayoshi Hatori
Age 33, married with children.
VP of Marketing.
Graduate of Futatsubashi University Literature department. His hobby is ceramics. The illegitimate son of current Yotsuba President, Dainosuke Yotsuba.

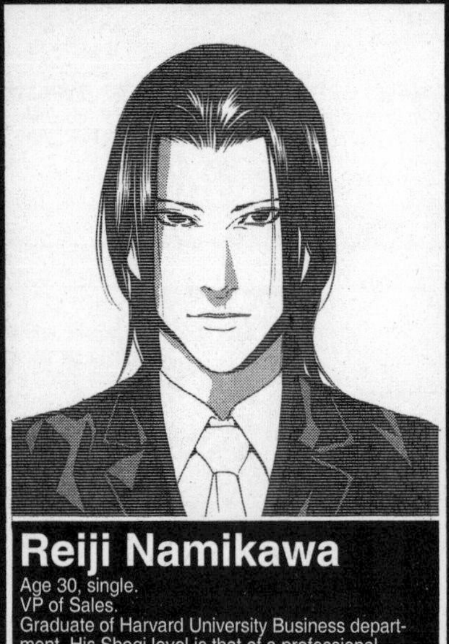
Reiji Namikawa
Age 30, single.
VP of Sales.
Graduate of Harvard University Business department. His Shogi level is that of a professional 4-dan. Son of the President of the Yotsuba American division. He's lived in America for 6 years.

chapter 43 Black

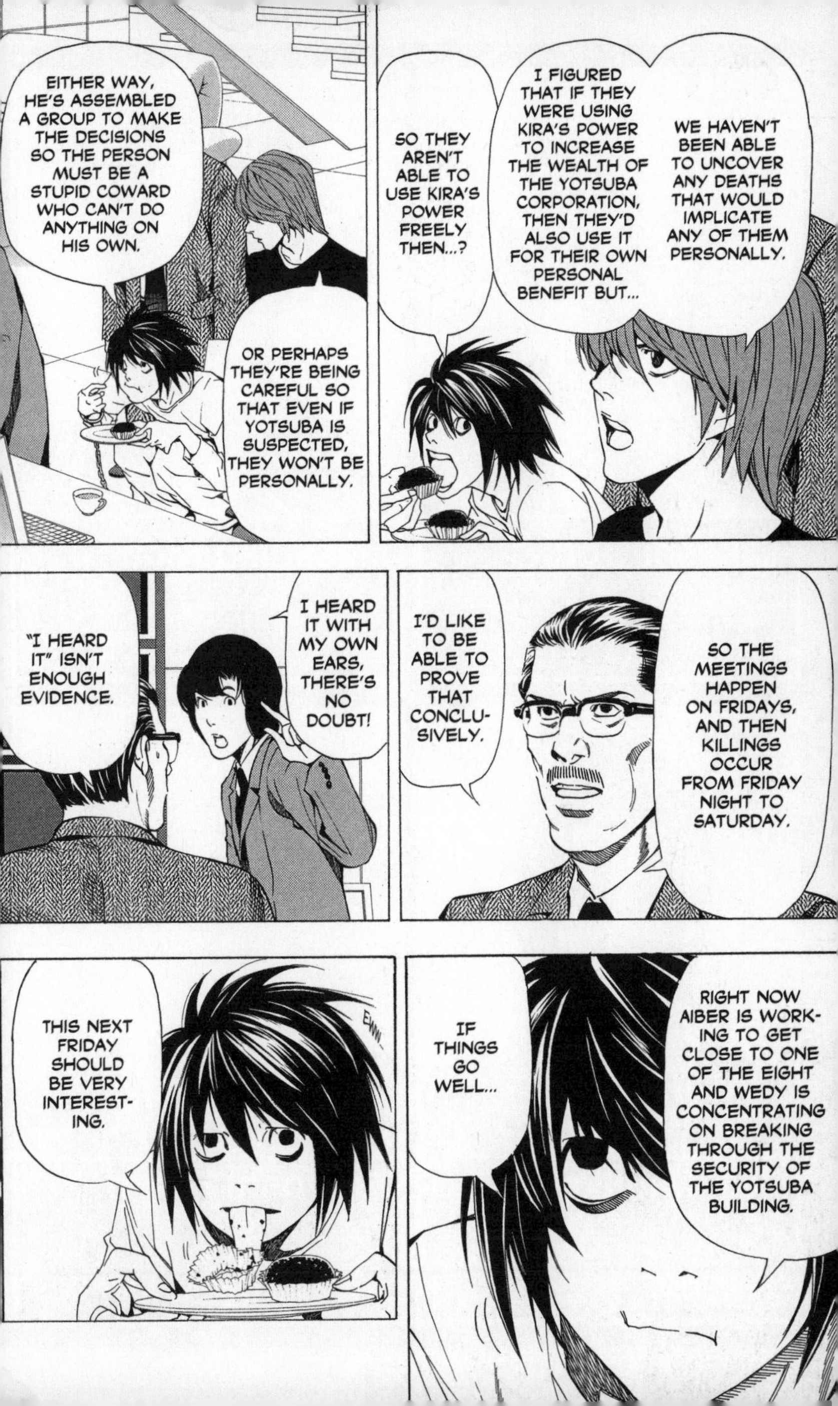
WE HAVEN'T BEEN ABLE TO UNCOVER ANY DEATHS THAT WOULD IMPLICATE ANY OF THEM PERSONALLY.
I FIGURED THAT IF THEY WERE USING KIRA'S POWER TO INCREASE THE WEALTH OF THE YOTSUBA CORPORATION, THEN THEY'D ALSO USE IT FOR THEIR OWN PERSONAL BENEFIT BUT...
SO THEY AREN'T ABLE TO USE KIRA'S POWER FREELY THEN...?
EITHER WAY, HE'S ASSEMBLED A GROUP TO MAKE THE DECISIONS SO THE PERSON MUST BE A STUPID COWARD WHO CAN'T DO ANYTHING ON HIS OWN.
OR PERHAPS THEY'RE BEING CAREFUL SO THAT EVEN IF YOTSUBA IS SUSPECTED, THEY WON'T BE PERSONALLY.
SO THE MEETINGS HAPPEN ON FRIDAYS, AND THEN KILLINGS OCCUR FROM FRIDAY NIGHT TO SATURDAY.
I'D LIKE TO BE ABLE TO PROVE THAT CONCLU-SIVELY.
I HEARD IT WITH MY OWN EARS, THERE'S NO DOUBT!
"I HEARD IT" ISN'T ENOUGH EVIDENCE.
RIGHT NOW AIBER IS WORK-ING TO GET CLOSE TO ONE OF THE EIGHT AND WEDY IS CONCENTRATING ON BREAKING THROUGH THE SECURITY OF THE YOTSUBA BUILDING.
IF THINGS GO WELL...
THIS NEXT FRIDAY SHOULD BE VERY INTEREST-ING.

READ THIS WAY

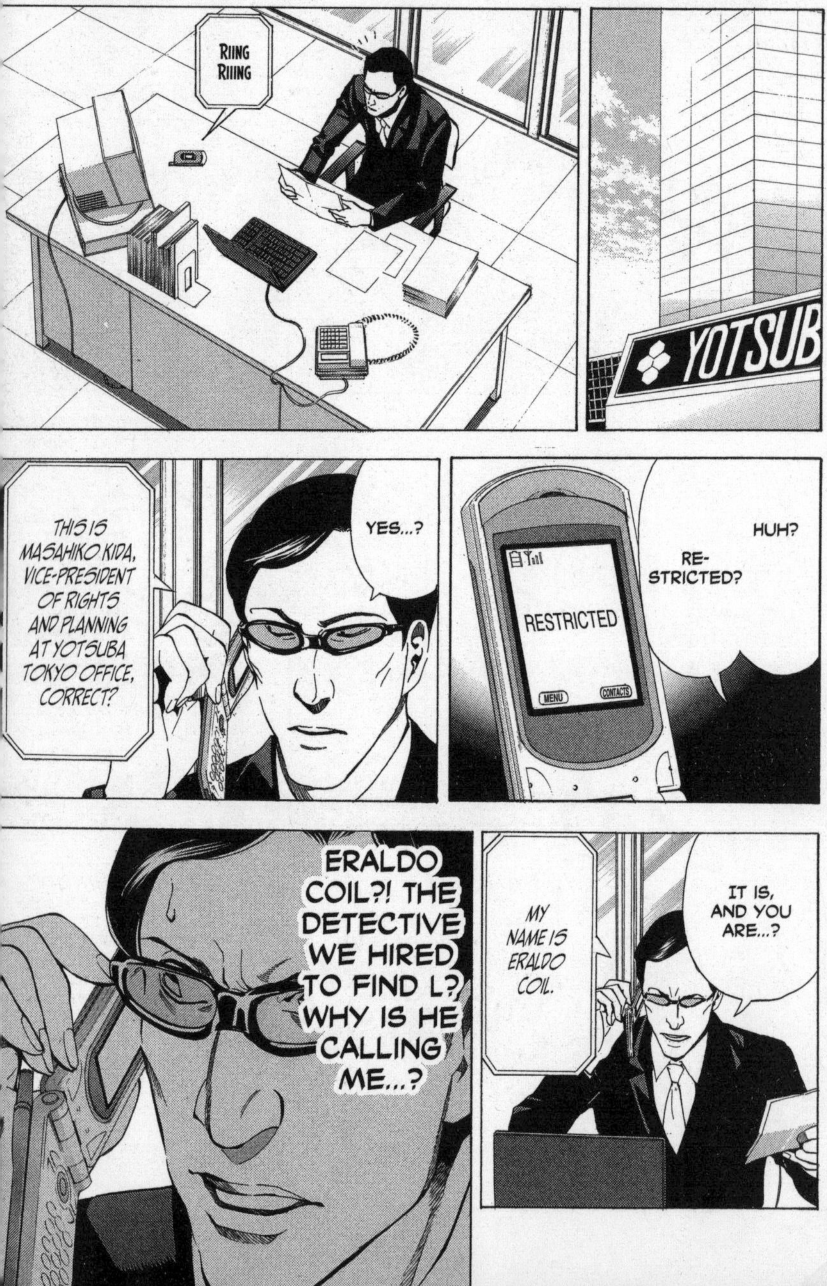

YOTSUB
RIING RIING
HUH?
RE-STRICTED?
RESTRICTED
MENU
CONTACTS
YES...?
THIS IS MASAHIKO KIDA, VICE-PRESIDENT OF RIGHTS AND PLANNING AT YOTSUBA TOKYO OFFICE, CORRECT?
IT IS, AND YOU ARE...?
MY NAME IS ERALDO COIL.
ERALDO COIL?! THE DETECTIVE WE HIRED TO FIND L? WHY IS HE CALLING ME...?

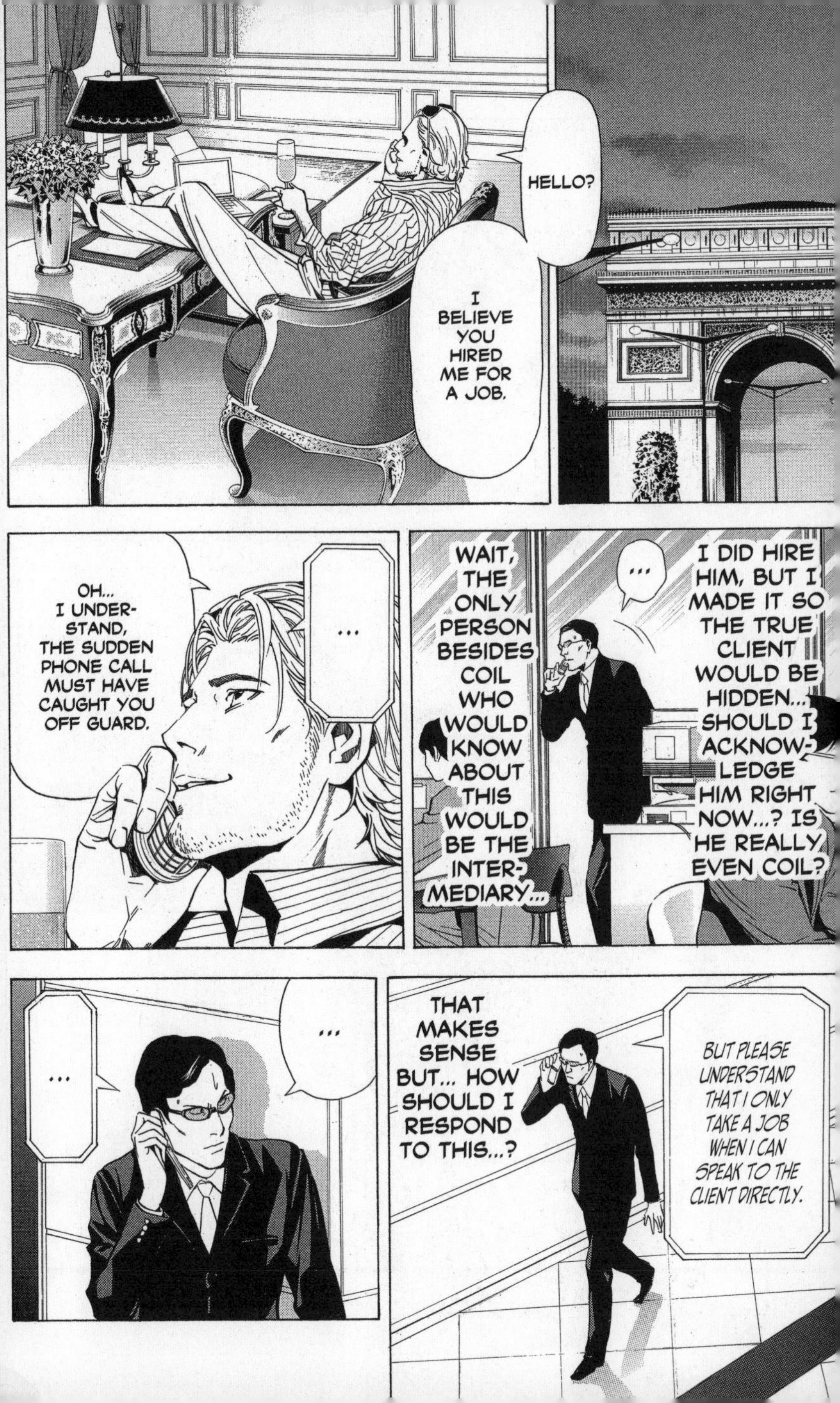
HELLO?
I BELIEVE YOU HIRED ME FOR A JOB.
I DID HIRE HIM, BUT I MADE IT SO THE TRUE CLIENT WOULD BE HIDDEN... SHOULD I ACKNOW-LEDGE HIM RIGHT NOW...? IS HE REALLY EVEN COIL?
...
WAIT, THE ONLY PERSON BESIDES COIL WHO WOULD KNOW ABOUT THIS WOULD BE THE INTER-MEDIARY...
...
OH... I UNDER-STAND, THE SUDDEN PHONE CALL MUST HAVE CAUGHT YOU OFF GUARD.
BUT PLEASE UNDERSTAND THAT I ONLY TAKE A JOB WHEN I CAN SPEAK TO THE CLIENT DIRECTLY.
THAT MAKES SENSE BUT... HOW SHOULD I RESPOND TO THIS...?
...
...

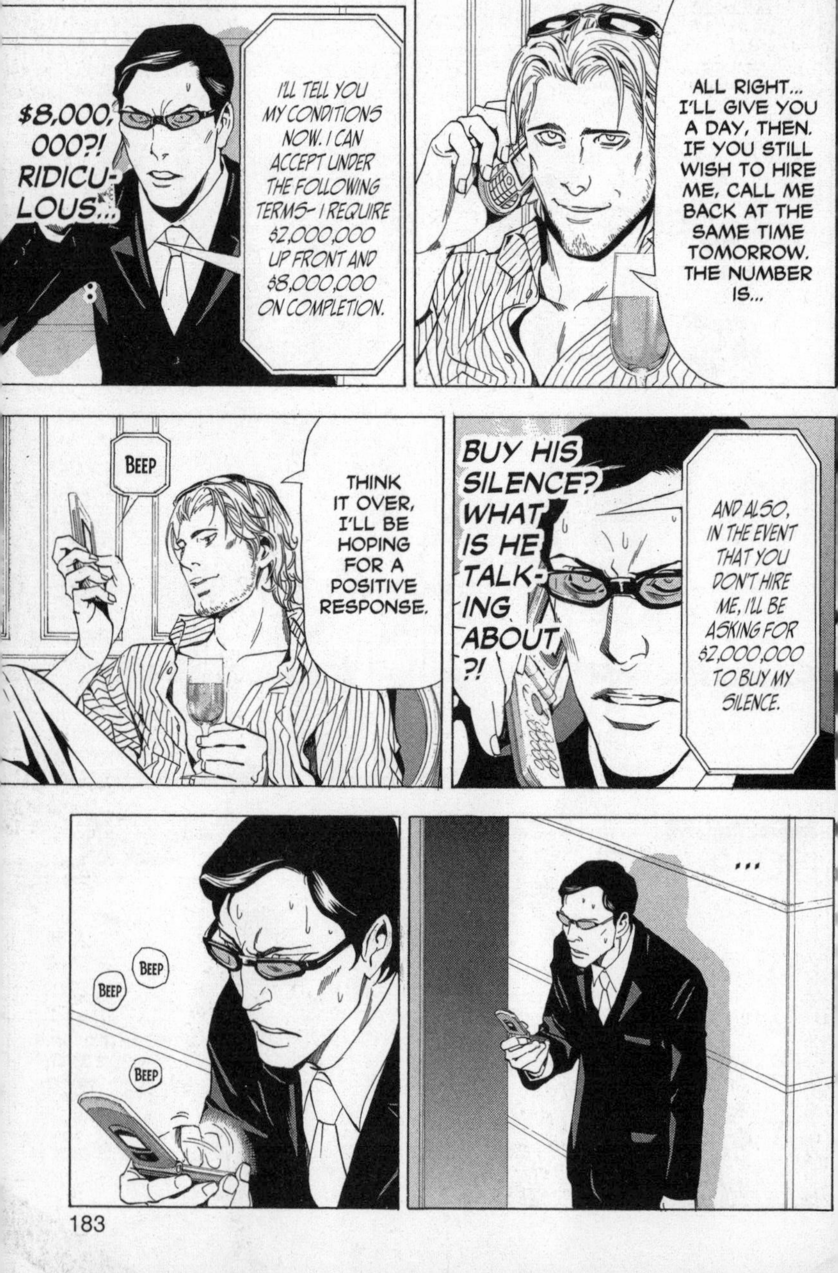

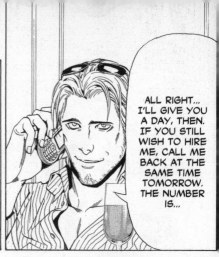

ALL RIGHT... I'LL GIVE YOU A DAY, THEN. IF YOU STILL WISH TO HIRE ME, CALL ME BACK AT THE SAME TIME TOMORROW. THE NUMBER IS...
I'LL TELL YOU MY CONDITIONS NOW. I CAN ACCEPT UNDER THE FOLLOWING TERMS- I REQUIRE $2,000,000 UP FRONT AND $8,000,000 ON COMPLETION.
$8,000,000?! RIDICULOUS...
AND ALSO, IN THE EVENT THAT YOU DON'T HIRE ME, I'LL BE ASKING FOR $2,000,000 TO BUY MY SILENCE.
BUY HIS SILENCE? WHAT IS HE TALKING ABOUT?!
THINK IT OVER, I'LL BE HOPING FOR A POSITIVE RESPONSE.
BEEP
...
BEEP
BEEP
BEEP

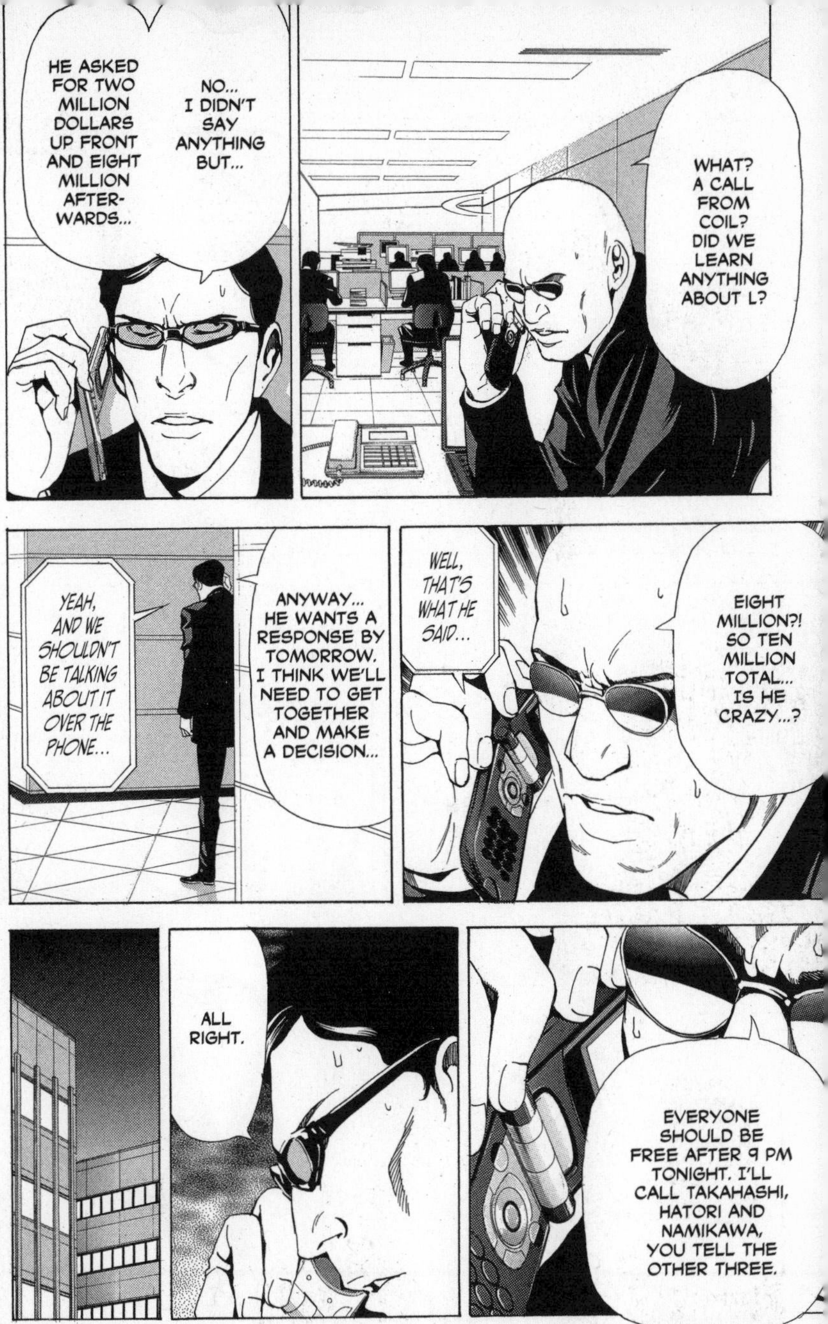
WHAT? A CALL FROM COIL? DID WE LEARN ANYTHING ABOUT L?
NO... I DIDN'T SAY ANYTHING BUT...
HE ASKED FOR TWO MILLION DOLLARS UP FRONT AND EIGHT MILLION AFTER-WARDS...
EIGHT MILLION?! SO TEN MILLION TOTAL... IS HE CRAZY...?
WELL, THAT'S WHAT HE SAID...
ANYWAY... HE WANTS A RESPONSE BY TOMORROW. I THINK WE'LL NEED TO GET TOGETHER AND MAKE A DECISION...
YEAH, AND WE SHOULDN'T BE TALKING ABOUT IT OVER THE PHONE...
EVERYONE SHOULD BE FREE AFTER 9 PM TONIGHT. I'LL CALL TAKAHASHI, HATORI AND NAMIKAWA, YOU TELL THE OTHER THREE.
ALL RIGHT.

READ THIS WAY

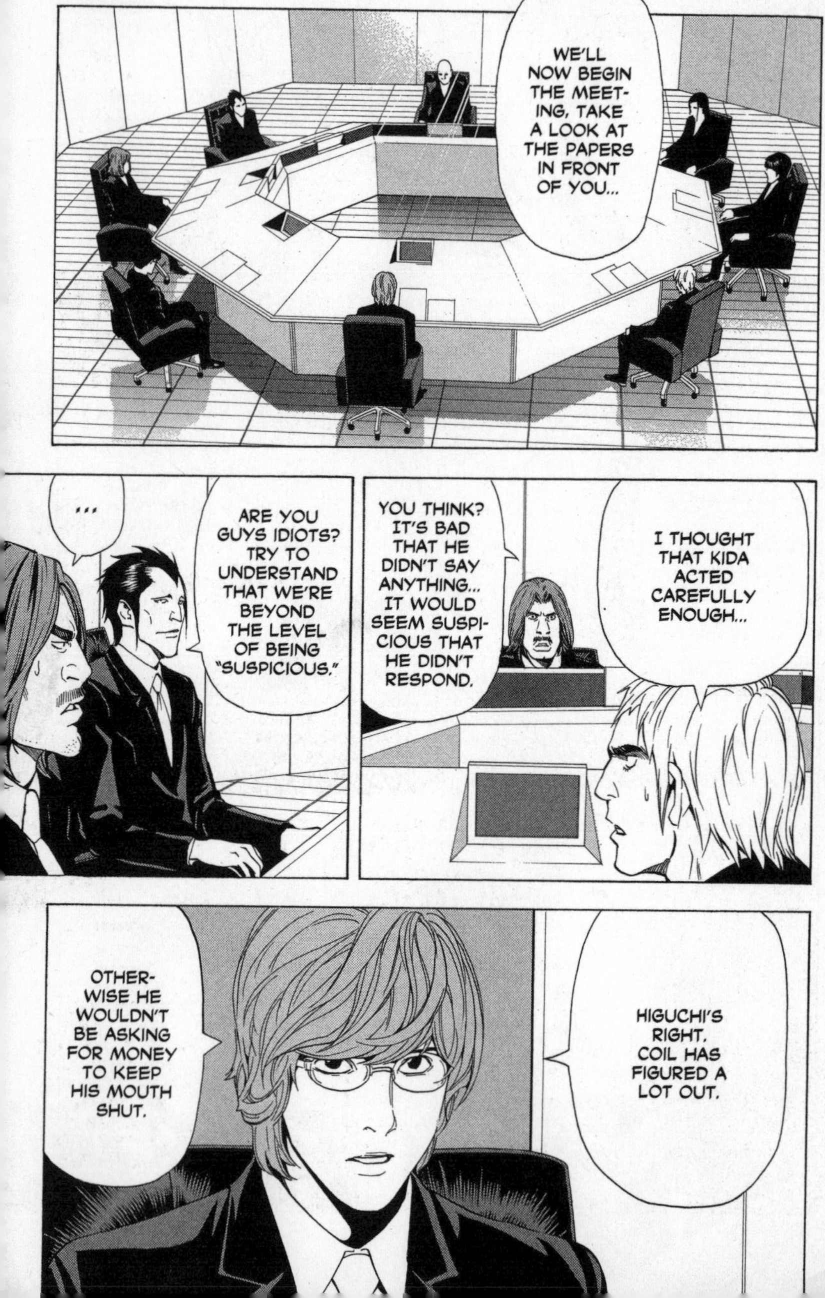
WE'LL NOW BEGIN THE MEET-ING, TAKE A LOOK AT THE PAPERS IN FRONT OF YOU...
I THOUGHT THAT KIDA ACTED CAREFULLY ENOUGH...
YOU THINK? IT'S BAD THAT HE DIDN'T SAY ANYTHING... IT WOULD SEEM SUSPI-CIOUS THAT HE DIDN'T RESPOND.
ARE YOU GUYS IDIOTS? TRY TO UNDERSTAND THAT WE'RE BEYOND THE LEVEL OF BEING "SUSPICIOUS."
...
HIGUCHI'S RIGHT. COIL HAS FIGURED A LOT OUT.
OTHER-WISE HE WOULDN'T BE ASKING FOR MONEY TO KEEP HIS MOUTH SHUT.

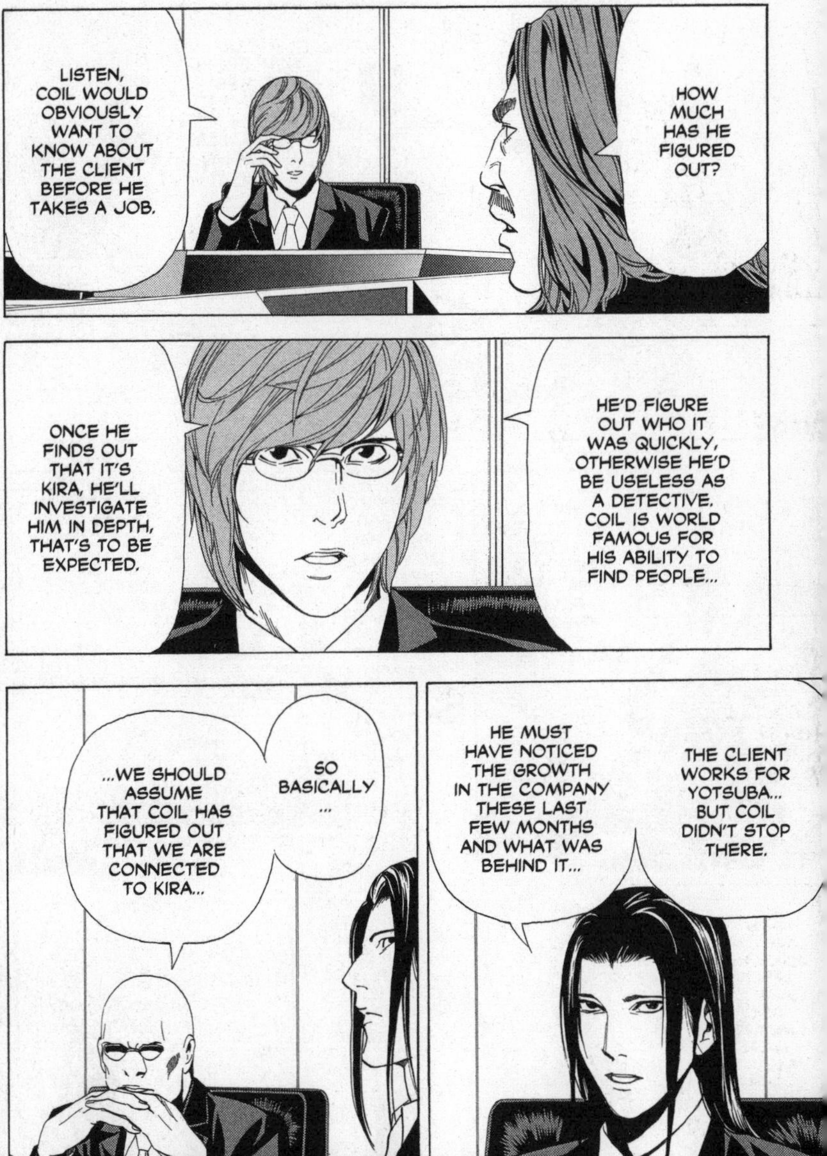
HOW MUCH HAS HE FIGURED OUT?
LISTEN, COIL WOULD OBVIOUSLY WANT TO KNOW ABOUT THE CLIENT BEFORE HE TAKES A JOB.
HE'D FIGURE OUT WHO IT WAS QUICKLY, OTHERWISE HE'D BE USELESS AS A DETECTIVE. COIL IS WORLD FAMOUS FOR HIS ABILITY TO FIND PEOPLE...
ONCE HE FINDS OUT THAT IT'S KIRA, HE'LL INVESTIGATE HIM IN DEPTH, THAT'S TO BE EXPECTED.
THE CLIENT WORKS FOR YOTSUBA... BUT COIL DIDN'T STOP THERE.
HE MUST HAVE NOTICED THE GROWTH IN THE COMPANY THESE LAST FEW MONTHS AND WHAT WAS BEHIND IT...
SO BASICALLY ...
...WE SHOULD ASSUME THAT COIL HAS FIGURED OUT THAT WE ARE CONNECTED TO KIRA...

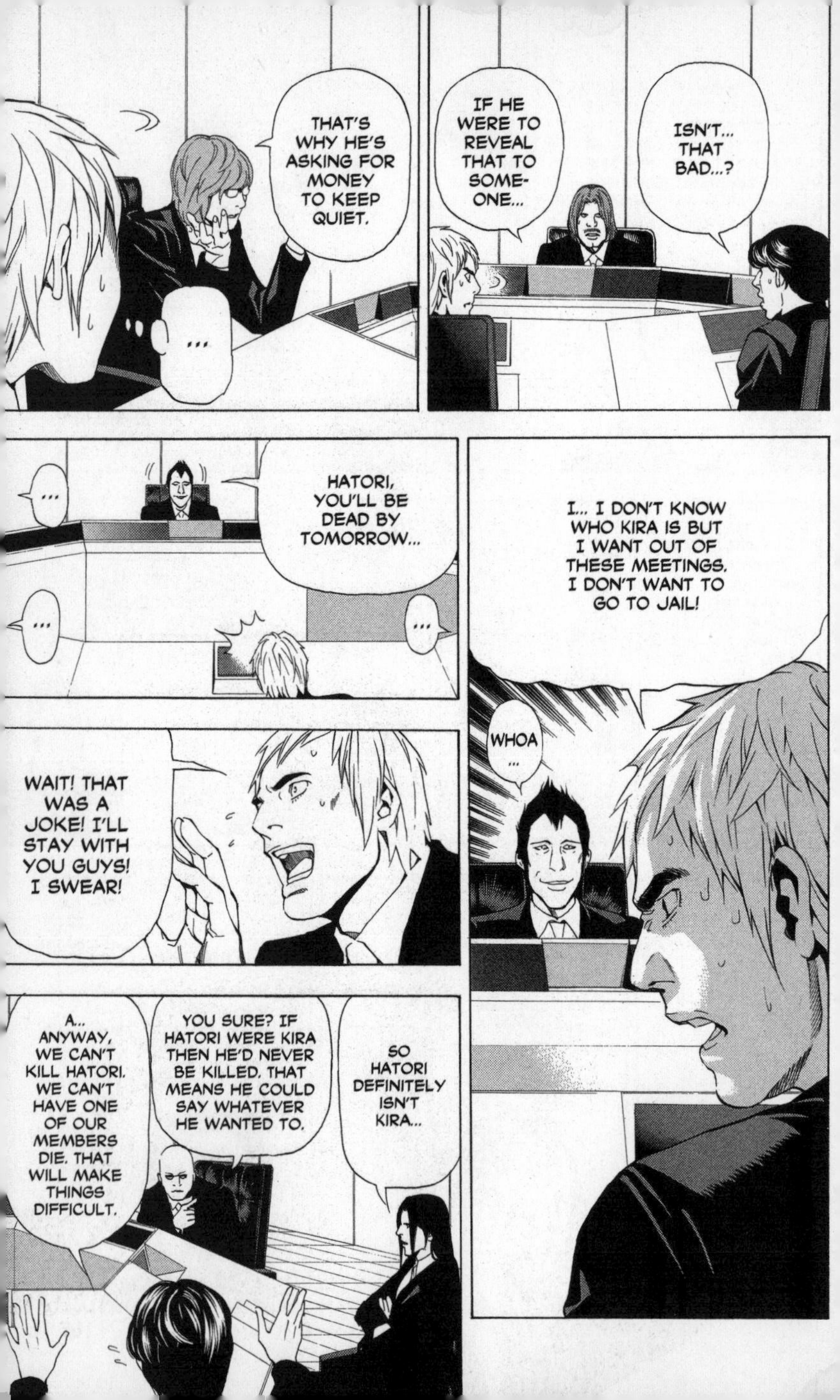
IF HE WERE TO REVEAL THAT TO SOME-ONE...
ISN'T... THAT BAD...?
THAT'S WHY HE'S ASKING FOR MONEY TO KEEP QUIET.
...
I... I DON'T KNOW WHO KIRA IS BUT I WANT OUT OF THESE MEETINGS. I DON'T WANT TO GO TO JAIL!
WHOA ...
HATORI, YOU'LL BE DEAD BY TOMORROW...
...
...
...
WAIT! THAT WAS A JOKE! I'LL STAY WITH YOU GUYS! I SWEAR!
SO HATORI DEFINITELY ISN'T KIRA...
YOU SURE? IF HATORI WERE KIRA THEN HE'D NEVER BE KILLED. THAT MEANS HE COULD SAY WHATEVER HE WANTED TO.
A... ANYWAY, WE CAN'T KILL HATORI. WE CAN'T HAVE ONE OF OUR MEMBERS DIE. THAT WILL MAKE THINGS DIFFICULT.

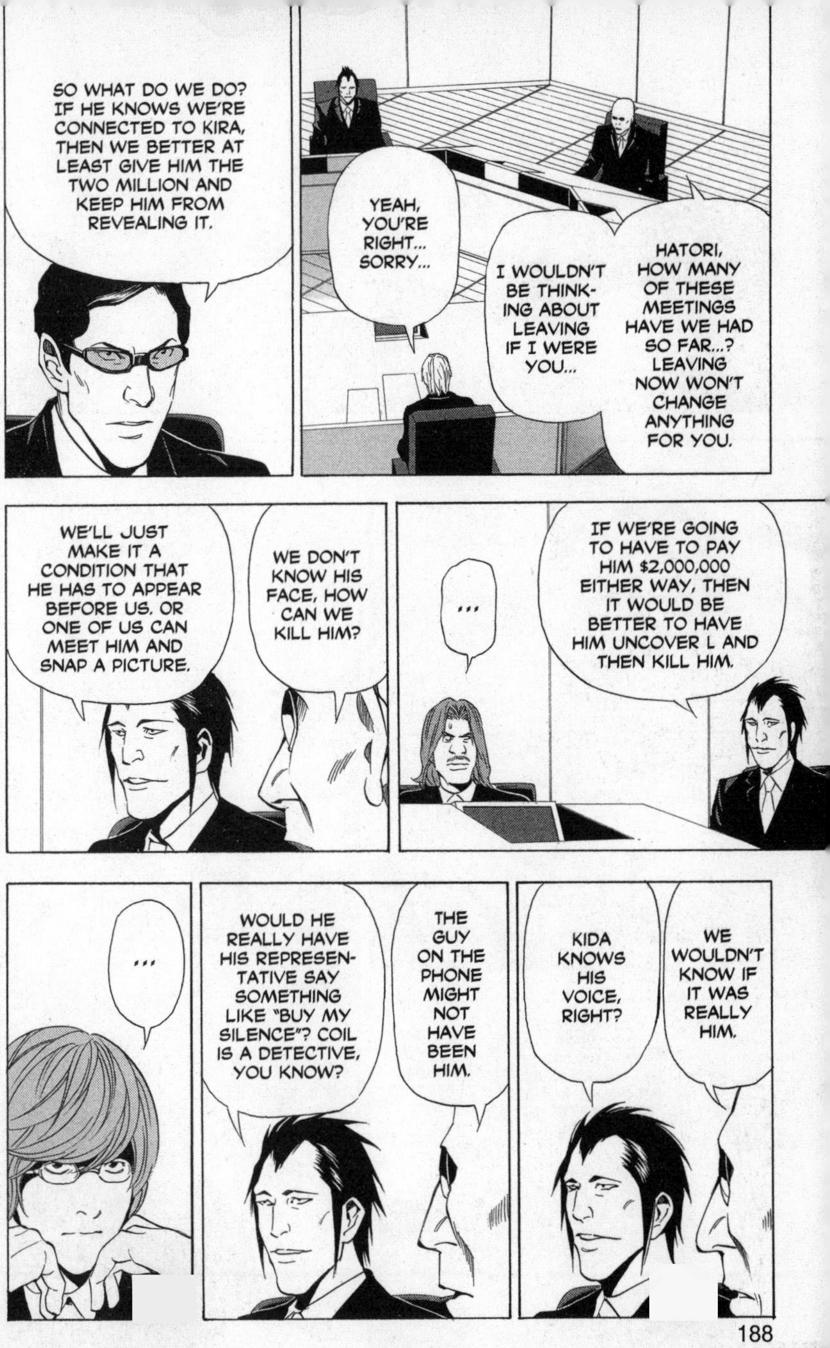
HATORI, HOW MANY OF THESE MEETINGS HAVE WE HAD SO FAR...? LEAVING NOW WON'T CHANGE ANYTHING FOR YOU.
I WOULDN'T BE THINK-ING ABOUT LEAVING IF I WERE YOU...
YEAH, YOU'RE RIGHT... SORRY...
SO WHAT DO WE DO? IF HE KNOWS WE'RE CONNECTED TO KIRA, THEN WE BETTER AT LEAST GIVE HIM THE TWO MILLION AND KEEP HIM FROM REVEALING IT.
IF WE'RE GOING TO HAVE TO PAY HIM $2,000,000 EITHER WAY, THEN IT WOULD BE BETTER TO HAVE HIM UNCOVER L AND THEN KILL HIM.
...
WE DON'T KNOW HIS FACE, HOW CAN WE KILL HIM?
WE'LL JUST MAKE IT A CONDITION THAT HE HAS TO APPEAR BEFORE US. OR ONE OF US CAN MEET HIM AND SNAP A PICTURE.
WE WOULDN'T KNOW IF IT WAS REALLY HIM.
KIDA KNOWS HIS VOICE, RIGHT?
THE GUY ON THE PHONE MIGHT NOT HAVE BEEN HIM.
WOULD HE REALLY HAVE HIS REPRESEN-TATIVE SAY SOMETHING LIKE "BUY MY SILENCE"? COIL IS A DETECTIVE, YOU KNOW?
...

READ THIS WAY

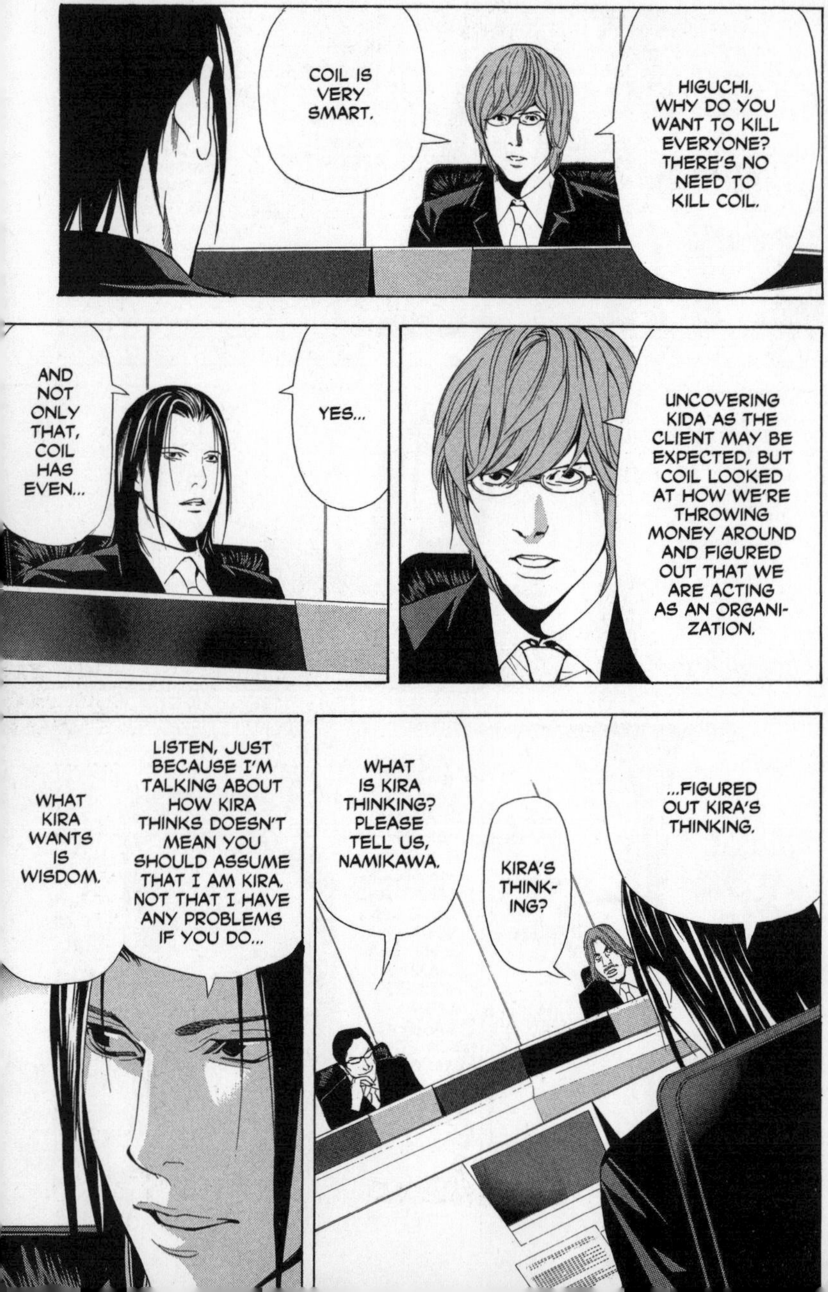
HIGUCHI, WHY DO YOU WANT TO KILL EVERYONE? THERE'S NO NEED TO KILL COIL.
COIL IS VERY SMART.
UNCOVERING KIDA AS THE CLIENT MAY BE EXPECTED, BUT COIL LOOKED AT HOW WE'RE THROWING MONEY AROUND AND FIGURED OUT THAT WE ARE ACTING AS AN ORGANI-ZATION.
YES...
AND NOT ONLY THAT, COIL HAS EVEN...
...FIGURED OUT KIRA'S THINKING.
KIRA'S THINK-ING?
WHAT IS KIRA THINKING? PLEASE TELL US, NAMIKAWA.
LISTEN, JUST BECAUSE I'M TALKING ABOUT HOW KIRA THINKS DOESN'T MEAN YOU SHOULD ASSUME THAT I AM KIRA. NOT THAT I HAVE ANY PROBLEMS IF YOU DO...
WHAT KIRA WANTS IS WISDOM.

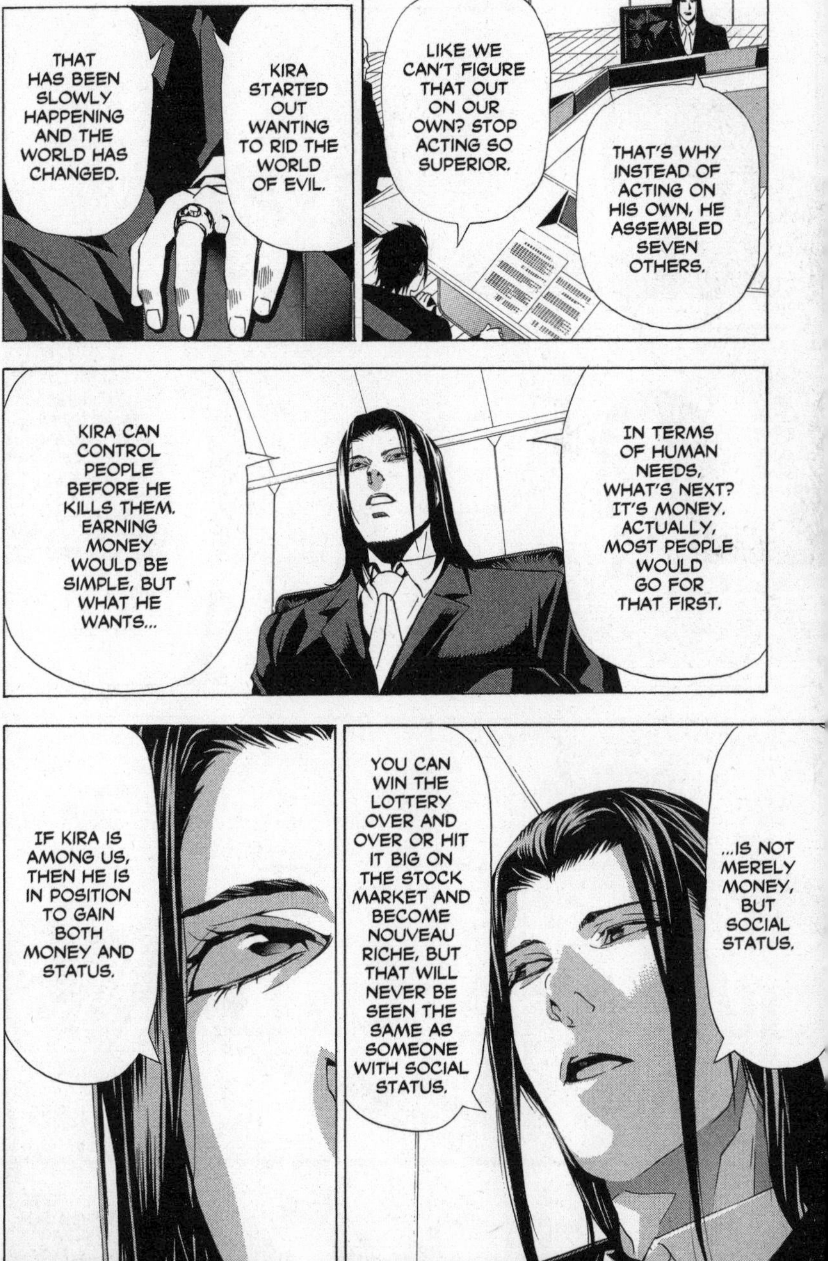
LIKE WE CAN'T FIGURE THAT OUT ON OUR OWN? STOP ACTING SO SUPERIOR.
THAT'S WHY INSTEAD OF ACTING ON HIS OWN, HE ASSEMBLED SEVEN OTHERS.
KIRA STARTED OUT WANTING TO RID THE WORLD OF EVIL.
THAT HAS BEEN SLOWLY HAPPENING AND THE WORLD HAS CHANGED.
IN TERMS OF HUMAN NEEDS, WHAT'S NEXT? IT'S MONEY. ACTUALLY, MOST PEOPLE WOULD GO FOR THAT FIRST.
KIRA CAN CONTROL PEOPLE BEFORE HE KILLS THEM. EARNING MONEY WOULD BE SIMPLE, BUT WHAT HE WANTS...
...IS NOT MERELY MONEY, BUT SOCIAL STATUS.
YOU CAN WIN THE LOTTERY OVER AND OVER OR HIT IT BIG ON THE STOCK MARKET AND BECOME NOUVEAU RICHE, BUT THAT WILL NEVER BE SEEN THE SAME AS SOMEONE WITH SOCIAL STATUS.
IF KIRA IS AMONG US, THEN HE IS IN POSITION TO GAIN BOTH MONEY AND STATUS.

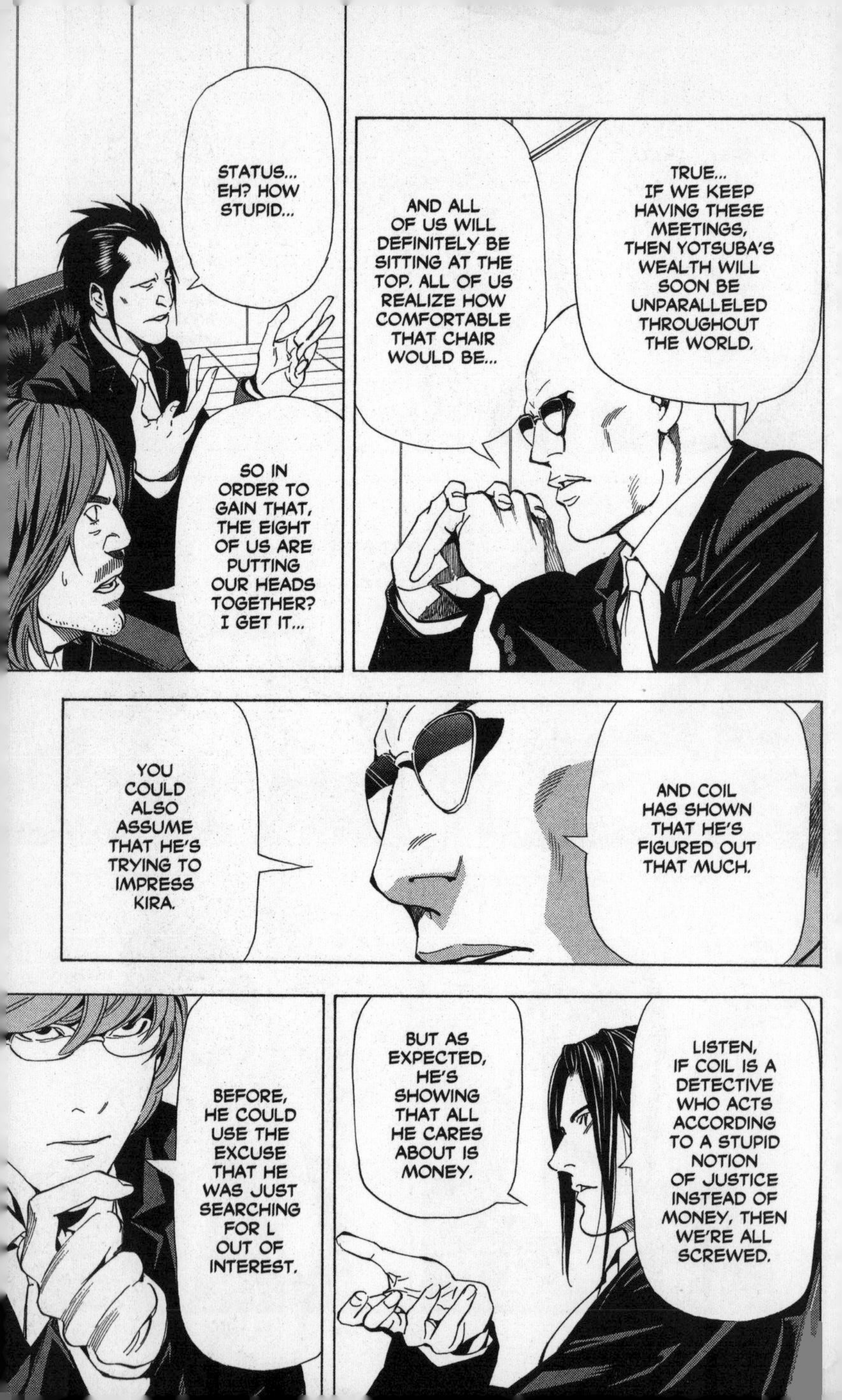
TRUE... IF WE KEEP HAVING THESE MEETINGS, THEN YOTSUBA'S WEALTH WILL SOON BE UNPARALLELED THROUGHOUT THE WORLD.
AND ALL OF US WILL DEFINITELY BE SITTING AT THE TOP. ALL OF US REALIZE HOW COMFORTABLE THAT CHAIR WOULD BE...
STATUS... EH? HOW STUPID...
SO IN ORDER TO GAIN THAT, THE EIGHT OF US ARE PUTTING OUR HEADS TOGETHER? I GET IT...
AND COIL HAS SHOWN THAT HE'S FIGURED OUT THAT MUCH.
YOU COULD ALSO ASSUME THAT HE'S TRYING TO IMPRESS KIRA.
LISTEN, IF COIL IS A DETECTIVE WHO ACTS ACCORDING TO A STUPID NOTION OF JUSTICE INSTEAD OF MONEY, THEN WE'RE ALL SCREWED.
BUT AS EXPECTED, HE'S SHOWING THAT ALL HE CARES ABOUT IS MONEY.
BEFORE, HE COULD USE THE EXCUSE THAT HE WAS JUST SEARCHING FOR L OUT OF INTEREST.

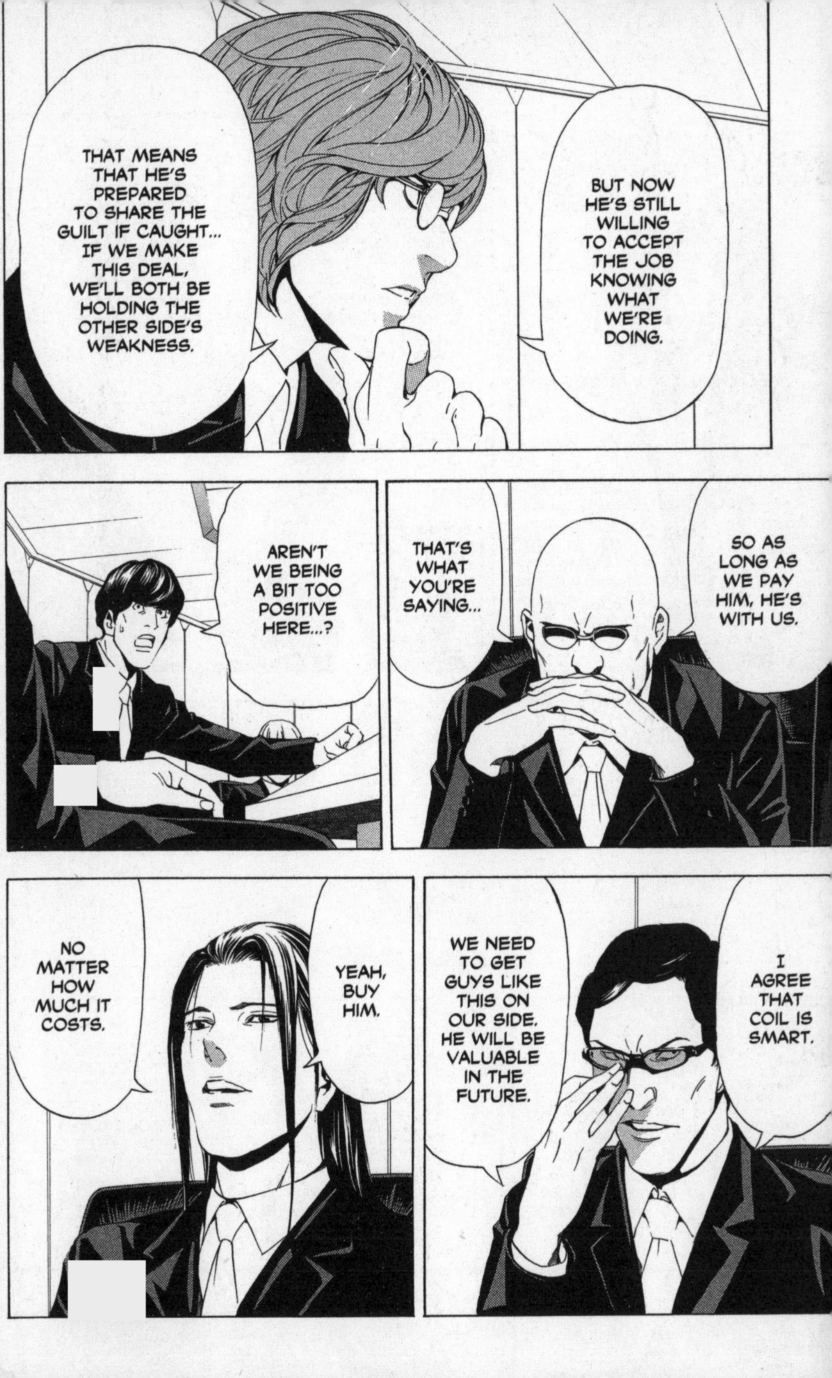
BUT NOW HE'S STILL WILLING TO ACCEPT THE JOB KNOWING WHAT WE'RE DOING.
THAT MEANS THAT HE'S PREPARED TO SHARE THE GUILT IF CAUGHT... IF WE MAKE THIS DEAL, WE'LL BOTH BE HOLDING THE OTHER SIDE'S WEAKNESS.
SO AS LONG AS WE PAY HIM, HE'S WITH US.
THAT'S WHAT YOU'RE SAYING...
AREN'T WE BEING A BIT TOO POSITIVE HERE...?
I AGREE THAT COIL IS SMART.
WE NEED TO GET GUYS LIKE THIS ON OUR SIDE. HE WILL BE VALUABLE IN THE FUTURE.
YEAH, BUY HIM.
NO MATTER HOW MUCH IT COSTS.

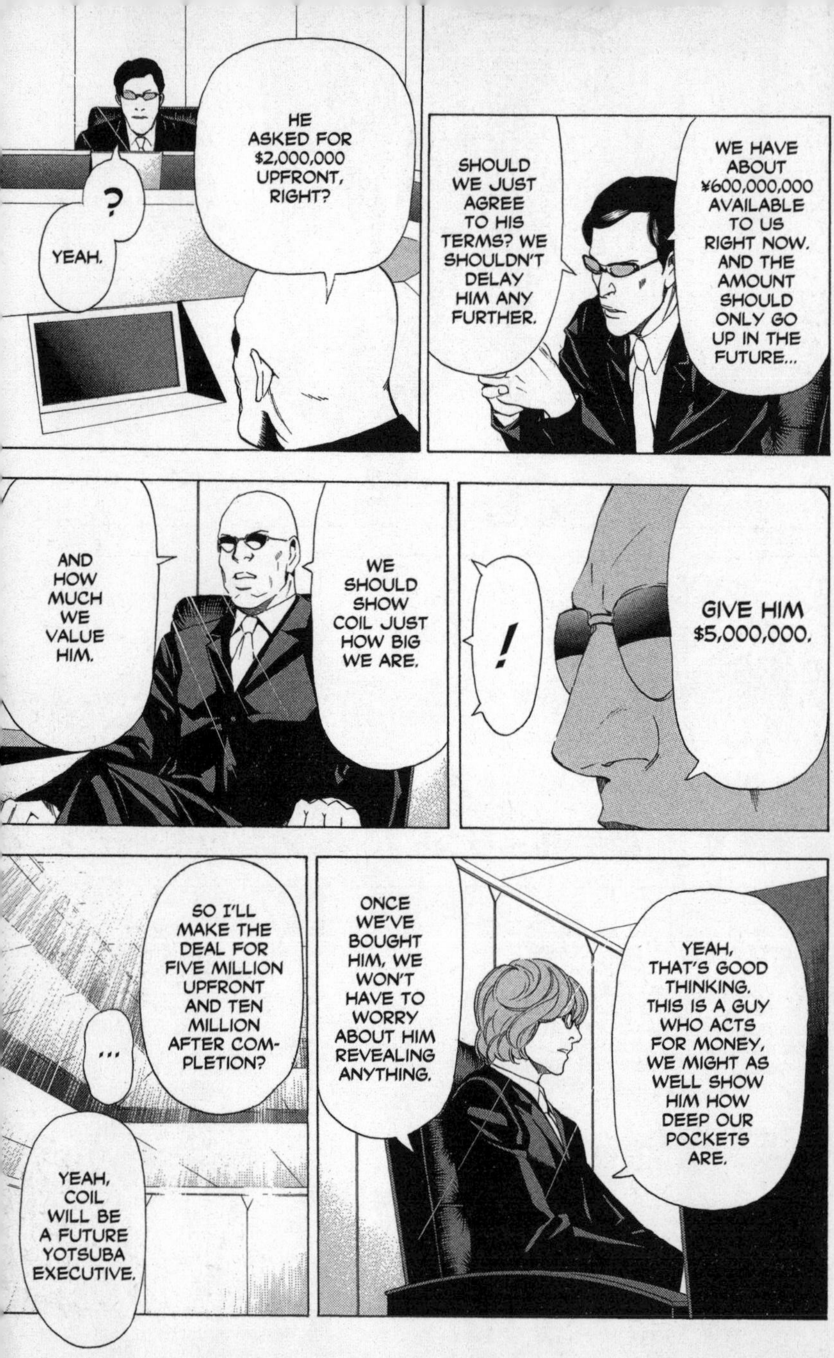
WE HAVE ABOUT ¥600,000,000 AVAILABLE TO US RIGHT NOW. AND THE AMOUNT SHOULD ONLY GO UP IN THE FUTURE...
SHOULD WE JUST AGREE TO HIS TERMS? WE SHOULDN'T DELAY HIM ANY FURTHER.
HE ASKED FOR $2,000,000 UPFRONT, RIGHT?
?
YEAH.
GIVE HIM $5,000,000.
!
WE SHOULD SHOW COIL JUST HOW BIG WE ARE.
AND HOW MUCH WE VALUE HIM.
YEAH, THAT'S GOOD THINKING. THIS IS A GUY WHO ACTS FOR MONEY, WE MIGHT AS WELL SHOW HIM HOW DEEP OUR POCKETS ARE.
ONCE WE'VE BOUGHT HIM, WE WON'T HAVE TO WORRY ABOUT HIM REVEALING ANYTHING.
SO I'LL MAKE THE DEAL FOR FIVE MILLION UPFRONT AND TEN MILLION AFTER COM-PLETION?
...
YEAH, COIL WILL BE A FUTURE YOTSUBA EXECUTIVE.

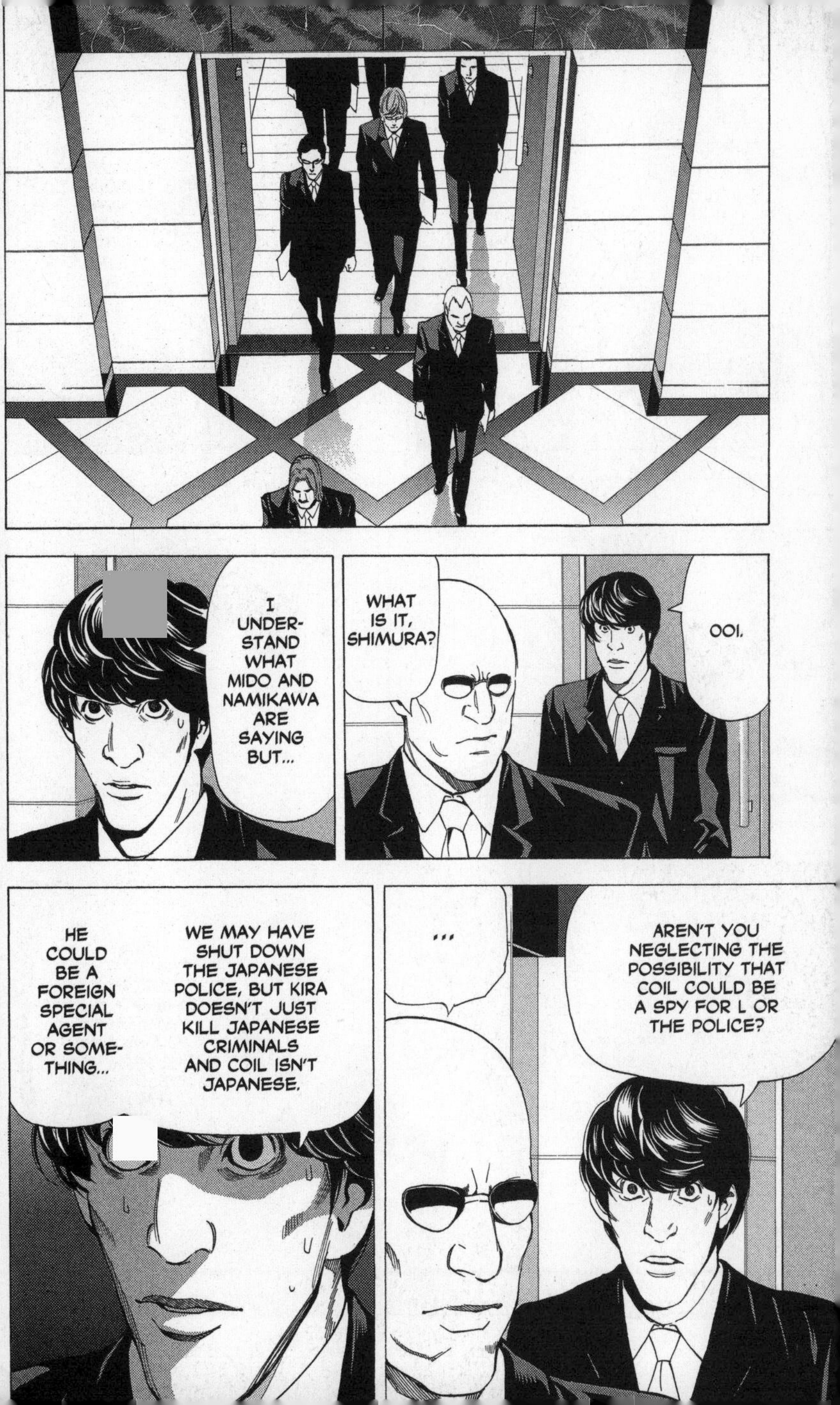
OOI.
WHAT IS IT, SHIMURA?
I UNDERSTAND WHAT MIDO AND NAMIKAWA ARE SAYING BUT...
AREN'T YOU NEGLECTING THE POSSIBILITY THAT COIL COULD BE A SPY FOR L OR THE POLICE?
...
WE MAY HAVE SHUT DOWN THE JAPANESE POLICE, BUT KIRA DOESN'T JUST KILL JAPANESE CRIMINALS AND COIL ISN'T JAPANESE.
HE COULD BE A FOREIGN SPECIAL AGENT OR SOMETHING...

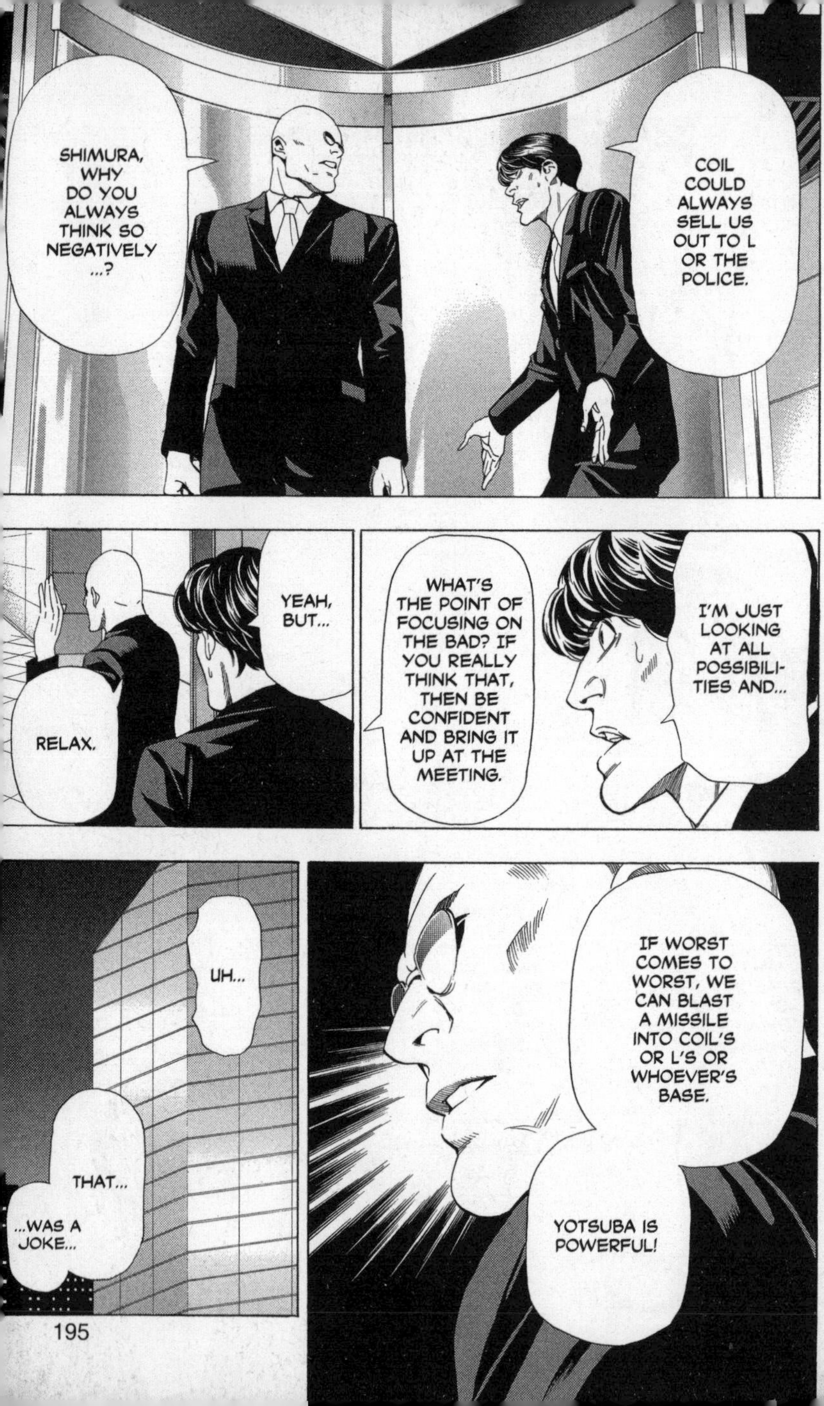
COIL COULD ALWAYS SELL US OUT TO L OR THE POLICE.
SHIMURA, WHY DO YOU ALWAYS THINK SO NEGATIVELY ...?
I'M JUST LOOKING AT ALL POSSIBILI-TIES AND...
WHAT'S THE POINT OF FOCUSING ON THE BAD? IF YOU REALLY THINK THAT, THEN BE CONFIDENT AND BRING IT UP AT THE MEETING.
YEAH, BUT...
RELAX.
IF WORST COMES TO WORST, WE CAN BLAST A MISSILE INTO COIL'S OR L'S OR WHOEVER'S BASE.
YOTSUBA IS POWERFUL!
UH...
THAT...
...WAS A JOKE...

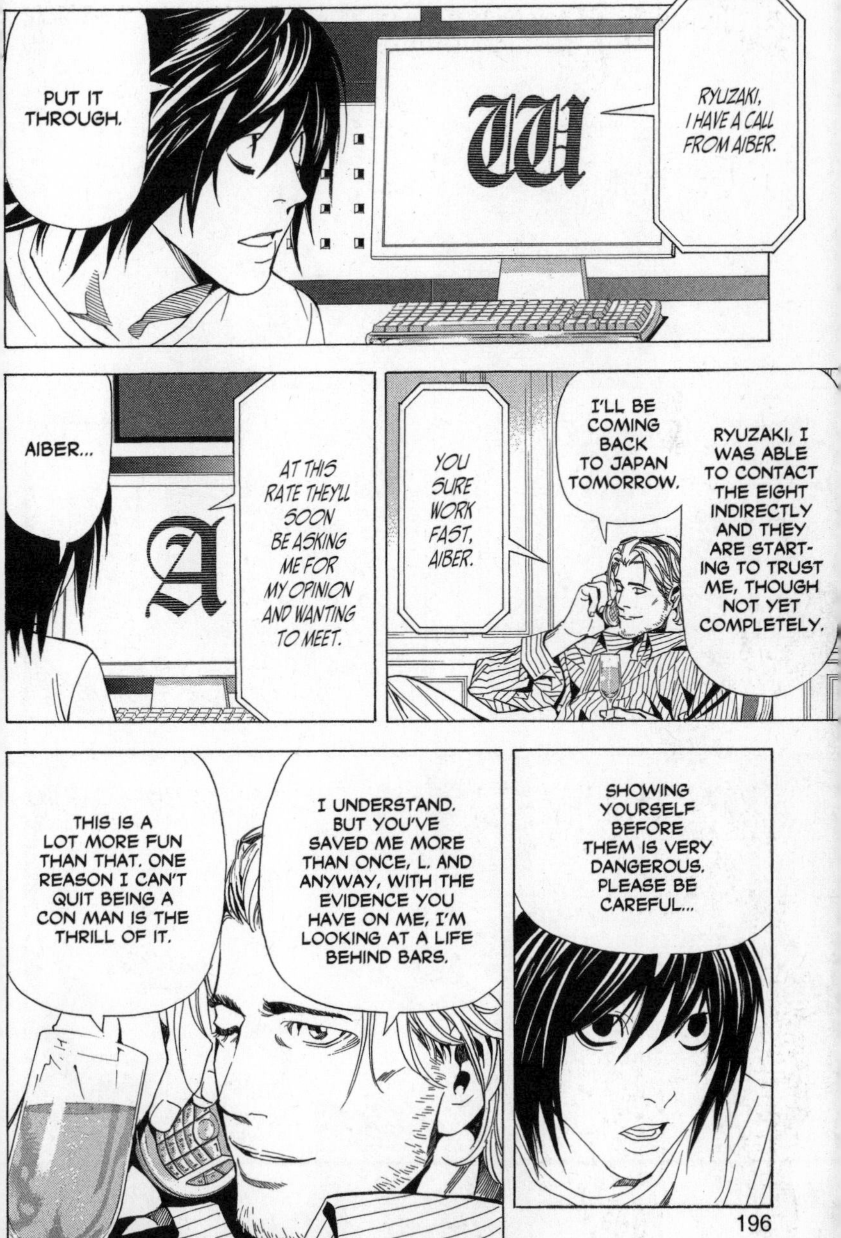

RYUZAKI, I HAVE A CALL FROM AIBER.
PUT IT THROUGH.
RYUZAKI, I WAS ABLE TO CONTACT THE EIGHT INDIRECTLY AND THEY ARE STARTING TO TRUST ME, THOUGH NOT YET COMPLETELY.
I'LL BE COMING BACK TO JAPAN TOMORROW.
YOU SURE WORK FAST, AIBER.
AT THIS RATE THEY'LL SOON BE ASKING ME FOR MY OPINION AND WANTING TO MEET.
AIBER...
SHOWING YOURSELF BEFORE THEM IS VERY DANGEROUS. PLEASE BE CAREFUL...
I UNDERSTAND. BUT YOU'VE SAVED ME MORE THAN ONCE, L. AND ANYWAY, WITH THE EVIDENCE YOU HAVE ON ME, I'M LOOKING AT A LIFE BEHIND BARS.
THIS IS A LOT MORE FUN THAN THAT. ONE REASON I CAN'T QUIT BEING A CON MAN IS THE THRILL OF IT.

READ THIS WAY

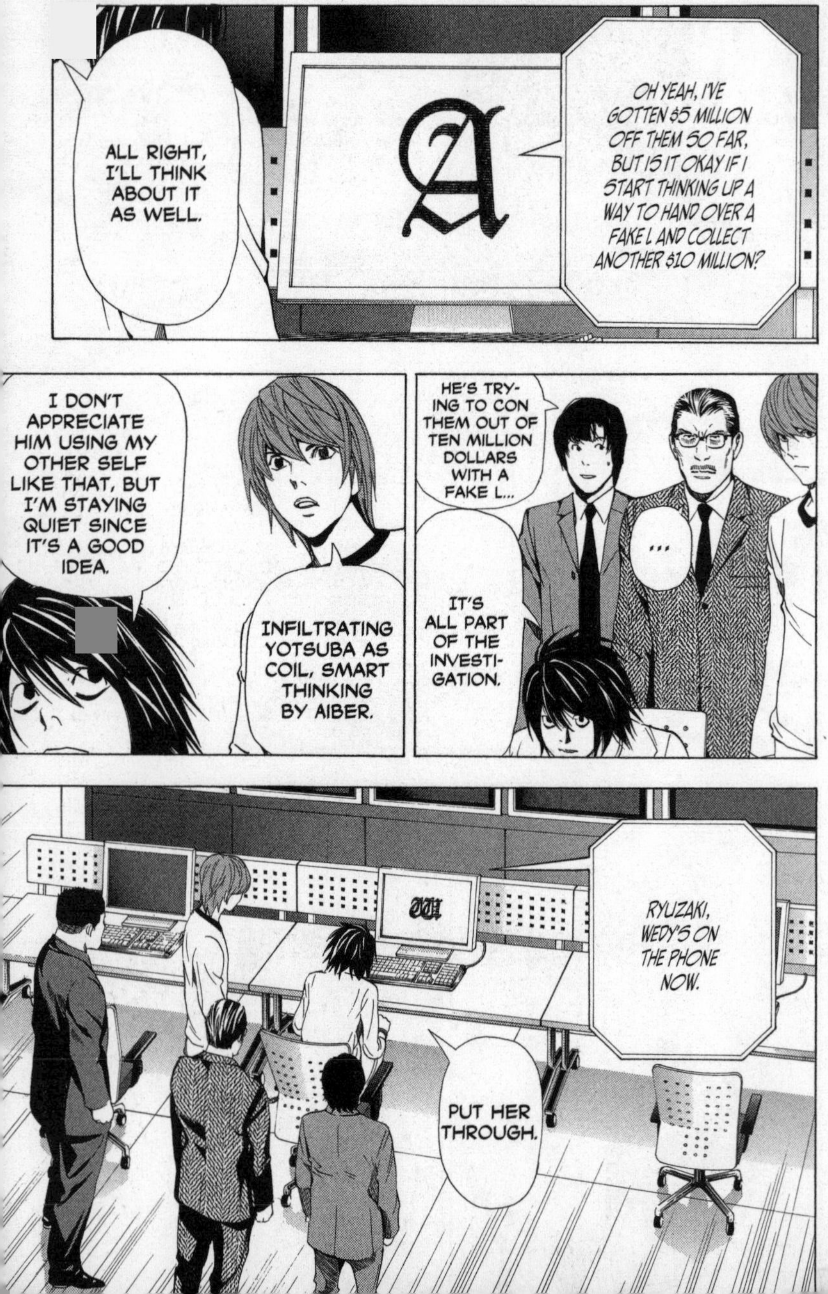
OH YEAH, I'VE GOTTEN $5 MILLION OFF THEM SO FAR, BUT IS IT OKAY IF I START THINKING UP A WAY TO HAND OVER A FAKE L AND COLLECT ANOTHER $10 MILLION?
ALL RIGHT, I'LL THINK ABOUT IT AS WELL.
HE'S TRYING TO CON THEM OUT OF TEN MILLION DOLLARS WITH A FAKE L...
...
IT'S ALL PART OF THE INVESTIGATION.
INFILTRATING YOTSUBA AS COIL, SMART THINKING BY AIBER.
I DON'T APPRECIATE HIM USING MY OTHER SELF LIKE THAT, BUT I'M STAYING QUIET SINCE IT'S A GOOD IDEA.
RYUZAKI, WEDY'S ON THE PHONE NOW.
PUT HER THROUGH.

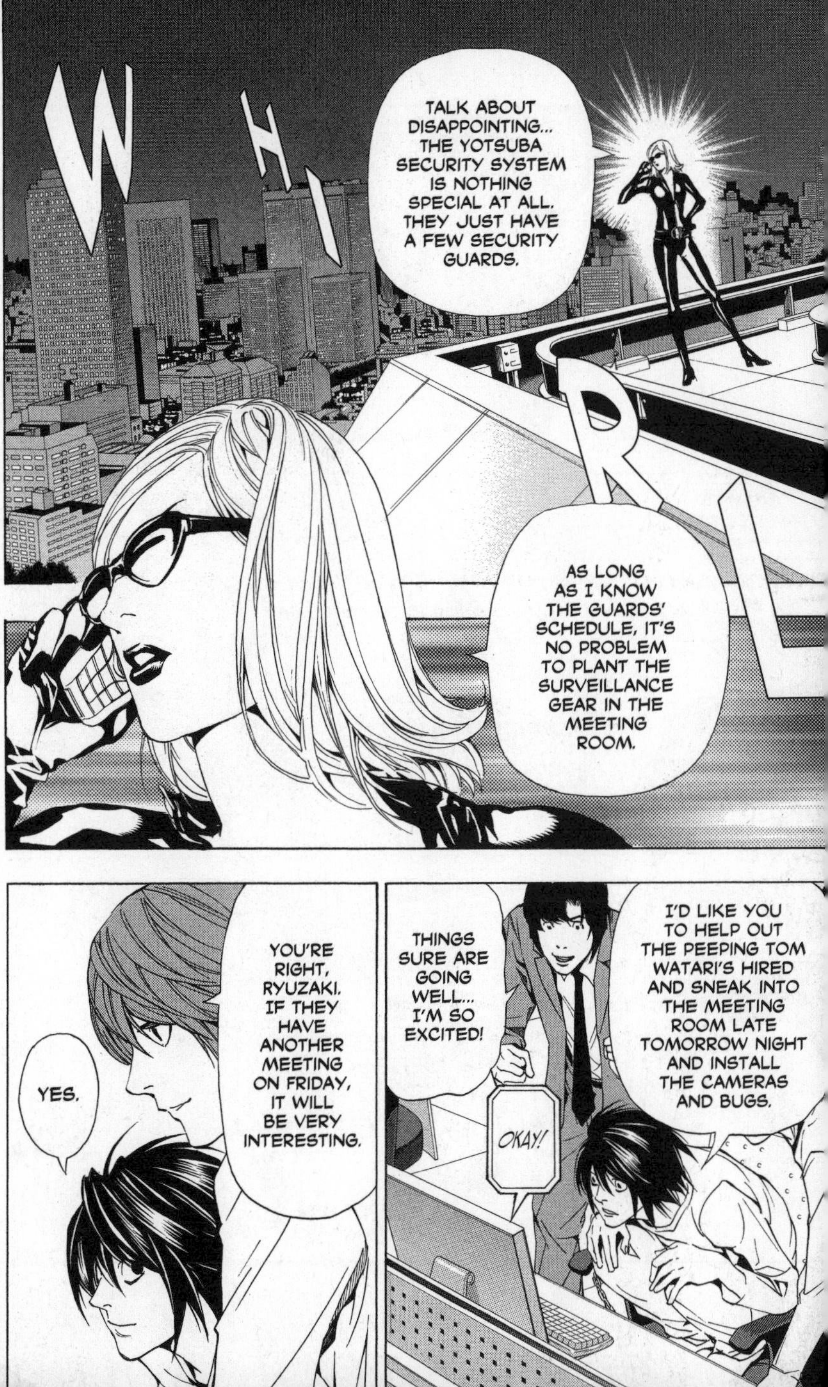

WHIRL
TALK ABOUT DISAPPOINTING... THE YOTSUBA SECURITY SYSTEM IS NOTHING SPECIAL AT ALL. THEY JUST HAVE A FEW SECURITY GUARDS.
AS LONG AS I KNOW THE GUARDS' SCHEDULE, IT'S NO PROBLEM TO PLANT THE SURVEILLANCE GEAR IN THE MEETING ROOM.
I'D LIKE YOU TO HELP OUT THE PEEPING TOM WATARI'S HIRED AND SNEAK INTO THE MEETING ROOM LATE TOMORROW NIGHT AND INSTALL THE CAMERAS AND BUGS.
THINGS SURE ARE GOING WELL... I'M SO EXCITED!
OKAY!
YOU'RE RIGHT, RYUZAKI. IF THEY HAVE ANOTHER MEETING ON FRIDAY, IT WILL BE VERY INTERESTING.
YES.

READ THIS WAY

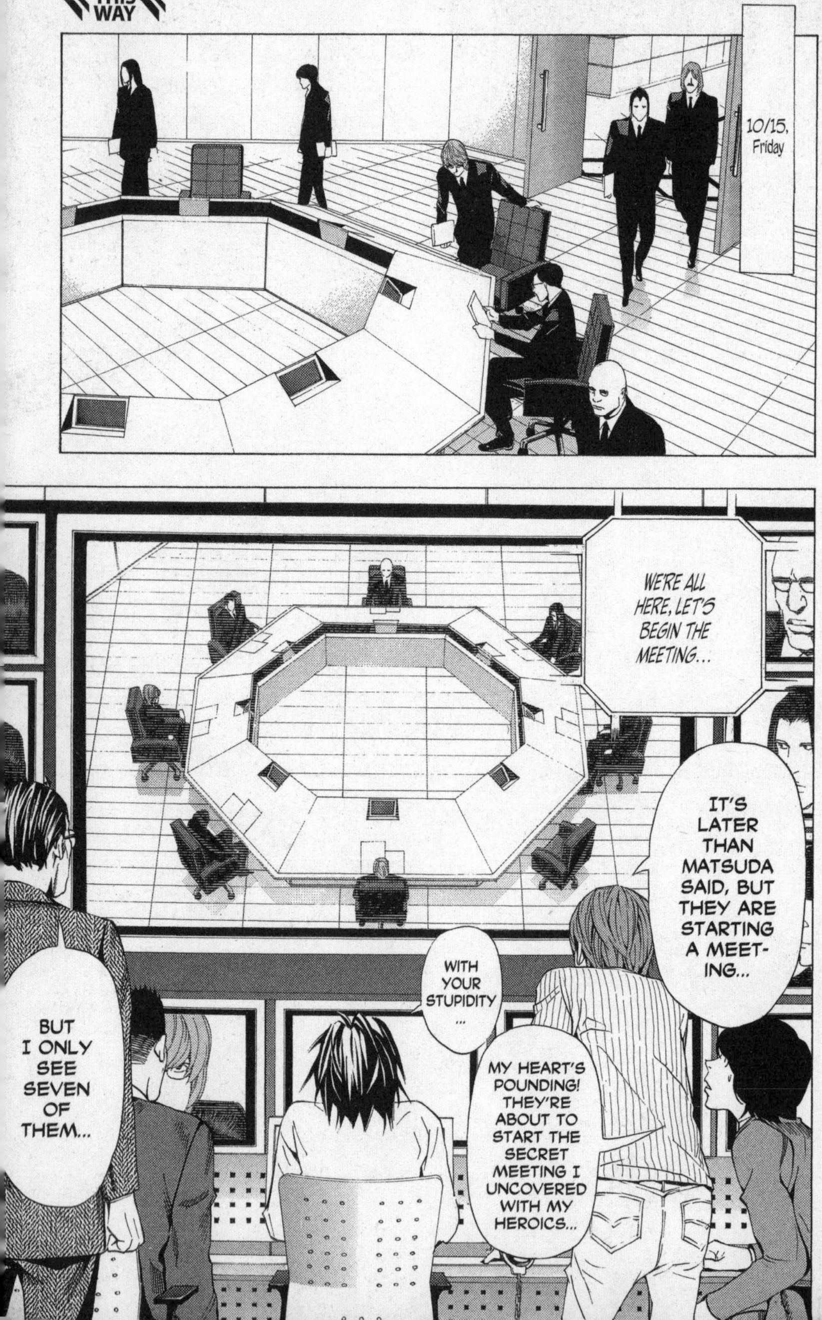
10/15, Friday
WE'RE ALL HERE, LET'S BEGIN THE MEETING...
IT'S LATER THAN MATSUDA SAID, BUT THEY ARE STARTING A MEET-ING...
MY HEART'S POUNDING! THEY'RE ABOUT TO START THE SECRET MEETING I UNCOVERED WITH MY HEROICS...
WITH YOUR STUPIDITY...
BUT I ONLY SEE SEVEN OF THEM...

# DEATH NOTE
## How to use it
## XXXI

○ The number of pages of the DEATH NOTE will never run out.

デスノートは、いくら名前を書いてもページがなくならない。

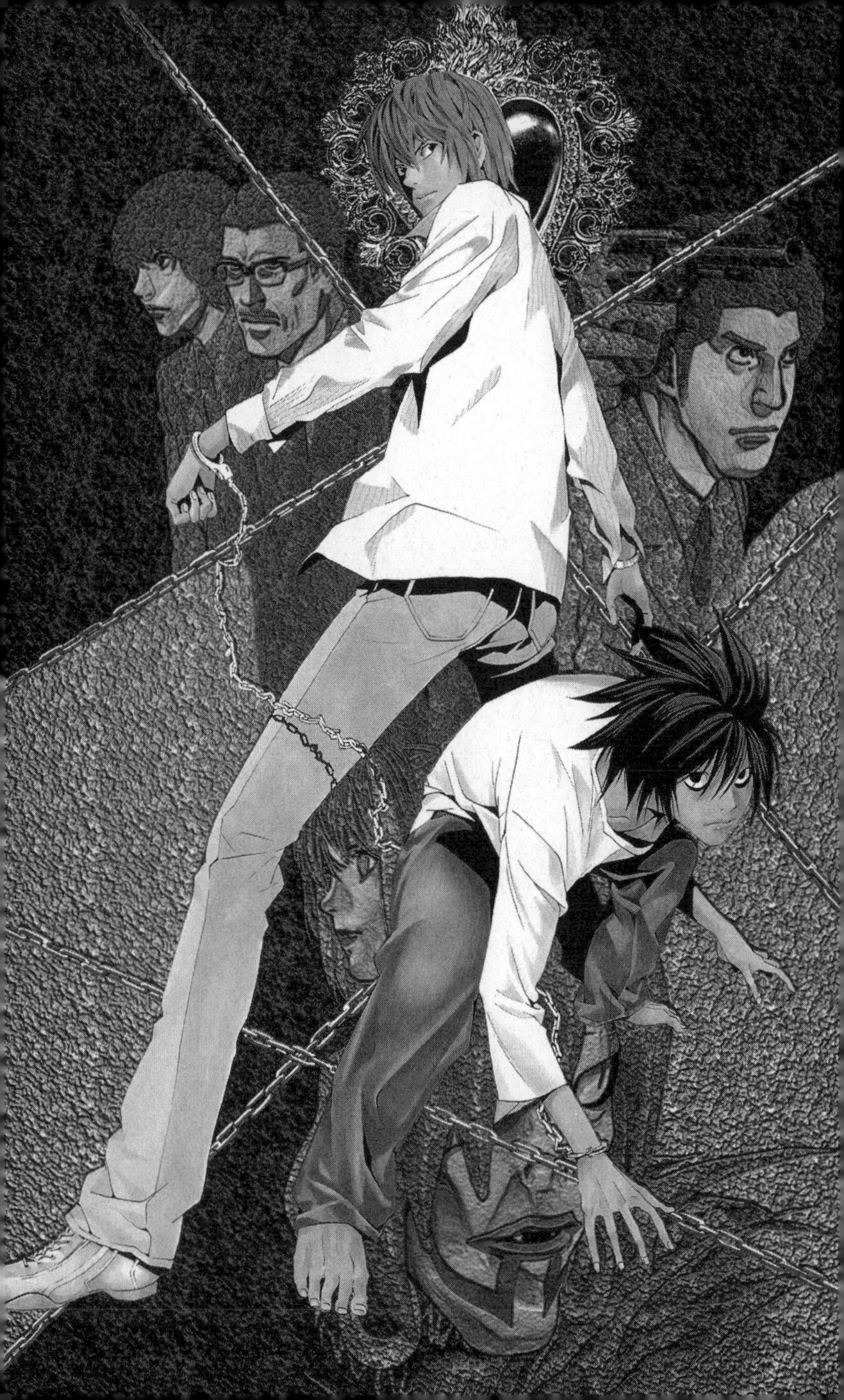

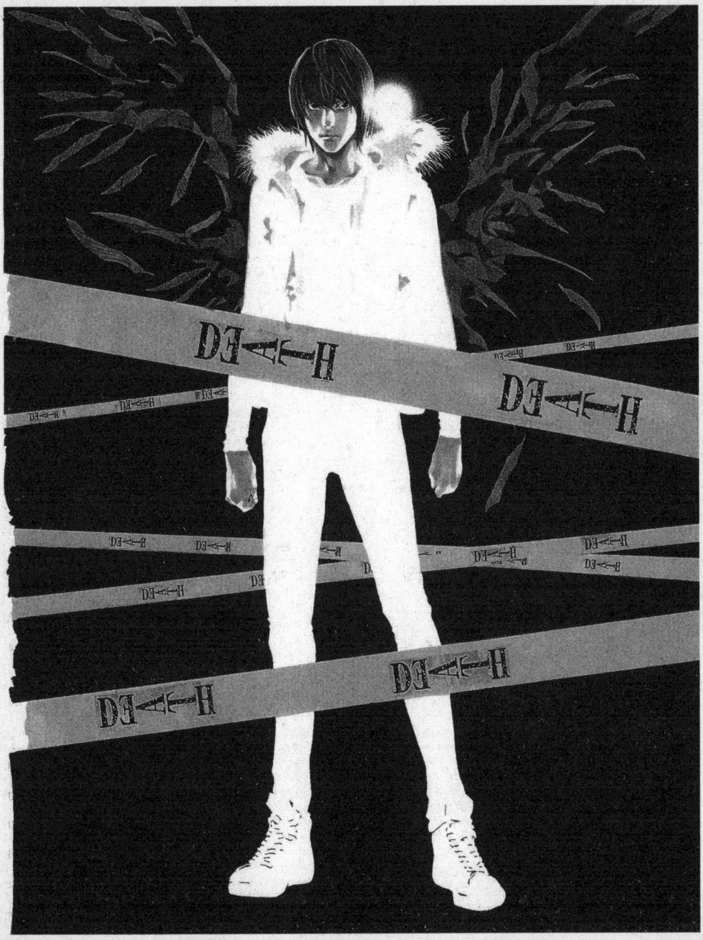
DEATH
DEATH
DEATH
DEATH

## In the Next Volume

L is ready to force the newest Kira out into the open, and he recruits Misa to help. But Misa discovers more than she expected when the Shinigami, Rem, reveals the identity of all three Kiras! Misa will do anything for Light, but what does that mean for L...?

**Available Now**

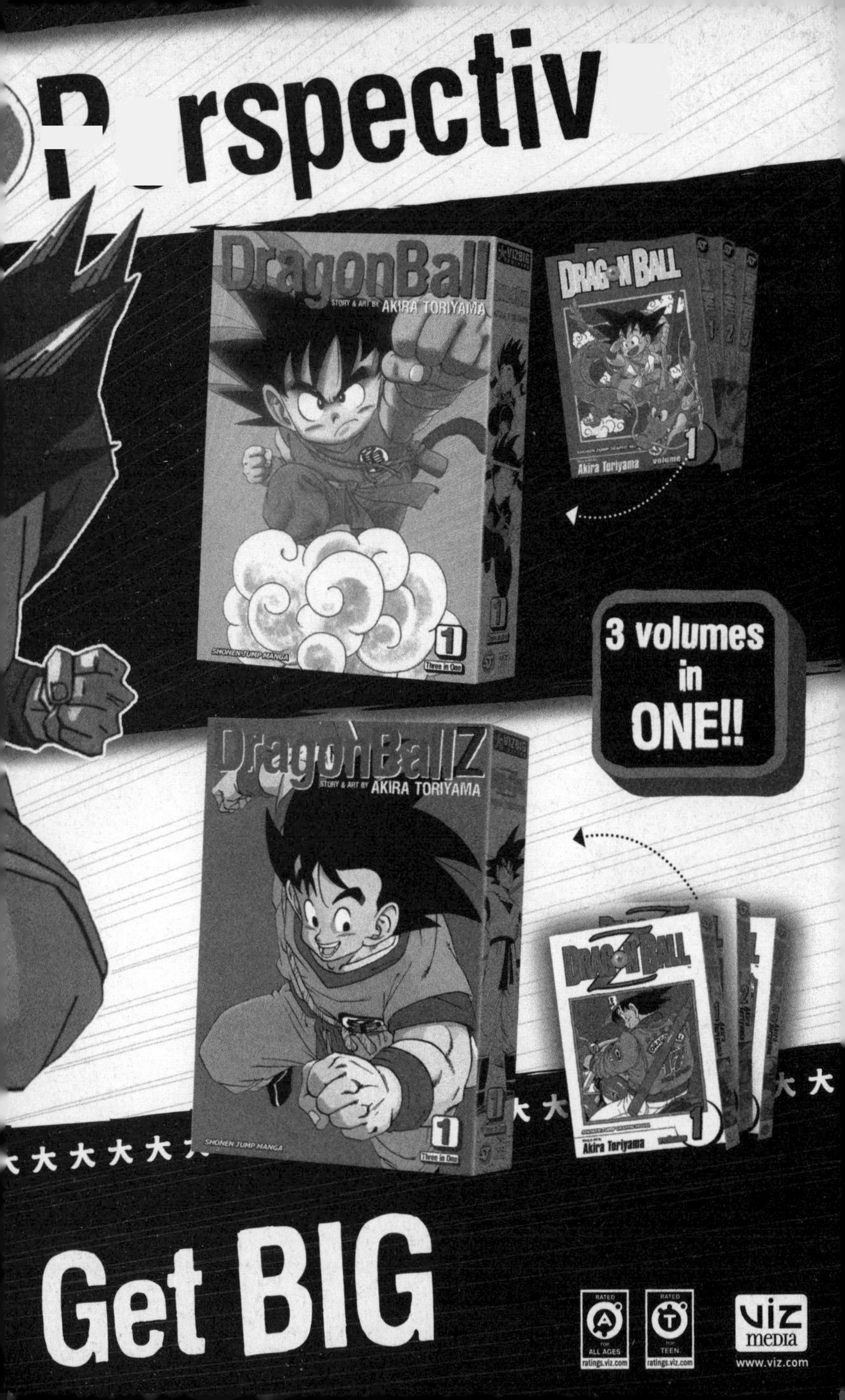

P rspectiv
DragonBall
STORY & ART BY AKIRA TORIYAMA
SHONEN JUMP MANGA
1
Three in One
DRAGON BALL
Akira Toriyama
volume 1
3 volumes in ONE!!
DragonBall Z
STORY & ART BY AKIRA TORIYAMA
SHONEN JUMP MANGA
1
Three in One
DRAGON BALL Z
Akira Toriyama
Get BIG
RATED A FOR ALL AGES ratings.viz.com
RATED T FOR TEEN ratings.viz.com
viz media
www.viz.com

# ⅤⅠⅭⅯⅤNGⅤ

## Read manga anytime, anywhere!

om our newest hit series to the classics you know
d love, the best manga in the world is now available
gitally. **Buy a volume\* of digital manga for your:**

iOS device (**iPad®, iPhone®, iPod® touch**)
through the **VIZ Manga app**

Android-powered device (**phone or tablet**)
with a browser by visiting **VIZManga.com**

**Mac or PC computer** by visiting VIZManga.com

**VIZ Digital has loads to offer:**

- 500+ ready-to-read volumes
- New volumes each week
- FREE previews
- Access on multiple devices! Create a log-in through the app
  so you buy a book once, and read it on your device of choice!\*

## To learn more, visit www.viz.com/apps

\* Some series may not be available for multiple devices.
  Check the app on your device to find out what's available.

RATED
T
FOR OLDER
TEEN
ratings.viz.com

ⅤⅰⅠ
mepia
viz.com/apps

# Re the wrong Direction!!

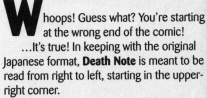

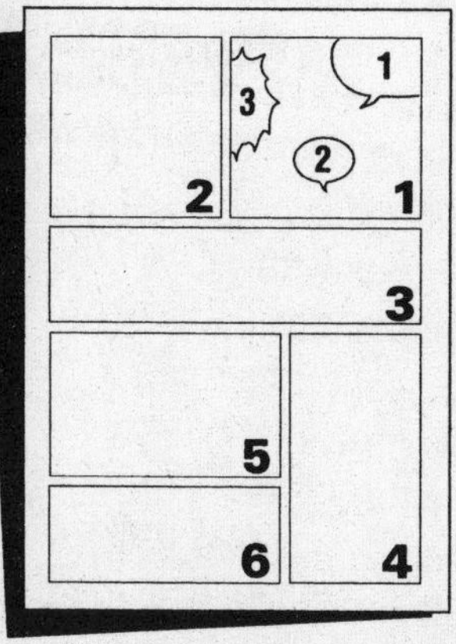

**W**hoops! Guess what? You're starting at the wrong end of the comic!

…It's true! In keeping with the original Japanese format, **Death Note** is meant to be read from right to left, starting in the upper-right corner.

Unlike English, which is read from left to right, Japanese is read from right to left, meaning that action, sound effects and word-balloon order are completely reversed… something which can make readers unfamiliar with Japanese feel pretty backwards themselves. For this reason, manga or Japanese comics published in the U.S. in English have sometimes been published "flopped"–that is, printed in exact reverse order, as though seen from the other side of a mirror.

By flopping pages, U.S. publishers can avoid confusing readers, but the compromise is not without its downside. For one thing, a character in a flopped manga series who once wore in the original Japanese version a T-shirt emblazoned with "M A Y" (as in "the merry month of") now wears one which reads "Y A M"! Additionally, many manga creators in Japan are themselves unhappy with the process, as some feel the mirror-imaging of their art alters their original intentions.

We are proud to bring you Tsugumi Ohba & Takeshi Obata's **Death Note** in the original unflopped format. For now, though, turn to the other side of the book and let the quest begin…!

–Editor